Inter-State Communications and Human Rights

Inter-State Communications and Human Rights

Developments and Prospects

Edited by

Rosana Garciandia and Jean-Pierre Gauci

BRILL | NIJHOFF

LEIDEN | BOSTON

Originally published, in part, as Volume 13, Issue 1 (2024) of Brill's journal International Human Rights Law Review.

Cover illustration: Photograph by Vojtech Bruzek on Unsplash.

Library of Congress Cataloging-in-Publication Data

Names: Garciandia, Rosana editor | Gauci, Jean-Pierre editor
Title: Inter-state communications and human rights : developments and prospects / edited by Rosana Garciandia and Jean-Pierre Gauci.
Description: Leiden; Boston: Brill/Nijhoff, 2025. | Includes index. |
Identifiers: LCCN 2025022876 (print) | LCCN 2025022877 (ebook) | ISBN 9789004712577 paperback | ISBN 9789004712584 ebook
Subjects: LCSH: International law and human rights | Convention for the Protection of Human Rights and Fundamental Freedoms (1950 November 5) | Inter-American Court of Human Rights | United Nations. Office of the High Commissioner for Human Rights
Classification: LCC KZ1266 .I589 2025 (print) | LCC KZ1266 (ebook) | DDC 341.4/8–dc23/eng/20250513
LC record available at https://lccn.loc.gov/2025022876
LC ebook record available at https://lccn.loc.gov/2025022877

Typeface for the Latin, Greek, and Cyrillic scripts: "Brill". See and download: brill.com/brill-typeface.

ISBN 978-90-04-71257-7 (paperback)
ISBN 978-90-04-71258-4 (e-book)
DOI 10.1163/9789004712584

Contents

Introduction: Inter-State Communications as a Tool for Promoting Human Rights

Rosana Garciandia and Jean-Pierre Gauci

Inter-state communications before UN treaty bodies have received renewed attention over the past decade, despite having been under-utilised and, consequently, under-studied for decades. This new interest emerges from the filing of the first ever of such cases in 2018 before the International Committee on the Elimination of Racial Discrimination (CERD Committee), *Qatar v Saudi Arabia,*[1] *Qatar v UAE*[2] and *Palestine v Israel*, the latter of which the *ad hoc* conciliation commission released its final report on in August 2024.[3] Other developments at the international level, including proceedings before the International Court of Justice (ICJ) initiated on an *erga omnes partes* basis by the Gambia,[4] South Africa[5] and Canada and the Netherlands,[6] and massive third party interventions before the ICJ and the European Court of Human Rights (ECtHR) in cases related to Ukraine,[7] have also contributed to the growing interest in the potential of the mechanism.

---

1 *Qatar v Saudi Arabia* (Decision on Jurisdiction) CERD/C/99/5 (19 October 2020).

2 *Qatar v United Arab Emirates* (Decision on Jurisdiction) CERD/C/99/3 (18 June 2020).

3 *State of Palestine v Israel* (Report of Ad Hoc Conciliation Commission) CERD/C/113/3 (21 August 2024). For an analysis of the ad hoc conciliation commission report, see David Keane, 'A Missed Opportunity: The Decision in Palestine v Israel' (*EJIL:Talk!*, 5 September 2024) <https://www.ejiltalk.org/a-missed-opportunity-the-decision-in-palestine-v-israel/> accessed 13 March 2025.

4 *Application of the Convention on the Prevention and Punishment of the Crime of Genocide (The Gambia v Myanmar)* (Pending) ICJ Press Release 2019/47 <https://www.icj-cij.org/sites/default/files/case-related/178/178-20191111-PRE-01-00-EN.pdf> accessed 4 September 2024.

5 *Application of the Convention on the Prevention and Punishment of the Crime of Genocide in the Gaza Strip (South Africa v Israel)* (Pending) ICJ Press Release 2023/77 <https://www.icj-cij.org/sites/default/files/case-related/192/192-20231229-pre-01-00-en.pdf> accessed 4 September 2024.

6 *Application of the Convention Against Torture and Other Cruel, Inhuman or Degrading Treatment or Punishment (Canada and the Netherlands v Syrian Arab Republic)* (Pending) (Application Instituting Proceedings) <https://www.icj-cij.org/sites/default/files/case-related/188/188-20230608-APP-01-00-EN.pdf> accessed 4 September 2024.

7 *Allegations of Genocide under the Convention on the Prevention and Punishment of the Crime of Genocide (Ukraine v Russian Federation)* (Pending) ICJ Order (2 June 2023) <https://www.icj-cij.org/sites/default/files/case-related/182/182-20230605-ORD-01-00-EN.pdf> accessed 4 September 2024; European Court of Human Rights, 'Update on the Third-Party

 | DOI:10.1163/9789004712584_002

Inter-state communications before treaty bodies allow States to bring cases against other States for violations of their human rights obligations. The possibility is available, *inter alia*, under the International Covenant on Civil and Political Rights,[8] the International Covenant on Economic, Social and Cultural Rights, the Convention Against Torture,[9] the International Convention on the Elimination of All Forms of Racial Discrimination (CERD),[10] the International Convention on the Protection of the Rights of All Migrant Workers and Members of their Families,[11] the Convention on the Rights of the Child (Optional Protocol 3)[12] and the International Convention for the Protection of All Persons from Enforced Disappearance.[13]

Given the strong human rights dimension of cases currently under consideration by the ICJ and other international disputes, as well as the numerous and significant cases being presently considered by human rights treaty bodies and other human rights courts, this edited volume seeks to consider the potential of inter-state communications for promoting and ensuring respect for human rights around the globe.

Like the special issue on which it is based, this volume seeks to take the reader on a journey through the features, opportunities, challenges and contradictions of inter-state communications before treaty bodies, offering thought-provoking arguments on how the existing mechanisms that States have at their disposal can be most effectively used to settle disputes with a human rights dimension. Through this journey, the volume seeks to identify lessons, prospects and perspectives as to what might be next for inter-state communications before human rights treaty bodies. It also furthers the discussion of if and how the features of inter-state communications (at the UN treaty body level and elsewhere) can help to achieve the perceived aims of the treaties in question.

Intervention Requests Granted in Inter-State Case *Ukraine and the Netherlands v Russia*' (Press Release No 082, 17 March 2023) <https://hudoc.echr.coe.int/app/conversion/pdf/?library=ECHR&id=003-7598878-10452070> accessed 13 March 2025.

8 International Covenant on Civil and Political Rights (ICCPR) arts. 41–42.

9 Convention Against Torture (CAT) art. 21.

10 International Convention on the Elimination of All Forms of Racial Discrimination (CERD) art. 11.

11 International Convention on the Protection of the Rights of All Migrant Workers and Members of their Families (CMW) art. 76.

12 Optional Protocol to the Convention on the Rights of the Child on a Communications Procedure (OPCRC) art. 12.

13 International Convention for the Protection of All Persons from Enforced Disappearance (ICAED) art. 32.

States and other international actors have traditionally seen those aims as limited to ensuring treaty compliance or avoiding human rights violations. But this could be progressively changing as the work of UN treaty bodies places greater emphasis on dispute settlement as an aim (e.g. CERD Committee), or as States decide to use inter-state communications to hold other States to account, or to signal themselves as 'good citizens' or signal others as failing to behave as such. How different actors understand those aims is likely to impact any decision on the features of inter-state communications and on the use of these mechanisms.

Setting the scene for the rest of the volume, in the first chapter Lawry-White focuses on the decision-making processes influencing State choices of dispute settlement options, building on the fact that inter-state communications do not exist in isolation but coexist with a number of alternatives. Drawing on international practice, and highlighting the importance of taking a contextual perspective, the chapter examines some of the factors that play into a choice of whether or not, and if so where and how, to bring an international – and particularly human rights – claim. The chapter concludes by providing a roadmap for States deciding whether and in which forum to bring forward an international dispute.

In the next chapter, Sthoeger explores the possibilities of inter-state conciliation in the human rights context, noting at the outset that despite provision for it in various human rights treaties, reliance thereon has been sparse. The chapter assesses the suitability of conciliation to advance the goals of inter-state communications in human rights treaties. It also identifies critical factors that may determine the success or failure of such conciliations, particularly by drawing on lessons learned from the conciliation between Timor Leste and Australia under the UN Convention for the Law of the Sea, which successfully concluded with a delimitation treaty.

Building on this exploration of possibilities and drawing on experiences and lessons from ongoing cases before the ICJ and other international fora, Garciandia and Gauci explore the potential of a collective approach before treaty bodies and the risks that would need to be mitigated in adopting such an approach, reflecting on how to make collective communications a viable option moving forward. This chapter posits that enabling collective inter-state communications before UN treaty bodies could strengthen the mechanism as an avenue for treaty compliance and the protection of human rights, and for amplifying sovereign voices as part of peaceful dispute settlement processes.

The next section of this volume turns to two substantive areas where inter-state communications seem to show potential. Keane's chapter explores whether inter-state communications before the CERD Committee can be an avenue to protect cultural heritage. Whilst both *Armenia v Azerbaijan*[14] *and Azerbaijan v Armenia*[15] by-passed the possibility of communications before the treaty body, choosing instead to refer the cases to the ICJ, Keane offers insights into the way in which the views of the CERD Committee may inform the determinations of the Court (including on the challenging question of whether the destruction of heritage in the context of conflict falls within the scope of the CERD). In doing so, the chapter draws attention to the dynamics of relationships between human rights treaty bodies and the ICJ.

In her chapter, Boticelli takes the reader to a particular situational context in exploring the possibilities for holding China to account for the denounced systematic mistreatment of Uyghur and other Muslim ethnic minorities in so-called 're-education camps' in Xinjiang. She argues that by examining the possibilities under alternative avenues, such as the inter-state quasi-judicial communication procedure under both the CERD and the Constitution of the International Labour Organization, as well as addressing the feasibility of requesting an ICJ advisory opinion as an inter-state case in disguise, it might be possible to overcome the barriers to international justice that emerge from China's reluctance to engage in dispute settlement mechanisms.

The volume then focuses in on each of the three key regional human rights systems. On the ECtHR, Risini and Eicke contextualise inter-state cases before the Court as a centrepiece of human rights supervision in Europe. The chapter traces the evolution of inter-state cases before the ECtHR through its 70-year history whilst also highlighting its strengths and drawing out its potential limitations, including in terms of the Court's resources. Focusing on the evidentiary dimension, the chapter highlights the value of establishing a judicial record of events under the ECtHR's scrutiny.

The other chapters focused on regional systems explore some of the reasons for the under-use of the mechanism. On the inter-American system, Contesse examines the limited inter-state communication practice before the Inter-American Court and Commission of Human Rights, highlighting that States in the region often utilise alternative avenues. The chapter argues that understanding how inter-state disputes before human rights bodies are addressed in

---

14 *Application of the International Convention on the Elimination of All Forms of Racial Discrimination* (*Armenia v Azerbaijan*) <https://www.icj-cij.org/case/180> accessed 04 September 2024.

15 *Application of the International Convention on the Elimination of All Forms of Racial Discrimination* (*Azerbaijan v Armenia*) <https://www.icj-cij.org/case/181> accessed 04 September 2024.

the region requires one to place inter-state communications within the broader repertoire of options that States will often utilise in seeking to resolve such disputes. In particular, the chapter explores how members of the Organisation of American States use advisory opinions as a covert inter-state dispute mechanism, and argues that the Inter-American Court should articulate a clear set of admissibility standards to address this practice.

Moving to the African context, Viljoen explores some of the features of the system and its potential in terms of the collective enforcement of human rights, including the compulsory nature of such processes. The chapter highlights the rarity with which these options have been exercised – with only three cases filed to date, all before the African Commission on Human and Peoples' Rights. The chapter then explores the question of why such a small number of inter-state cases have been submitted under the African system. In doing so, it points to the influence of a general culture of non-intervention and a preference for non-confrontational dispute mechanisms among African States; the existence of alternative channels to resolve cases involving massive or widespread violations; the confidence placed in the ICJ; the delays associated with particular decisions; and a pervasive ignorance of inter-state complaints processes under the African system.

As outlined in various chapters of this volume, inter-state communications are simply one of a plethora of options available to States in resolving disputes that have a human rights dimension. As the understanding of and engagement with these mechanisms evolves, they will develop features likely to impact their potential to achieve what is also a moving range of objectives that States, treaty bodies themselves and the human rights movement more broadly ascribe to these processes.

This introduction is a slightly modified version of the editorial note to the special issue on which the volume is based.[16] This edited version of the special issue includes the contributions as they were published online, before the ad hoc conciliation commission convened for *Palestine v Israel* had released its report on the case, and therefore the contributions do not incorporate reflections on the outcome of this conciliation process.

This work is the culmination of exploratory research on inter-state communications led by the editors at King's College London and the British Institute of International and Comparative Law (BIICL). The findings build on an

16 Rosana Garciandia and Jean-Pierre Gauci, 'Editorial Note' (2024) 13(1) International Human Rights Law Review 1.

event hosted by BIICL[17] and on an expert workshop hosted by the Centre for International Governance and Dispute Resolution and BIICL on the aims and features of inter-state communications. As editors, we remain grateful to the authors who have contributed their time, ideas, and insights through their articles (and now chapters), to Stefanos Arvanitakis for his research assistance in the project and in pulling together the special issue and this edited volume and to King's College for financially supporting the research that preceded and underpinned this work.

17 British Institute of International and Comparative Law, 'Inter-State Complaints in International Human Rights Law' (27 April 2022) <https://www.biicl.org/publications/inter-state-complaints-in-international-human-rights-law> accessed 13 March 2025.

CHAPTER 1

Inter-State Human Rights Disputes

Mapping Dispute Resolution Options Including Conciliation

*Merryl Lawry-White**

Abstract

This paper maps the factors that States consider when deciding whether to raise inter-State disputes to an international dispute resolution body. It focuses particularly on these factors in the context of human rights disputes, including whether such disputes will be brought before the mechanisms provided for under the universal human rights treaties, and notably conciliation commissions. While traditionally negotiation has been seen as the most appropriate way to resolve inter-State disputes, there are times that human rights disputes may benefit from a different approach. It discusses (i) the general trend to negotiate or mediate disputes; (ii) the importance of taking a contextual perspective; (iii) the patchwork of international norms; (iv) key legal and factual considerations; (v) choice of mechanism/process; and (vi) palatability of the potential dispute resolution options. The paper concludes by providing a roadmap for States deciding whether to commence an international dispute and which forum to choose.

Keywords

inter-state disputes – human rights disputes – conciliation – decision-making – strategy

* The author is grateful for the research assistance of Laura Anaya-Quintero. This article is up to date as at the end of 2023.

 DOI:10.1163/9789004712584_003

1 Introduction

This article maps the factors that States consider when deciding whether to raise inter-State disputes to an international dispute resolution body. In line with the theme of the special issue, the paper focuses particularly on these factors in the context of human rights disputes and whether they will be brought before the mechanisms provided for under the universal human rights treaties, and notably conciliation commissions. The discussion provides a roadmap for States deciding whether to commence an international complaint or case and which forum to choose. In doing so, it highlights that, while traditionally negotiation has been seen as the most appropriate way to resolve inter-State disputes, there are times that human rights disputes may benefit from a different approach.

There are many different theories of what underpins decision-making in a foreign policy context and which factors matters most in coming to a decision, These theories demonstrate the multiple factors and relationships that contribute to how and why options are narrowed and chosen.[1] Decisions about dispute resolution options, and international relations in general, are not made in a theoretical context; they are moulded and evaluated by the relevant actors, in line with their psychology, the different institutions, the situation and the decision-process chosen.[2] This is not a paper on decision-making theory, nor foreign policy analysis. Instead, it draws on international practice to examine some of the factors within these categories (psychology, institutional history and processes, culture, etc.) that play into a choice of whether or not to bring an international – and particularly human rights claim – and, if so, to what type of dispute resolution body. The factors discussed in this paper are not exhaustive, nor – as many decision-making theories do – does the paper cover the ways that the factors will be weighed up against each other. In addition, international situations are always evolving, with the context shifting and new facts and factors coming to light. This is also true of international disputes – they evolve as situations change, new facts come to light and priorities shift.

1 *See, e.g.,* R Synder, HW Bruck & B Sapin (eds), *Foreign Policy and Decision Making: The Decision-Making Approach to the Study of International Politics, New York: The Free Press* (1962), pp. 60–74, reprinted at: https://www.acsu.buffalo.edu/~fczagare/PSC%20346/SnyderBruckSapin.PDF. J Levy, 'Psychology and Foreign Policy Decision Making and Psychology' in L Huddy, D Sears & J Leavy, *The Oxford Handbook of Political Psychology* (OUP, 2013, 2nd ed.), Ch. 10. G L Scarborough, 'Polarity, Power, and Risk in International Disputes' (1988) 32(3) *The Journal of Conflict Resolution*, pp. 511–533.

2 *See, e.g.,* L. Andy Afinotan, 'Decision Making in International Relations: A theoretical Analysis' (2014) 10(5) *Canadian Social Science* 249–256. DOI: <http://dx.doi.org/10.3968/4970> accessed 30 April 2024.

The interplay of the factors underlying a decision therefore also shifts over time.

A key vantage point in understanding why and how decisions are made is the complexity of objectives involved in the resolution of inter-State disputes. The objectives and intended outcome drive the options and methodology chosen to achieve those objectives, including how the options are assessed, adapted and implemented. The objectives are often multiple and variable. For example, while one intended outcome may be based on a drive to put an end to and/or obtain reparation for human rights violations, any claim will likely implicate a composite of considerations, whether personal or collective, from reputational to economic, from geopolitical to identity-driven ideologies. As soon as a dispute is raised to the international level and third-party decision makers are involved, the interests and objectives of that body are also implicated in the outcome.

The different sections of this article discuss: (i) a starting point: the general trend to negotiate or mediate disputes; (ii) the importance of taking a contextual perspective; (iii) the patchwork of international norms: substantive and those affording international jurisdiction and admissibility; (iv) key legal and factual considerations; (v) choice of mechanism/process; and (vi) palatability of the potential dispute resolution options. The paper then looks at how conciliation maps onto these different factors, especially in the context of human rights disputes. Conciliation of human rights disputes forms one potential option for certain States – retaining significant State control but using a third party to assist in finding a solution. The conclusion includes a flowchart of certain factors a State may want to consider when bringing an international claim.

These elements interweave to define the dispute resolution options and the potential inflection points underlying the choices made along the way. All claims are a process, involving planning, reactivity and adjustments. International claims are therefore crafted and moulded by these multiple factors – including international politics and relations – and are usually dynamic. In a human rights context, this can, of course, raise complexities when lined up against obligations that are not subject to compromise at will. However, it can also lead to creative claims and prevention and accountability efforts in an area of international law in which these can be hard to achieve.

2 The Starting Point: Negotiation and Mediation

Studies and scholars have long emphasised the tendency and preference for States to resort to negotiation or mediation to resolve their international disputes. Scholars have explained that: '[n]egotiation is the oldest and most elementary method for settling international disputes apart from arbitration and by far the method most referred to by states'.[3] Further, that '[i]ndeed, negotiation is used more frequently than all other dispute resolution methods combined'. The author goes on to explain why: 'negotiation allows the parties to maintain maximum control over the outcome; a negotiated settlement is more likely to be accepted by the parties; and negotiation is simpler and less costly than other methods'.[4]

In their book published in 2004, Bercovitch and Fretter surveyed the choice of conflict management methods for 343 international conflicts (occurring between 1945 and 2003) and found that states employed mediation in 59.3% of all cases, negotiation in 32.2%, and arbitration in 0.6%. Like other authors, they also emphasised the preference for dispute resolution methods that maximise state control, such as mediation or negotiation. Further, that, while 'allowing states to maintain control over the process', 'mediation and negotiation seem to offer a relatively high chance of success'. On the other hand, there is a 'reluctance to use international organizations [to assist in solving conflicts] as the organizations appear to be far less effective at settling conflicts'.[5]

Almost 40 years ago, Richard Bilder explained some of the key factors underlying States' preference for negotiation to other forms of dispute resolution involving third parties, including that 'negotiation is the least risky way of trying to deal with disputes', as both parties retain 'maximum control' over the process and outcome and the 'option of simply walking away from the negotiation and not agreeing'. Further that: '[n]egotiation places responsibility for resolving the dispute on the parties themselves, who are in the best

3 Manuel Indlekofer, 'Public International Arbitration in Today's Dispute Settlement Framework' in *International Arbitration and the Permanent Court of Arbitration* (vol 27, Kluwer Law International, 2013) 111–232, at 117.

4 Carla Copeland, 'The Use of Arbitration to Settle Territorial Disputes' (1999) 67(6) *Fordham Law Review* 3073–3108, at 3103. See also Richard Bilder, 'An Overview of International Dispute Settlement' (1986) 1(1) Legal Studies Research Paper Series Archival Collection Emory Journal of International Dispute Resolution 1–32, at 22 ('[n]egotiation is clearly the predominant, usual and preferred method of resolving international disputes. Except in cases where the dispute is submitted directly to settlement by binding adjudication or conciliation, or where settlement is otherwise imposed by a third party, negotiation is normally an essential component of any dispute settlement process'.), and B. S. Murthy, 'Diplomacy and Resolution of International Disputes' in United Nations, *International Law as a Language for International Relations* (Kluwer International Law, The Hague 1997), at 163 ('negotiation is the most preferable method of settlement of disputes'.)

5 Jacob Bercovitch and Judith Fretter, *Regional Guide to International Conflict and Management from 1945 to 2003* (SAGE Publications, California 2004), at 29.

position to develop a sensible, workable and acceptable solution' that – as a freely-agreed to solution – will presumably have 'maximum acceptability and stability'. Bilder explained that '[n]egotiation favors compromise and accommodation between the parties', which is most likely to preserve good long-term relations between the parties and meets their priorities for the process, for example, a process that simple, less costly than other options and easy to carry out without publicity.[6]

Murthy echoed these sentiments a decade later in his book on international law as a language for international relations, particularly emphasising that a negotiated settlement is more likely to be seen as balanced and respected: 'since the resolution of the dispute is by mutual consent, reached after free bargaining, there is a high degree of probability of both the parties carrying out the agreement faithfully .... arbitration and judicial settlement are, in game-theoretic terms, zero-sum games. One party's gain is the other party's loss and the total pay-off is zero'.[7]

The preference on the part of States to resort to negotiation or mediation is also reflected in international practice: for example, through the many compromissory clauses in treaties that require States parties to a dispute to engage in negotiation for a period of time before resorting to third party adjudication, such as, arbitration or the International Court of Justice (the ***Court***).[8] As Bilder noted '[i]ndeed, the use of other techniques [than negotiation] including adjudication, is usually preceded, accompanied by and arranged through some kind of negotiation process'.[9]

For example, in *Application of the International Convention on the Elimination of All Forms of Racial Discrimination* (*Georgia v. Russian Federation*), the Court explained that: 'it is not unusual in compromissory clauses conferring jurisdiction on the Court and other international jurisdictions to refer to resort to negotiations'. It went on to explain the rationale behind such clauses: first,

6 Bilder, *supra* n 4 at 36.

7 Murthy, *supra* n 4 at 22.

8 The six methods of peaceful inter-State dispute settlement envisaged in the UN Charter are: negotiation, medication, conciliation, fact-finding, arbitration and resort to the international court of justice. Article 30(1) of the Convention against Torture and Other Cruel, Inhuman or Degrading Treatment or Punishment 1984 provides one example of this ratcheting mechanism: '[a]Any dispute between two or more States Parties concerning the interpretation or application of this Convention which cannot be settled through negotiation shall, at the request of one of them, be submitted to arbitration. If within six months from the date of the request for arbitration the Parties are unable to agree on the organization of the arbitration, any one of those Parties may refer the dispute to the International Court of Justice by request in conformity with the Statute of the Court.'

9 Bilder, *supra* n 4 at 36.

'it gives notice to the respondent State that a dispute exists and delimits the scope of the dispute and its subject-matter;' second, 'it encourages the parties to attempt to settle their dispute by mutual agreement, thus avoiding recourse to binding third-party adjudication;' and, third, 'prior resort to negotiations or other methods of peaceful dispute settlement performs an important function in indicating the limit of consent given by States'.[10]

It is within this context that we understand that resort to dispute resolution involving a third party – and especially international adjudication by an international body – will be the exception and not the rule. Certain States make more use of international adjudication than others.[11] This may reflect a more general political and cultural acceptance of international adjudication (see final section). There is also a sense in which a third-party decision-making body may level the playing field in a context where more powerful States could have more leverage in negotiations. Binding dispute resolution has benefits that may be absolutely key in certain situations, for example, where it might be easier to sell an 'imposed' solution to a domestic audience.

The factors that propel States towards negotiation also help us understand some of the considerations at play in resorting to other adjudication methods, including: time, timing and cost; State control over the process (with its concomitant impact on risk); limited derogation of sovereignty; the ability to craft a solution that is acceptable to both parties and accounts for factors that there is no appetite to broadcast in a public, international or national forum; and, the ability to address multiple factors rather than only the likely narrow set of norms subject to the jurisdiction of an international body. How much these factors matter in each situation depends on the specific context.

In a complex context – including the majority in which inter-State human rights claims arise (see next section) – diplomatic efforts, including negotiation, will also often continue alongside any third-party resolution procedure that is launched. The different dispute resolution mechanisms influence the other. While negotiations may be a precursor to triggering a different dispute resolution mechanism under a treaty, they will also often continue in parallel or rise and fall alongside the proceedings. As is discussed further below,

---

10 Application of the International Convention on the Elimination of All Forms of Racial Discrimination (*Georgia v. Russian Federation*), Preliminary Objections, Judgment, I.C.J. Reports 2011, at 70, para. 131.

11 *See E.g.,* Jin-Hyun Paik, Asian States' Participation in International Adjudication: Comments, EJIL Talk, 18 January 2017, <https://www.ejiltalk.org/asian-states-participation-in-international-adjudication-comments/> accessed 30 April 2024.

international proceedings may also be a leverage point in negotiations or an impulse to find a settlement.

3 A Contextual Perspective

Human rights disputes between States will usually arise as part of larger, multifaceted context; not in a vacuum.[12] They are often tied up with economic considerations, trade, boundaries, conflict, and/or the sharing (or not) of natural resources. This stands in contrast to human rights disputes raised by individuals to the international level, many of which concern a specific (often structural) human rights violation(s) decoupled from other violations of international law. There must therefore be an incentive for a State to raise a concern about what is happening in another jurisdiction to the international level, and that incentive will likely be found in a broader context of mass violations, cross-border implications, or the potential violation of other international law norms – or all of these factors together.

A brief survey of inter-State disputes brought under human rights treaties before the ICJ over the last 15 years illustrates this point. The *Georgia v. Russia, Ukraine v. Russia, Qatar v. UAE, Armenia v. Azerbaijan* and *Azerbaijan v. Armenia* disputes, under the Convention on the Elimination of All Forms of Racial Discrimination (**CERD**), concern or concerned allegations of mass violations arising in a broader context of conflict, political or diplomatic isolation, the transition to peace, and sitting alongside other allegations of international law violations either before other courts and tribunals or at the international level more generally.[13] The same can be seen in disputes under the 1948 Convention on the Prevention and Punishment of the Crime of Genocide (***Genocide Convention***) and the Convention against Torture and

12 There are, of course, exceptions to this pattern. The *Diallo* case before the ICJ was based on the diplomatic espousal by one State of human rights violations against one of its citizens against another State. See Ahmadou Sadio Diallo (*Republic of Guinea v. Democratic Republic of the Congo*), Merits, Judgment, I.C.J. Reports 2010, at 639.

13 Application of the International Convention on the Elimination of All Forms of Racial Discrimination (*Georgia v. Russian Federation*); Application of the International Convention for the Suppression of the Financing of Terrorism and of the International Convention on the Elimination of All Forms of Racial Discrimination (*Ukraine v. Russian Federation*); Application of the International Convention on the Elimination of All Forms of Racial Discrimination (*Qatar v. United Arab Emirates*); Application of the International Convention on the Elimination of All Forms of Racial Discrimination (*Armenia v. Azerbaijan*); Application of the International Convention on the Elimination of All Forms of Racial Discrimination (*Azerbaijan v. Armenia*).

Other Cruel, Inhuman or Degrading Treatment or Punishment 1984 (CAT). *Gambia v. Myanmar*, for example, concerns atrocities against the Rohingya that has led to a mass displacement from Myanmar to Bangladesh and other countries.[14] However, the broader context of this dispute is decades of military dictatorship, isolationism, attempts to transition to democracy (at the time) and – although largely forgotten by the international community – sporadic and sustained conflicts against different ethnic peoples that have included atrocities, including systematic sexual and gender-based violence and displacement. The same applies to the case under the Genocide Convention between Ukraine and Russia, which arises in the context of an ongoing conflict, and that between Canada and the Netherlands against Syria under the Torture Convention.[15] In the Application commencing proceedings, Canada and the Netherlands describe:

> Syria has committed countless violations of international law, beginning at least in 2011, with its violent repression of civilian demonstrations, and continuing as the situation in Syria devolved into a protracted armed conflict. These violations include the use of torture and other cruel, inhuman or degrading treatment or punishment ('CIDTP'), including through abhorrent treatment of detainees, inhumane conditions in places of detention, enforced disappearances, the use of sexual and gender-based violence, and violence against children. These violations also include the use of chemical weapons which has been a particularly abhorrent practice to intimidate and punish the civilian population, resulting in numerous deaths, injuries and severe physical and mental suffering. Syria's actions, which have resulted in severe pain and suffering, and the deaths of tens of thousands of people, have been met with widespread condemnation by the international community.[16]

We see a similar picture in inter-State cases brought before the European Court of Human Rights – human rights violations are part of a broader context. A

---

14 Application of the Convention on the Prevention and Punishment of the Crime of Genocide (*The Gambia v. Myanmar*).

15 Allegations of Genocide under the Convention on the Prevention and Punishment of the Crime of Genocide (*Ukraine v. Russian Federation: 32 States intervening*); Application of the Convention against Torture and Other Cruel, Inhuman or Degrading Treatment or Punishment (*Canada and the Netherlands v. Syrian Arab Republic*).

16 Application of the Convention against Torture and Other Cruel, Inhuman or Degrading Treatment or Punishment (*Canada and the Netherlands v. Syrian Arab Republic*), Joint Application Instituting Proceedings, 8 June 2023, para. 2.

conference report published by the Council of Europe and other institutions in 2022 stated: '[a]n increasing number of inter-State applications have been brought before the European Court of Human Rights recent years ... they often relate to conflict situations ...'.[17]

The context of any human rights dispute has obvious implications for the available dispute resolution options. A State will need to decide whether to consider all the implicated violations holistically, or to raise pieces of the dispute to a dispute resolution body in line with the patchwork of international jurisdiction (discussed in the next section). The multi-faceted context includes, not only the broader factual scenario in which the human rights violations arise, but also the historical background of relations and diplomacy between the two (or more) States and future projections. The channels of communication, priorities in the relationship between the States involved and the trade off on what comes next also add to the option-narrowing process.

4 Patchwork of International Norms

4.1 *Substantive Obligations*

International law consists of a patchwork of norms, developed and evolving iteratively over time, and premised on State consent. As such, there are scenarios not covered by international norms (a precursor to an international 'dispute') and not every State is bound by every international norm. A snapshot of ratifications of universal human rights conventions illustrates this point (see https://indicators.ohchr.org/): for example, CERD, which has formed the basis of multiple international proceedings has been ratified by 182 States, signed by 3 States and 12 States have taken no action.[18]

However, ratifications do not represent a full picture of the available substantive obligations. A State may have entered reservations to the substantive provisions of a treaty – and therefore the number of States parties does not necessarily represent the number of States bound by each protection.

17 Summary, Inter-state cases under the European Convention on Human Rights – Experiences and current challenges (2022), <https://edoc.coe.int/en/european-convention-on-human-rights/11067-inter-state-cases-under-the-european-convention-on-human-rights-experiences-and-current-challenges.html> accessed 30 April 2024. For additional discussion on inter-State cases before the ECHR see Isabella Risini and Tim Eicke, 'Inter-State Applications under the European Convention on Human Rights – situating the instrument in the current human rights landscape' (2024) 13(1) *International Human Rights Law Review*.

18 United Nations Human Rights Office of the High Commissioner, 'Status of Ratification Interactive Dashboard' <https://indicators.ohchr.org/> accessed 30 April 2024.

Reservations 'purport[s] to exclude or alter the legal effect of certain provisions of the treaty in their application to [the reserving] state'.[19]

However, there are specific limits on the nature and extent of reservations that States may make and therefore the scope to exclude obligations under a treaty. Certain treaties do not permit reservations at all or permit only specific reservations.[20] For example, Article 16 of the Treaty on the Prohibition of Nuclear Weapons states: '[t]he Articles of this Treaty shall not be subject to reservations'.[21] Even if the treaty is silent on whether reservations are permissible, reservations cannot be incompatible with the object and purpose of the relevant treaty.[22] The Human Rights Committee (***HRC***) has clarified that reservations to norms within the International Covenant on Civil and Political Rights (***ICCPR***) that 'represent customary international law (and a fortiori when they have the character of peremptory norms) may not be the subject of reservations'. It has also analysed whether reservations to other norms would be justified, clarifying, for example, that reservations to non-derogable rights would put a 'heavy onus' on the reserving State to justify its reservations.[23] Further, for example, that 'supportive' 'guarantees provide the necessary framework for securing the rights in the Covenant and are thus essential to its object and purpose … Reservations designed to remove these guarantees are thus not acceptable. Thus, a State could not make a reservation to article 2, paragraph 3, of the Covenant, indicating that it intends to provide no remedies for human rights violations. Guarantees such as these are an integral part of the structure of the Covenant and underpin its efficacy'.[24]

---

19 United Nations Treaty Collection, 'Glossary of terms relating to Treaty actions' <https://treaties.un.org/pages/overview.aspx?path=overview/glossary/page1_en.xml#:~:text=of%20Treaties%201969%5D-,Reservation,their%20application%20to%20that%20state> accessed 30 April 2024. Reservations are: 'declaration[s] made by a state by which it purports to exclude or alter the legal effect of certain provisions of the treaty in their application to that state. A reservation enables a state to accept a multilateral treaty as a whole by giving it the possibility not to apply certain provisions with which it does not want to comply. Reservations can be made when the treaty is signed, ratified, accepted, approved or acceded to. Reservations must not be incompatible with the object and the purpose of the treaty. Furthermore, a treaty might prohibit reservations or only allow for certain reservations to be made'.

20 *See* Article 19, Vienna Convention on the Law of Treaties 1969.

21 Treaty on the Prohibition of Nuclear Weapons, 7 July 2017, <https://ihl-databases.icrc.org/en/ihl-treaties/tpnw-2017/article-16> accessed 30 April 2024.

22 *See* Article 19, Vienna Convention on the Law of Treaties 1969.

23 CCPR/C/21/Rev.1/Add.6, 11 November 1994, para. 8.

24 CCPR/C/21/Rev.1/Add.6, 11 November 1994, para. 11.

States also use declarations[25] (or sometimes 'understandings') to clarify their understanding of treaty obligations, although, unlike reservations they do not alter the binding legal effect of the obligations in question. However, some 'declarations', in fact, purport to alter the legal effects of a treaty – a practice that has been described as widely used.[26] Regardless of its name, if the statement 'purports to limit the obligations imposed on it by the treaty',[27] it will be treated as a reservation and will be subject to the customary rules concerning reservations' validity.

In their article published in *International Studies Quarterly* in 2020, Zvobgo, Sandholtz and Mulesky published statistics on declarations and reservations, 'Human rights treaty reservations and declarations, 1948–2014' (see figure below reproduced from their article).[28] They note that '[t]reaty reservations introduce flexibility for states, potentially reducing the constraining power of treaties'.[29] The HRC has explained that reservations to the ICCPR serve specific functions:

> The possibility of entering reservations may encourage States which consider that they have difficulties in guaranteeing all the rights in the Covenant none the less to accept the generality of obligations in that instrument. Reservations may serve a useful function to enable States to adapt specific elements in their laws to the inherent rights of each person as articulated in the Covenant.[30]

However, Zvobgo, Sandholtz and Mulesky explain that 'reservations to human rights treaties are rare. States do not make widespread use of reservations to dilute their obligations'.[31]

---

25 *Ibid.* Sometimes states make 'declarations' as to their understanding of some matter or as to the interpretation of a particular provision. Unlike reservations, declarations merely clarify the state's position and do not purport to exclude or modify the legal effect of a treaty. Usually, declarations are made at the time of the deposit of the corresponding instrument or at the time of signature.

26 Anthony Aust, *Modern Treaty Law and Practice* (Cambridge University Press, Cambridge 2004) 101.

27 Report of the International Law Commission on the Work of its Fifty-First Session, 3 May23 July 1999 (A/54/10) (1999 ILC Report), Chapter VI, 1 (1) (5).

28 Suzie Mulesky et al, 'Reserving Rights: Explaining Human Rights Treaty Reservations' (2020) 64(4) 785–797, at 788 figure 1. DOI: https://doi.org/10.1093/isq/sqaa070.

29 Suzie Mulesky et al, Do Human Rights Treaty Obligations Matter for Ratification? (2020) 1–42, at 38. DOI: http://dx.doi.org/10.2139/ssrn.3383165.

30 CCPR/C/21/Rev.1/Add.6, 11 November 1994, para. 4.

31 Mulesky et al, *supra* n 28.

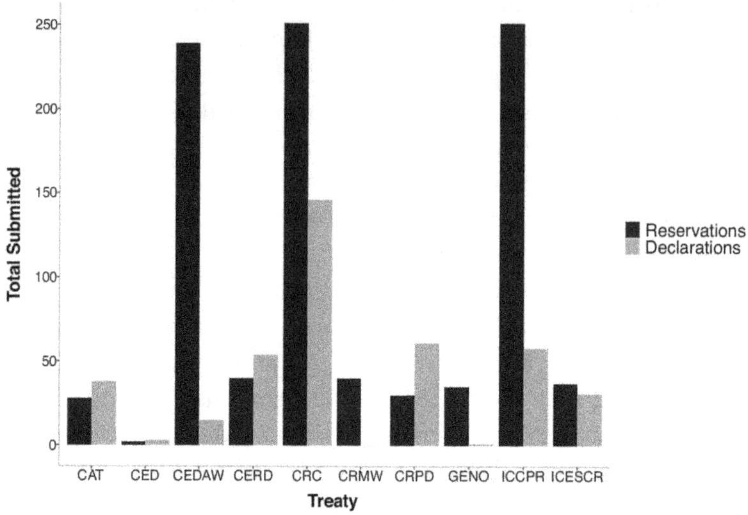

FIGURE 1 Human rights treaty reservations and declarations, 1948–2014. Reproduced from Figure 1 in 'Reserving Rights: Explaining Human Rights Treaty Reservations' Mulesky, Sandholtz and Zvobgo. *International Studies Quarterly*, Volume 64, Issue 4, December 2020, Pages 785–797.

The CEDAW, the CRC and the ICCPR have invited the largest number of reservations. They are, however, three of the most ratified treaties. This search for 'flexibility' means that States need to consider which norms bind their potential opponent in an international dispute before they map their options.[32]

32 Examples of reservations to these treaties include Slovenia's reservation to Article 9(1) of the CRC ('The Republic of Slovenia reserves the right not to apply paragraph 1 of article 9 of the Convention since the internal legislation of the Republic of Slovenia provides for the right of competent authorities (centres for social work) to determine on separation of a child from his/her parents without a previous judicial review' (Slovenia, 6 July 1992)) and Gambia's reservation to Article 14(3)(d) of the ICCPR ('For financial reasons free legal assistance for accused persons is limited in our constitution to persons charged with capital offences only. The Government of the Gambia therefore wishes to enter a reservation in respect of article 14 (3) (d) of the Covenant in question' (Gambia, 22 March 1979)). The Genocide Convention 1948 has also invited a variety of reservations, including, for example, that of Venezuela to Article 7 ('With reference to article VII, notice is given that the laws in force in Venezuela do not permit the extradition of Venezuelan nationals' (Venezuela, 12 July 1960)) and Singapore's reservation to the dispute resolution provision in Article 9 ('That with reference to article IX of the Convention, before any dispute to which the Republic of Singapore is a party may be submitted to the jurisdiction of the International Court of Justice under this article, the specific consent of the Republic of Singapore is required in each case' (Singapore, 18 August 1995)).

Another source of international law obligations is customary international law – these norms bind all States, aside from those that qualify as 'persistent objectors'.[33] A persistent objector is a State that has persistently rejected a new rule even before it emerged as such to avoid its application. There is of course a relationship between treaties and customary international law – the former codifying or often contributing to the crystallisation of the latter and the latter developing the former. Most human rights norms found in customary international law are also codified in treaties. In addition, there are a series of norms – many relating to human rights protections – that bind all States and trump any other obligations they may have made. These *jus cogens* norms are defined by the International Law Commission as follows:

> Peremptory norms of general international law (*jus cogens*) reflect and protect fundamental values of the international community. They are universally applicable and are hierarchically superior to other rules of international law.
>
> A peremptory norm of general international law (*jus cogens*) is a norm accepted and recognized by the international community of States as a whole as a norm from which no derogation is permitted and which can be modified only by a subsequent norm of general international law having the same character.[34]

That these norms bind all States does not mean there is jurisdiction (see next sub-section), but in the patchwork of international substantive norms, they are truly universal.

4.2 *Jurisdiction and Admissibility*

This patchwork of applicable norms also extends to jurisdiction. The fact that State A is bound by a particular obligation under international law does not mean there is jurisdiction for State B to raise a dispute against State A to the international level. Jurisdiction flows from State consent – both as to whether a claim can be brought and where and how that claim can be raised. To understand the options on the table, a State would need to analyse the relevant

33 For example, the ICRC's study concluded in 2005 found 161 norms of customary international humanitarian law. University of Cambridge, 'Customary International Law Project' <https://www.lcil.cam.ac.uk/researchcollaborative-projects-housed-lcil/customary-international-humanitarian-law-project accessed> 30 April 2024.

34 United Nations, *Report of the International Law Commission* (Seventy-third session, Supplement No. 10 (A/77/10), 2022), at 11–12.

substantive obligations and then any associated jurisdictional provisions. States may also enter reservations to the dispute resolution provisions of the treaty (subject to the caveats set out above regarding reservations, although, reservations to compromissory clauses will not generally be seen as incompatible with a treaty's object and purpose.). A State may therefore be bound by all the substantive obligations contained in a treaty, but there is no option for another State to compel resolution of a dispute about that substantive obligation.

Dispute resolution provisions are a frequent target of reservations. In fact, Zvobgo, Sandholtz and Mulesky suggest a reverse relationship between the strength of the substantive provisions in a human rights treaty and a State's willingness to accept jurisdiction of an international body to look at it:

> Related to this point, one might argue that another design feature of international [human rights treaties] relevant to their demandingness is whether or not states accept the jurisdiction of a treaty body, court, or committee to receive submissions from other states or from individuals, to interpret the treaty, or to initiate inquiries.[35]

For example, multiple States have entered reservations to Article 22 of the CERD, which provides:

> Any dispute between two or more States Parties with respect to the interpretation or application of this Convention, which is not settled by negotiation or by the procedures expressly provided for in this Convention, shall, at the request of any of the parties to the dispute, be referred to the International Court of Justice for decision, unless the disputants agree to another mode of settlement.[36]

Each reservation is formulated in its own unique language, but there are two clear trends. Some States, for example, Bahrain, have entered reservations to Article 22 that state that consent to apply Article 22 or to the Court's jurisdiction would have to be given by both parties once the dispute is envisaged.[37]

35 Mulesky et al, *supra* n 28, at 786.

36 International Convention on the Elimination of All Forms of Racial Discrimination (adopted 21 December 1965, entered into force 4 January 1969) (*cerd*), Article 22.

37 Bahrain's reservation reads: '[w]ith reference to article 22 of the Convention, the Government of the State of Bahrain declares that, for the submission of any dispute in terms of this article to the jurisdiction of the International Court of Justice, the express consent of all the parties to the dispute is required in each case'. CERD, Bahrain's reservation.

Others, such as China, do not envisage the operation of Article 22 under any circumstances.[38]

There are other ways that consent to jurisdiction may be provided aside from a compromissory clause in the treaty, for example: (i) the parties may consent to a particular form of dispute resolution at the time the dispute arises (or later); (ii) there may be a general form of submissions to disputes before a particular institution, such as the optional declarations deposited by certain States at the ICJ (often subject to conditions, including reciprocity);[39] (iii) the parties may have agreed to a more general form of jurisdiction that covers the subject matter of the specific dispute, for example, the American Treaty on Pacific Settlement, also known as the Pact of Bogota, which provides for various dispute resolution options and has been invoked as the basis for ICJ jurisdiction in multiple disputes between its States parties.[40]

Once a State has verified that there is a *potential* basis for jurisdiction to hear a dispute, it will need to satisfy any conditions that precede the parties' consent to the exercise of that jurisdiction. The jurisprudence of the ICJ has frequently discussed different contours of consent-based jurisdiction. The Court's jurisprudence has, for example, treated in some depth what Article 22 of the CERD requires before the Court can claim jurisdiction to decide the

---

38 China's reservation reads: '[t]he People's Republic of China has reservations on the provisions of article 22 of the Convention and will not be bound by it'. CERD, China's reservation.

39 The ICJ Statute envisages that the States parties to the Statute of the Court may 'at any time declare that they recognize as compulsory *ipso facto* and without special agreement, in relation to any other State accepting the same obligation, the jurisdiction of the Court'. See Statute of the International Court of Justice, Article 36(2). At present, 74 States have deposited declarations. See International Court of Justice, 'Declarations recognizing the jurisdiction of the Court as compulsory' <https://www.icj-cij.org/declarations> accessed 30 April 2024.

40 Territorial and Maritime Dispute between Nicaragua and Honduras in the Caribbean Sea (*Nicaragua v. Colombia*); Dispute regarding Navigational and Related Rights Case (*Costa Rica v. Nicaragua*); Maritime Dispute (*Peru v. Chile*); Aerial Herbicide Spraying (*Ecuador v. Colombia*) (discontinued); Certain Questions concerning Diplomatic Relations (*Honduras v. Brazil*) (discontinued); Certain Activities carried out by Nicaragua in the Border Area (*Costa Rica v. Nicaragua*); Construction of a Road in Costa Rica along the San Juan River (*Nicaragua v. Costa Rica*); Obligation to Negotiate Access to the Pacific Ocean (*Bolivia v. Chile*); Question of the Delimitation of the Continental Shelf between Nicaragua and Colombia beyond 200 nautical miles from the Nicaraguan *Coast* (*Nicaragua v. Colombia*); Alleged Violations of Sovereign Rights and Maritime Spaces in the Caribbean Sea (*Nicaragua v. Colombia*); Maritime Delimitation in the Caribbean Sea and the Pacific Ocean (*Costa Rica v. Nicaragua*); Land Boundary in the Northern Part of Isla Portillos (*Costa Rica v. Nicaragua*); Dispute over the Status and Use of the Waters of the Silala (*Chile v. Bolivia*).

dispute – *first,* and obviously, that the dispute must concern the 'interpretation or application' of the CERD (i.e., the subject matter of the treaty); *second,* that the phrase 'which is not settled by' in Article 22 (see citation of Article 22 above) indicated that the procedures envisaged in Article 22 are a precondition to seisin of the Court;[41] and *third,* in *Ukraine v. Russia,* the Court clarified that 'not settled by negotiation' or 'not settled by […] the procedures expressly provided for' are alternative not cumulative conditions to access the Court's jurisdiction.[42] In *Georgia v. Russia,* the Court also explained the content of the 'negotiation' requirement. Not only must the negotiations concern the subject matter of treaty:

> In determining what constitutes negotiations, the Court observes that negotiations are distinct from mere protests or disputations. Negotiations entail more than the plain opposition of legal views or interests between two parties, or the existence of a series of accusations and rebuttals, or even the exchange of claims and directly opposed counter-claims. As such, the concept of 'negotiations' differs from the concept of 'dispute', and requires – at the very least – a genuine attempt by one of the disputing parties to engage in discussions with the other disputing party, with a view to resolving the dispute.
>
> […]
>
> Manifestly, in the absence of evidence of a genuine attempt to negotiate, the precondition of negotiation is not met. However, where negotiations are attempted or have commenced, the jurisprudence of this Court and of the Permanent Court of International Justice clearly reveals that the precondition of negotiation is met only when there has been a failure of negotiations, or when negotiations have become futile or deadlocked.[43]

41 Application of the International Convention on the Elimination of All Forms of Racial Discrimination (*Georgia v. Russian Federation*), Preliminary Objections, Judgment, I.C.J. Reports 2011, at 70, para. 141.

42 Application of the International Convention for the Suppression of the Financing of Terrorism and of the International Convention on the Elimination of All Forms of Racial Discrimination (*Ukraine v. Russian Federation*), Preliminary Objections, Judgment, I.C.J. Reports 2019, at 558, para. 113.

43 Application of the International Convention on the Elimination of All Forms of Racial Discrimination (*Georgia v. Russian Federation*), Preliminary Objections, Judgment, I.C.J. Reports 2011, at 70, paras 157, 159.

A case that illustrates clearly all the different limits to jurisdiction discussed in this section is *DRC v. Rwanda*.[44] The DRC filed its case against Rwanda before the ICJ under the compromissory clauses 'in many legal instruments', including the 1979 Convention on the Elimination on All Forms of Discrimination against Women, the CERD, the Genocide Convention, the Constitution of the WHO, the Constitution of UNESCO, the CAT and the 1971 Montreal Convention for the Suppression of Unlawful Acts against the Safety of Civil Aviation. The DRC further contended in its Application that Article 66 of the Vienna Convention on the Law of Treaties of 23 May 1969 established the jurisdiction of the Court to settle disputes arising from the violation of peremptory norms (jus cogens) in the area of human rights, as those norms were reflected in a number of international instruments.[45]

The Court declined jurisdiction over the dispute under each of these instruments on one or more of each of the conditions just discussed: that either (i) Rwanda was not a signatory to the relevant treaty; (ii) Rwanda had entered reservations to the dispute resolution clause; or (iii) DRC could not show that the preconditions for seisin of the Court specified in the treaties had not been satisfied.

In relation to the DRC's objections to the validity of Rwanda's reservation to compromissory clauses encapsulating treaty norms, and the DRC's attempt to found its jurisdiction on the Vienna Convention and the invocation of *jus cogens* norms, the Court said:

> The Court observes, however, as it has already had occasion to emphasize, that 'the *erga omnes* character of a norm and the rule of consent to jurisdiction are two different things' (*East Timor (Portugal v. Australia), Judgment, I.C.J. Reports 1995*, p. 102, para. 29), and that the mere fact that rights and obligations *erga omnes* may be at issue in a dispute would not give the Court jurisdiction to entertain that dispute. The same applies to the relationship between peremptory norms of general international law (*jus cogens*) and the establishment of the Court's jurisdiction: the fact that a dispute relates to compliance with a norm having such a character, which is assuredly the case with regard to the prohibition of genocide, cannot of itself provide a basis for the jurisdiction of the Court to entertain that

44 Armed Activities on the Territory of the Congo (New Application: 2002) (*Democratic Republic of the Congo v. Rwanda*).

45 Armed Activities on the Territory of the Congo (New Application: 2002) (*Democratic Republic of the Congo v. Rwanda*), Jurisdiction and Admissibility, Judgment, I.C.J. Reports 2006, at 6, para. 1.

> dispute. Under the Court's Statute that jurisdiction is always based on the consent of the parties.[46]

Another jurisdictional hurdle that presents itself frequently in inter-State human rights cases, especially concerning conflict, is whether a State exercises 'jurisdiction' or 'authority' in areas outside of its territory such that its human rights obligations apply. The European Court of Human Rights has considered this question in various different conflict scenarios, including in territories where the Convention does or does not apply. This includes in the European Court of Human rights's ruling on admissibility in *Ukraine v. Russia* (*Crimea*), in which it found: 'Eu égard à l'ensemble des considérations qui précèdent, la Cour estime qu'elle dispose de suffisamment d'éléments pour pouvoir conclure que, pendant la période considérée, l'État défendeur exerçait un contrôle effectif sur la Crimée'.[47] This subject is treated in more detail in Risini and Eicke's contribution to this special issue on inter-State cases before the European Court of Human Rights.[48]

Therefore, a patchwork of potentially applicable international norms has to be overlayed with a picture of limited consent-based jurisdiction. The boundaries carved by the applicable and relevant international law obligations and consent to jurisdiction can result in disputes that emphasise a very specific aspect of a much broader situation. In relation to the *Georgia v. Russia* dispute before the ICJ under the CERD, Phoebe Okawa wrote:

> From a litigant's perspective, the strategic decision to base the dispute on the jurisdictional provisions of CERD is not hard to fathom. As is well known, the International Court's jurisdiction is based on state consent, and none of the relevant instruments that were binding on the two states provided a jurisdictional basis for disputes on the use of force. CERD provided a convenient peg for the public articulation of Georgia's grievances, even if the substance of the dispute was only peripherally concerned with racial discrimination.[49]

---

46 *Ibid.* para. 64. This conclusion was reiterated at para. 125.

47 *Grand Chamber Admissibility Decision in the case of Ukraine v. Russia* (*re Crimea*) (app nos 20958/14 and 38334/18), 16 December 2020, para. 335.

48 Isabella Risini and Tim Eicke, 'Inter-State Applications under the European Convention on Human Rights – situating the instrument in the current human rights landscape' (2024) 13(1) *International Human Rights Law Review*.

49 Phoebe Okawa, 'The International Court of Justice and the Georgia/Russia Dispute' (2011) 11(4) *Human Rights Law Review* 739–757, at 740. DOI: https://doi.org/10.1093/hrlr/ngr039.

Okawa explained that the *Georgia* case was one of a 'long line of cases' where the jurisdictional clause of a convention had more to do with 'drawing international attention to their plight than the settlement of the dispute that had arisen'.[50]

Sitting alongside jurisdiction, admissibility is another potential hurdle when considering bringing an inter-State dispute (it is worth noting that jurisdiction and admissibility are not categorised in the same way by all international bodies). In human rights cases, especially where diplomatic protection is concerned, admissibility requirements will involve exhausting local remedies. However, there are some key exceptions to the requirement to exhaust domestic remedies, including, of particular relevance to inter-State cases, where there is a pattern of violations. In *Ukraine v. Russia,* the Court found that:

> The Court notes that, according to Ukraine, the Russian Federation has engaged in a sustained campaign of racial discrimination, carried out through acts repeated over an appreciable period of time starting in 2014, against the Crimean Tatar and Ukrainian communities in Crimea. The Court also notes that the individual instances to which Ukraine refers in its submissions emerge as illustrations of the acts by which the Russian Federation has allegedly engaged in a campaign of racial discrimination. It follows, in the view of the Court, that, in filing its Application under Article 22 of CERD, Ukraine does not adopt the cause of one or more of its nationals, but challenges, on the basis of CERD, the alleged pattern of conduct of the Russian Federation with regard to the treatment of the Crimean Tatar and Ukrainian communities in Crimea. In view of the above, the Court concludes that the rule of exhaustion of local remedies does not apply in the circumstances of the present case.[51]

Another key factor in determining admissibility is whether there is an interest at play that gives the applicant state standing. For example, in the South West Africa Cases (*Ethiopia v. South Africa* and *Liberia v. South Africa*) concerning South Africa's apartheid measures conducted in Namibia, the ICJ affirmed its jurisdiction to hear the cases in 1962, but, in 1966, determined that Ethiopia and Liberia 'cannot be considered to have established any legal right or

50 Ibid.

51 Application of the International Convention for the Suppression of the Financing of Terrorism and of the International Convention on the Elimination of All Forms of Racial Discrimination (*Ukraine* v. *Russian Federation*), Preliminary Objections, Judgment, I.C.J. Reports 2019, at 558, para. 130 (emphasis added).

interest appertaining to them in the subject-matter of the present claims'.[52] However, there is a broader notion of the standing of States to bring claims where obligations are obligations *erga omnes* or *erga omnes partes*, as has already been declared to be the character of various human rights obligations (jurisdiction to adjudicate human rights disputes usually arises under human rights treaties and so *erga omnes partes* is a more common basis to request standing in such cases). For example, in Questions relating to the Obligation to Prosecute or Extradite (*Belgium v. Senegal*), under the Convention Against Torture, the Court found that:

> The common interest in compliance with the relevant obligations under the Convention against Torture implies the entitlement of each State party to the Convention to make a claim concerning the cessation of an alleged breach by another State party. If a special interest were required for that purpose, in many cases no State would be in the position to make such a claim. It follows that any State party to the Convention may invoke the responsibility of another State party with a view to ascertaining the alleged failure to comply with its obligations *erga omnes partes*, such as those under Article 6, paragraph 2, and Article 7, paragraph 1, of the Convention, and to bring that failure to an end.[53]

A similar ground for admissibility has been pleaded in recent cases, including *Gambia v. Myanmar* and *Canada and the Netherlands v. Syria*, demonstrating that obligations of this nature open up a much wider swathe of 'interested' parties than in cases that do not implicate obligations *erga omnes* or *erga omnes partes*.

Although not the specific subject of this article, another strategic factor worth bearing in mind is the possibility of international advocacy to other international institutions that can be appealed to uphold certain norms. These routes apply whether or not dispute resolution provisions are available, or jurisdiction or admissibility conditions are satisfied, and may therefore arise alongside or aside from a claim. The findings that might be issued by these bodies and the potential associated leverage adds another layer of complexity to any inter-State dispute strategy. Such findings are very likely to form part of any evidential record (see next section) and perhaps add impetus to bringing related international proceedings. For example, at its 17th Special Session, the

---

52 South West Africa, Second Phase, Judgment, ICJ Reports 1966, at 6, para. 99.

53 Questions relating to the Obligation to Prosecute or Extradite, (*Belgium* v. *Senegal*), Judgment, I.C.J. Reports 2012, at 422, para. 69.

Human Rights Council issued Resolution S-17/1 concerning the 'Situation of human rights in the Syrian Arab Republic', which involved establishing an 'independent international commission of inquiry' 'to investigate all alleged violations of international human rights law since March 2011 in the Syrian Arab Republic, to establish the facts and circumstances that may amount to such violations and of the crimes perpetrated and, where possible, to identify those responsible with a view to ensuring that perpetrators of violations, including those that may constitute crimes against humanity, are held accountable'.[54] The commission of inquiry subsequently issued numerous reports on the situation in Syria, some of which have been relied on as evidence by Canada and the Netherlands in its case against Syria at the ICJ and drawn on by the ICJ in issuing provisional measures in the case in November 2023.[55]

5 Legal and Factual Considerations

Once a State knows that there is an available cause of action – applicable substantive obligations, jurisdiction, admissibility – there is another layer of strategic assessments to make relating to facts and law. In relation to the law, namely: what is the state of the substantive law? How settled is that law? What is the power of the relevant body to interpret the law? How likely is that body to stay consistent with what has gone before? What is the risk that the state of the law will be determined or reinterpreted in the State's favour or against it? These factors may well influence the type of dispute resolution body that a State chooses or whether to bring a claim at all – will a particular body take a more progressive position on the law and is that in the State's favour?

Further, in relation to evidence, what are the key points the State will need to show to arrive at the outcome it seeks? What evidence is required to prove these points? What are the potential sources of that evidence? Where is the evidence? What is the state of the evidence (if known)? How easy and costly will it be to gather, organise and assess the evidence? These questions are both immediately relevant to the merits, but also to quantum and potentially also key jurisdictional questions. There are questions of jurisdiction that are highly factual and will often be determined by a Court alongside the merits, rather

54 Human Rights Council, Resolution S-17/1, <https://www.ohchr.org/sites/default/files/Documents/HRBodies/HRCouncil/CoISyria/ResS17_1.pdf> accessed 30 April 2024.

55 Application of the Convention against Torture and Other Cruel, Inhuman or Degrading Treatment or Punishment (*Canada and the Netherlands v. Syrian Arab Republic*), Order of the Court on the Request for Provisional Measures, 16 November 2023, paras. 67, 72–75.

than as a preliminary issue. Article 79*ter*(4) of the Court's Rules, for example, provides:

> After hearing the parties, the Court shall decide upon a preliminary question or uphold or reject a preliminary objection. The Court may however declare that, in the circumstances of the case, a question or objection does not possess an exclusively preliminary character.

This is a common approach adopted by dispute resolution bodies. For example, in its decisions on the admissibility of the Article 11 communications submitted by Qatar with respect to the UAE and Saudi Arabia, the Committee adopted a similar approach, determining that:

> [...] To substantiate their conflicting views on the requirement of the exhaustion of domestic remedies, the State parties concerned invoke a multitude of factual elements which can only be verified at the stage of the examination of the merits of the communication. Moreover, the Committee considers that exhaustion of domestic remedies is not a requirement where a 'generalized policy and practice' has been authorised.
>
> For the above-mentioned reasons, the Committee decides that the exception of the non-exhaustion of domestic remedies has to be examined jointly with the examination of the merits of the communication.[56]

It is worth noting that the goal of an international claim may not always be ultimate success on the merits or to win on quantum. Claims may be used for other reasons, such as a pressure point in negotiations or other forms of dispute settlement, as mentioned above, or for reputational reasons. It is rare that a State's strategy is unconcerned with winning on jurisdiction, but sometimes even initiating a claim can trigger a result – including pressure and leverage in negotaitions – that a State considers desirable, especially as even jurisdictional phases in some dispute resolution fora might take some time. Or States may be focused on winning on jurisdiction and the merits, but not be seeking financial compensation. For example, in *Australia v. Japan,* Australia asked the Court to declare that Japan shall:

---

56 Committee on the Elimination of Racial Discrimination, Admissibility of the Inter-State communication submitted by Qatar against the United Arab Emirates, CERD/C/99/4, 30 August 2019, paras 40–41.

(*a*) refrain from authorizing or implementing any special permit whaling which is not for purposes of scientific research within the meaning of Article VIII;
(*b*) cease with immediate effect the implementation of JARPA II; and
(*c*) revoke any authorization, permit or licence that allows the implementation of JARPA II.[57]

Similarly, in the conciliation proceedings between Israel and Palestine under the CERD, Palestine has not sought monetary compensation. Palestine requested the conciliation commission to declare certain specific findings, including:

A. Israel practices a policy of systemized racial discrimination throughout the occupied territory of the State of Palestine amounting to violations of Arts. 2, 3 and 5 CERD;
B. Israel's policies and practices in the occupied territory of the State of Palestine constitute apartheid within the meaning of Art. 3 CERD;

And that, accordingly:

C. Israel is under an obligation to cease these violations of CERD, as well as to provide an assurance and guarantee of non-repetition;[58]

Alternatively, States may be seeking to win all different phases of a claim: jurisdiction, merits and quantum. The objectives of any claim will, of course determine how the legal and factual elements of any strategy hang together.

Evidence gathering is a particularly important exercise in almost any case strategy. The nature of the dispute resolution forum in question will determine the way evidence is adduced and where the burden falls. Mediation and conciliation are likely to structure the evidentiary process differently from a contentious proceeding – given that the objectives of the proceedings are very different. The ICJ, for example, has determined that the standard of proof will vary depending on the allegations, which may be particularly relevant in a human rights case:

> The Court has long recognized that claims against a State involving charges of exceptional gravity must be proved by evidence that is fully conclusive (cf. *Corfu Channel (United Kingdom v. Albania), Judgment, I.C.J. Reports 1949*, p. 17). The Court requires that it be fully convinced that allegations made in the proceedings, that the crime of genocide or the other

57 Whaling in the Antarctic (*Australia v. Japan*), Judgment, I.C.J. Reports 2014, at 226, para. 244.

58 Communication submitted to the CERD by Palestine pursuant to article 11 of the International Convention on the Elimination of All Forms of Racial Discrimination, 23 April 2018, para. 660.

> acts enumerated in Article III have been committed, have been clearly established. The same standard applies to the proof of attribution for such acts.[59]

And, per the *Diallo* case, the Court emphasised that the burden of proof will normally fall on the party 'alleg[ing] a fact in support of its claims', but this is not a blanket rule:

> As a general rule, it is for the party which alleges a fact in support of its claims to prove the existence of that fact. However, it would be wrong to regard this rule, based on the maxim *onus probandi incumbit actori*, as an absolute one, to be applied in all circumstances. The determination of the burden of proof is in reality dependent on the subject-matter and the nature of each dispute brought before the Court; it varies according to the type of facts which it is necessary to establish for the purposes of the decision of the case.
>
> [...]
>
> It is for the Court to evaluate all the evidence produced by the two Parties and duly subjected to adversarial scrutiny, with a view to forming its conclusions. In short, when it comes to establishing facts such as those which are at issue in the present case, neither party is alone in bearing the burden of proof.[60]

In contrast, given the nature of the proceedings, the Palestine-Israel Conciliation Commission procedural rules provide:

> The States Parties are expected to co-operate in good faith with the Commission and are invited to comply with requests by the Commission to submit written materials, provide evidence and attend meetings.[61]

---

59 Application of the Convention on the Prevention and Punishment of the Crime of Genocide (*Bosnia and Herzegovina v. Serbia and Montenegro*), Judgment, I.C.J. Reports 2007, at 43, para. 209.

60 Ahmadou Sadio Diallo (*Republic of Guinea v. Democratic Republic of the Congo*), Merits, Judgment, I.C.J. Reports 2010, at 639, paras 54–56 (internal citations omitted).

61 Committee on the Elimination of Racial Discrimination, Rules of Procedure of the ad hoc Conciliation Commission on the interstate communication submitted by the State of Palestine against Israel under article 11 of the International Convention on the Elimination of All Forms of Racial Discrimination, 25 April 2022, Rule 15.

Any party considering international proceedings will want to understand what the standard of proof is, and where the burden of proof falls, in assessing the strength of its claim. Even in conciliatory proceedings without any 'formal' burdens or standards, any future party will, of course, want to ensure that it is putting forward strong evidence in support of its position – especially where that body is making findings of fact and for the ultimate framing of recommendations. The State will want to consider the types of evidence available, what kind of weight might be attached to that type of evidence (depending on timing, nature, content, etc.) and whether further evidence is required in light of the nature and probative value of the available evidence. In *Nicaragua v. USA*, the Court explained the different weight it would attach to different types of evidence, including press articles, statements made by State representatives and statements of opinion.[62]

From this, a State can build a picture on which to assess a claim. It is often an iterative process to build and assess the evidence, but it is usually the basis on which a claim stands or falls.

In addition to the evidence itself, there are some key questions around evidence that may be influential. These include whether the proceedings, or specific pieces of evidence, will be kept confidential – and, if so, how exigent the test is to do so. One example of particular importance: there may be questions around the security of human rights witnesses and confidentiality can be an important way of helping to ensure that security.

6 Logistical, Political and Cultural Considerations

Logistical considerations are largely situation and case specific and are therefore unsuited to a lengthy analysis. However, they are worth mentioning as a key factor in decisions about if, where, when and how to engage with international proceedings. Engaging in and gathering evidence about multiple human rights abuses may be a costly and time-consuming exercise and may require an array of specific expertise. As noted above, a State may be assisted by relevant fact finding that has already been conducted by an international fact-finding body. For example, in its provisional measures order in *Gambia v. Myanmar*, the Court drew frequently on the findings of the United Nations Independent International Fact-Finding Mission on Myanmar and General

62 Military and Paramilitary Activities in and against Nicaragua (*Nicaragua v United States of America*), Merits, Judgment, I.C.J. Reports 1986, at 14, paras 62–64, 68.

Assembly Resolutions (including some Resolutions citing to the Fact-Finding Mission's Report).[63]

In addition, State officials will need to be involved and dedicate time to the case. As a result, a State will want to determine whether it has the resources or capacity to bring the claim in the first place – or, at least, if that is how it wishes to allocate them. The time a particular dispute resolution option takes, and its associated costs, may impact the choice of that dispute mechanism.

Another driving factor in approaching a claim is cultural attitudes to resolving disputes and the type of dispute resolution mechanism that may therefore seem more familiar and appealing – with, for example, some States more adapted to 'discussion' and others to 'confrontation'.[64] States also have varying levels of experience and familiarity with different international dispute resolution bodies, which contributes to distinct attitudes to the devolution of sovereignty to a decision-making body. Much attention has been paid in recent times to the cultural approaches of the US and China to dispute resolution and engaging with international dispute resolution bodies.[65] Last century, some scholars focused on 'new' states and their attitude and approaches to international law.[66] There is still discussion as to whether international institutions are welcomed by some of these States as a way to help level the

---

63 Application of the Convention on the Prevention and Punishment of the Crime of Genocide (*The Gambia v. Myanmar*), Provisional Measures, Order of 23 January 2020, I.C.J. Reports 2020, at 3, paras 27, 54, 55.

64 *See, e.g.,* Chatham House, H Moynihan, 'China's Evolving Approach to International Dispute Settlement', March 2017,<https://www.chathamhouse.org/sites/default/files/publications/research/2017-03-29-chinas-evolving-approach-international-dispute-settlement-moynihan-final.pdf> accessed 30 April 2024.

65 *See, e.g.,* S D Murphy, 'The United States and the International Court of Justice: Coping with Antinomies' in *The United States and International Courts and Tribunals* (Cesare Romano, ed., 2008).

Ibid., p. 3. 'At the Beijing Roundtable, it was observed by some Chinese participants that China's wariness of international dispute resolution is partly informed by Chinese culture and tradition, which is more inclined towards discussion (and thus negotiation) than towards the confrontation involved in litigation. But China's attitude is also informed by its lack of experience and expertise in interstate litigation. China's legal profession has only developed relatively recently, and there are linguistic and technical barriers to engagement in international litigation for domestic Chinese lawyers. The fact that many Western states have long engaged with international tribunals, whereas China has not, has led to a sense in China that international dispute settlement is 'foreign made', and as such does not always offer a level playing field'.

66 *See, e.g.,* IFI Shihata, 'The Attitude of New States Towards the International Court of Justice', 1965 19(2), *International Organization,* 203–222. S. Prakash Sinha, 'Perspective of the Newly Independent States on the Binding Quality of International Law', *The International and Comparative Law Quarterly* (1965) 14(1), 121–13.

playing field in international relations.[67] What is clear is that a variety of States are increasingly using international mechanisms as a way to profile issues important to them.[68]

Finally, the role of domestic politics – within and between a government, its institutions and ministries, and between political leaders and their constituencies – also affect what is palatable. International claims may bolster or undermine government popularity and any notable settlement agreement will usually need to be 'sell-able' domestically.[69] Sometimes a binding decision can be easier to 'sell' to a domestic audience as any concessions were not made voluntarily.[70]

7 Conciliation

Conciliation is envisaged as a means to resolve interstate disputes in several human rights treaties, including the CEDAW, the CAT, the ICCPR and the CERD. It is also part of the inter-State dispute resolution mechanism in many other international treaties, including the Vienna Convention on the Law of Treaties and various environmental agreements, such as the Paris Agreement and the Biodiversity Convention.

Within the scope of state consent, conciliation is an inherently flexible process, in which a third party assists the parties in examining elements of a dispute and finding an amicable settlement to their dispute. The UN Handbook on the Peaceful Settlement of International Disputes describes conciliation as 'the peaceful settlement procedure which combines the elements of both inquiry and mediation'.[71] The procedure would: '[...] on the one hand, provide [the parties] with a better understanding of each other's case ... and, on the other hand, provide them with an informal third-party machinery for the negotiation and non-judicial appraisal of each other's legal and other claims,

67 J McIntyre, 'Great Hall, Small States', NUS CIL Blog, 10 July 2023, <https://cil.nus.edu.sg/blogs/great-hall-small-states/> accessed 30 April 2024.

68 *See, e.g.,* Application of the Convention against Torture and Other Cruel, Inhuman or Degrading Treatment or Punishment (*Canada and the Netherlands v. Syrian Arab Republic*); Application of the Convention on the Prevention and Punishment of the Crime of Genocide (*The Gambia v. Myanmar*).

69 TL Allee and PK Huth, 'Legitimizing Dispute Settlement: International Legal Rulings as Domestic Political Cover', 100(2) May 2006, The American Political Science Review, pp. 219–234.

70 Ibid.

71 United Nations Office of Legal Affairs, Codification Division, Handbook on Peaceful Settlement of International Disputes, UN Doc. OLA/COD/2394 (1992), para. 140.

including the opportunity for defining the terms for a solution susceptible of being accepted by them'.[72] There is a more in-depth discussion of the nature of conciliation in and conciliation commissions' powers (including to interpret the law) in Sthoeger's contribution to this special issue.[73]

How do the factors set out above map onto conciliation proceedings? Conciliation – like other forms of dispute resolution – is based on the consent of the relevant States, either provided in advance, for example, through a treaty, or once the dispute has arisen, in an effort to resolve it. All of the key threshold questions set out above therefore apply.

While conciliation is provided for in many treaties, it has rarely been invoked in the context of any international dispute.[74] Some commentators have noted that conciliation is a convenient way to avoid binding dispute resolution in a treaty, suggesting that conciliation was not included as a potential option with the intention of frequently deploying the procedure.[75] That may be the case, but there are other risks associated with conciliation that may also dissuade

72 The approach of the UN Handbook is consistent with the approach in many other rules devoted to conciliation. For example, Article 1 of the Regulations on Conciliation of the Institut de Droit International's 1961 Resolution provides: 'For the purpose of the present provisions, 'conciliation' means a method for the settlement of international disputes of any nature according to which a Commission set up by the Parties, either on a permanent basis or on an ad hoc basis to deal with a dispute, proceeds to the impartial examination of the dispute and attempts to define the terms of a settlement susceptible of being accepted by them, or of affording the Parties, with a view to its settlement, such aid as they may have requested'. Institut de Droit International, Resolution on International Conciliation (1961), Article 1. *See* also Eran Sthoeger, 'The Path Less Taken? Interstate Conciliation and Human Rights' (2024) 13(1) *International Human Rights Law Review*.

73 Eran Sthoeger, 'The Path Less Taken? Interstate Conciliation and Human Rights' (2024) 13(1) *International Human Rights Law Review*.

74 *See, e.g.,* Henri Rolin, *Une Conciliation Belgo-Danoise* (*Affaire des ss "Gorm" et "Svava"*), 57 REVUE GÉNÉRALE DE DROIT INTERNATIONAL PUBLIC 353 (1953); Timor Sea Conciliation (*Timor-Leste v. Australia*), PCA Case No. 2016-10, Report and Recommendations of the Compulsory Conciliation Commission between Timor-Leste and Australia on the Timor Sea, 9 May 2018, para. 295; Conciliation Commission on the Continental Shelf area between Iceland and Jan Mayen: Report and recommendations to the governments of Iceland and Norway, Decision, June 1981, R.I.A.A. Vol. XXVII, at 23.

75 Jean-Pierre Cot, 'Conciliation' (2006), in Rüdiger Wolfrum (ed), *Max Planck Encyclopedia of Public International Law*, para. 38 ('so-called compulsory conciliation [...] look[s] like a convenient excuse for eluding compulsive adjudication'.). He also quotes Hersch Lauterpacht ('[i]nsofar as [conciliation] is in effect used as a pretext for concealing the determination of the States to remain free from the obligation of obligatory judicial settlement, it is harmful [...] [the trend] lends ample support to the view that conciliation, although non-existent in practice, has become an obstacle to progress by reducing the fundamental postulate of the obligatory rule of law to one of many means of settlement of equivalent nature'.)

parties from invoking it as a dispute resolution mechanism. The lack of precedent and inherent flexibility, along with the discretion usually afforded to conciliation commissions, adds to the uncertainty surrounding the procedure – for example, how will it work in practice? How long might it take? What range of outcomes could there be? What evidence might be requested and examined? How will it be treated? (Again, for a deeper assessment of existing and potential procedures around conciliation, see Sthoeger's contribution to this special issue – the discussion here has been kept short to reduce repetition throughout the volume). Any form of settlement requires the exercise of personal and institutional authority, and the associated risks in doing so (both domestic and international) as well as these elements of uncertainty can obstruct successful settlement.

These risks may be seen by some parties to increase where there is partial or total transparency. The CERD, for example, prescribes certain features of the conciliation mechanism in the treaty: the Commission will make findings of 'questions of fact relevant to the issue between the parties' and 'recommendations as it may think proper for the amicable solution of the dispute'[76] and the CERD envisages that the final report will be circulated to all States parties.[77] As such, the CERD provides for greater transparency than might be envisaged with other conciliation mechanisms, and seemingly unfavourable findings of fact and recommendations may be circulated to (at time of writing) 182 States Parties.

Quantum is another point of uncertainty that would be relevant to parties seeking compensation, and it will be interesting to see how conciliation commissions assessing human rights claims might address quantum claims. Which standards will they use? Especially in claims representing multiple victims. Will they adopt the standards used by human rights courts, or committees, and, if so, which one? One likely outcome – which would reduce uncertainty for States – is that a commission recommend that the States in question establish a mechanism to determine reparation for victims – perhaps with certain specified standards to be applied or safeguards – if they deem appropriate to recommend reparation.

At the same time, there are a few signs of greater willingness to resort to conciliation as a mode of dispute settlement at the international level.[78]

---

76 CERD, Article 13(1).

77 *Ibid.* Article 13(3).

78 In recent years, the following have been constituted for example: Timor Sea Conciliation (*Timor-Leste v. Australia*), PCA Case No. 2016-10; Ad hoc Conciliation Commission, Inter-State communication submitted by Qatar v. the Kingdom of Saudi Arabia, 8 March 2018; Ad hoc Conciliation Commission, Inter-State communication submitted by Qatar v. the United Arab Emirates, 8 March 2018; Ad hoc Conciliation Commission, Inter-State communication submitted by the State of Palestine v. Israel, 23 April 2018.

Certain elements of conciliation that might be seen as adding to its 'riskiness' for some parties, may be highly attractive to parties, for example, its flexibility and therefore the ability to mould the procedure in line with the nature of the dispute and the parties' wishes. In line with the discussion in the first section, conciliation also allows the parties retain significant control, which, as many commentators noted is an attraction of negotiation and mediation, including because any outcome is not binding and because they can walk away. Parties are able to express and have their views heard as part of the process, particularly in crafting workable recommendations for settlement – again, an advantage that commentators have noted from their study of negotiation and mediation (see above). They likely avoid the costs and time associated with binding adjudication, while at the same time, utilising the assistance of a qualified third party to broker agreement in line with the objectives of the parties and underlying treaty. Where negotiation is not yielding results, an alternative procedure with the assistance of a neutral decision maker may be particularly important in a situation where fundamental rights are at stake, to try to redress the situation as far as possible. The conciliation commission constituted pursuant to Article 298 and Annex V of the United Nations Convention on the Law of the Sea to resolving a dispute between Timor Leste and Australia as to the maritime boundary between the states (***Timor Leste/ Australia Commission***) provided an insight into the value that a neutral third party can have in opening up different communication channels:

> Many of the principal steps that were instrumental to bringing the Parties together occurred as much in late night conversations with various members of each delegation as in any formal meeting.[79]

As any final recommendations or other outcome is non-binding, this may be attractive to parties that do not want to derogate sovereignty to be bound by the decision of a third party. Conciliation proceedings are usually confidential, largely to facilitate the objective of finding an amicable solution, although elements may be public (usually following discussion with the parties). For many parties, this might be more attractive rather than public court proceedings.

As is explained in detail in other parts of this special issue, the signs of greater willingness to use conciliation extend to human rights disputes. In

79 Timor Sea Conciliation (*Timor-Leste v. Australia*), PCA Case No. 2016-10, Report and Recommendations of the Compulsory Conciliation Commission between Timor-Leste and Australia on the Timor Sea, 9 May 2018, para. 295.

2018, the procedure under Articles 11–13 of the CERD was invoked for the first time in more than 50 years, and three conciliation committees have since been constituted. One commission continues to be active. Each of the other human rights treaties that envisage conciliation as a dispute resolution mechanism requires specific State consent over and above what exists in the treaty, adding one more hurdle to its use.

There are elements of the conciliation process that are well-suited to human rights proceedings. The outcomes of conciliation are focused on the future, restoring the relations of the parties and compliance with the norms in question. As such, there will be a significant emphasis on ensuring that human rights are respected going forward (i.e., prevention, cessation and ensuring non-repetition). A commission and the parties can craft practical solutions to embed protection of human rights into the polity, with the input of the relevant party as to how this can best be done within their jurisdiction. A commission can also put in place a monitoring mechanism – either between the parties or with this assistance of another third party – which can both monitor and help build capacity where this is necessary. Like negotiation and mediation (see above), the flexibility and confidential free-flow exchange with the parties (both *ex parte* and in a group) can therefore lead to solutions well-tailored to the situation and likely more effective.

At the same time, there are some key elements of human rights treaties that may not be immediately suited to conciliation proceedings. Human rights protections are not susceptible to compromise at will.[80] While States have flexibility in *how* they respect and protect human rights, they do not have flexibility in whether to respect the human rights by which they are bound at the international level. The line between flexibility and rigidity is one that conciliation commissions and the parties will need to walk in finding a solution. By contrast, there is often greater flexibility for States to agree on realities and rules that may apply between them on a bilateral basis, as long as the agreement does not undermine rights of third States or contravene broader principles of international law – this was the case for the *Timor Leste/ Australia Commission*, for example, which sought 'agreement on the basis

80 Fundamental rights are non-derogable, for example, the prohibition on the arbitrary deprivation of life, as well as of torture and cruel and inhumane treatment. Other rights may be derogated from in the case of public emergency and subject to strict conditions, or may be subject to limitations based on the nature and content of the right itself – for example, the right to freedom of expression may be limited in accordance with law, and are necessary 'for respect of the rights or reputations of others' or 'for the protection of national security or of public order (ordre public), or of public health or morals'. Articles 4 and 19 ICCPR. *See* also Sthoeger (n 73).

of international law ... in order to achieve an equitable solution.'[81] However, because of the nature of human rights obligations – protecting fundamental rights and applying between multiple States – it is unlikely that there will be the same room for manoeuvre that some other international obligations may provide. Whether conciliation is an appropriate mechanism in such circumstances was raised by at least one delegate during the negotiation of the CERD. The *travaux preparatoires* show that Mr. Waldron-Ramsey of Tanzania explained: '[c]onciliation ... was not particularly appropriate to the subject matter of the convention. He did not see how complaints concerning human rights violations could be settled by conciliation'.[82] Other commentators have also noted the complexities of friendly settlements under the European Convention on Human Rights and the complexities for bodies supervising negotiated solutions between States.[83] However, as noted above, it is not an impossible task – the line between flexibility and rigidity can be walked carefully by commissions and States and must be part of the rules of the game. Ultimately, this is an explicit part of the mandate, governing the commission and accepted by the parties – conciliation commissions established under the CERD are to render their 'good offices shall be made available to the States concerned with a view to an amicable solution of the matter *on the basis of respect for this Convention*'.[84]

Another point of tension is between transparency and confidentiality. Many different stakeholders may have an interest in the progress and outcome of the proceedings. At the same time, as noted above, confidential proceedings (and outcome) may engender freer discussions between the parties and concessions leading to an agreement and upholding of rights where that might otherwise not be achieved. The CERD recognises the interest of other States parties in the outcome of the conciliation commission through its requirement that the final report be circulated to all States parties – including an interest to ensure consistency of interpretation and implementation of the underlying treaty.[85] From a victim perspective, there may be huge benefits (including reparative)

81 Timor Sea Conciliation (*Timor-Leste v. Australia*), PCA Case No. 2016-10, Report and Recommendations of the Compulsory Conciliation Commission between Timor-Leste and Australia on the Timor Sea, 9 May 2018, para. 69.

82 U.N. General Assembly, 20th session, Official Records, Third Committee, Record of the 1345th meeting, U.N. Doc. A/C.3/SR.1345 (17 November 1965), p.323, para. 41.

83 H Keller and R Piskóty, Friendly Settlements as the Sleeping Beauty in Inter-State Cases, 28 April 2021, <https://voelkerrechtsblog.org/friendly-settlements-as-the-sleeping-beauty-in-inter-state-cases/> accessed 30 April 2023.

84 CERD, Article 12(1)(a) (emphasis added).

85 The Timor Sea Conciliation Commission stated: '... there is a question regarding the extent to which a conciliation commission should engage with the parties concerning questions of international law. [...] The function of a commission is to assist the parties to reach an

gained from publicity; at the same time, victims may have very real concerns – including relating to security and/or stigmatisation and discrimination – that only strict confidentiality can cater to.

Another potential challenge for conciliation commissions is reflecting the realities of the victims themselves. This can be a challenge in any inter-State case, and reflects the way that international human rights norms and international jurisdiction is structured. As discussed above, although a State may espouse the claim of one or multiple nationals at the international level,[86] many inter-State human rights disputes will affect the rights of many victims and will not necessarily implicate the rights of that State's citizens. In addition, there is no requirement for the voices of victims to be heard in inter-State proceedings – it is up to the States what evidence they present and in what form, in an effort to obtain the outcome they are looking for. However, depending on the circumstances, victims' voices may be important to understand the facts on the ground, and particularly to understand how to 'repair' violations[87] – what are the victims themselves looking for – and to better respect rights on

---

amicable settlement, not to pronounce for its own sake on questions of international law ... It follows, for the Commission, that a conciliation commission need not as a matter of course engage with the parties on their legal positions but may engage with these matters to the extent that so doing will likely facilitate the achievement of an amicable settlement'. Timor Sea Conciliation (*Timor-Leste v. Australia*), PCA Case No. 2016-10, Report and Recommendations of the Compulsory Conciliation Commission between Timor-Leste and Australia on the Timor Sea, 9 May 2018, para. 70. In the prior paragraph, the Timor Sea Commission noted that prior conciliation commissions had 'historically taken varying approaches' on the question 'regarding the extent to which a conciliation commission should engage with the parties concerning questions of international law'.

86 Ahmadou Sadio Diallo (*Republic of Guinea v. Democratic Republic of the Congo*), Merits, Judgment, I.C.J. Reports 2010, at 639.

87 While the ICC is concerned with international criminal violations rather than international human rights violations, its structure in giving victims a voice in proceedings and a reparations mechanism reflects both the academic study and years of international justice experience demonstrating the importance of giving victims a voice. For example, see Vahida Nainar, 'Giving Victims a Voice in the International Criminal Court' (1999) 36(4) *UN Chronicle*. The Basic Principles, Preamble also note: 'the Rome Statute of the International Criminal Court requires the establishment of "principles relating to reparations to, or in respect of, victims, including restitution, compensation and rehabilitation", requires the Assembly of States Parties to establish a trust fund for the benefit of victims of crimes within the jurisdiction of the Court, and of the families of such victims, and mandates the Court "to protect the safety, physical and psychological well-being, dignity and privacy of victims" and to permit the participation of victims at all "stages of the proceedings determined to be appropriate by the Court"'. General Assembly, Basic Principles and Guidelines on the Right to a Remedy and Reparation for Victims of Gross Violations of International Human Rights Law and Serious Violations of International Humanitarian Law, Resolution adopted on 16 December 2005, Preamble.

the ground. The opportunity to be heard and acknowledged may be inherently reparative.[88]

Witness statements are one way that victims can play a part in proceedings, as long as they are envisaged in the procedural rules and as long as the security of victims is assured (see above). In an effort to uphold the objectives of the treaty under which the conciliation is established, the States parties and conciliation commissions should also be vigilant about upholding victims' dignity. Respecting the dignity of victims applies all the way through the process – from soliciting information, their absolute right to refuse to participate at any point, in the interviewing process (including providing psychological assistance if necessary), ongoing communication, obtaining consent to use their information, in the manner in which the information is used and in the process of presenting and testing the evidence.[89] Commissions will need to consider carefully how this works within the context of their mandate to find an amicable solution, and also the powers and procedural modalities laid down in the treaty and procedural rules. If victims' evidence is to be used, one idea may be to appoint one or several victims' representatives who portray the evidence. Another way to hear victims' voices is through third party publications, where those third parties have spent time with and interviewed the community (perhaps a fact-finding commission or inquiry, as in the case of the *Gambia v. Myanmar* case mentioned above). This will usually be more impactful, however, if there is a channel of communication with the victims. The flexibility afforded to the parties and conciliation commission means that, as part of the amicable settlement or recommendations, victims' voices may be included in the proceedings or implementation phase.

8 Conclusions

This article has surveyed some of the key factors that States consider in the roadmap of whether an inter-State dispute is (i) available; and (ii) palatable,

88 M Lawry-White, 'The Reparative Effect of Truth Seeking In Transitional Justice', (2015) 64(1) ICLQ, 141–177.

89 The Basic Principles note that, in providing Access to Justice, States shall '[t]ake measures to minimize the inconvenience to victims and their representatives, protect against unlawful interference with their privacy as appropriate and ensure their safety from intimidation and retaliation, as well as that of their families and witnesses, before, during and after judicial, administrative, or other proceedings that affect the interests of victims'. General Assembly, Basic Principles and Guidelines on the Right to a Remedy and Reparation for Victims of Gross Violations of International Human Rights Law and Serious Violations of International Humanitarian Law, Resolution adopted on 16 December 2005, Principle 12(b).

with a focus on human rights disputes. A roadmap of the factors discussed in this paper is set out below:

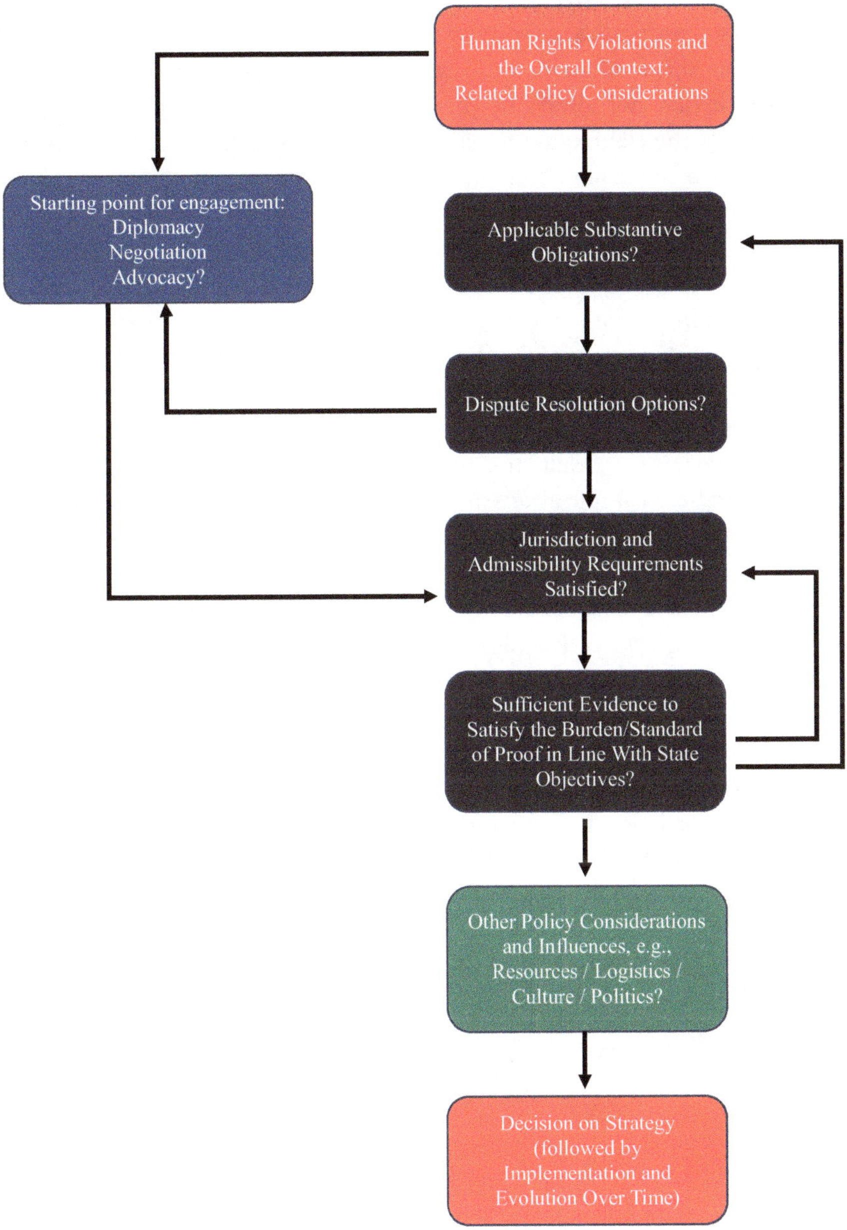

FIGURE 2 Factors that States Consider in the Roadmap of Whether an Inter-State Dispute is Available and Palatable.

The article then looks at how the features of conciliation – one form of inter-State dispute resolution previewed in certain human rights treaties, following a communication to a UN treaty body – might map onto this picture. Scholars have explained that the majority of inter-State disputes are resolved through negotiation and mediation, with or without third party diplomatic efforts. However, it may not always be the most effective route, depending on the objectives of the claim and the realities of the international polity, as recent State practice has made clear. Conciliation provides a more formal structure and third-party assistance in which dialogue and cooperation may take place, and yet, without the full devolution of power to a third-party adjudicative body. States may still decide not to abide by final recommendations (which are not binding unless the parties agree otherwise). However, the CERD envisages the circulation of the decision to other States' parties and therefore does not provide the same degree of confidentiality in accepting or rejecting a commission's recommendations as is normally the case outside of a human rights context. As a result, the issuance of formal recommendations may have reputational implications if a State rejects them after engaging in a conciliation process.

The choices made along each step of the process – and therefore how frequently we see inter-State dispute resolution under human rights treaties and concerning UN treaty bodies – will depend upon the peculiarities of each situation, and the institutions, people and decision-making process involved, amongst other factors. Overall, we have seen increasing public inter-State dispute resolution concerning alleged human rights violations over the last two decades. In addition, the three conciliation processes constituted under the CERD, not long after the successful Timor Leste/Australia conciliation administered by the PCA, represent the appearance of more formal and public conciliation proceedings at the international level after decades of silence. They are also a representation of the advent of the use of the UN treaty body/ conciliation commission process envisaged in certain human rights treaties.

CHAPTER 2

Inter-State Applications under the European Convention on Human Rights – Situating the Instrument in the Current Human Rights Landscape

Isabella Risini and Tim Eicke

Abstract

Recent events and developments in Europe have called for the use of the inter-State application under Article 33 the European Convention on Human Rights (ECHR, the Convention), a challenging situation (1) for the European Court of Human Rights (ECtHR, the Court) on many levels, including the resource situation of the Court. The inter-State application was the centerpiece of international human rights supervision in the original 1950 Convention. This contribution sketches out the evolution of the inter-State application over some seven decades of history (2) of the ECHR. It highlights strengths and raises awareness of existing limitations (3). One aspect that merits attention is the evidential side in this type of proceedings. Establishing a judicial record of the events under the Court's scrutiny is a value to be appraised here in its aims and complexities.

Keywords

inter-State application – European Convention on Human Rights – facts – collective enforcement

 DOI:10.1163/9789004712584_004

1 Europe – a Troubled Continent and Associated Challenges for the European Court of Human Rights

The European Convention on Human Rights provides for inter-State applications in Article 33 ECHR which provides that '[a]ny High Contracting Party may refer to the Court any alleged breach of the provisions of the Convention and the Protocols thereto by another High Contracting Party.'[1] By comparison with other regional and universal human rights mechanisms, the inter-State application has been used with remarkable frequency both historically as well as in the recent past.[2]

At the time of writing, the Russian Federation is the main respondent to such applications. Ukraine has brought no fewer than ten applications against the Russian Federation between 2014 and 2022 and Georgia has lodged a total of four applications, also against the Russian Federation, since 2007. A number of further applications principally involving Azerbaijan and Armenia concern the situation in Nagorno Karabakh.[3] In numerical terms, the majority of the current batch of inter-State applications pending before the Court are at relatively early stages of the proceedings. The tenth set of proceedings brought by Ukraine against Russia concerns the Russian war of aggression in Ukraine initiated by the attacks on 24 February 2022, covering the period during which the Convention applies *ratione temporis* after Russia's expulsion from the Council of Europe.[4] The Court remains competent to deal with applications

1 The authors would like to make use of the opportunity to remember Mark Villiger, who passed away in December 2023. In his own view, the witness hearing conducted in Strasbourg from 31 January to 4 February 2011 in the case of *Georgia v Russia I* was among the most important tasks he performed as judge at the European Court of Human Rights.

2 A full list of all pending and completed applications is available on the Court's website at <https://www.echr.coe.int/inter-state-applications>.

3 Dean Spielmann, John Darcy, 'The European Court of Human Rights as Guarantor of a Peaceful Public Order in Europe' (2014) 3 Cyprus HumRtsLRev 106.

4 The membership of the Russian Federation in the European Convention on Human Rights ended on 16 September 2022; for futher detail see Philip Leach, 'A time of reckoning? Russia and the Council of Europe' (2022) EHRLR 219; Wolfgang Benedek, 'Der Ausschluss Russlands aus dem Europarat', NLMR 2022, 81; Andrew Drzemczewski, Rick Lawson, 'The Exclusion of the Russian Federation from the Council of Europe and the ECHR: An Overview, Baltic

directed against the Russian Federation in relation to acts or omissions capable of constituting a violation of the Convention provided that they occurred up to 16 September 2022.[5] This residual jurisdiction of the Court derives from Article 58 of the Convention.[6]

The case of *Ukraine and the Netherlands v Russia*, concerning events in Eastern Donbas in 2014 and the downing of flight MH17,[7] has passed the admissibility stage.[8] In the proceedings in *Ukraine v Russia re Crimea*, following the admissibility decision of 16 December 2020,[9] the merits hearing as well as a hearing on the admissibility and the merits of the joined "transfer of convicts" complaint under application no. 38334/18, took place on 13 December 2023.[10] The Court enjoys a discretion to join admissibility issues to the merits under Article 29 § 2 ECHR. The tenth application has been joined to three previously pending sets of inter-State proceedings combined in what is now *Ukraine and the Netherlands v. Russia*.[11]

The tenth set of inter-State proceedings between Ukraine and the Russian Federation is unprecedented in the history of the European Convention on Human Rights in that 31 third party interveners, including 26 ECHR member States, the first of whom were The Netherlands, as well as Canada have joined

Yearbook of International Law' (2022–23, forthcoming); Norman Weiß, Theresa Lanzl, 'Die wechselvolle Geschichte der Mitgliedschaft Russlands im Europarat', HJIL 2022, 801. For a detailed consideration of the Court's (temporal) jurisdiction with respect to acts or omissions spanning across the date on which the Russian Federation ceased to be a Party to the Convention, see *Pivkina and Others v Russia* (dec.), 2134/23, 2156/23, 4556/23 et al., 6 June 2023.

5 Resolution of the European Court of Human Rights on the consequences of the cessation of membership of the Russian Federation to the Council of Europe in light of Article 58 of the European Convention on Human Rights, 22.3.2022, <https://www.echr.coe.int/documents/d/echr/Resolution_ECHR_cessation_membership_Russia_CoE_ENG> accessed 30 April 2024, as confirmed by the Court in *Fedotova and Others v. Russia* (GC), 40792/10 and 2 others, § 72, 17 January 2023; *Ukraine and the Netherlands v Russia* (dec., GC), 8019/16, 43800/14 and 28525/20, §§ 36 and 389, 25 January 2023 and *Georgia v. Russia (II)* (just satisfaction) (GC), no. 38263/08, §§ 19–24, 28 April 2023).

6 See press release ECHR 036 (2023) 03.02.2023; *Fedotova and others v Russia* (GC), 17 January 2023, §§ 68 et seq; *Ukraine and the Netherlands v Russia* (GC, dec.), 8019/16, 43800/14 and 28525/20, 25 January 2023, § 389.

7 Kanstantsin Dzehtsiarou, Vassilis Tzevelekos, 'The Aggression Against Ukraine and the Effectiveness of Inter-state Cases in Case of War', Editorial, ECHLR 2022, 165–173.

8 *Ukraine and The Netherlands v Russia*, 8019/16 43800/14 28525/20 (dec.,GC) 30 November 2022.

9 *Ukraine v Russia (re Crimea)* (dec.,GC), 20958/14 and 38334/18, 16 December 2020.

10 *Ibid.* § 446.

11 *Ukraine and the Netherlands v Russia*, 8019/16, 43800/14, 28525/20 and 11055/22.

the proceedings in 2022.[12] The 26 member States of the ECHR have been requested to coordinate their work in order not to delay the proceedings by the sheer volume of interventions.[13] In this context, it is worthwhile recalling that the Grand Chamber, in the 2021 *Georgia v Russia II* judgment, held that:

> .., having regard in particular to the large number of alleged victims and contested incidents, the magnitude of the evidence produced, the difficulty in establishing the relevant circumstances and the fact that such situations are predominantly regulated by legal norms other than those of the Convention (specifically, international humanitarian law or the law of armed conflict), the Court considers that it is not in a position to develop its case-law beyond the understanding of the notion of "jurisdiction" as established to date.
> If, as in the present case, the Court is to be entrusted with the task of assessing acts of war and active hostilities in the context of an international armed conflict outside the territory of a respondent State, it must be for the Contracting Parties to provide the necessary legal basis for such a task.[14]

The interventions of the 26 ECHR member states have recently been analysed by Marco Milanovic.[15] The procedural instrument of third party interventions under Article 36 § 2 ECHR provides States with an opportunity to express their views on the interaction between international humanitarian law and human rights law in the wake of *Georgia v. Russia II*.[16] However, as the Court

12 Austria, Belgium, Bulgaria, Croatia, the Czech Republic, Denmark, Estonia, Finland, France, Germany, Iceland, Ireland, Italy, Latvia, Lithuania, Luxembourg, the Netherlands, Norway, Poland, Portugal, Romania, Slovakia, Slovenia, Spain, Sweden and the United Kingdom; see also their interventions in the ICJ proceedings in *Allegations of Genocide under the Convention on the Prevention and Punishment of the Crime of Genocide* (Ukraine v. Russian Federation: 32 States intervening), in which the hearing took place in September 2023.

13 Update on the third-party intervention requests granted in Inter-State case Ukraine and the Netherlands v Russia, ECHR press release ECHR 082 (2023) 17.03.2023.

14 *Georgia v Russia* (*II*), 38263/08 (GC), 21 January 2021, §§ 141–142.

15 Marko Milanovic, 'The Mariupol Test: Analysing the Briefs of Third States Intervening in Ukraine and the Netherlands v. Russia', EJIL:Talk!, 9.1.2024, <https://www.ejiltalk.org/the-mariupol-test-analysing-the-briefs-of-third-states-intervening-in-ukraine-and-the-netherlands-v-russia/> accessed 30 April 2024. The blog post contains a link to all third-party briefs.

16 Justine Batura, Isabella Risini, 'Of Parties, Third Parties, and Treaty Interpretation: Ukraine v. Russia (X) before the European Court of Human Rights', 26.9.2022, <https://www.ejiltalk.org/of-parties-third-parties-and-treaty-interpretation-ukraine-v-russia-x-before-the-european-court-of-human-rights/> accessed 30 April 2024.

clarified in its practice direction on third party interventions, "third parties are not entitled to express support directly for one or the other party".[17] Some of the non-governmental third-party interveners have published the texts of their interventions. The Geneva Academy, for example, published its third-party intervention in April 2023.[18] The authors, Francesco Romani and Gloria Gaggioli, focus on the extra-territorial application of the ECHR in the active phase of hostilities, the interplay between the ECHR and *jus ad bellum* and international humanitarian law. The Human Rights Law Centre of the University of Nottingham, which had already submitted a brief authored by Marko Milanovic and Sangeeta Shah in 2021 concerning the shooting down of flight MH 17 over Ukrainian Territory,[19] submitted and published a further third-party intervention for merits stage also in April 2023.[20] Further third parties include the individual applicants, who are relatives of the victims of the Malaysian Airline's flight MH 17 destruction.[21]

This is unprecedented in that other inter-State proceedings affecting European public order as well as (whether directly or indirectly) the interests of other member States, whether in the context of armed conflict in Europe or the alleged 'ongoing administrative practice by the Russian Federation consisting of targeted assassination operations against perceived opponents of the Russian Federation, in Russia and on the territory of other States' (including

17 Practice direction issued by the President of the Court in accordance with Rule 32 of the Rules of Court on 13 March 2023, para 2; see also Justine Batura, 'The Objective Friends of the Court – New Insights into the Role of Third Parties before the European Court of Human Rights', 19.4.2023, EJIL:Talk!, <https://www.ejiltalk.org/the-objective-friends-of-the-court-new-insights-into-the-role-of-third-parties-before-the-european-court-of-human-rights/> accessed 30 January 2024.

18 Francesco Romani, Gloria Gaggioli, Third-Party Intervention on Behalf of the Geneva Academy of International Humanitarian Law and Human Rights, Ukraine and the Netherlands v. Russia (nos. 8019/16, 43800/14, 28525/20 & 11055/22), <https://www.geneva-academy.ch/joomlatools-files/docman-files/Third%20party%20intervention%20ECtHR%20Geneva%20Academy.pdf> accessed 30 April 2024.

19 Marko Milanovic, Sangeeta Shah, 'Ukraine and the Netherlands v. Russia re MH17, Amicus Curiae Brief on behalf of the Human Rights Law Centre of the University of Nottingham, University of Reading – School of Law', (January 25, 2021), Ukraine and the Netherlands v. Russia, Merits Amicus Curiae Brief Submitted on behalf of the Human Rights Law Centre of the University of Nottingham, 4 May 2023, <https://ssrn.com/abstract=3775402 or http://dx.doi.org/10.2139/ssrn.3775402> accessed 30 April 2024.

20 Marko Milanovic, Sangeeta Shah, Ukraine and the Netherlands v. Russia, Merits Amicus Curiae Brief Submitted on behalf of the Human Rights Law Centre of the University of Nottingham, <https://papers.ssrn.com/sol3/papers.cfm?abstract_id=4427214> accessed 30 April 2024.

21 *Ayley and Others v Russia* (25714/16), *Angline and Others v Russia* (no. 56328/18), *Bakker and Others v Russia* (22729/19) and *Warta and Others v Russia* (3568/20).

Germany and the United Kingdom),[22] have to date not attracted a comparable interest amongst potential third party intervenors – with the exception, in the latter case, of the governments of Poland and Lithuania.

Previous inter-State proceedings against the Russian Federation have not led to other third-party interventions by member State. The only exception here is The Netherlands, which intervened in the proceedings brought by Ukraine (indirectly) in support of the relatives of the victims of the downing of flight MH 17 over Ukrainian territory in 2014 as well as bringing its own inter-State proceedings in 2020.[23] The Dutch government has used the inter-State proceedings twice before.[24] In 1967, it lodged a case against the Greek Colonel rule together with Denmark, Norway and Sweden.[25] While the Netherlands did not join a second set of proceedings against Greece,[26] it joined forces with Denmark, France, Norway, Sweden against Turkey's military regime in 1982.[27]

While the Russian Federation, despite repeated invitations to do so,[28] no longer appears to be actively participating in proceedings before the Court, it previously also sought to make use of the inter-State mechanism as an applicant.[29] In its application of 22 July 2021 against Ukraine, the Russian Government alleged that since 2014 there existed an administrative practice in Ukraine of, among other things, killings, abductions, forced displacement, interference with the right to vote, restrictions on the use of the Russian language and attacks on Russian embassies and consulates. Russia also complained that the water supply to Crimea via the North Crimean Canal had been cut off and alleged that Ukraine was responsible for the deaths of those on board Malaysia Airlines flight MH17 because it had failed to close its airspace. The Russian application was struck off the list by a decision of 4 July 2023.[30] The Court concluded that the Russian Government no longer wished to pursue their application as they had repeatedly failed to reply to its

22 *Ukraine v Russia IX*, 10691/21, see ECHR press release 069 (2021) 23.02.2021.

23 Previously *The Netherlands v Russia*, 28525/20, now *Ukraine and The Netherlands v Russia* (8019/16, 43800/14 and 28525/20).

24 The Netherlands have again, more recently, shown their willingness to bring inter-State proceedings in order to enforce fundamental international human rights norms when they, together with Canada, initiated proceedings in the ICJ against Syria in *Application of the Convention against Torture and Other Cruel, Inhuman or Degrading Treatment or Punishment* (Canada and the Netherlands v. Syrian Arab Republic), in which interim measures were indicated in November 2023.

25 *Denmark, Norway, Sweden and the Netherlands v Greece (I)*, 3321–23, 3344/67.

26 *Denmark, Norway and Sweden v Greece (II)*, 4448/70.

27 *France, Norway, Denmark, Sweden and the Netherlands v Türkiye*, 9940-44/82.

28 See e.g. *Georgia v Russia (II)*, 38263/08 (GC, Just Satisfaction), 28 April 2023, §§ 8 and 10.

29 *Russia v Ukraine*, 36958/21, lodged on 22 July 2021.

30 *Russia v Ukraine*, 36958/21, decision of 4 July 2023.

correspondence and that it could find no grounds related to respect for human rights which would require it to continue the examination of the application in light of the fact that the events which unfolded in 2014 in various parts of Ukraine, including the Autonomous Republic of Crimea and the city of Sevastopol, as well as various parts of eastern Ukraine, had already given rise to some 8,500 pending individual applications under Article 34 ECHR, some of which overlaped with those raised by the Russian Federation in its application.

The proceedings concerning Ukraine, along with several thousand individual applications concerning the conflict, are certainly one of the central challenges the Court and the credibility of the European human rights system itself currently faces.

The conflict concerning Nagorno Karabakh and its consequences further add to the heavy workload for the Court. While the most recent escalation of violence in autumn 2023 and the ensuing displacement of some 100.000 persons[31] has not (or not yet) triggered a further set of inter-State proceedings under Article 33 ECHR, seven sets of inter-State application centre around the region. They involve Azerbaijan, Armenia and Türkiye.[32] Like the above cases, these cases are also seen as a challenge to the credibility of the European human rights oversight mechanisms.[33]

It may, in this context, be worthwhile mentioning that it is open to any member States to bring an inter-State application even if the applicant country is not directly affected by the allegations made, and regardless of the nationality of the alleged victims. After all, as the Court has repeatedly emphasised, the purpose of the High Contracting Parties in concluding the Convention was not to concede to each other reciprocal rights and obligations in pursuance of their individual national interests but to realise the aims and ideals of the Council of Europe, as expressed in its Statute, and "to establish a common public order of

31 Council of Europe Commissioner for Human Rights concludes her visit to Armenia and Azerbaijan with a focus on the human rights situation of people affected by the conflict in and around the Karabakh region, <https://www.coe.int/en/web/commissioner/-/council-of-europe-commissioner-for-human-rights-concludes-her-visit-to-armenia-and-azerbaijan-with-a-focus-on-the-human-rights-situation-of-people-affected-by-the-conflict-in-and-around-the-karabakh-region> accessed 30 April 2024, 16.10.2023.

32 *Azerbaijan* v Armenia (II) (39912/22), *Armenia v Azerbaijan* (IV) (no 15389/22), *Armenia v Azerbaijan* (III) (42445/21), *Armenia v Azerbaijan* (II) (33412/21), *Azerbaijan v Armenia* (47319/20), *Armenia v Türkiye* (43517/20), *Armenia v Azerbaijan* (42521/20).

33 Andrew Forde, Nagorno Karabakh – 'A Stark Reminder of the Council of Europe's Operational 'Grey Zones'', <http://opiniojuris.org/2021/02/11/nagorno-karabakh-a-stark-reminder-of-the-council-of-europes-operational-grey-zones/> accessed 30 April 2024, 11.2.2021; see also Andrew Forde, *European Human Rights Grey Zones: The Council of Europe and Areas of Conflict* (Cambridge University Press, forthcoming 2024).

the free democracies of Europe with the object of safeguarding their common heritage of political traditions, ideals, freedom and the rule of law".[34]

Interim measures were an important part of many inter-State proceedings. The request by the now defunct Commission to stay the execution of Nicolas Sampson in the proceedings between Greece and the United Kingdom was the very first interim measure indicated by the Strasbourg organs.[35] It was honoured by Greece. Interim measures were also requested in the context of the proceedings between Ireland and The United Kingdom. In March 1972, at a time prior to the admissibility decision, the Irish government asked the Commission "to request the respondent Government to take interim measures", relying on the argument that a power to grant or request interim measures "was the necessary attribute of its judicial functions and therefore covered by the doctrine of implied powers.[36] The applicant Government requested the Commission to seek an undertaking from the respondent Government that 'all such treatment of persons in custody as had been complained of [the so-called five techniques] in the application as constituting a breach of Article 3 ECHR should be discontinued.'[37] The applicant also requested that Commission-nominated observers be granted permission to monitor the situation in detention facilities. Having considered the request and the respondent Government's observations thereon, the Commission decided that it did 'not have the power, consistent with its functions under the Convention, to meet the request made.'[38] Many of the recent inter-State proceedings concerning armed conflicts started with requests for interim measures, most of which the court granted, and more promptly than any other international court.[39] Where considered urgent, interim measures are normally provisionally granted *ex parte*, which means that the respondent State was not necessarily able to be heard, either in writing or orally, before the measures are adopted. However, as the Court has made clear, it is always open for the respondent Government to apply to the Court to ask for a review of the decision to grant an interim measure and for an interim measure to be lifted following reconsideration. Where such

34 *Ukraine and the Netherlands v Russia* (dec., GC), 8019/16, 43800/14 and 28525/20, § 385, 25 January 2023.

35 *Greece v United Kingdom (I)*, 176/56, 1958-report (as published in1997 in HRLJ 1197 348, 358; see also Brian Simpson *Human Rights and the End of Empire* (2004) 973.

36 *Ireland v United Kingdom*, 5310/71 (dec), Yearbook 15 (1972), 82.

37 *Ibid.* 84.

38 *Ibid.* 88.

39 For example: "The European Court grants urgent interim measures in application concerning Russian military operations on Ukrainian territory", ECHR 068 (2022); 1.3.2022; "Expansion of interim measures in relation to Russian military action in Ukraine", ECHR 116 (2022), 1.4.2022

a request is made, it is communicated to the applicant and a decision on this request will be reached following consideration of both parties' submissions and the material before the Court. The Court's modern practice in this regard began on 12 August 2008, when Jean-Paul Costa, the then President of the Court acting as President of the competent Chamber, decided to apply Rule 39 of the Rules of the Court upon the request of Georgia. The Court called upon *both* Russia and Georgia to comply with their engagements under the Convention, particularly with respect to Articles 2 and 3. The measures are usually coupled with requests for information under Rule 39 § 3 of the Rules of the Court. Russia itself had also requested interim measures on this basis.

Overall, while the recent admissibility decisions have already clarified significant aspects of Convention law relevant to these inter-State proceedings, both in terms of sheer volume and in terms of individual outstanding issues of law, significant work in these inter-State proceedings still lies ahead of the Court. In addition to the cases above, there is also pending before the Court an inter-State application brought by Liechtenstein against the Czech Republic concerning the respondent State's classification of Liechtenstein citizens as persons with German nationality for the purposes of applying the Decrees of the President of Republic of 1945 (also known as the Beneš decrees), which, among other things, confiscated property belonging to all ethnic Germans and Hungarians after the Second World War.[40] Furthermore, there has been recent press reporting that the government of Ireland has decided to initiate a new inter-State application against the United Kingdom over the Northern Ireland Troubles (Legacy and Reconciliation) Bill.[41]

Inter-State applications provide a real challenge for the Court due to their sheer size and the scarce resources the Court has to ascertain disputed facts, a difficulty which is, of course, exacerbated in cases involving active armed hostilities. The failure of a respondent State to engage with the proceedings

40 *Liechtenstein v the Czech Republic* (35738/20), Isabella Risini, Geir Ulfstein, Liechtenstein v Czech Republic before the European Court of Human Rights, 7.9.2020, EJIL:Talk!, <https://www.ejiltalk.org/liechtenstein-v-czech-republic-before-the-european-court-of-human-rights/> accessed 30 April 2024. Mark Villiger co-advised the government of Liechtenstein.

41 Statement by the Tánaiste, Micheál Martin, on the Government decision to initiate an inter-State case against the United Kingdom, 20.12.2023, <https://www.gov.ie/en/press-release/82232-statement-by-the-tanaiste-micheal-martin-on-the-government-decision-to-initiate-an-inter-state-case-against-the-united-kingdom/> 30 April 2024; Daniel Holder, Andrew Forde, Avoiding the Legacy of Impunity, Ireland lodges a new Inter-State case against the UK at the ECtHR over amnesty legislation ending investigations into the Northern Ireland conflict, Verfassungsblog, 21.12.2023, <https://verfassungsblog.de/avoiding-the-legacy-of-impunity/> accessed 30 April 2024.

provides further challenges. Furthermore, the more than 10,000 individual applications and several inter-State applications that stem from armed conflict are, of course, also not the only issue the Court has to deal with. After all, the principal and overwhelming number of cases come before the Court by way of individual applications under Article 34 of the Convention. At the time of writing, there are some 71,450 applications pending.[42] These, of course, also include a significant number of cases arising out of the fallout of the attempted coup d'État in Türkiye in 2016, the Covid-19 pandemic, the unresolved question of migration into Europe, democratic backsliding[43] and the overarching challenge of climate change.[44]

In relation to the challenge of meeting these demands, the president of the Court, *Síofra O'Leary*, made it clear in her speech for the opening of the judicial year in January 2023, that "[i]n terms of organisation, however, there is no leeway for further improvement. We as a Court are currently dealing with multiple complex inter-State cases, while simultaneously processing tens of thousands of individual applications lodged in some 40 languages. ... Political support for the Council of Europe's values and for the Convention system itself ... must imperatively be translated into the provision of appropriate material resources and more sustainable funding to further the implementation of a Convention which, for over 70 years, has contributed to stability, security and peace in Europe."[45]

The Court has re-emphasised the insufficiency of its funding again in the context of the Summit of the Heads of State and Government of the Council of Europe in Reykjavik.[46] The overall only fourth summit of its kind in the history of the Council of Europe of Europe was warranted by the profound crisis the war of aggression by Russia against Ukraine has caused. The Summit

---

42 Pending Applications Allocated To A Judicial Formation, 30 November 2023, <https://www.echr.coe.int/documents/d/echr/stats_pending_month_2023_bil> accessed 30 April 2024.

43 See for example *Wałęsa v Poland*, 50849/21, 23.11.2023.

44 *Verein Klimaseniorinnen Schweiz and Others v Switzerland*, (53600/20), *Carême v France* (7189/21) and *Duarte Agostinho and Others v Portugal and 32 Others* (39371/20).

45 Speech by Síofra O'Leary, President of the European Court of Human Rights, 27 January 2023, <https://www.echr.coe.int/documents/d/echr/Speech_20230127_OLeary_JY_ENG> accessed 30 April 2024, p. 3.

46 Memorandum of the European Court of Human Rights, Fourth Summit of Heads of State and Government of the Council of Europe, Strasbourg, 20 March 2023, <https://www.echr.coe.int/documents/d/echr/memorandum_summit_reykjavik_2023_eng> accessed 30 April 2024, p. 2, para 16 and conclusion 2 on page 6: "The European Court of Human Rights calls on the States Parties to ... 2. Pledge sufficient financial resources to enable the Court to exercise effectively its judicial functions and handle its caseload expeditiously."

Declaration[47] contains a commitment "to strengthening the work of the Council of Europe, to support and promote national and international efforts, including the work of the European Court of Human Rights ...". It is noteworthy in this context that the Council of Europe's Ordinary Budget for 2025, adopted on a provisional basis on 23 November 2023,[48] already seeks to translate this commitment[49] by providing for a real increase in the Court's budget; however, it will remain to be seen if and how this commitment will be maintained and fulfilled in the coming years and decades.

The Court of Justice of the European Union (CJEU) has, in the past, identified the possibility of inter-State applications as one of the obstacles for the accession of the EU to the ECHR. In its Opinion 2/13, the CJEU saw the inter-State application as a threat to the autonomy of the law of the European Union under Article 344 TFEU.[50] The CJEU has expressed similar views with regard to other international dispute settlement mechanisms.[51] In its Opinion, the Luxembourg Court has postulated the 'express exclusion of the ECtHR's jurisdiction under Article 33 ECHR over disputes between Member States or between Member States and the EU in relation to the application of the ECHR within the scope *ratione materiae* of EU law'. This concern is now reflected in Article 4 § 3a of the Consolidated version of the latest Draft revised agreement on the accession of the European Union to the Convention for the Protection of Human Rights and Fundamental Freedoms (as of 2 February 2023). This provides that "The European Union and its member States in their relations with each other shall not avail themselves of Article 33 of the Convention.

47 4th Summit of Heads of State and Government of the Council of Europe, Reykjavík Declaration, United around our values, 16–17 May 2023, <https://rm.coe.int/4th-summit-of-heads-of-state-and-government-of-the-council-of-europe/1680ab40c1> accessed 30 April 2024.

48 CM/Res(2023)22, https://rm.coe.int/0900001680ad50b1&format=native accessed 30 January 2024.

49 See paragraph 3 of CM/Del/Dec(2023)1481/11.1-Part1 (<https://rm.coe.int/0900001680ad50ad&format=native> accessed 30 April 2024).

50 CJEU Opinion 2/13 (Full Court), 18 December 2014, ECLI:EU:C:2014:2454; the opinion should be read together with the view of GA Juliane Kokott, 13 June 2014, ECLI:EU:C:2014:2475; see also Christian Tomuschat, 'Der Streit um die Auslegungshoheit: Die Autonomie der EU als Heiliger Grahl/das EuGH-Gutachten gegen den Beitritt der EU zur EMRK', EuGRZ 2015, 133, 137; Daniel Halberstam, 'It's the autonomy, stupid!' German Law Journal 2015, 106, 111.

51 E.g. *Slovak Republic v Achmea BV* C-284, 6 March 2018, ECLI:EU:C:2018:158, and *Republic of Moldova v Komstroy LLC*, C-741/19, 2 September 2021, ECLI:EU:C:2021:655.

Nor shall the member States of the European Union avail themselves of Article 33 of the Convention insofar as a dispute between them concerns the interpretation or application of European Union law".[52] In this context, it is perhaps noteworthy that, of course, the EU itself does not, as things stand, have any general competence for the supervision of human rights standards in EU member States and the CJEU's jurisdiction is, in principle, confined to allegations of a failure to fulfil an obligation under the EU Treaties.

Overall, the current docket of inter-State applications raises challenges, inter alia concerning issues of jurisdiction and admissibility, multi-forum litigation, competing sovereignty claims, the relationship to international humanitarian law, the overlap of individual and inter-State cases, and fact-finding in inter-State proceedings, as well as questions of just satisfaction under Article 41 ECHR.

In the following three sections, we reflect upon recent events and developments in Europe which have led to the use of the inter-State application under Article 33 the European Convention on Human Rights. We show how and why this results in a challenging situation for the European Court of Human Rights on many levels, including the resource situation of the European Court of Human Rights. In the second of three main subsections we sketch out how the inter-State application was the centerpiece of international human rights supervision in the original 1950 Convention. We then highlight the evolution of the inter-State application over some seven decades of history of the ECHR. In the third main section, we highlight some of the strengths and raise awareness of existing limitations of the mechanism. One aspect that we highlight in a cross-cutting fashion is the evidential aspects of this type of proceedings. Establishing a judicial record of the events under the Court's scrutiny is a separate and free-standing value of such proceedings to be appraised here in its aims and complexities.

2 The Evolution of the Inter-State Application Over Some Seven Decades of History

An overview of the evolution of inter-State applications over time can facilitate an understanding of how the mechanism was set up, and how it has worked in practice. It is worthwhile to underline that the inter-State application

52 Appendix 1 to the Consolidated version of the draft Accession Instruments (as of 2 February 2023) (Doc No 46 + 1(2023)31) <https://rm.coe.int/consolidated-version-of-the-draft-accession-instruments-as-of-2-februa/1680aa3443> accessed 30 April 2024.

procedure was, at the very beginning, conceived as the default oversight mechanism in the European Convention on Human Rights as finalised in 1950. Former Article 24 ECHR, which in the initial text of the Convention provided for the referral of inter-State complaints to the (former) Commission, was the minimum exposure to international human rights supervision States had to accept upon becoming a member of the Convention; it was and is an indispensable centerpiece of the public order of Europe. The availability of such international human rights oversight was no small achievement. The departure from the law of diplomatic protection and international minimum standards through the Convention as a human rights treaty was described in the emblematic *Barcelona Traction* judgment of 1970 by the International Court of Justice. In an *obiter dictum*, the Hague Court described the characteristics and the potential of the inter-State application procedure.

> [...] on the universal level, the instruments which embody human rights do not confer on States the capacity to protect the victims of infringements of such rights irrespective of their nationality. It is therefore still on the regional level that a solution to this problem has had to be sought; thus, within the Council of Europe, of which Spain is not a member, the problem of admissibility encountered by the claim in the present case has been resolved by the European Convention on Human Rights, which entitles each State which is a party to the Convention to lodge a complaint against any other contracting State for violation of the Convention, irrespective of the nationality of the victim.[53]

The idea of "collective enforcement" of human rights, which is identified in the preamble as one of the purposes of the Convention (i.e. to be a "first step[...] for the collective enforcement of certain rights stated in the Universal Declaration") and the way the supervision has been organised can be traced back to the Teitgen-report during the Convention's drafting process.[54] That document affirms the 'usefulness of such a collective guarantee' and details that 'this guarantee will demonstrate clearly the common desire of the Member States to build a European Union in accordance with the principles of natural law, of humanism and of democracy; (...) it will allow Member States to prevent – before it is too late – any new member who might be threatened

53 *Case Concerning the Barcelona Traction, Light and Power Company* (*Belgium v Spain*), ICJ Reports 1970, 3, 47.

54 Brian Simpson, *Human Rights and the End of Empire* (2004), 657.

by a rebirth of totalitarianism from the succumbing to the influence of evil, as has already happened in general conditions of apathy.'[55]

The Convention entrusted three bodies with the supervision of the Convention's obligations: the European Commission of Human Rights (the Commission), the European Court of Human Rights (the Court) and the Committee of Ministers of the Council of Europe. The Commission's task under the Convention was to decide on the admissibility of both individual and inter-State applications according to ex-Articles 26 and 27 ECHR. As mentioned above, inter-State applications to the Commission under ex-Article 24 ECHR were the very minimum of international oversight States had to accept when becoming a member State. The jurisdiction of the European Court of Human Rights as well as the right to individual application, on the other hand, where options which States could choose to accept, and did so usually for periods of two or three years.

At the merits stage of inter-State proceedings under the arrangements prior to Protocol 11, the Commission had the duty to establish the facts and to work with the parties towards a friendly settlement under ex-Article 28 ECHR. If a settlement was reached, the Commission was to prepare a report, under ex-Article 30 ECHR, which was confined to a brief statement of facts. If a settlement could not be reached, the Commission would prepare a report under ex-Article 31 ECHR which included its findings of fact and law. In this non-binding report, the Commission stated its opinion whether the established facts disclosed a violation of the Convention. The Commission could also, under ex-Article 31 § 3 ECHR, 'make such proposals as it [thought] fit'. Any such proposals were, like the report as a whole, not binding on the parties. The Commission's reports were confidential documents, and were only to be published by decision of the Committee of Ministers, or if the case was referred to the Court. Only one set of inter-State proceedings reached the Court before Protocol 11 entered into force: *Ireland v United Kingdom*.[56] Famously, the Commission and the Court diverged in their interpretation of Article 3 ECHR with regard to the so-called five techniques during the Troubles in Northern Ireland. The divergence concerned the question whether the interrogation methods employed during the conflict in Northern Ireland amounted to torture or were to be seen as inhuman and degrading treatment contrary to Article 3.

---

55 Arthur Robertson (ed), *Travaux Préparatoires I* (1975), 192.

56 *Ireland v United Kingdom*, 5310/71; Commission Report of 25 January 1976, judgment (Plenary) of 18 January 1978; see also *Ireland v the United Kingdom* (revision), 5310/71, 20 March 2018.

All the other early inter-State cases were handled by the Commission and the Committee of Ministers of the Council of Europe. This is not to say that the non-binding reports of the Commission lacked in rigor, judicial tone or effect; quite the contrary. While not all cases can be mentioned here, and not all cases had the same impact, one example that stands out is the so-called Greek case.[57] In 1967, four applicant governments, Denmark, Norway, Sweden and the Netherlands joined forces to address the situation in Greece after the military had taken over governmental powers. The Commission's report runs over 1,100 pages and occupies a special edition of the 1969 yearbook.[58] The Commission found numerous violations of the Convention, and held that Greece could not avail itself of derogations under Article 15 ECHR to justify the measures taken. For the first time, the Commission found that torture within the meaning of Article 3 ECHR had been practiced in a member State of the Convention.[59] Acting under ex-Article 31 § 3 ECHR, the Commission included ten proposals in its report.[60] The non-binding proposals addressed the detention practices as well as the independence of the judiciary, and as the Commission was not itself able to award just satisfaction under Article 50 (now Article 41) ECHR, called for compensation for the cases in which torture and ill treatment were found. The Commission also proposed to hold free elections at the earliest date possible. In November 1969, the final report of the Commission was leaked to the European press and *Le Monde* and *The Sunday Times* revealed its contents.[61] The Committee of Ministers met in December 1969 in order to discuss a possible suspension of Greece from the Council of Europe under Article 8 of the Statute of the Council of Europe. However, on 12 December 1969, the Greek foreign minister announced the Greek withdrawal from the Council of Europe under Article 7 of the Statute of the Council of Europe and

---

57 Wolfgang Benedek, 'The Effectiveness of the Tools of the Council of Europe Against Democratic Backsliding: What Lessons Can be Learned from the "Greek Case"?', *Austrian Law Journal* 2020, 1.

58 Indicated by the roman number 'II'; *Denmark, Norway, Sweden and the Netherlands v Greece (I)*, report of the Commission of 5 November 1969, Yearbook 12 II (1969). The total documents for the proceedings ran to over 20,000 pages; see also Ed Bates, *The Evolution of the European Convention on Human Rights* (2011), 265.

59 See also James Becket, *Barbarism in Greece* (1970); Becket, who worked for Amnesty International, was also heard as a witness in the fact-finding proceedings before the Commission. He was the husband of Maria Hary Becket, a Greek activist, see www.mariabecketreport.com; see also the conference recordings of 50 years of the Greek Case, with his intervention, available on youtube at www.youtube.com/@greekcase6671.

60 Proposals made by the European Commission of Human Rights, appendix to report of the Commission under Article 31 § 3 ECHR, Yearbook 12 (1969), 514, 515.

61 Alexandre Kiss, Phédon Végléris, 'L'affaire grecque devant le Conseil de l'Europe et la Commission européenne des droits de l'homme', AFDI 1971, 889, 902.

the dununciation of the ECHR under ex-Article 65 ECHR.[62] As a consequence, Greece ceased to be a member of the ECHR on 13 June 1970.[63] On 15 April 1970, the Committee of Ministers decided, in accordance with ex-Article 32 § 3 ECHR, to publish the report of the European Commission on Human Rights.[64] In 1974, Greece was readmitted to the Council of Europe and again became a party to the ECHR once democracy had been restored, a development closely connected to the events in Cyprus that summer. The Committee of Ministers decided in November 1974 to discontinue the examination of the 1967 inter-State application in view of the 'fundamental changes' that had occurred in Greece.[65]

An example that shows the long shadow of the inter-State application procedure in its initial setup are the first three *Cyprus v Türkiye* cases. *Türkiye* had not accepted the jurisdiction of the European Court of Human Rights under ex-Article 46 ECHR before 1990 and it was thus for the Committee of Ministers to decide on the merits of the inter-State applications. Under ex-Article 32 ECHR, the Committee of Minister's task was to decide, by a two-thirds majority, in a 'confidential peer review procedure', whether there had been a violation of the Convention.[66] The way the duties under ex-Article 32 ECHR were to be discharged concerning the first two inter-State cases was subject to lengthy discussions within the political body.[67] While *Türkiye* had refused to cooperate in the proceedings on the merits before the Commission, in May 1977 it submitted a detailed memorial to the Committee of Ministers.[68]

62 See for a comprehensive documentation Herbert Petzold, 'Der Gegenwärtige Wirkungsbereich der Europäischen Menschenrechtskonvention und ihrer Zusatzprotokolle, der Konvention zur Beseitigung aller Formen von Rassendiskriminierung sowie der Menschenrechtspakte der Vereinten Nationen', HJIL 1970, 400.

63 See documentation in Yearbook 13 (1970), 4.

64 *Denmark, Norway, Sweden and the Netherlands v Greece (I)*, Committee of Ministers res DH (70) 1, 15.4.1970, Yearbook 12 II (1969), 511, 513.

65 *Denmark, Norway, Sweden and the Netherlands v Greece (I)*, Committee of Ministers, res DH 74 (2) 26.11.1974.

66 Frederick Sundberg, 'Control of Execution of Decisions under the European Convention on Human Rights – A Perspective on Democratic Security, Intergovernmental Cooperation, Unification and Individual Justice in Europe' in Gudmundur Alfredsson et al (eds), *International Monitoring Mechanisms: Essays in Honor of Jacob Th. Möller* (2nd ed, 2009) 465, 466.

67 See eg *Cyprus v Türkiye* (*I*) and (*II*), 6780/74, 6950/75, Committee of Ministers, Del/Concl (77)274 of 17 October 1977.

68 Memorandum of the Government of the Republic of *Türkiye* on the Question of Human Rights in Cyprus, Doc CM (77) 11, 24 May 1977; the document remains confidential but see Gérard Cohen Jonathan, Jean-Paul Jacqué, 'Activité de la Commission Européenne des Droits de l'Homme' (1979) 25 *AFDI* 382, 389.

In October 1977, the Committee of Ministers took note of the Commission's report and decided that the events in Cyprus constituted violations of the Convention. The Committee of Ministers, however, left open which State was responsible for the violations. The text of the decision remains confidential.[69] The report of the Commission was rendered public after it had also been leaked.[70] In January 1979, the Committee of Ministers urged the parties to resume inter-communal talks under the auspices of the Secretary General of the United Nations.[71] The Committee's Resolution of January 1979 met with stark criticism.[72] *Ed Bates* describes the decision of the political body as a 'low point in the Convention's history'.[73] In more graphic terms, *Brice Dickson* called the Committee of Ministers 'pusillanimous in face of serious human rights violations committed by one member State of the Council of Europe on the territory of another.'[74] The criticism was unanimous except for a Turkish commentator, who opined that '… the Committee of Ministers, like the Commission of Human Rights in its Reports on the two Greek Applications against the United Kingdom, has very rightly made a practical and realistic approach to the matter by recognizing the inescapable fact that enduring protection of human rights in Cyprus can only be brought about through the re-establishment of peace and confidence between the two communities, that is to say, by the finding of a political settlement of the Cyprus problem and not by protracted litigation in the human rights tribunals of the Council of Europe or other international fora.'[75]

Just as after the end of the proceedings in the first two inter-State applications between Cyprus and *Türkiye*, the comments about the Committee of Ministers' actions with respect to the third Cyprus cases were also mainly negative.[76]

69 The contents of the decision is corroborated in Committee of Ministers res DH (79), 20.1.1979.

70 The report was in part published by *The Sunday Times* in early 1977; the full report had been published by the private initiative 'Friends of Cyprus' in 1978, see Hans Jürgen Bartsch, 'Ministerkomitee des Europarats (MKER) Straßburg', EuGRZ 1979, 86.

71 Committee of Ministers resolution DH (79), 20.1.1979.

72 Jacques Velu, 'Report on Responsibilities for States Parties to the European Convention' in *Proceedings of the Sixth International Colloquy about the European Convention on Human Rights organized by the Secretariat General of the Council of Europe* (1988) 532, 612; Leo Zwaak, 'Turkey and the European Convention on Human Rights' in Monique Castermans-Holleman et al (eds), *The Role of the Nation State in the 21st Century* (1998) 209, 211.

73 Ed Bates, *The Evolution of the European Convention on Human Rights* (2011) 283.

74 Brice Dickson, *The European Convention on Human Rights and the Conflict in Northern Ireland* (2010) 371.

75 Münir Ertekün, 'Inter-State Applications and Article 27 (2) of the European Convention on Human Rights and Fundamental Freedoms', Turkish Yearbook of Human Rights 1980, 5, 9.

76 Ed Bates, *The Evolution of the European Convention on Human Rights* (2011) 283; Menno Kamminga, 157.

Christian Tomuschat stated that '[t]he procedure under Article 24 is not meant to end up in a diplomatic communiqué which carefully accommodates the susceptibilities of the parties involved.'[77] The Committee of Ministers published the 1983 report in 1992, at a time when the two groups on the island were making attempts of finding a peaceful settlement.[78] In its 2001 judgment in the *Cyprus v Türkiye* (IV) case, the Court noted that 'neither Resolution DH (79) 1 nor Resolution DH 92 (12) resulted in a 'decision' by the Committee of Ministers within the meaning of Article 32 § 1.'[79]

The sobering performance of the Committee of Ministers in the Cyprus cases can be identified as one of the possible disincentives for lodging further inter-State proceedings under the old structures and may explain the relative scarcity of inter-State applications after these early experiences.

This tripartite setup of the Convention's supervisory regime gave way to the single Court in 1998 by virtue of Protocol No 11 to the Convention.[80] The idea of reforming the Convention had been discussed for a number of years, and had been accelerated by the Vienna Summit in 1993.[81] The Summit was the first meeting of heads of States and Governments of the Council of Europe in the history of the organisation, and must be seen in the context of the significant changes in Eastern Europe that were underway following the fall of the Berlin wall.

The Vienna Declaration specified with regard to a reform of the Conventions supervisory architecture that:

> "Since the Convention entered into force in 1953 the number of contracting States has almost tripled and more countries will accede after becoming members of the Council of Europe. We are of the opinion that it has become urgently necessary to adapt the present control mechanism to this development in order to be able to maintain in the future effective international protection for human rights. The purpose of this reform is to

77 Christian Tomuschat, 'Quo Vadis, Argentoratum? The Success Story of the European Convention on Human Rights – and a Few Dark Stains', HRLJ 1992, 401, 402.

78 Christian Rumpf, ‚Nochmals: Zypern und Türkei vor den Straßburger Menschenrechtsorganen', EuGRZ 1992, 457.

79 *Cyprus v Türkiye* (IV), 25781/94 (GC, merits), 10 May 2001, § 67.

80 Protocol No. 11 to the Convention for the Protection of Human Rights and Fundamental Freedoms, restructuring the control machinery established thereby, ETS 155, 11 May 1994.

81 Explanatory Report to Protocol No. 11 to the Convention for the Protection of Human Rights and Fundamental Freedoms, restructuring the control machinery established thereby, 11 May 1994, rm.coe.int/CoERMPublicCommonSearchServices/DisplayDCTMContent?documentId=09000016800cb5e9, paras 1–5.

enhance the efficiency of the means of protection, to shorten procedures and to maintain the present high quality of human rights protection."[82]

The drafters of the initial Convention, of course, had worked under the weight of the memory of a war that had shaken the continent and the world. As sketched out above, their intention was to prevent the further rise of tyranny in Europe by establishing a legally binding framework of human rights protection. By contrast, while the early 1990s were marked by the conflict in former Yugoslavia, this was also a period of enthusiasm in the aftermath of the fall of the Berlin wall and the dissolution of the Soviet Union. Some even proclaimed the end of history.[83]

This context is one possible explanation why the inter-State application procedure was not considered in more depth when the single Court was conceived as a court which would have compulsory jurisdiction both for individual and inter-State applications. It may well be that any future need for inter-State proceedings was not readily apparent. In any event, the focus of the reform process therefore centered very much around individual applications. At the time of the drafting of Protocol 11, inter-State applications had for a long time not been part of the Strasbourg realties. It appears that in those years leading up to the reform, inter-State applications were largely absent from the docket of the Commission. While *Cyprus v Türkiye III* had been lodged in 1977, *Cyprus v Türkiye IV* was not lodged until November 1994. In the meantime, however, Protocol 11 had been opened for signature in May 1994 and entered into force in 1998. As a consequence, the mechanism was only mentioned very few times – and then more in passing – in the explanatory report to Protocol 11 to the Convention. Para 83 of the explanatory report to Protocol 11 states:

> The text of Article 33 is based on that of former Article 24 of the Convention. This Article on inter-State cases reflects the former system whereby proceedings could be instituted before the Commission by one or more States against another State that had ratified the Convention, without the necessity for any additional acceptance of competence on the latter's part. States are, of course, bound only by the protocols they have ratified.

The decisive difference between the old and the new supervisory structure of the Convention was that the Court would now enjoy compulsory jurisdiction

82 Vienna Declaration, Appendix I, Reform of the control mechanism of the European Convention on Human Rights, 9.10.1993.

83 Francis Fukuyama, *The End of History and the Last Man* (1992).

not only in individual cases, but also in inter-State applications. The shortcomings of the role of the Committee of Ministers in the initial setup had been "remedied" by the judicialisation of the machinery through Protocol No 11 to the Convention. This compulsory jurisdiction would soon be extended to the new member States. Protocol 11 was opened for signature in May 1994, two years before Russia became a member, and two years after Russia had applied for membership in the Council of Europe. While Russia's membership in the Council of Europe was seen as challenging in Strasbourg,[84] again it appears that at the time the inter-State mechanism was not considered to be an issue requiring any detailed consideration in this context.

Furthermore, on a formal level, the way overlapping individual and inter-State applications should be dealt with is not addressed by the Convention.[85] Both have an important function and do not exclude each other, as the Court has underlined in *Varnava*.[86] This means, for example, that individuals or the next of kin who wish to complain under Article 2 ECHR, the right of life, are in principle free to lodge their applications subject to the terms of Articles 34 and 35 ECHR even if similar (or even identical) allegations made by a state under Article 2 ECHR were declared inadmissible, as for example in the admissibility decision of *Ukraine v Russia* (*re Crimea*).[87] After all, the reason for inadmissibility in those proceedings frequently derived from the lack of evidence of the necessary "administrative practice". The next of kin of individuals who were killed are therefore not prevented from "having their day in Court". The fact that the Convention does not regulate this relationship further supports the assumption that little thought was given to the inter-State application when Protocol 11 was drawn up.

The current docket of inter-State cases, which started to fill up again in 2007 with the first set of inter-State proceedings between Georgia and Russia, was briefly sketched out above and shall not be repeated here. Worth mentioning here is, however, that a decade or so later the instrument of the inter-state application under Article 33 ECHR was the subject of a reflection process in the framework of the Steering Committee of Human Rights (CDDH). This body was set up by the Committee of Ministers in 1976 to conduct the

84 Interview with Daniel Tarschys, former Secretary General of the Council of Europe, 28.2.2016, on the occasion of the 20th anniversary of the Russian Federation's accession to the Council of Europe, <https://www.coe.int/en/web/human-rights-rule-of-law/daniel-tarschys> accessed 30 April 2024.

85 Elena Carpanelli, 'Il rapporto tra ricorsi interstatali e individuali dinnanzi alla Corte europea dei diritti umani', Diritti Umani e Diritto Internazionale, 389–411.

86 *Varnava and Others v Turkey*, 16064/90 et al, 18.9.2009.

87 *Ukraine v Russia* (re Crimea, GC, dec.), 20958/14 and 38334/18, 20 December 2020, §§ 398–400.

intergovernmental work of the Council of Europe and to give legal expertise to the Committee of Ministers on all questions within its field of competence. At the time the reflection process started, the Russian Federation was, of course, still a member of the Council of Europe and actively, albeit perhaps not most constructively, participated in most of the process. In any event, the idea of the reflection never contemplated a change to the wording of the Convention. The 2018 Copenhagen Ministerial Declaration[88] commissioned the Committee of Ministers, before the end of 2019, to finalise its analysis of 'obtaining a balanced case load', including by:

> exploring ways to handle more effectively cases related to inter-State disputes, as well as individual applications arising out of situations of inter-State conflict, without thereby limiting the jurisdiction of the Court, taking into consideration the specific features of these categories of cases inter alia regarding the establishment of facts.

In the context of this follow-up work by the CDDH, the Plenary of the Court also adopted and presented a document addressing the question of a more efficient processing of inter-State cases.[89] However, in its meeting on 18–21 June 2019 the CDDH was ultimately not able to agree on a set of recommendations. In its meeting on 26–29 November 2019, the Committee decided to set up a Drafting Group on the effective processing and resolution of cases relating to inter-State disputes (DH-SYSC-IV) with a view to submitting proposals to the Committee of Ministers before 31 December 2021.[90] In this context, a conference entitled "Inter-State cases under the European Convention on Human Rights" was organised by the German Presidency of the Committee of Ministers in co-operation with the CDDH on 12 and 13 April 2021 and its proceedings were published in book format under the auspices of the Council of Europe.[91]

---

88 Council of Europe, Committee of Ministers of the Council of Europe, *Copenhagen Declaration* (12–13 April 2018) <https://rm.coe.int/copenhagen-declaration/16807b915c> accessed 30 April 2024 (para. 54 c).

89 Council of Europe, Steering Committee for Human Rights (CDDH), *Proposals for a more efficient processing of inter-State cases* (6 June 2019) <https://rm.coe.int/steering-committee-for-human-rights-cddh-proposals-for-a-more-efficien/168094e6e1 accessed 30 April 2024.

90 All documents are available here: https://www.coe.int/en/web/human-rights-intergovernmental-cooperation/effective-processing-and-resolution-of-inter-state-disputes accessed 30 April 2024.

91 Council of Europe, Inter-state cases under the European Convention on Human Rights – Experiences and current challenges (Proceedings of the Conference organised under the aegis of the German Presidency of the Committee of Ministers, Berlin, 12–13 April 2021)

Ultimately, these reflection efforts culminated in a Declaration by the Committee of Ministers on the effective processing and resolution of cases relating to inter-State disputes of 5 April 2023, i.e. one month before the fourth Summit in Reykjavik. In this declaration, the Committee of Ministers invited "the Court to continue to reflect on its working methods and allocate appropriate human resources so as to ensure effective and speedy examination and resolution of applications stemming from interstate disputes which often involve large-scale human rights violations, including by taking into account the consequences of the fact that whilst the Russian Federation ceased to be a member of the Council of Europe as from 16 March 2022 it remained bound by obligations under the Convention, including to implement judgments of the Court, in accordance with Article 58 of the Convention, Resolution CM/Res(2022)3, and the Court's Resolution of 22 March 2022; and in this context, welcomes the Court's approach to proceeding with examination of applications lodged against the Russian Federation even in the absence of co-operation from the Russian authorities, in order to best preserve the effective functioning of the Convention system."[92] Beyond that, however, most of the questions that motivated the reflection process remain open at the time of writing.

3 Strengths and Limitations of the Inter-State Procedure under Article 33 ECHR

The third part of this contribution highlights the strengths and raises awareness of the existing limitations of the inter-State application under the European Convention on Human Rights.[93] One aspect that merits particular attention is the evidential aspect of this type of proceedings. Establishing a judicial record

<https://edoc.coe.int/en/european-convention-on-human-rights/11067-inter-state-cases-under-the-european-convention-on-human-rights-experiences-and-current-challenges.html> accessed 30 April 2024; see also the online Symposium hosted by Justine Batura and Isabella Risini in April 2014, with pieces by Angelika Nußberger, Laurence Burgorgue-Larsen, Geir Ulfstein, Andreas Zimmermann, Hélène Tigroudja, Philip Leach, Alina Miron,Nicola Wenzel, Helen Keller, Réka Piskóty, Jorge Contesse, Peter Tzeng, https://voelkerrechtsblog.org/de/symposium/inter-state-cases/ accessed 30 April 2024.

92 Declaration by the Committee of Ministers on the effective processing and resolution of cases relating to inter-State disputes, 5 April 2023, <https://search.coe.int/cm/Pages/result_details.aspx?ObjectId=0900001680aad39a> accessed 30 April 2024.

93 See also Geir Ulfstein, Isabella Risini, Human Rights, State Complaints in MPEIL 2022 online; Geir Ulfstein, Isabella Risini, Inter-State Applications under the European Convention on Human Rights: Strengths and Challenges, 24.1.2020, https://www.ejiltalk.org/inter-state-applications-under-the-european-convention-on-human-rights-strengths-and-challenges/ accessed 30 April 2024.

of the events under the Court's scrutiny is a separate and free-standing value these proceedings which will be appraised here in its aims and complexities.

3.1 *Jurisdiction*

Article 33 ECHR gives access to a comparatively broad jurisdiction. After all, the Strasbourg Court enjoys compulsory jurisdiction and, by comparison with other fora like the International Court of Justice (ICJ) or the dispute settlement procedures provided for under the United Nations Convention on the Law of the Sea, provides a readily accessible forum. The ICJ by contrast can be accessed only via a compromissory clause in a substantive international agreement or an optional protocol, a special agreement under Article 36 § 1 ICJ-Statute, or likewise without limitations on the subject matter where parties have reciprocally accepted the compulsory jurisdiction of the Court under Article 36 § 2 ICJ-Statute. However, only about 1/3 of the UN member States have done so.[94]

Where the jurisdiction of the ICJ is based on a compromissory clause, the Hague Court requires the existence of a "dispute" between the parties.[95] In Strasbourg, a genuine allegation of a human rights violation is sufficient to lodge an inter-State application under Article 33 ECHR.[96] That said, it appears that the ICJ is witnessing an increase in what might be termed "public interest" litigation initiated by non-affected States Parties to the underlying treaties *inter alia* based on the assertion of obligations *erga omnes partes*.[97]

An inevitable limitation to the Court's jurisdiction lies in the subject matter of the application. After all, the Court is limited to the four corners of the Convention, Article 33 ECHR expressly providing that it must concern an "alleged breach of the provisions of the Convention and the Protocols thereto by another High Contracting Party". That said, the applicability and relationship to the Convention of other parallel legal regimes frequently arises in inter-State proceedings and especially international humanitarian

94 Declarations recognising the jurisdiction of the Court as compulsory, <https://www.icj-cij.org/declarations> accessed 30 April 2024.

95 *Application of the International Convention on the Elimination of All Forms of Racial Discrimination* (*Georgia v Russian Federation*), Preliminary Objections, Judgment 1 April 2011, §§ 23 et seq; see also the contribution by David Keane in this special issue.

96 *Georgia v Russia (I)*, 13255/07 (dec)30 June 2009, § 44.

97 Eugenio Carli, 'Community Interests Above All: The Ongoing Procedural Effects of Erga Omnes Partes Obligations Before the International Court of Justice', EJIL:Talk!, 29.12. 2023, see also Christian Tams, 'Individual States as Guardians of Community Interests', in Ulrich Fastenrath et al (eds), *From Bilateralism to Community Interest, Essays in Honour of Judge Bruno Simma* (2011); Francois Voeffray, *L'actio popularis ou la défense de l'intérêt collectif devant les juridictions internationales* (2004).

law, which (deliberately) does not provide for judicial mechanisms for its enforcement, has featured heavily in this aspect of the Court's work. As the Court's jurisprudence shows, there is, however, no "one size fits all" way to deal with the implications of IHL on a given case. It is useful to recall the position of the ICJ in this context. The Hague Court stated that "[a]s regards the relationship between international humanitarian law and human rights law, there are thus three possible situations: some rights may be exclusively matters of international humanitarian law; others may be exclusively matters of human rights law; yet others may be matters of both these branches of international law."[98] With that said, systemic integration may offer one method for reconciling the two bodies of law in some instances.[99]

It has been noted that some of the interim measures indicated by the Court in the context of inter-State proceedings, in fact, include language borrowed from international humanitarian law.[100] In *Georgia v Russia II*, for example, the Court used the term "prisoners of war", a term borrowed from international humanitarian law to describe the fate of 30 men who had been detained in Tskhinvali. Building on the fact that the prohibition of torture and ill-treatment under Article 3 ECHR is a non-derogable guarantee and has a homologue in international humanitarian law, the Court added that "[t]hose acts are particularly serious given that they were perpetrated against prisoners of war, who have a special protected status under international humanitarian law".[101] The situation is thus the opposite to that which arose in the *Hassan v United Kingdom* case, which concerned Article 5 ECHR.[102] In that case, the implication of IHL was that Article 5 of the Convention was applied, despite the fact that no derogation under Article 15 had been notified, in a more open

98 *Armed Activities on the Territory of the Congo (Democratic Republic of the Congo v Uganda)* 19 December 2005, § 216, with reference to its advisory opinion of 9 July 2004 on Legal Consequences of the Construction of a Wall in the Occupied Palestinian Territory.

99 Jean D'Aspremont, 'Articulating international human rights and international humanitarian law: conciliatory interpretation under the guise of conflict of norms resolution', in Malgosia Fitzmaurice, Panos Merkouris (eds), The Interpretation and Application of the European Convention of Human Rights: Legal and Practical Implications, 3,6; *Hassan v the United Kingdom* (GC), 29750/09, 16 September 2014, § 104; *Ukraine and the Netherlands v Russia* (GC), 8019/16, 43800/14 and 28525/20, 25 January 2023, § 396 set seq. § 718.

100 For example: The European Court grants urgent interim measures in application concerning Russian military operations on Ukrainian territory, ECHR 068 (2022) speaks of "civilians", see also *Ukraine v Russia* (re Crimea, GC, dec.), 20958/14 and 38334/18, 20 December 2020, § 5.

101 *Georgia v Russia II*, § 278.

102 *Hassan v the United Kingdom* (GC), 29750/09, 16 September 2014, § 104.

textured manner in order to make allowance for the norms of IHL under which the respondent State was operating.[103]

Concerning the negative obligation to protect the right to life under Article 2 ECHR, apart from the obvious evidential difficulties if it were to apply, as identified in *Georgia v Russia II*, one of the legal difficulties – in addition to the absence of any derogation under Article 15 ECHR – lies in the fact that, unlike e.g. Article 6 § 1 ICCPR,[104] Article 2 §1 ECHR states in absolute terms that "[n]o one shall be deprived of his life intentionally" and none of the permissible exceptions under Article 2 § 2 ECHR ("Deprivation of life shall not be regarded as inflicted in contravention of this article when it results from the use of force which is no more than absolutely necessary ...") would seem to apply in the context of armed hostilities. However, even where the substantive negative obligation under Article 2 ECHR may not apply, Article 2 ECHR may arguably make a real difference inasmuch as it also includes a positive obligation to investigate.[105] While these issues remain to be resolved by the Court it has been noted that Article 15 § 2 ECHR expressly provides that, while in principle no derogation from Article 2 ECHR is permissible, the one exception to this prohibition is "in respect of deaths resulting from lawful acts of war".

3.2 *Admissibility*

Overall, the admissibility requirements for an inter-State application have, so far, shown themselves to be only moderate obstacles to access to the Court. Very few inter-State applications have failed to overcome the hurdles set by the Convention.[106] However, it is worth noting that, while the Court has historically limited itself at the admissibility stage to determining whether, *prima facie*, the allegations of the applicant Government were not 'wholly unsubstantiated' or 'lacking the requirements of a genuine allegation in the sense of Article 33 of the Convention',[107] in its more recent admissibility decisions, the Court appears to have sought to decide as many of the important admissibility issues as early as possible. This has included questions such as that of jurisdiction under Article 1 as well as compliance with the admissibility requirements of Article 35 § 1 and the existence of sufficient *prima facie* evidence to make good the violations complained of. Where the complaint of an applicant Government is not based on an allegation of an "administrative practice", the question of

---

103 An approach which, however, was criticised at the time in the Partly Dissenting Opinion of Judge Spano Joined by Judges Nicolaou, Bianku and Kalaydjieva in that case.

104 Article 6 § 1 ICCPR provides that "No one shall be arbitrarily deprived of his life".

105 See also *Hanan v Germany* (GC), 4871/16, 16 February 2021.

106 *Slovenia v Croatia*, 54155/16, (dec) 12 June 2019.

107 *Georgia v Russia I*, 13255/07 (dec), 30 June 2009, § 44.

the exhaustion of domestic remedies and compliance with the four-month rule contained in Article 35 § 1 ECHR may also raise further procedural issues capable of being decided at the admissibility stage. However, Article 35 § 2 also makes clear that the remaining admissibility requirements contained therein only apply to individual applications.

While in principle the requirement to exhaust domestic remedies applies to inter-State applications, substantial exceptions to the rule have been developed in the case law of the Convention organs. These concern both legislative measures as well as alleged administrative practices. First, the Court has held that the requirement of exhaustion of domestic remedies may be dispensed with if the applicant State alleges that legislation "which introduces, directs or authorises measures incompatible with the rights and freedoms safeguarded", even absent a specific individual victim, and the legislation being "challenged ... is couched in terms sufficiently clear and precise to make the breach immediately apparent".[108] As the Court explained in the 1978 judgment in *Ireland v United Kingdom*, this approach is confirmed unequivocally by the *travaux préparatoires* to the Convention.[109] However, the Court went on to say that, "otherwise, the decision of the Convention institutions must be arrived at by reference to the manner in which the respondent State interprets and applies in concreto the impugned text or texts".[110]

Secondly, the notion of "administrative practice" was developed to address situations where a sufficient repetition of acts constituting the alleged violation and an official tolerance of those acts has been shown to exist and is of such a nature as to make domestic proceedings futile or ineffective.[111] The notion of administrative practice dispenses with the need to exhaust domestic remedies where a systemic issue appears to curtail the Convention rights. However, the Court has also consistently highlighted the fact that, while the exhaustion rule 'does not in principle apply where the applicant Government ... complain[s] of a practice as such, with the aim of preventing its continuation or recurrence, [it] does not ask ... the Court to give a decision on each of the cases put forward as proof or illustrations of that practice'.[112]

108 *Ireland v United Kingdom (Plenary)*, 5310/71, 18 January 1978 § 240.

109 *Ireland v United Kingdom (Plenary)*, 5310/71, 18 January 1978 § 240 et seq. and *Cyprus v Türkiye IV* (GC, merits), 25781/94,10 May 2001, § 357.

110 *Ibid.*

111 *Georgia v Russia (I)* (GC, merits), 3 July 2014, 13255/07, § 122 et seq.

112 *Ibid.* § 125.

3.3 *Merits*

The issue of fact-finding and the way in which the Court deals with the evidence in the context of inter-State proceedings merits detailed (academic) attention in the context of inter-State proceedings.[113] As sketched out above, the now defunct Commission was originally the body tasked with ascertaining the facts. As the explanatory report to Protocol 11 specifies, once the Commission had been abolished, it was generally expected that "[t]he facts will be established by the Court, with the co-operation of the parties."[114] These facts are, however, often in dispute in inter-State proceedings. As a consequence, where the exhaustion of domestic remedies is not possible or not required, the Court is, in turn, put in the position of having to act as if it were a Court of first instance. Such fact-finding is highly resource-intensive both in terms of the potential amount of evidence to be collected as well as the resources the Court would have to expend in order to conduct this exercise. For example, the Court provided a glimpse of the sheer volume of the factual dimension of the case in the admissibility decision in the case of *Ukraine and the Netherlands v. Russia* where it indicated that, by reference only to the evidence submitted by the parties, "one thousand different pieces of evidence have been produced in annexes or cited in footnotes to support the respective positions of the three parties and many thousands of pages of supporting documentation have been submitted."[115] The relevant evidence was then summarised in an Annex attached to the admissibility decision which itself runs to some 811 pages.[116]

113 *Ukraine and the Netherlands v. Russia* (GC, dec.), 8019/16, 43800/14 and 28525/20, 25 January 2023, § 396 set seq.; Philip Leach, 'Enhancing Fact-finding in Inter-State Cases: A Critical Challenge for the European Court of Human Rights'; Thilo Marauhn, 'Less is More: Limited Fact-Finding to Avoid Overburdening the European Court of Human Rights in inter-State Cases', both in Justine Batura and Isabella Risini (eds), 'Symposium on Inter-State Cases Under the European Convention on Human Rights; special issue in European Convention on Human Rights Law Review, 'The Evidentiary System of the European Court of Human Rights in Critical Perspective', edited by Marie-Bénédicte Dembour, 2023 (forthcomimg); Philip Leach, 'Fact-Finding: European Court of Human Rights (ECtHR)' (2018) in Max Planck Encyclopedia of International Procedural Law, Hélene Ruiz Fabri, Rüdiger Wolfrum (eds), (online edn).

114 Explanatory Report to Protocol No. 11 to the Convention for the Protection of Human Rights and Fundamental Freedoms, restructuring the control machinery established thereby, 11 May 1994, rm.coe.int/CoERMPublicCommonSearchServices/DisplayDCTMContent?documentId=09000016800cb5e9, para. 44.

115 *Ukraine and the Netherlands v Russia* (GC, dec.), 8019/16, 43800/14 and 28525/20, 25 January 2023, § 396.

116 Annex to the Decision in the case of *Ukraine and the Netherlands v Russia* (GC, dec.), 8019/16, 43800/14 and 28525/20, 25 January 2023, available at https://www.echr.coe.int/Documents/HUDOC_8019_16_Annexes_Decision_ENG.pdf, accessed 30 April 2024.

The Court's fact-finding role is, of course, even more difficult in cases where the territory in question was or continues to be the theater of an armed conflict and/or the respondent State is uncooperative or altogether absent. The fact that the budget of the Court has, until very recently, been on the decline in real terms also did not help.

While the Court is, in principle, free to adopt the evidentiary rules and practices which it deems suitable, the difficult role the Court is having to play in this context was highlighted in the case of *Georgia v Russia II*. In its judgment, the Court cites the "difficulty in establishing the relevant circumstances" (§ 141) in that part of its judgment addressing the jurisdiction of the Russian Federation during the active phase of hostilities, a jurisdiction which the Court was unable to establish. The Court also referred to the "magnitude of the evidence produced" as adding to the difficulty. Judge Keller, in her Concurring Opinion in that case, observed that "the Court's usual fact-finding methodology is ill-suited, in its flexibility and forbearance, to inter-State cases" (§ 11). However, perhaps building both on its (and the former Commission's) vast fact-finding experience as well as on the "lessons learned" in *Georgia v Russia II*, the Court has more recently tried to set out in some detail the methodological approach it would take to the assessment of the evidence in such inter-State cases.[117] In any event, what is certain is that the methods of fact-finding and the possibilities of today's forensics are not mere technicalities. They may well lay the groundwork for the Court's work. In this context, the Court is, of course, also able to seek to take direct evidence such as through witness hearings, as was done in *Georgia v Russia II*,[118] and/or, where appropriate, to take any other investigatory measures considered necessary and/or appropriate under the provisions set out in the Annex (concerning investigations) to the Rules of Court.

While the Court has no formal powers to compel witnesses to appear before it, the Court has increasingly referred to the duty to cooperate with the Court under Article 38 ECHR and Rules 44A and 44C(1), and the power to draw the necessary inferences. In *Georgia v Russia II (Merits)* the Grand Chamber held that the Russian Federation was in violation of its duty to cooperate under Art. 38 ECHR because it did not disclose the combat reports requested (para. 345). In *Georgia v Russia (I) (Merits)* (2014), Russia's violation of its duty to cooperate was the first operative paragraph of the judgment. As recently

117 *Ukraine and the Netherlands v Russia* (GC, dec.), 8019/16, 43800/14 and 28525/20, 25 January 2023, §§ 396–481 and *Ukraine v Russia (Crimea)* (GC, dec.), 20958/14 38334/18, 16 December 2020, §§ 249–266.

118 *Georgia v Russia (II), 38263/08 (GC, merits), 21 January 2021,* §§ 20 -25.

as its admissibility decision in *Ukraine and the Netherlands v the Russian Federation*,[119] the Court set out in a number of paragraphs its approach to the drawing of inferences; an approach which may assume increased importance in cases where the respondent government does not engage with the Court and/or the complaints brought against it.

Previous inter-State cases, such as the Greek case mentioned above, have derived their relevance and authority from the meticulous fact-finding effort of the former Commission. It is, however, also important to note that the Greek case used up almost all resources of the Commission at the time. The Commission heard live witnesses on site with members of the Commission having travelled to Greece. As Judge O'Donoghue, who had been a member of the Commission in the Greek Case and had travelled to Greece at the time, explained in his dissenting opinion in the 1978 *Ireland v United Kingdom* judgment: 'The value of hearing evidence in a local venue cannot be overestimated. (…) No written description, however colorful, could have been as informative as the visit to Bouboulinos Street in Athens.' For the reasons identified above as well as the considerable backlog of some 74,000 pending individual cases (as of the autumn of 2023),[120] the ECtHR today is unable to match these efforts in relation to fact-finding, as desirable as it might be for it to be able to do so.

3.4 *Just Satisfaction, Article 41 ECHR*

So far, the Court has rendered three judgments on just satisfaction under Article 41 ECHR in inter-State cases: in *Cyprus v Türkiye IV* in 2014, *Georgia v Russia I* in 2019 and *Georgia v Russia II* in April 2023.[121]

In the 2014 *Cyprus v Türkiye IV*[122] just satisfaction judgment, the Court awarded ninety million euros in non-pecuniary damages to certain Greek-Cypriot victims of large-scale human rights violations in the northern part of Cyprus, attributable to *Türkiye* following a judgment on the merits rendered in 2001. Until recently, the award was nominally the largest award in the history of the European Convention on Human Rights in terms of non-pecuniary

119 *Ukraine and the Netherlands v Russia* (GC, dec.), 8019/16, 43800/14 and 28525/20, 25 January 2023, §§ 436–438, 440–441, 454–459, 477 and 479.

120 Pending Applications Allocated to a Judicial Formation, 30 November 2023, https://www.echr.coe.int/documents/d/echr/stats_pending_month_2023_bil, accessed 30 April 2024.

121 *Cyprus v Türkiye IV* (GC, Just Satisfaction), 25781/94, 12 May 2014, 25781/94; *Georgia v Russia (I)* (GC; Just Satisfaction), 31 January 2019, 13255/07, *Georgia v Russia (II)(GC, Just Satisfaction)*, 38263/08, 28 April 2023.

122 *Cyprus v Türkiye IV* (*GC, Just Satisfaction*), 25781/94, 12 May 2014, 25781/94.

damages. Out of the ninety million euros awarded, thirty million euros were earmarked for an unknown number of relatives of the 1,456 persons identified as missing. The remaining sixty million euros were destined for the enclaved Greek Cypriot residents of the Karpas peninsula in northern Cyprus. Their number was likewise not clear. While Türkiye has honored the just satisfaction awards in some individual cases, such as for example the *Loizidou v Türkiye*[123] case, it has not yet paid the award in this inter-State case. The secondary obligation to pay just satisfaction does not alter the obligation to comply with the *Cyprus v Türkiye IV* 2001 judgment on the merits and to put an end to the breaches found. An eventual payment of the award would also not absolve *Türkiye* from the obligation to investigate the fate of the missing persons or to change the treatment of the inhabitants of the Karpas peninsula.

The case of *Georgia v Russia (I)* concerned the arrest, detention and expulsion from Russia of large numbers of Georgian nationals from the end of September 2006 to the end of January 2007, in a series of events which were largely unrelated to the armed conflict in 2008. The Court rendered judgment on the merits in 2014, and found that a coordinated policy of arresting, detaining and expelling Georgian nationals had been put in place in the Russian Federation amounting to an administrative practice of collective expulsion of aliens, contrary to Article 4 of Protocol No. 4. The Court also found that the practice had infringed Article 5 §§ 1 and 4, Article 3 and Article 13 of the Convention, owing in particular to the arbitrary nature and conditions of detention of the persons arrested.[124] In its 2019 just satisfaction judgment, the Court awarded ten million euros in non-pecuniary damage to be paid to the applicant Government to be distributed as follows to the victims, a group of at least 1,500 Georgian nationals, (i) EUR 2,000 to each of the victims of a violation of Article 4 of Protocol No. 4 alone; (ii) between EUR 10,000 and 15,000 to those of them who had also been victims of a violation of Article 5 § 1 and Article 3 of the Convention, taking into account the length of their respective periods of detention. In late 2021, Georgia and Russia finalised a Memorandum of Understanding to enable payment to take place through a Council of Europe bank account held in escrow.[125] However, the payment

123 *Varnava and Others v Türkiye* (GC), 16064/90, 18 September 2009 (12,000 euros as non-pecuniary damages) as well as *Loizidou v Türkiye*, 15318/89 28 July 1998 (20,000 Cypriot pounds (approx. 34,000 euros) of non-pecuniary damages).

124 *Georgia v Russia (I)*, 13255/07 (GC) 3 July 2014.

125 Georgia v. Russia (I), 13255/07, Supervision of the execution of the European Court's judgments, 1419th meeting, 30 November – 2 December 2021 (DH) H46-30, Reference document CM/Notes/1419/H46-30: "3. noted with satisfaction that the Secretary General of the Council of Europe and the Georgian authorities have now signed the

ultimately did not occur due to Russia having launched its attacks against Ukraine in February 2022 and its ensuing expulsion from the Council of Europe in March 2022. Russia continues to be under an obligation to pay the award.

In the recent just satisfaction judgment in *Georgia v Russia (II)*, following its merits judgment of January 2021 concerning the events during the eight-day war in 2008, the Court awarded just satisfaction under the following headings: three million two hundred and fifty thousand euros in respect of non-pecuniary damage suffered by a group of at least fifty victims of the administrative practice of killing of civilians in Georgian villages in South Ossetia and in the "buffer zone" and of the respondent Government's failure to comply with their procedural obligation to carry out an adequate and effective investigation into those killings; two million six hundred and ninety-seven thousand five hundred euros in respect of non-pecuniary damage suffered by a group of at least 166 victims of the administrative practice of inhuman and degrading treatment and arbitrary detention of Georgian civilians detained by the South Ossetian forces in the basement of the "Ministry of Internal Affairs of South Ossetia" in Tskhinvali between approximately 10 and 27 August 2008; six hundred and forty thousand euros in respect of non-pecuniary damage suffered by a group of at least 16 victims of the administrative practice of torture of Georgian prisoners of war detained by the South Ossetian forces in Tskhinvali between 8 and 17 August 2008; one hundred and fifteen million euros in respect of non-pecuniary damage suffered by a group of at least 23,000 victims of the administrative practice of preventing the return of Georgian nationals to their respective homes in South Ossetia and Abkhazia; and eight million two hundred and forty thousand euros in respect of non-pecuniary damage suffered by a group of at least 412 victims of the respondent Government's failure to comply with their procedural obligation to carry out an adequate and effective investigation into the deaths which occurred during the active phase of the hostilities. As in its previous just satisfaction judgments, the Court also left it to the applicant Government to distribute the sums awarded decided that it should be left to the applicant Government, under the supervision of the Committee of Ministers, to set up an effective mechanism to do so within eighteen months from the date of the payment by the respondent Government or within any other period deemed appropriate by the Committee of Ministers.

Memorandum of Understanding; looked forward also to the swift signature of the Memorandum of Understanding by the Russian authorities and the payment of the funds to the Council of Europe bank account held in escrow in the shortest possible timeframe and in any event by the end of the year, as well as to the completion of the remaining steps to execute the Court's judgment as soon as possible".

The Court's reasoning as to why Article 41 ECHR applies in the inter-State context can be found in §§ 39–47 of the *Cyprus v Türkiye* just satisfaction judgment, most recently restated in the *Georgia v Russia II* just satisfaction judgment at § 30. The award is an emanation of the engagements undertaken by the Contracting States of the ECHR within the meaning of Article 19 ECHR, authoritatively defining the scope of the treaty obligations flowing from the Convention. The Contracting States to the ECHR have consented to abide by the Court's judgments under Article 46 ECHR. Thus, they have removed these matters from the merely political arena and have entered into binding treaty obligations, which includes the obligation under Article 41 ECHR to afford such just satisfaction to the injured party as determined by the Court.

As in its recent *Georgia v Russia II* just satisfaction judgment, the Court usually leaves the ensuing questions concern the identification of the individual beneficiaries of the awards and the distribution of the award to the applicant State under the supervision of the Committee of Ministers. Of course, just satisfaction most acutely raises the issue of how the Court should deal with overlapping individual applications. In this context, it has been suggested that, as an alternative approach, the Court, in its judgment on an inter-State-application, should at the same time decide on the compensation to be granted to all victims of the underlying systemic violations of the Convention which it considers to have occurred, regardless of whether the individuals concerned have simultaneously filed individual applications or not.[126] This suggestion, however, in turn raises the question of how "all victims" should be identified by the Court at the time of rendering its judgment in the inter-State case and, on the other hand, whether such an approach would justify the Court thereafter striking out all related individual applications under Article 37.

In May 2023, the Council of Europe held its overall fourth summit in the history of the Council of Europe in Reykjavik, which addressed the Russian aggression in Ukraine. There, a register of damage for Ukraine was created as a first step towards an international compensation mechanism for the victims of Russian aggression.[127] How this new mechanism might relate to the Courts work remains to be seen. According to Article 2 of the mechanism,

---

126 Isabella Risini, Geir Ulfstein, Andreas Zimmermann, 'Of Foxes Guarding Chickens, and Their Fellow Foxes, An Outlook on the Reform Process Concerning Inter-State Applications Under the ECHR', 30.4.2021,Völkerrechtsblog, https://voelkerrechtsblog.org/de/of-foxes-guarding-chickens-and-their-fellow-foxes/ accessed 30 April 2024.

127 Resolution CM/Res(2023)3 establishing the Enlarged Partial Agreement on the Register of Damage Caused by the Aggression of the Russian Federation against Ukraine, adopted by the Committee of Ministers on 12 May 2023 at the 1466th meeting of the Ministers' Deputies.

"[t]he Register shall receive and process information on claims of damage and evidence; categorise, classify and organise such claims, assess and determine the eligibility of claims for inclusion in the Register and record the eligible claims for the purposes of their future examination and adjudication".

4 In Conclusion: of Root Causes and Other Effects

In our contribution we have sought to show how the inter-State application is a centerpiece of international human rights supervision in Europe. We sketched out the challenges related to inter-State applications, and have focused on the dimension of facts and evidence. We hope to highlight that it is of utmost importance to provide a judicial record of the evidence provided and judicially assessed by the Court in the context of the allegations of serious human rights violations brought before the Court by one or more member States against another member State. The related question raised by inter-State applications is whether the European Court is equipped to deal with large-scale abuses of human rights in Europe. Its mandate to provide the mechanism for the collective enforcement of human rights emerges clearly from the Convention. On the other hand, the resources to do so are clearly finite. Given the importance of inter-State proceedings, as well as the thousands of overlapping individual applications, the conscious dedication of resources to these proceedings is worthwhile to ensure the effective application of the Convention; something which was clearly recognised in the conclusions of the Council of Europe Summit in Reykjavik.

The erosion of a rule-based framework respected and internalised by all must be addressed. The expectations towards the Court, which depends on the initiative and the support of the member States of the Council of Europe, has to be managed carefully. One of the root causes for said erosion being a democratic decline within member States, it is important that the effect of these erosions should be more and not less rigor in the administration of justice including via inter-State applications in Strasbourg.

CHAPTER 3

Inter-States Disputes Under the Inter-American Human Rights System

Jorge Contesse

Abstract

Under the inter-American human rights system, inter-State disputes seem largely irrelevant. Such irrelevance contrasts with the European human rights system, where the amount of inter-State disputes is significant (and growing), and is similar to the African human rights regime, where there is a very low number of inter-State disputes. In more than four decades since the entry into force of the American Convention on Human Rights, there are only two inter-State disputes brought before the Inter-American Commission on Human Rights—one of the two bodies that, along with the Inter-American Court, make up the regional human rights system. The virtual inexistence of inter-State complaints, however, does not mean an absence of human rights disputes among members of the Organization of American States (OAS). In fact, States resort to other mechanisms to process their disputes. Therefore, to explore how inter-States disputes actually operate under inter-American human rights law, it is necessary to broaden the view and look beyond the specific mechanism of inter-State communications established in the American Convention. This chapter discusses the two inter-State communications that the Inter-American Commission on Human Rights has so far examined, and analyses other mechanisms—typically, advisory opinions by the Inter-American Court—that serve as a substitute for inter-State communications. The chapter shows how OAS States use advisory opinions as a covert inter-State dispute mechanism and argues that the Inter-American Court should articulate a clear set of admissibility standards to address this practice.

 | DOI:10.1163/9789004712584_005

Keywords

inter-state disputes – American Convention on Human Rights – admissibility standards – advisory opinions – friendly settlements – Inter-American Commission on Human Rights

1 Introduction

Unlike the European human rights system, where the amount of inter-State disputes is significant –and growing—, and similar to the situation in the African human rights regime, the inter-State disputes mechanism under the inter-American human rights system has had virtually no relevance. There have only been two inter-State disputes—called 'communications'—brought before the Inter-American Commission on Human Rights—one of the two bodies that, along with the Inter-American Court, make up the regional human rights system. One of those cases was declared inadmissible and the second one ended in a friendly settlement. The dearth of inter-State communications in Latin America, however, does not mean that there are no human rights disputes among members of the Organization of American States. Therefore, to explore how inter-States disputes actually operate under inter-American human rights law, it is necessary to broaden the view. This chapter examines how certain mechanisms—typically, advisory opinions by the Inter-American Court—serve as a substitute for inter-State communications, and how the Inter-American Court should articulate a clear set of admissibility standards to address what seems to be an increasing practice among Latin American States.

The chapter proceeds as follows. First, I explain the legal regime on inter-State communications under the American Convention on Human Rights. Here, I discuss the two communications that the Inter-American Commission has addressed so far. I then turn to a discussion of five advisory opinions that Latin American States have requested to the Inter-American Court and analyse them as a covert way to address human rights violations committed by other States. The opinions, which are nominally brought to address legal questions, are in fact a device that States use to hold other OAS members accountable for human rights violations, even member States that are not parties to the American Convention and, consequently, are not subject to the jurisdiction of the Inter-American Court. I conclude by offering reflections on the use of the Inter-American Court's advisory jurisdiction as a mechanism to uphold a regional public order of human rights, which calls for the active engagement of all States, whether or not they are parties to the American Convention.

2 Legal Regime

The American Convention on Human Rights establishes the inter-State dispute mechanism in Article 45.[1] Unlike the European human rights regime, members of the Organization of American States must expressly 'recognize[] the competence of the Commission to receive and examine communications in which a State Party alleges that another State Party has committed a violation of a human right set forth in this Convention', with an addition that 'the Commission shall not admit any communication against a State Party that has not made such a declaration'.[2]

Of the thirty-four countries that make up the Organization of American States, twenty-four are parties to the American Convention on Human Rights, and nine—eight, after Venezuela's denunciation of the American Convention, in 2012—have ratified the competence of the Inter-American Commission on Human Rights under Article 45 of the Convention.[3] Five States—Argentina,

1 Article 45:

1. Any State Party may, when it deposits its instrument of ratification of or adherence to this Convention, or at any later time, declare that it recognizes the competence of the Commission to receive and examine communications in which a State Party alleges that another State Party has committed a violation of a human right set forth in this Convention.
2. Communications presented by virtue of this article may be admitted and examined only if they are presented by a State Party that has made a declaration recognizing the aforementioned competence of the Commission. The Commission shall not admit any communication against a State Party that has not made such a declaration.
3. A declaration concerning recognition of competence may be made to be valid for an indefinite time, for a specified period, or for a specific case.
4. Declarations shall be deposited with the General Secretariat of the Organization of American States, which shall transmit copies thereof to the member States of that Organization.

2 Article 33 of the European Convention of Human Rights states that, 'Any High Contracting Party may refer to the [European] Court [of Human Rights] any alleged breach of the provisions of the Convention and the Protocols thereto by another High Contracting Party'.

3 See American Convention on Human Rights, Declarations, Reservations, Denunciations and Withdrawals <https://www.cidh.org/Basicos/basicos3.htm> accessed 30 January 2024. The chart lists Venezuela as both a party to the American Convention and as recognizing the Commission's competence under article 45. However, in September 2012, Venezuela withdrew from the American Convention. In its Diplomatic Notice of Denunciation submitted to the OAS Secretary General, Venezuela stated that the Convention's 'international effects' and the jurisdiction of both the Inter-American Court and the Inter-American Commission would 'cease' as regards Venezuela. As a consequence, inter-State communications may not be brought against it. See Minister of Popular Power for Foreign Affairs of the Bolivarian Republic of Venezuela, Notice of Denunciation at 11–12 (6 September 2012). In July 2019, Venezuela's self-proclaimed interim president Juan Guaidó (2019–22) submitted

Chile, Colombia, Ecuador and Peru—have recognized the Commission's Article 45 competence under a principle of reciprocity, that is, if and only if another State has also done so. The remaining four States (three, after Venezuela's exit) have recognized the Commission's competence to hear inter-State communications unconditionally (Costa Rica, Jamaica and Nicaragua).

The Inter-American Commission's Rules of Procedure also regulate inter-State communications. Article 50.1 of the Rules of Procedure states:

> A communication presented by a State Party to the American Convention on Human Rights that has accepted the competence of the Commission to receive and examine such communications against other States Parties shall be transmitted to the State Party in question, whether or not it has accept (*sic*) the Commission's competence in this respect. If that competence has not been accepted, the communication shall be transmitted in order that the State concerned may exercise its option under Article 45, paragraph 3 of the Convention, to recognize that competence in the specific case that is the subject of the communication.

Interestingly, the Rules of Procedure seem to be in tension with the text of the Convention. The Convention stipulates that the Commission '*shall not admit* any communication against a State Party that *has not* made such a declaration' (emphasis added). Under the Commission's Rules of Procedure, however, the Commission may in fact admit a communication against a State that has not accepted the Commission's inter-State competence, subject to a *subsequent* act of recognition of the Commission's competence with respect to a present dispute.

3 Two Communications

In line with the low number of countries that have recognized the Commission's competence under Article 45, inter-State disputes are virtually non-existent, and have had no significant impact on the inter-American human rights system. As of 2023, there have only been two instances in which States have used this mechanism—and neither one has led to a decision on the merits by the Inter-American Commission. First, in 2006, Nicaragua lodged a

an instrument of ratification of the American Convention with retroactive effect. See <http://www.oas.org/es/sla/ddi/docs/B-32_venezuela_RA_7-31-2019.pdf> accessed 30 January 2024. The legal implications of the submission are beyond the scope of this chapter.

communication against Costa Rica, alleging Costa Rica's failure to guarantee the rights of Nicaraguans immigrants, which resulted in the violation of several provisions of the American Convention on Human Rights.[4] Second, in 2009, Ecuador filed a communication against Colombia for the extra-judicial killing of an Ecuadorean citizen in the context of a military operation conducted by the Colombian army in Ecuadorean soil.[5] Regarding the first communication, the Commission found the communication inadmissible.[6] With respect to the second communication, Ecuador desisted from it after four years of negotiations.[7]

3.1 *Nicaragua v Costa Rica*

On 6 February 2006, the OAS General Secretariat received Nicaragua's instrument of recognition of the Inter-American Commission's competence to hear inter-State complaints.[8] That same day, Nicaragua lodged the first inter-State communication under the American Convention on Human Rights. The communication, filed against Costa Rica, argued that Costa Rica was in violation of several provisions of international human rights instruments due to Costa Rica's failure to guarantee the rights of Nicaraguan immigrants.[9] The parties made multiple written submissions to the Commission, and the Commission convened a hearing in July 2006.[10] After the hearing, the Commission invited the parties to seek a friendly settlement. Nicaragua responded positively, but

---

4 *Nicaragua v Costa Rica*, Report No. 11/07, Inter-State Case 01/06, Inter-American Commission on Human Rights (8 March 2007).

5 *Ecuador v Colombia*, Report No. 112/10, Inter-State Petition IP-02 Admissibility, Franklin Guillermo Aisalla Molina, Inter-American Commission on Human Rights (21 October 2010).

6 *ibid.*

7 *Ecuador v Colombia*, Report No. 96/131, Inter-State Case 12.779, Inter-American Commission on Human Rights (4 November 2013).

8 See American Convention on Human Rights (n. 3).

9 Nicaragua argued that Costa Rica was in violation of Articles 1(1) (Obligation to respect rights), 8 (Right to a fair trial), 24 (Right to equal protection), and 25 (Right to judicial protection) of the American Convention; Articles 2, 7, 8, and 28 of the Universal Declaration of Human Rights; Articles II (Right to equality before law) and XVIII (Right to a fair trial) of the American Declaration of the Rights and Duties of Man; and Article 9 of the Inter-American Democratic Charter, concerning the elimination of all forms of discrimination.

10 Remarkably, Nicaragua claimed that the procedure under which the communication should be processed was *not* the Article 45 inter-State mechanism, but pursuant to the general rules set forth for individual communications. The Commission did not address the matter until it issued its final report, on both admissibility and merits.

Costa Rica declined. The Commission decided 'to open the case ... and defer its treatment of admissibility until the debate and decision on the merits',[11] and to convene a new hearing on the merits of the case.[12]

Nicaragua's claim was based first on the killing of Mr. Natividad Candia Mairena, who was mauled by two Rottweiler dogs in an incident that, according to the State's communication, 'lasted approximately two hours and was witnessed by the owner of ... the two dogs ... the security guard ... the head of the security company ... armed policemen, firefighters, and curious onlookers'.[13] The second incident giving rise to the communication concerned 'grievous' injuries inflicted on two other Nicaraguan citizens; the third incident concerned the 'injuries sustained by stoning' of two more nationals; and lastly, the communication made a general complaint on behalf of 'the Nicaraguan migrant population' in Costa Rica who are in a 'vulnerable situation'.[14]

As regards the first incident, Nicaragua argued that Costa Rica violated the right to due process and to judicial protection, by failing to investigate the killing; and that it discriminated against the Nicaraguan national, as in a similar incident involving a Costa Rican child, the investigation had been promptly carried out, and the dog that attacked the child was killed. Similarly, in the second incident, Nicaraguan nationals who were at a bar, were attacked by a group of Costa Rican patrons who verbally abused them with xenophobic insults. According to the communication, a group of patrons followed the Nicaraguans outside the bar and attacked them with stones and a knife, resulting in the death of one of the Nicaraguan nationals and the serious injury of the others.[15] Nicaragua labelled the incidents as 'hate crimes'.[16] Finally, concerning the general complaint on behalf of 'the Nicaraguan migrant population in Costa Rica', Nicaragua argued that the circumstances surrounding said incidents were 'merely outward symptoms of a much deeper underlying situation rooted in sentiments of xenophobia, intolerance, and rejection that reign in some sectors in Costa Rica, despite the solidarity and generosity that prevails in the vast majority of the noble Costa Rican people'.[17]

11 *Nicaragua v Costa Rica* [32].

12 *ibid.* [33].

13 *ibid.* [51].

14 *ibid.* [49]. The Commission broke down Nicaragua's claims into 'three separate situations': the killing of a Nicaraguan national by two dogs; the killing and injury of five individuals, and the general situation of the Nicaraguan migrant population. *ibid.* [50].

15 *ibid.* [60]-[62].

16 *ibid.* [62].

17 *ibid.* [64]. Nicaragua further noted that 'the inaction of the [Costa Rican] justice system and of the State itself in the investigation, prosecution, and punishment of those responsible in the horrific death of Natividad Canda Mairena, which occurred in a context

To bolster its claim that Costa Rica violated the rights of Nicaraguans 'in general', Nicaragua produced evidence of public manifestations of derision and mockery against the Nicaraguan population. Nicaragua also presented the findings of polls which showed that 88 percent of Costa Ricans admitted that Nicaraguan immigrants suffer discrimination,[18] and that 77 percent of the population believed that there was 'much' discrimination against Nicaraguan migrants;[19] a book documenting how the Costa Rican media portrays the Nicaraguan community as a 'problem' and a 'threat', and 'how the Nicaraguan population in Costa Rica is frequently "racialized" and criminalized', analysing 'different ways in which Nicaraguan women have been associated with prostitution'.[20] Finally, Nicaragua argued that immigration legislation adopted by Costa Rica had a discriminatory effect on Nicaraguans, as it allowed the deportation of immigrants unable to show that they are in the country legally; the criminalization of individuals and business that employ illegal immigrants; and the violation of due process guarantees as the immigration law failed to provide recourse against certain decisions of immigration authorities.[21]

Costa Rica rejected the claims made by Nicaragua. First, it argued that the killing of Mr. Canda Mairena by two dogs was under criminal investigation and, while it recognized that there had been public messages mocking the death, the Costa Rican government had issued a formal statement expressing 'its profound disapproval for the contents of said messages'.[22] Second, Costa Rica argued that Nicaragua had failed to exhaust domestic remedies, as the incidents concerning the attacks at the bar were being thoroughly investigated and that victims and their next-of-kin could resort to the Costa Rican courts.[23] Finally, concerning the general claim about discrimination against the Nicaraguan migrant population, Costa Rica argued that these incidents were 'isolated cases in Costa Rican society and in no circumstances were they framed by (*sic*) a context of xenophobia or discrimination'.[24] The State argued that Nicaraguans, and any other foreigners, are protected by the equal protection clause enshrined in Costa Rica's constitution, a right that the

of xenophobia that prevails in certain sectors in Costa Rica [...] intensified the climate of intolerance and discrimination in certain segments of Costa Rican society, which led to an atmosphere of "permissiveness" toward any attack on a Nicaraguan'. *ibid.* [67].

18 *ibid.* [73].

19 *ibid.* [75].

20 *ibid.* [76].

21 *ibid.* [86].

22 *ibid.* [93].

23 *ibid.* [97].

24 *ibid.* [100].

country's Constitutional Court has embraced 'as a fundamental right held by nationals and foreigners alike'.[25] With respect to the immigration law, Costa Rica observed that the law 'is founded on the legitimate exercise by Costa Rica of its sovereignty and the discretion enjoyed by all States to determine the rules authorizing or governing the conditions under which foreigners may stay in their territory [pursuant to the standards set forth by] the Inter-American Court of Human Rights in Advisory Opinion OC-18/03'.[26] Costa Rica then addressed the protection of many fundamental rights for immigrants, such as the right to health, education, work and housing, arguing that 'the allegations, while regrettable and requiring the due attention of the Costa Rican authorities, are not sufficient to assert that there exists in Costa Rica the climate of discrimination and xenophobia that the State of Nicaragua seeks to create'.[27]

In February 2007, the Commission found the communication inadmissible because Nicaragua had failed to exhaust available remedies at the domestic level,[28] and 'failed to prove the existence of a generalized practice of discrimination by Costa Rica against the Nicaraguan population'.[29] First, the Commission rejected Nicaragua's argument that the communication should be processed as an individual petition (pursuant to Articles 48 to 51 of the American Convention), noting that 'application of Article 45 of the Convention is an obligatory and logical prerequisite since otherwise the competence to be exercised by the Commission would not exist'.[30] Second, the Commission found that, despite the inter-American human rights system's caselaw on the need to identify individual victims of human rights violations, 'if a State party considers that another State party has committed generalized human rights violations it may turn to the Commission to denounce this situation without the need to individually identify each possible victim'.[31] Crucially, the Commission noted that '[t]he American Convention enshrines a system that constitutes a genuine regional public order the preservation of which is in the interests of each and every State party',[32] thus making an argument for a sort of *erga omnes* inter-State mechanism.[33]

25 *ibid.* [104].
26 *ibid.* [106].
27 *ibid.* [118].
28 *ibid.* [308].
29 *ibid.* [305].
30 *ibid.* [131].
31 *ibid.* [196].
32 *ibid.* [197].
33 In fact, the Commission notes that the inter-State mechanism set forth in Article 45 of the American Convention may be understood as a 'collective guarantee' mechanism, as

On the general context of discrimination, the Commission observed that Nicaragua had established a practice of discrimination against Nicaraguans among sectors of Costa Rican society. However, the Commission found that 'the perceptions of the population do not constitute a practice that could be said to be grounds for establishing the international responsibility of the State', unless such perceptions 'translate into discriminatory acts or omissions'.[34] The Commission agreed with Nicaragua that 'the law on migration and nationality is oriented toward protecting public security rather than human rights, and grants broad, discretionary powers to the administrative authorities in Costa Rica'.[35] However, it noted that Costa Rica 'acted within its powers in adopting the law',[36] and that Nicaragua failed to show 'that this law has been applied to the detriment of the rights of the Nicaraguan migrant population in Costa Rica'.[37] Therefore, the Inter-American Commission deemed the communication inadmissible and moot as an inter-State dispute.

3.2 *Ecuador v Colombia*

The second inter-State case under the inter-American human rights system was submitted in June 2009. In its communication, Ecuador argued that Colombia violated several provisions of the American Convention on Human Rights, including the provisions on the right to life, the right to humane treatment, judicial guarantees and due process as a result of the extrajudicial execution of Ecuadorian citizen Franklin Guillermo Aisalla Molina by agents of Colombia's security forces, in the context of a military operation on Ecuadorian soil, known as 'Operation Phoenix'. During the operation, the Colombian army bombed a camp of the Colombian Revolutionary Armed Forces ('FARC') located in Ecuador, near the Colombian-Ecuadorean border. According to the communication, members of the Colombian secret police had liaised with CIA agents in Ecuador, who shared information that a high-rank member of the FARC would be in Ecuador. Ecuador argued that, in the context of the military incursion, which was facilitated by the U.S. government, members

described by the UN Human Rights Committee in General Comment No. 31. *ibid.* [201]. In General Comment No. 31, the UN Human Rights Committee observed that 'every State Party has a legal interest in the performance by every other State Party of its obligations [which] follows from the fact that the "rules concerning the basic rights of the human person" are *erga omnes* obligations ...'. UNCHR, 'General Comment No. 31, The Nature of the General Legal Obligation Imposed on States Parties to the Covenant' (29 March 2004) UN Doc CCPR/C/21/Rev.1/Add. 1326, [2].

34 *Nicaragua v Costa Rica* [295].

35 *ibid.* [297].

36 *ibid.*

37 *ibid.* [301].

of the Colombian army extrajudicially executed Ecuadorian citizen Franklin Guillermo Aisalla Molina, who was in the bombed camp.[38]

Colombia rejected the communication on several grounds. First, it argued that the Commission lacked jurisdiction as the events had taken place on Ecuadorean soil. The Commission, however, following inter-American human rights caselaw, as well as the jurisprudence of other human rights bodies—such as the UN Human Rights Committee and the European Court of Human Rights—and the International Court of Justice, found that there was sufficient evidence to 'conclude that in the present case the State of Colombia exercised extraterritorial jurisdiction over the area attacked'.[39] Second, Colombia argued that Ecuador had failed to exhaust domestic remedies before lodging its inter-State complaint,[40] as Colombia 'initiated the corresponding criminal investigation and that this advanced by all possible means given the complexity of the facts'.[41] However, the Commission found that Colombia failed to explain how 'the complexity of the facts' had impacted on the investigations, and that there was in fact 'an unwarranted delay in the criminal investigation'.[42] Having met all admissibility requirements, the Commission declared the communication admissible and the proceedings moved forward, with the Commission placing itself 'at the disposal of the parties with a view to reaching a friendly settlement of the matter'.[43]

In March 2011, Colombia asked the Commission to 'suspend the proceedings since a direct dialogue had been initiated among the two parties'.[44] Ecuador initially agreed, and the parties engaged in efforts to reach a solution, but months later Ecuador decided to withdraw from the friendly settlement procedure.[45] The Commission put an end to the settlement procedure, but Ecuador changed its mind and the two States communicated their intention to resume the friendly settlement procedure and asked the Commission to suspend its decision on the merits.[46] The Commission agreed, and in August 2013, Ecuador withdrew its inter-State communication, informing that the parties had reached 'an agreement for social and economic development and reparations and investment for social compensation along the border'.[47] The

38 *Ecuador v Colombia* [28]-[33] (n. 5).
39 *ibid.* [102].
40 *ibid.* [141]-[143].
41 *ibid.* [155].
42 *ibid.* [160].
43 *Ecuador v Colombia* [7] (n. 7).
44 *ibid.* [9].
45 *ibid.* [11].
46 *ibid.* [13].
47 *ibid.* [14].

Commission archived the communication, and the States went on to agree on the terms of their settlement.

The fact that this communication ended in an amicable solution raises some important questions. First, inter-State communications can have a relevant political dimension.[48] As noted by the former Inter-American Commission on Human Rights Executive Secretary, it can be costly for States to sue another State for human rights violations.[49] In fact, Latin American States seem reluctant to use this mechanism because, in the words of Mr. Cantón, 'States often seek to debilitate the Commission' and inter-State communications give the Commission a crucial role in addressing political disputes, which, in many States' view, should not fall under the Commission's competence, but rather the political organs of the Organization of American States. Second, under friendly settlement mechanisms, third parties do not routinely participate.[50] But, as the Commission noted in *Nicaragua v Costa Rica*, all OAS States have an interest in preserving the 'regional public order' set up by the American Convention.[51] If all States have such interest, then the inter-State communications that are subject to friendly settlement (that is, to inter-State negotiations) should be open to all OAS States—or at least, all States that are parties to the American Convention.[52]

4 Advisory Opinions as Inter-States Cases

As described in the previous section, Latin American States have largely overlooked the inter-State dispute mechanism contemplated in the American Convention on Human Rights. Whether the dearth of inter-State disputes is

48 See Section 4.5.

49 Interview with Santiago Cantón, former Executive Secretary of the Inter-American Commission on Human Rights (25 January 2024).

50 See Jorge Contesse, 'Settling Human Rights Violations' (2019) 60(2) *Harvard International Law Journal* 317.

51 *Nicaragua v Costa Rica* [197].

52 In *Ecuador v Colombia*, Colombia requested that the admissibility hearing convened by the Inter-American Commission be held *in camera*. See *Inter-State Petition IP-02 Admissibility, Franklin Guillermo Aisalla Molina (Ecuador-Colombia)*, Report No. 112/10, Inter-American Commission on Human Rights (21 October 2010) [14]. The Commission, however, rejected Colombia's request, based on Article 68 of the Commission's Rules of Procedure, which states: 'Hearings shall be public. When warranted by exceptional circumstances, the Commission, at its own initiative or at the request of an interested party, may hold private hearings and shall decide who may attend them. This decision pertains exclusively to the Commission, which shall notify the parties in this regard prior to the beginning of the hearing, either orally or in writing ...'.

due to the political nature of inter-State communications or to the preference to use other judicial forums, such as the International Court of Justice, the fact is that the two cases that Latin American States have pursued so far do not allow for the articulation of a general theory of inter-States disputes under inter-American human rights law.[53] This does not mean, however, that no human rights disputes among Latin American States exist; such disputes are channelled through different mechanisms, for example, through the use of advisory opinions requested to the Inter-American Court of Human Rights. In this section, I discuss five cases and show how Latin American countries resort to the Inter-American Court's advisory powers to address human rights violations committed by other OAS States. Under this view, advisory opinions in Latin America are effectively inter-State disputes 'in disguise'.

4.1 *Mexico v United States I*

In 1997, Mexico sought the Inter-American Court's opinion concerning 'the issue of minimum judicial guarantees and the requirement of the due process when a court sentences to death foreign nationals whom the host State has not informed of their right to communicate with and seek assistance from the consular authorities of the State of which they are nationals'.[54] Mexico submitted its request 'on behalf of some of its nationals, whom the host State had allegedly not informed of their right to communicate with Mexican

---

53 Latin American States have had a number of international disputes, many of them concerning border disputes, the use of river waters, environmental issues, and of course, human rights. Yet, Latin American States have historically resorted to the International Court of Justice to address these matters, pursuant to specific dispute settlement clauses or to the general 1948 American Treaty on Pacific Settlement, known as 'Pact of Bogotá', which has been ratified by sixteen out of thirty-five OAS members. Among these cases, it is worth mentioning the disputes between Colombia and Peru, regarding the interpretation of an asylum treaty (1950); Honduras and Nicaragua (1958) regarding the binding authority of the Arbitral Award that delineates the borders between the two countries; Costa Rica and Nicaragua's 2009 dispute over navigational rights; Argentina and Uruguay's 2010 dispute over a pulp mill in the Uruguay River; Colombia and Nicaragua's 2012 territorial and maritime dispute; Chile and Peru's 2014 maritime dispute; Costa Rica and Nicaragua's 2015 dispute over the rights to wetlands on the San Juan River and the construction of a road along the river; Colombia and Nicaragua's case in 2016, in which the ICJ handed down a new judgement to aforementioned 2012 case over the delimitation of the continental shelf between the two countries; Costa Rica and Nicaragua's 2018 dispute over land boundary; Bolivia and Chile's 2018 dispute over Chile's alleged obligation to facilitate access to the Pacific Ocean; and Chile and Bolivia's 2022 dispute over the use of the waters of the Silala River.

54 *The Right to Information on Consular Assistance in the Framework of the Guarantees of the Due Process of Law*, Advisory Opinion OC-16/99, Inter-American Court of Human Rights Series A No 16 (1 October 1999) [1].

consular authorities and who had been sentenced to death in ten States in the United States'.[55] As this was not an inter-State communication, the fact that the United States is not a party to the American Convention had no relevance. However, Mexico based its request on other international instruments, such as the Vienna Convention on Consular Relations, the American Declaration of the Rights and Duties of Man, and the International Covenant on Civil and Political Rights, in order to render the Court's expected opinion somehow relevant—if not applicable—to the United States.

In October 1999, the Inter-American Court issued its opinion and found that the 1963 Vienna Convention on Consular Relations 'confers rights upon detained foreign nationals, among them the right to information on consular assistance, and that said rights carry with them correlative obligations for the host State'.[56] During the proceedings, several States intervened, including the United States. The United States accused Mexico of abusing the Court's advisory jurisdiction, noting that '[t]he request is patently an attempt to subject the United States to the contentious jurisdiction of this Court, even though the United States is not a party to the American Convention and has not accepted the Court's contentious jurisdiction; Mexico has presented a contentious case in the guise of a request for an advisory opinion'.[57]

To situate the request as a *human rights* inter-State dispute, it is worth mentioning Judge Antonio Cançado Trindade's concurring opinion. In his opinion, Judge Cançado Trindade noted that the United States was the only intervening State to reject the 'relationship between the right to information on consular assistance and human rights'.[58] More significantly, Judge Cançado Trindade noted, the United States did this in contravention to what it had itself argued in a previous case before the International Court of Justice.[59] The request was not only clearly directed *against* the United States—a non-party to the regional human rights treaty—but it also put the United States as a 'respondent State', forced to take a minoritarian and defensive position.

---

55 *ibid.* [2].

56 *ibid.* dispositif 1.

57 *ibid.* 14.

58 *ibid.* (separate opinion of Cançado Trindade J) [16].

59 In the words of Cançado Trindade: the United States adopted 'a position with an orientation manifestly distinct from that which they sustained themselves in the case—filed against Iran—of the *Hostages (United States Diplomatic and Consular Staff) in Tehran* (1979–1980) before the International Court of Justice (ICJ) [where the United States argued that its nationals held hostages] had been held incommunicado "in the grossest violation of consular norms and *accepted standards of human rights*"'. *ibid.* [18]-[19] (footnotes omitted; emphasis in original).

4.2 *Mexico v United States II*

In 2002, Mexico submitted a new request for an advisory opinion, again concerning the rights of migrants under international law. In its submission, Mexico expressed its 'profound concern' with 'the incompatibility with the OAS human rights system of the interpretations, practices and enactment of laws by *some States* in the region'.[60] Mexico did not mention the obvious: 'some States' were in fact *one* single OAS member—the United States—and 'the interpretations of laws' were in fact a single decision by the U.S. Supreme Court, rendered only months earlier.[61]

In *Hoffman Plastic Compounds*, the U.S. Supreme Court held that undocumented workers are not entitled to remedies for violations of their rights to unionize under the National Labor Relations Act.[62] Human rights advocates and immigration lawyers criticized the decision as it allowed for further discrimination against undocumented migrants.[63] Mexico, whose nationals were gravely affected by the court's decision, reacted by filing a request for an advisory opinion. Unlike the previous case, the United States did not participate in the proceedings in this new request.[64] However, multiple U.S.-based human rights organizations filed *amici* briefs in support of Mexico's position.[65]

The Inter-American Court found that States have a duty to respect workers' right to equality and non-discrimination despite their undocumented status, and laid out guidelines for the treatment of undocumented workers.[66] Remarkably, the Court noted that its opinion did not only encompass 'those OAS Member States that are parties to the American Convention'.[67] To do so, the

60 *Juridical Condition and Rights of the Undocumented Migrants*, Advisory Opinion OC-18/03, Inter-American Court of Human Rights Series A No 18 (17 September 2003) [2] (emphasis added).

61 *Hoffman Plastic Compounds, Inc. v NLRB*, 535 US 137 (2002).

62 *ibid.*

63 See Christopher David Ruiz Cameron, 'Borderline Decisions: *Hoffman Plastic Compounds*, the New Bracero Program, and the Supreme Court's Role in Making Federal Labor Policy,' (2003) 51 *UCLA Law Review* 1; Maria L. Ontiveros, 'Immigrant Workers Rights in a Post-*Hoffman* World-Organizing Around the Thirteenth Amendment,' (2004) 18 *Georgetown Immigration Law Journal* 651; Thomas J. Walsh, '*Hoffman Plastic Compounds, Inc. v NLRB*: How the Supreme Court Eroded Labor Law and Workers in the Name of Immigration Policy,' (2003) 21(2) *Law and Inequality* 313.

64 *Juridical Condition* (n 60) [17].

65 The U.S. interveners included human rights law clinics, immigration lawyers and advocates, and more than fifty labor, civil rights and immigrants' rights organizations. Organizations from Latin American countries and UN agencies, such as the United Nations High Commissioner for Refugees also intervened by filing *amicus* briefs.

66 *Juridical Condition* (n 60) [113]-[114].

67 *ibid.* [59].

Court held, 'would not be in the general interest of the request'.[68] Consequently, it determined that 'everything indicated in this Advisory Opinion applies to the OAS Member States that have signed either the OAS Charter, the American Declaration, or the Universal Declaration [of Human Rights], or have ratified the International Covenant on Civil and Political Rights, regardless of whether or not they have ratified the American Convention ...'.[69] The message was clear: the opinion was applicable to Latin American States but also, and more importantly, to the United States.

The Court also advanced a substantive argument to reach the United States (or any State not a party to the American Convention). The Court held that the principle of non-discrimination was 'applicable to all States, regardless of whether or not they are a party to a specific international treaty',[70] and that said principle had attained the status of a *jus cogens* norm.[71] As a consequence, the right to non-discrimination—in the present case, of undocumented migrants—'entails obligations *erga omnes* of protection that bind all States and generate effects with regard to third parties, including individuals'.[72] As one commentator aptly noted, the Court's articulation of *jus cogens* 'may have been instrumental in reaching the United States'.[73] The nature of the request for an advisory opinion was once again a disguised or 'covert' inter-State complaint.

4.3 *Mexico v United States III*

The latest request for an advisory opinion involving Mexico and the United States concerns 'the activities of private companies engaged in the firearms industry and their effects on human rights', submitted to the Inter-American Court in November 2022.[74] In its request, Mexico asked the Court 'to rule' on the international responsibility of firearms companies for 'careless, negligent and/or intentional marketing activities';[75] the international responsibility of States for their failure to regulate such activities; the appropriate remedies for victims of gun violence, and the compatibility of laws that grant procedural immunity to gun manufacturers.[76] The background for the request, as explained

68 *ibid.*
69 *ibid.* [60].
70 *ibid.* dispositif 4.
71 *ibid.*
72 *ibid.* dispositif 5.
73 Andrea Bianchi, 'Human Rights and the Magic of *Jus Cogens*,' (2008)(3) 19 *European Journal of International Law* 491.
74 Request for an Advisory Opinion submitted by Mexico to the Inter-American Court of Human Rights (11 November 2022).
75 *ibid.* 6.
76 *ibid.*

by Mexico, is the pervasive situation of gun violence in the Americas, and, in particular, the role of the U.S. gun industry in the increase of gun violence and criminal activity in Mexico.[77] As noted in its request, Mexico argues that:

> the flow of weapons into our country, and their subsequent illicit use, is the foreseeable result of deliberate and informed decisions to design, advertise, distribute and sell weapons in ways that they know, with utmost certainty, will attract and supply criminals in Mexican territory … U.S. gun companies are aware of the massive illicit trafficking of their weapons into Mexico.[78]

Mexico adds that the request also rests on the developments in the area of business and human rights, insofar one of the key questions posed to the Inter-American Court is whether or not private manufacturers have responsibilities under international human rights law.[79] Finally, in its request, Mexico 'emphasizes' that it 'does not focus on the sovereign right that some States confer on their citizens to acquire and possess firearms for personal protection', but on 'the legal implications of negligent practices on the part of private actors'.[80] The reference to 'some States' may once again be read as referring if not exclusively, at least principally, to the United States and the right to bear arms guaranteed by the Second Amendment of the U.S. Constitution.[81]

Following Mexico's submission, the Inter-American Court 'invited all those who were interested to submit their written opinion' on the matter.[82] Four OAS States intervened: Bolivia, Colombia, Costa Rica and the United States.[83]

---

77 Mexico notes that more than 500,000 guns are illegally trafficked into Mexico each year from the United States. Of the guns recovered at crime scenes in Mexico, between 70–90% were trafficked from the United States. *ibid.* 8.

78 *ibid.*

79 *ibid.* [10]-[11].

80 *ibid.* [11]-[12].

81 The Second Amendment of the U.S. Constitution reads: 'A well regulated Militia, being necessary to the security of a free State, the right of the people to keep and bear Arms, shall not be infringed'. The provision is the subject of significant political and legal debate, especially in light of the severe crisis—or 'epidemic', as many call it—of gun violence. See, *e.g.*, Adam Winkler, 'Scrutinizing the Second Amendment,' (2007) 105 *Michigan Law Review* 683; see also American Medical Association, *AMA calls gun violence 'a public health crisis'*, Press Release (14 June 2016).

82 *Order of the President,* Request for Advisory Opinion OC-30 submitted by the United Mexican States, Inter-American Court of Human Rights (13 October 2023) [4].

83 Also, a dozen non-governmental organizations and regional, national and international associations, more than twenty academic institutions and individuals submitted written opinions. *ibid.* [9]-[12].

The United States, in line with its submission in the first advisory opinion discussed in this section, rejected the Court's jurisdiction, and criticized Mexico's submission on several grounds. First, as there is pending domestic litigation before U.S. courts initiated by Mexico, and the Inter-American Court has held that advisory proceedings should not be used as a mechanism to obtain a ruling on a matter disputed at the domestic level; second, that Mexico's request invites the Court to resolve questions of fact, a matter that is outside the scope of the Court's advisory jurisdiction.[84] Third, the United States rejected Mexico's effort to hold private companies accountable for human rights violations, as it is 'the United States' longstanding position that as a general matter, with notable exceptions such as slavery, a human rights violation entails state action'.[85] Ultimately, the United States accused Mexico of once again using the Court's advisory powers 'to exercise jurisdiction over a contentious case in the guise of a request for an advisory opinion'.[86]

In contrast to the U.S. position, Bolivia, Colombia and Costa Rica all supported Mexico's submission, and encouraged the Court to process the request and address the questions submitted to it.[87] As the time of writing this chapter, the Inter-American Court had held a public hearing and the proceedings were still pending.

4.4 *Colombia v Nicaragua*

Colombia is another State that has resorted to advisory proceedings to process international disputes, with at least two other OAS States, Nicaragua and Venezuela.

Colombia and Nicaragua have brought several matters over territorial and maritime disputes to the International Court of Justice. In 2012, the ICJ ruled that Colombia had sovereignty over disputed maritime features, and Nicaragua's claim for a continental shelf beyond 200 nautical miles was rejected due to

84 *ibid.* 3.

85 *ibid.*

86 Request for an Advisory Opinion by the Government of the United Mexican States, CDH-SOC-1-2022, Written Observations of the United States, 2 (21 August 2023). The U.S. government note adds: 'Although the United States is not explicitly identified in the questions posed, the background section makes clear that the request is focused specifically on the United States'. *ibid.*

87 See Plurinational State of Bolivia, *Escrito de Observaciones a la Opinión Consultiva SOC-1-2022 presentada por los Estados Unidos Mexicanos,* PGE-DESP No. 1365/2023 SPDRLE-DGDDHHMA (31 July 2023); Colombia, Nota Diplomática S-DIDHD-23-018225: *Amicus Curiae de la República de Colombia sobre la Opinión Consultiva de México relacionada con 'Empresas privadas de armas y sus efectos sobre los DDHH'* (18 August 2023); Ministerio de Relaciones Exteriores, República de Costa Rica, DM-DJO-1498-2023 (29 May 2023).

insufficient evidence.[88] The following year, Nicaragua filed two applications: first, a case against Colombia asking the ICJ to 'definitively determine the question of the delimitation of the continental shelf between Nicaragua and Colombia in the area beyond 200 nautical miles from the Nicaraguan coast'.[89] In July 2023, the Court handed down its merits judgment, ruling against Nicaragua. Second, Nicaragua instituted proceedings against Colombia over a 'dispute concern[ing] the violations of Nicaragua's sovereign rights and maritime zones' declared by the Court's in its 2012 judgment, 'and the threat of the use of force by Colombia in order to implement these violations'.[90] In 2022, the ICJ ruled in favour of Nicaragua, finding that Colombia had in fact violated Nicaragua's sovereign rights and jurisdiction in the latter's exclusive economic zone.[91]

While the ICJ proceedings were pending, Colombia requested an advisory opinion to the Inter-American Court on the right to a healthy environment.[92] As noted by a Colombian scholar, the request was largely related to the ICJ cases, as Colombia had filed counter-claims on environmental matters before the ICJ and presumably expected to use a favourable opinion by the Inter-American Court to buttress its case before the World Court.[93] The case before the Inter-American Court also allowed States that had unsuccessfully attempted to intervene in the ICJ proceedings to do so, as was the case of Honduras.

During the public hearing convened by the Inter-American Court, Guatemala emphasized the importance of considering the dispute between

88 *Territorial and Maritime Dispute (Nicaragua v Colombia)* (Merits) [2012] ICJ Rep 624.

89 *Question of the Delimitation of the Continental Shelf between Nicaragua and Colombia beyond 200 nautical miles from the Nicaraguan Coast (Nicaragua v Colombia)* (Application Instituting Proceedings) General List No 154 [2013] ICJ.

90 *Alleged Violations of Sovereign Rights and Maritime Spaces in the Caribbean Sea (Nicaragua v Colombia)* (Application Instituting Proceedings) General List No. 155 (2013) ICJ 2.

91 *Alleged Violations of Sovereign Rights and Maritime Spaces in the Caribbean Sea (Nicaragua v Colombia)* (Merits) [2022] ICJ Rep 266.

92 *The Environment and Human Rights (State obligations in relation to the environment in the context of the protection and guarantee of the rights to life and to personal integrity—interpretation and scope of Articles 4(1) and 5(1) of the American Convention on Human Rights)*, Advisory Opinion OC-23/17, Inter-American Court of Human Rights Series A No 23 (15 November 2017).

93 Nicolás Carrillo-Santarelli, 'The Politics behind the Latest Advisory Opinions of the Inter-American Court of Human Rights' (I·CONnect Blog, 24 February 2018). Carrillo-Santarelli argues that 'it is clear that the state of Colombia considered that, had [its counter-claims] been declared admissible, the opinion of the IACtHR –which foreseeably would be favorable to environmental human rights concerns, as it indeed was—could increase the chances of having a successful case before the ICJ …'.

Nicaragua and Colombia before the ICJ.[94] Despite neither Colombia nor Nicaragua mentioning the ICJ proceedings, Guatemala made explicit what was understood: that the advisory proceedings before the San José court had implications for Nicaragua which should be taken into account, stressing the need for the Inter-American Court's opinion to align with the outcomes of the ICJ case while respecting human rights and state sovereignty.[95] Additionally, the Inter-American Court noted that the Inter-American Commission was examining a petition related to Nicaragua's alleged violations of the American Convention in the context of the Grand Interoceanic (or 'Nicaragua') Canal project, a project heavily resisted by Colombia.[96] The Court responded by reiterating its doctrine whereby the existence of petitions before the Inter-American Commission or the ICJ related to an advisory request's subject matter does not justify the Court's abstention from responding to the submitted questions.[97]

The Inter-American Court released its advisory opinion in February 2018. Commentators praised the Court's opinion as 'the most significant decision in a series of high-profile international judicial rulings that acknowledge legal consequences for environmental harm'.[98] The opinion had several key aspects, such as the articulation of a healthy environment as a human right. One of those aspects was the Court's doctrine of transboundary environmental harm, in the context of the precautionary principle—clearly an *inter*-State matter.[99]

4.5 *Colombia v Venezuela*

In November 2020, the Inter-American Court issued an advisory opinion also requested by Colombia addressing the human rights obligations of States

94 *The Environment and Human Rights* (n 92) [25].

95 *ibid.*

96 *ibid.*

97 *ibid.* [26]. See also Jorge Contesse, 'The Rule of Advice in International Human Rights Law,' (2021) 115(3) *American Journal of International Law* 367.

98 Monica Feria-Tinta & Simon C. Milnes, 'The Rise of Environmental Law in International Dispute Resolution: The Inter-American Court of Human Rights Issues a Landmark Advisory Opinion on the Environment and Human Rights,' (2016) 27 *Yearbook of International Environmental Law* 64.

99 According to Angeliki Papantoniou, '[o]ne of the most important aspects of the Advisory Opinion is the Court's finding that in relation to large-scale transboundary infrastructure projects, state parties to the Convention can exercise extraterritorial jurisdiction under certain circumstances'. Angeliki Papantoniou, 'Advisory Opinion on the Environment and Human Rights,' (2018) 112(3) *American Journal of International Law* 460.

that have denounced the American Convention.[100] Although the request was formulated in a seemingly neutral way, the subtext was obvious: Colombia was referring a case on Venezuela, which, as previously noted, pulled out of the system in 2012 after a long standoff with both the Court and the Commission.[101] Lixinski notes that, as a neighbouring state to Venezuela, 'and one with a much stronger human rights record and to where a number of Venezuelan refugees [were] flocking', Colombia had a direct interest in the results of the opinion.[102]

In a sweeping opinion, the Court held that '[t]he effective exercise of democracy in the Americas is an international legal obligation ... [and] is no longer solely a matter of domestic, internal or exclusive jurisdiction'.[103] In the Court's view, when a State denounces the American Convention, other States must act 'as collective guarantors of its efficacy', and are called upon 'to express any observations or objections deemed pertinent regarding denunciations that do not withstand scrutiny in light of the democratic principle and that undermine the inter-American public interest'.[104] In short, the Court, through this opinion, enhanced the notion of a collective interest to respect and promote the rights protected under the American Convention—even as regards a State that has withdrawn from the system.

In a dissenting opinion, which reads more like an essay on Latin American politics than a judicial pronouncement, Judge Eugenio Zaffaroni declared that the Court should have refrained from issuing an opinion. In his view, there was no preventive function for the Court to play in the case, as it was 'unquestionable that the Court [was] being asked to provide answers directly and solely regarding the situation posed by the Bolivarian Republic of Venezuela'.[105] Judge Zaffaroni stated that the Court was being 'invited, under the guise of abstract questions ... to rule on a matter that is inseparable from the greatest and most serious international political conflict in the region at

100 *Denunciation of the American Convention on Human Rights and the Charter of the Organization of American States and the consequences for State human rights obligations (interpretation and scope of articles 1, 2, 27, 29, 30, 31, 32, 33, 65 and 78 of the American Convention on Human Rights and 3(l), 17, 45, 53, 106 and 143 of the Charter of the Organization of American States)*, Advisory Opinion OC-26/20, Inter-American Court of Human Rights Series A No 26 (9 November 2020).

101 See Jorge Contesse, 'Resisting the Inter-American Human Rights System,' (2019) 44 *Yale Journal of International Law* 179, 206.

102 Lucas Lixinski, 'The "collective guarantee" of international human rights: Creating, reinforcing, and undoing legitimacies and mandates between law and politics,' (2021) 80 *Questions of International Law* 5, 6.

103 *Denunciation of the American Convention* (n 100) [72].

104 *ibid.* [71].

105 *ibid.* (dissenting opinion of Zaffaroni J) [4].

present'.[106] In his view, the conflict belonged to the realm of international politics, not adjudication.[107] Judge Zaffaroni's concerns are consistent with the remarks by former Inter-American Commission Executive Secretary, Santiago Cantón, who, as noted, explains the dearth of inter-State disputes in the fact that States see these matters as essentially political.

One aspect that the latest opinion reveals perhaps with more prominence than previous cases is the Court's reference to the notions of 'inter-American public interest' and 'collective guarantee' of human rights.[108] The Court notes that the 'collective guarantee' notion 'underlies the entire inter-American system, and in particular to the solidarity and good neighbourliness among the States of the Americas [which must] cooperate with each other in order to comply with their international obligations, both regional and universal'.[109] This reference to the inter-American public interest suggests that all OAS States have a stake in ensuring the protection and promotion of human rights in the region. This suggestion can have important normative implications: on the one hand, it connects with the emphasis that the Inter-American Commission placed on this notion in the *Nicaragua v Costa Rica* communication, as explained above.[110] Therefore, through the use of advisory proceedings, the Court seems to return to the idea that, underlying the use of inter-States communications, it is the region's interest that should drive the mechanism, rather than the defence and representation of particular State interests.

Second, the Court seems to advance a theory of *erga omnes* obligations coupled with a mechanism that allows for greater participation of States—and other stakeholders, as seen in the multiple interventions by civil society

---

106 *ibid.* [6].

107 *ibid.* [27], [31]. Judge Zaffaroni's view sharply contrasts with his colleague Patricio Pazmiño, who filed a separate opinion, expressing his frustration with the Court's tepid articulation of the 'collective guarantee' notion. In his view: 'given the high and extreme volatility and radicalization of the political conflict in our countries ... we should seek to rationalize, from a regulatory perspective, the solution of these conflicts ... The power to substantively analyze a denunciation should belong to the Inter-American Court and not to the General Assembly'. *Denunciation of the American Convention* (partially dissenting opinion of Pazmiño Freire J) (n 100) [15]. Judge Pazmiño added that any State who wishes to withdraw from the American Convention should 'be required to submit a petition for an advisory opinion ... requiring the Court to analyze the compatibility of the denunciation with the instrument from which the State is seeking to withdraw'. *ibid.* [18].

108 See, especially, Chapter VI of the Opinion.

109 *ibid.* [163].

110 See (n 32). In the *Nicaragua v Costa Rica* admissibility report, the Commission noted that '[t]he American Convention enshrines a system that constitutes a genuine regional public order the preservation of which is in the interests of each and every State party'.

organizations and academic institutions. In this sense, the Court seems eager to not only render advisory proceedings a substitute for inter-State communications, but to do it in a way that calls and requires the active participation of all OAS States, not just those that are parties to the American Convention—and therefore fall under the Court's jurisdiction. If the inter-American system is to be conceived as a regional order of law and human rights, then the role of all affected and interested actors seems like a necessary requirement for such order's legitimacy.

However, one problem with the Court's use of its advisory powers is the lack of clear admissibility standards.[111] If States turn to the Court's advisory function to address inter-State disputes, such admissibility requirements, as well as sound methods to engage with States, are even more in order. *Mexico v United States III*, concerning the legal obligations of gun manufacturers, is a good example of the tensions that may arise from the lack of clear admissibility standards. The United States challenges the Court's jurisdiction on the very grounds that the Court has articulated: there is a pending domestic litigation and it is clear that the issue—gun control—may be used as an instrument of domestic politics. The Court must make an effort to strike a proper balance between its interest and its role in protecting human rights in the Americas and offering guidelines to States with the necessary tools to protect and enhance the Court's (and, more generally, the inter-American system's) legitimacy and authority. That a single issue is of utmost relevance does not automatically mean that the Court must issue an opinion on it.

5 Conclusion

The practice of inter-State communications under inter-American human rights law is virtually non-existent. With only two such cases, none of which have obtained a decision on the merits, the analysis necessarily needs to be broadened. Looking at the Inter-American Court's advisory practice can help us better understand how Latin American States, when they do not litigate before the ICJ, may prefer to use the non-contentious mechanism of advisory opinions. This chapter has described the phenomenon of inter-State disputes 'in disguise'. Further research will help us elucidate how the advisory role of the Inter-American Court may in fact serve as a substitute for the mechanism of inter-State communications, and what the consequences of using such disguised mechanism can be for the regional human rights regime.

111 I address this problem in Contesse (n 97) at 367.

CHAPTER 4

Inter-State Complaints under the African Human Rights System: a Breeze of Change?

Frans Viljoen

Abstract

An inter-state procedure is provided for explicitly in the 1981 African Charter on Human and Peoples' Rights, on which the African regional human rights system is based, but the mechanism remains underused. Exploring the question why such a small number of inter-state cases have been submitted under the Africa system, the article points to the influence of a general culture of non-intervention and a preference for non-confrontational dispute mechanisms among African States; the existence of alternative channels to resolve cases involving massive or widespread violations cases; African States have over the years placed growing confidence in the ICJ; the delays associated with the DRC decision; and a pervasive ignorance of inter-state complaints processes under the African system. To overcome some of these impediments, the article notes, inter-states cases may be masked as cases brought by individuals or NGOs whose interests overlap with those of States.

Keywords

African Charter on Human and Peoples' Rights – inter-state proceedings – non-confrontational dispute resolution – NGOs – culture of non-intervention

 | DOI:10.1163/9789004712584_006

1 Introduction

An inter-state procedure is provided for explicitly in the 1981 African Charter on Human and Peoples' Rights (African Charter), on which the African regional human rights system is based.

When the African Charter was established, a quasi-judicial body, the African Commission on Human and Peoples' Rights (African Commission), with a mandate of promotion and protection, was its only supervisory body. A judicial body, the African Court on Human and Peoples' Rights (African Court), complementing the Commission's protective mandate, has been in operation since 2006. Although both these bodies can deal with inter-state complaints or cases, the submission of these complaints or cases has been a rarity. An child-specific treaty, the African Charter on the Rights and Welfare of the Child (African Children's Charter), with its own supervisory body, the African Committee of Experts on the Rights and Welfare of the Child (African Children's Committee), completes the 'African human rights system'. While inter-state complains are mentioned under the African Children's Charter,[1] this possibility has not been further elaborated in the African Children's Committee guidelines, and has not been used.

While the rationale of inter-state complaints or cases is contested, this article adopts the premise that, ideally, it provides a mechanism for a State party, in the name of and on behalf of a collective of States parties to a human rights treaty, and by extension, humanity as a whole, to call out a State for transgressing its treaty promises in respect of human rights.[2] In practice, however, inter-state complaints have been instituted mostly when a government's interests have been impaired. The handful of inter-state cases submitted so far has mostly sought to draw attention to the violation of its citizens' rights abroad, to protest the violation of the rights of 'persons belonging to minorities' which it 'feels responsible for',[3] or more broadly in the national interest. However, the inter-state mechanism is distinguishable from diplomatic protection, which allows for a State to intervene at the inter-state level in respect of injury to its own citizens by another State.

---

1 Art 44 of the African Children's Charter.

2 See Søren C Prebensen, 'Inter-state complaints under treaty provisions–the experience under the European Convention on Human Rights' in G Alfredsson et al (eds) *International Human Rights Monitoring Mechanisms* (Brill Nijhoff, 2009) 533–559 at 539, noting that the first of these procedures, set up under the European Convention on Human Rights, was aimed at establishing a 'common public order of the free democracies in Europe'.

3 Manfred Nowak, *Introduction to the International Human Rights Regime* (Martinus Nijhoff, Leiden, 2003) at 100.

It remains a rarity for States to submit a human rights case against another State not motivated to act by their conflict with the other State, or by concern for its own nationals, but on the basis of the collective responsibility that all States have to uphold agreed upon human rights norms as a common public good. When a confluence of some of the following factors occur, the likelihood of such cases increases: the presence of widespread, serious and persistent human rights violations in the respondent State; deterioration in the relations between the two States, in the context of a charged political or legal dispute; the existence of conflict in the form of a declared or undeclared war between the two States; and the failure of attempts to amicably resolve the matter.

Although the purpose of inter-state complaints under the African Charter is not explicitly articulated, it appears to fluctuate, as it does under other international human rights treaty regimes, between serving the common interest of upholding a shared standard ('collective enforcement'), and enforcement where the complaining State has a 'direct interest in the outcome'.[4] As a measure of 'collective enforcement', an inter-state complaint is brought to address human rights violations in a State party to uphold the integrity of the system as a whole, by making real the treaty promises to victims of violations. This is therefore the quintessence of the inter-state system under human rights treaties. Experience in other systems has shown that the use in pursuance of a general public interest is often undertaken by multiple rather than single States, allowing them to 'share the diplomatic burden of instituting proceedings with other States', and only when a high threshold of human rights violations has been reached.[5]

There is little scholarly writing about the inter-state procedure under the African regional system.[6] This contribution, based on a desk review and analysis of relevant primary and secondary sources, aims to explore aspects

4 Prebensen (n 2) 556; see also Dai Tamada, 'Inter-State Communication under ICERD: From ad hoc Conciliation to Collective Enforcement?', (2021) 12(3) *Journal of International Dispute Settlement* 405–426.

5 Ibid (exemplified by the complaint to the European Commission of Human Rights in Applications 3321-3323/67 and 3344/67, *Denmark, Norway, Sweden and the Netherlands v. Greece*.

6 See eg Frans Viljoen *International Human Rights Law in Africa* (2nd edn, OUP, 2012) at 343–344; Murray (n 12) 655–663; Frans Viljoen, 'A Procedure Likely to Remain Rare in the African System: An Introduction to Inter-State Communications Under the African Human Rights System', Völkerrechtsblog, 27.04.2021, doi: 10.17176/20210427-221127-0; Adoga-Ikong J. Adams, Edidiong Jacob Udo, and Aboh Pascal Bekonfe 'The Inter-State Complaint under the African Charter on Human and Peoples' Rights: a Lesson from the European Regional System', 2.2 *GNOSI: An Interdisciplinary Journal of Human Theory and Praxis* (2019) 126–133; Isabella Risini, and Geir Ulfstein 'Human Rights, State Complaints' in *Max Planck Encyclopedias of International Law* (2022), Oxford Public International Law (http://opil.ouplaw.com), para 23.

of this neglected topic. It starts off by locating the inter-state mechanism under the African regional system within a global context, emphasising the automatic acceptance by States parties to relevant African treaties of both inter-state and individual communications procedures. The article then explores the African Commission and African Court as avenues through which States may submit inter-state complaints, and indicates that these avenues have been sparsely used. Only three cases have thus far been submitted to the African Commission, and one to the African Court.[7] Only one of these cases, submitted to the African Commission by the DRC against Burundi, Rwanda and Uganda (the *DRC* case),[8] has been decided on its merits. The article analyses the Commission's decision in this matter, with reference to admissibility, the substantive findings, the simultaneous submission of an inter-state to the International Court of Justice (ICJ), conciliation and friendly settlement, the non-submission of individual claims arising from the same situation, fact-finding, and reparations and implementation.

Although there has, in recent times, been an increase in the use of inter-state complaints and cases within the United Nations (UN) human rights treaty system,[9] and under the European human rights systems;[10] and African States have been at the vanguard of submitting cases to the ICJ based on the principle of 'collective enforcement',[11] these developments do not necessarily presage a

---

7 See section 3 below.

8 *Democratic Republic of Congo v Burundi, Rwanda and Uganda* case Communication 227/99, (2004) AHRLR 19 (ACHPR 2003) (20th Activity Report) (*DRC* case).

9 Just about a half a century since it became a possibility, the first-ever inter-state communications under the UN human rights system were submitted in 2018, to the Committee on the Elimination of Racial Discrimination (CERD), which has been in place since 1969: two by Qatar (against Saudi Arabia and United Arab Emirates) and one by Palestine (against Israel). While the complaints submitted by Qatar have been terminated, the one by Palestine was, at the end of 2023, ongoing (Inter-State communication submitted by the State of Palestine against Israel, CERD/C/100/5, 12 December 2019; decision on admissibility, 30 April 2021); see also Dai Tamada, 'Inter-State Communication under ICERD: From ad hoc Conciliation to Collective Enforcement?' (2021) 12(3) *Journal of International Dispute Settlement* 405–426.

10 Kinga Machowicz & Robert Tabaszewski 'The Inter-State Application to the European Court of Human Rights in Strasbourg–Potential Revival' (2023) 174(1) *Przeglad Sejmowy* 175–197.

11 By The Gambia against Myanmar (*Application of the Convention on the Prevention and Punishment of the Crime of Genocide* (*The Gambia v. Myanmar*), Preliminary Objections, Judgment, I.C.J. Reports 2022, p. 477) (*Rohingya Genocide* case); *Application of the Convention on the Prevention and Punishment of the Crime of Genocide* (*The Gambia v. Myanmar*), Provisional Measures, Order of 23 January 2020, I.C.J. Reports 2020, p. 3) and by South Africa against Israel (*Application of the Convention on the Prevention and Punishment of the Crime of Genocide in the Gaza Strip* (*South Africa v. Israel*) (*Gaza Genocide* case)).

steady stream of inter-state cases in the African regional human rights system. The ICJ may well be a very specific strategic choice for African States to achieve broad geopolitical objectives, almost exclusively against non-African States.

Exploring the question why such a small number of inter-state cases have been submitted under the Africa system, the article points to the influence of a general culture of non-intervention and a preference for non-confrontational dispute mechanisms among African States; the existence of alternative channels to resolve cases involving massive or widespread violations cases; African States have over the years placed growing confidence in the ICJ (as a possible alternative to African processes); the delays associated with the *DRC* decision; and a pervasive ignorance of inter-state complaints processes under the African system. To overcome some of these impediments, the article notes, inter-states cases may be masked as cases brought by individuals, or NGOs whose interests overlap with those of States.

2 Automatic Nature of Inter-state cases under the African Charter

Acceptance of inter-state communications is automatic upon ratification of or accession to the African Charter.[12] No opt-in is required; and no opt-out is allowed. The Charter inter-state procedure largely mirrors that in the International Convention on the Elimination of Racial Discrimination (ICERD).[13] None of these States parties to the African Charter has entered a reservation in respect of the relevant Charter provisions. This means that submitting inter-state communications under the African Charter was, by the end of 2023, within the competence of 54 African States.[14]

12 Arts 47–52 of the African Charter. Murray (Rachel Murray, *The African Charter on Human and Peoples' Rights: A Commentary* Oxford University Press 2019 at 656) indicates that the Mbaye draft, on which the drafting of the African Charter is anchored, made the acceptance of inter-state complaints optional. The drafting history gives no indication why the drafters made it compulsory in the final version of the Charter.

13 See ICERD arts 11–13; the important exception is that there is no provision under the African Charter for referral to the International Court of Justice (ICJ). The drafters of the African Charter also drew on the European Convention, which in its original article 24, 'provided a model of a compulsory and working inter-state referral mechanism' not only to ICERD, (See David Keane, 'Inter-state cases under the International Convention on the Elimination of All Forms of Racial Discrimination' in Norman Weiss and Andreas Zimmermann (eds) *Human Rights and International Humanitarian Law* Edward Elgar (Cheltenham, 2022) 199–224 at 208) but indirectly, at least, also to the African Charter.

14 All African Union (AU) member States that are also States parties to the African Charter, with the exception of Morocco.

The African Charter is one of only three out of all regional or UN human rights treaties to make inter-state communications 'compulsory'. In addition to the Charter, only ICERD and the European Convention of Human Rights make acceptance of the inter-state complains procedure a necessary consequence of treaty ratification.[15] In this respect, the European and African regional human rights systems differ from the inter-American, which under article 45 of the American Convention of Human Rights requires States parties to opt into accepting the possibility of inter-state cases. At the time of the adoption of the African Charter, four UN human rights treaties were in force (ICERD, ICCPR, ICESCR and CEDAW). Of these, only the ICERD contains a compulsory inter-state mechanism. The subsequent treaties (CRC, CAT, CMW, CRPD, CED) make inter-state communications optional.

The African system is the only international human rights system (at UN and regional level) which from its inception made *both inter-state and individual communications* a necessary consequence of treaty acceptance. Among UN treaties, ICERD makes inter-state communications automatic, but requires States' explicit acceptance of individual communications.[16] While inter-state communications were automatic under the European Convention of Human Rights, as it was adopted in 1950, at that time the competence of both the Commission and Court to accept individual communications was optional. For a communication to be heard by the European Commission of Human Rights, the State had to accept the Commission's competence in the matter;[17] and the matter could be referred to the European Court of Human Rights only if the State had, in addition, declared that it recognised the Court's jurisdiction.[18] This position changed in 1998,[19] when the Court became the single Convention organ, and individual submission were made automatic.

3 Avenues for Submitting Inter-state Complaints

Under the African system, there are two main avenues through which States may submit inter-state complaints: either to the African Commission or (directly or indirectly) to the African Court.

15 Arts 11–13 of ICERD and arts 24 of the 1950 European Convention of Human Rights.

16 Art 14 of ICERD.

17 Art 25 of the 1950 Convention.

18 Art 46 of the 1950 Convention.

19 With the entry into force of Protocol 11 to the European Convention.

3.1 *African Commission*

Inter-state communications to the African Commission may be initiated along two pathways, the one conciliatory ('communications negotiations'), and the other directly confronting the State complained against ('communications complaints').

The first option is the conciliatory procedure under articles 47 and 48 of the Charter.[20] In this instance, the complaining State 'may draw, by written communication', the respondent State's attention to its complaint or communication.[21] The State against which a communication is directed has three months to engage with the complaining State to reach an amicable resolution of the dispute, through 'bilateral negotiation or by any other peaceful procedure'.[22] The avenue is premised on the ideal or desirability of avoiding a formal approach to and potential decision by the African Commission settling an inter-state dispute. However, if the matter is not settled amicably, any of the States involved may submit the matter to the Commission.[23] Hansungule points out that 'the formal contact between the States, before the Commission's intervention, is a singularly distinctive feature of the African Charter'.[24]

This avenue foregrounds conciliation as one of the animating features of African approaches to resolving disputes.[25] It offers the respondent State an opportunity to 'decide whether to settle the complaint amicably or not', thus avoiding to 'surprise' the State with a formal communication.[26] However, the feasibility of 'communications negotiations' depends on the particular circumstances. In a situation of 'undeclared war' between two States, for example, the 'type of diplomatic contact' associated with this option would be misplaced.[27] To the extent that a successful outcome of this mediatory process would involve the Commission's facilitating role, the Commission's lacklustre practice in respect on amicable settlements does not inspire confidence.

The second option, direct inter-state communications provided for under article 49 of the Charter, allows a State to submit a communication alleging that another State has violated the provisions of the Charter directly to the Commission. This approach does not require any attempt to settle the matter

20 Under arts 47 and 48 of the Charter.
21 Art 47 of the Charter.
22 Art 48 of the Charter.
23 Art 48 of the African Charter.
24 Michelo Hansungule 'The African Charter on Human and Peoples' Rights' in Abdulqawi A. Yusuf and Fatsah Ouguergouz (eds) *The African Union: Legal and Institutional Framework: A Manual on the Pan-African Organization* (Leiden Martinus Nijhoff, 2012) 417 at 440.
25 See eg art 4(e) and (i) of the AU Constitutive Act.
26 *DRC* case (n 8), para 60.
27 *DRC* case (n 8), para 61.

amicably. This makes for a quicker process of acquiring a finding from a quasi-judicial body, but excludes the possibility of a mediated settlement before approaching the Commission.

The trigger for the negotiated-settlement route is the reasonable belief by the complaining State that another State party has violated the Charter.[28] Direct inter-state communications complaints may be triggered if the complaining State 'considers that another State party' has violated the Charter.[29] The wording in both these instances suggests that the aim of the inter-state procedure is 'collective enforcement', in the sense that a complaint by a State is provoked not by self-interest, but by the public or collective State party interest in addressing human rights violation by another State party.[30] The standing of a complaining State is thus located in the joint obligation that the treaty imposes on all parties to the treaty – *erga omnes partes* – such as in respect of the core obligations under ICERD to prevent and punish genocide under the Genocide Convention.

3.2 *African Court*

The Court has jurisdiction over inter-state cases. Its potential personal jurisdictional scope of application is narrower than that of the Commission. While all the 54 States parties to the Charter may submit an inter-state communication to the Commission,[31] submission to the Court is possible only if *both* the complaining and respondent States are parties to *both* the African Charter and the Protocol to the African Charter on the Establishment of an African Court on Human and Peoples' Rights (Court Protocol).[32]

An inter-state case can reach the African Court if the Commission, under its mandate of complementarity, refers such a communication or case to the

---

28 Art 47 of the Charter.

29 Art 49 of the Charter.

30 *Application of the Convention on the Prevention and Punishment of the Crime of Genocide (The Gambia v. Myanmar)* - Provisional measures, [2020] ICJ Reports 5 (Order of 23 January 2020), para 41 ('any State party to the Genocide Convention, and not only a specially affected State, may invoke the responsibility of another State party with a view to ascertaining the alleged failure to comply with its obligations *erga omnes partes*, and to bring that failure to an end'); CERD Committee, Inter-State communication submitted by the State of Palestine against Israel: decision on jurisdiction, para 67: 'the Committee finds that it has jurisdiction to hear the inter-State communication lodged by the applicant against the respondent' because the 'core provisions of the Convention have an *erga omnes* nature'.

31 By 31 December 2023, the number of States parties stood at 54 (www.au.int/treaties/), with Morocco the only AU member State not party to the Charter.

32 By 31 December 2023, the number of States parties to the Court Protocol stood at 34 (www.au.int/treaties/).

Court. In other words, an inter-state case can reach the Court indirectly, after its initial submission to the Commission, if the Commission decides to transfer such a case to the Court.[33] In the European system, the erstwhile European Commission of Human Rights, in the process of indirect submission to the Court that was in place at the time, referred two inter-state cases to the European Court of Human Rights.[34] The African Commission has by the end of 2023 not referred to the African Court any of the three inter-state cases submitted to it. The Commission's 2020 Rules do not expressly deal with the referral of inter-state cases by the Commission to the Court. However, this silence should not be understood as negating the Commission's competence under article 5(1)(a) of the Court Protocol to submit, at any stage of the proceedings before it, an inter-state case to the Court. While no criteria exist to guide what is essentially a discretionary competence, such referral would only be possible if all States involved are States parties to the Court Protocol. A lack of clear guidance does not account for the non-referral by the Commission to the Court of the *Democratic Republic of Congo v Burundi, Rwanda and Uganda* case (*DRC* case),[35] which the Commission concluded on the merits in May 2003. While this form of referral was specifically contemplated under the Commission's 2010 Rules, which were in force at the time when the case was decided,[36] the DRC was at the time not a party to the Court Protocol.[37] The Commission therefore lacked the competence to refer the complaint to the Court.

But it is not only the Commission that may refer to the Court inter-state cases submitted to it. Any of the States involved in an inter-state dispute may also do so. While neither the Court Protocol nor the Court's 2020 Rules expressly mention inter-state cases, the Protocol clarifies that both the State that has 'lodged a complaint to the Commission' (under article 5(1)(b) of the

33 Under art 5(1) of the Court Protocol, the Commission has an unqualified 'entitlement' to submit cases to the Court; this form of access logically also covers inter-state cases.

34 See *Ireland v United Kingdom*, Ser A 25, in which the Court on 18 January 1978 found violations of the European Convention in respect of a case referred by the European Commission, based on its 'report' of January 1976; and *Cyprus v Turkey*, Application 25781/94, referred by the European Commission to the new (post-1998) European Court based on its 'report' of 1 June 1999.

35 *DRC* case (n 8).

36 Rule 118(1) of the Commission's 2010 Rules of Procedure (If the Commission has taken a decision with respect to a communication submitted under articles 48, 49 of the Charter and the Commission considers that the State has not complied or is unwilling to comply with its recommendations … the Commission may submit the case to Court pursuant to article 5(1)(a)).

37 The DRC deposited its instrument of ratification by 2020 (having ratified the Court Protocol in 2017); Burundi ratified and deposited its instrument of ratification in 2003; Rwanda in 2003; and Uganda in 2001.

Court Protocol) and the State 'against which the complaint has been lodged at the Commission' (under article 5(1)(c) of the Court Protocol) are entitled to 'submit' the relevant inter-state case to the Court.[38] Article 5(1)(b) is applicable only to inter-state communications, since that is the only way in which a State may 'lodge' a 'complaint' to the Commission. Article 5(1)(c) comes into play both in respect of inter-state and individual communications, because a State may be subjected to a 'complaint' by other States or by individuals/NGO s.

A complaining State may want to have the matter decided by a body with the authority to issue binding decisions, and may thus opt to refer the case lodged with the Commission to the Court. A respondent State facing a complaint by either an individual, NGO or by another State, may be less likely to approach the African Court. However, such a State may well submit to the Court an inter-state case in which the Commission arrived at an adverse decision against it. In this scenario, the Court would be approached with a view to reversing the Commission's finding.

At what stage of the proceedings before the Commission can this referral (whether by the Commission or any of the States involved) be made?[39] One possible answer to this question is that referral to the Court may take place immediately after seizure by the Commission.[40] Another possible answer is that referral would be a form of 'appeal', following only once the Commission has finalised the communication before it.[41] Such an approach would indeed pre-empt the concern that a referral at an earlier stage (for example, just after seizure) would effectively exclude the role of the Commission.[42] However, the wording of the Protocol does not require that any particular stage of the proceedings has to be reached prior to referral. In this respect, the position

38 Art 5(1)(b) and (c) of the Court Protocol.

39 See Fatsah Ouguergouz, 'The establishment of an African Court of Human and Peoples' Rights: a judicial premiere for the African Union' (2003) 11 *African Yearbook of International Law Online/Annuaire Africain de droit international Online* 79, 110; and Dan Juma, 'Access to the African Court on Human and Peoples' Rights: A Case of the Poacher Turned Gamekeeper?' (2007) 4(2) *Essex Human Rights Review* 1, 10; also available at SSRN 1391482 (2007).

40 See Ouguergouz (supra n 39) at 110 (noting the Protocol's silence on the issue, he concludes that – without a contrary position in the Rules of Court – the States involved in an inter-state dispute can refer the case to the Court 'as soon as a case is brought before the Commission … on the sole condition that they are parties to the Protocol').

41 As above, contending that 'it may appear that the intention was to afford a State Party … a forum for appealing a decision of the Commission'.

42 It may be argued that since the Charter (under arts 47 and 49) provides for communications to be submitted to the Commission, the Commission should not become a mere conduit for referral of these complaints to the Court, but should at least to some extent be involved in their resolution.

under the African system differs from that under the Inter-American system, where the American Convention explicitly requires that petitions must be *finalised* by the Inter-American Commission before possible referral to the Inter-American Court.[43]

Although not explicitly stated, submission to the African Court of inter-state cases also appears to be possible under art 5(1)(d) of the Court Protocol, which allows a State party 'whose citizen is a victim of a human rights violation' to submit a case to the Court. This avenue to the Court is in part based on the principle of diplomatic protection, which entails the protection by a State of the rights of its own citizens while they are abroad,[44] rather than 'collective enforcement'.[45] This 'avenue' is similar to that allowed for under article 5(1)(b), but here, the rationale is clearly stated. Juxtaposed against article 5(1)(d), the 'collective enforcement' rationale of article 5(1)(b) is foregrounded.

The formulation in article 5(1)(d) does not require the cases to have been submitted to the Commission (as articles 5(1)(a) to (c) do). On a literal and common sense reading, article 5(1)(d) allows a State party to the Protocol to submit a case against another State party to the Protocol when its citizens are victims of human rights violations – whether on the territory of the complaining State or on the territory of any other State party. Both the complaining State and the State complained against need to fall under the Court's jurisdiction for the Court's personal jurisdiction to be vested. If these conditions are met, the State may refer the case directly to the Court. The only difference between articles 5(1)(b) and (d) is that the motive for referral under the latter provision is explicit, thus restricting the application of this provision to cases involving the citizen of the complaining State. The *DRC v Rwanda* case submitted to the Court in 2023, discussed below, seems to fall within the ambit of article 5(1)(d), based on the alleged violation of the rights of the people of the DRC by Rwanda on the territory of the DRC.

43 See art 61(1) of the American Convention: 'Only the States Parties and the Commission shall have the right to submit a case to the Court.'; and art 61(2); 'In order for the Court to hear a case, it is necessary that the procedures set forth in Articles 48 and 50 shall have been completed.'

44 Edwin Borchard, *The Diplomatic Protection of Citizens Abroad: Or, The Law of International Claims* (Banks law publishing Company, 1915) vi; See also Isabella Risini, 'The Inter-State Application Under the European Convention on Human Rights: More Than Diplomatic Protection' *The Influence of Human Rights on International Law*, (Brill/Nijhoff, 2018), <https://brill.com/display/title/35940> accessed 30 April 2024, 69–77.

45 See Juma (n 39) at 12, noting that diplomatic protection is based on the principle that an injury to its nationals is an injury to the State; he refers to art 5(1)(d) as introducing a 'variant of the inter-state complaints mechanism'.

There is no legal impediment that precludes a State, under articles 47 to 49 of the Charter, from submitting an inter-state communication to the African Commission, complaining of human rights violations of its citizens by the other State.

4 Extent of Use Thus Far

Despite the fact that the inter-state complaints mechanism is available to all States parties to the African Charter, and the possibility of submitting such cases to both the African Commission and the African Court, only four cases has thus far been submitted, three to the African Commission, and one to the African Court. This number excludes a complaint submitted by Libya against the United States, reported by a previous Chairperson to the Commission but not available in the public records, which the Commission declared 'inadmissible'.[46] One of the cases submitted to the Commission, the *DRC* case, relates to the conflict in the Great Lakes region in the aftermath of the 1994 genocide in Rwanda. It was decided on the merits at the 33rd Ordinary Session of the Commission held in May 2003. However, the Commission only made public this finding three years later – in 2006. This finding is discussed in more depth below.

It was also the Democratic Republic of Congo that submitted, on 20 August 2023, the only inter-state case to the Court, *Democratic Republic of Congo v Rwanda*, against one of the respondent States in the earlier *DRC* case.[47] On 7 March 2024, the African Court dismissed the DRC's request for an 'expedited procedure', but decided to deal with the case on a priority basis.[48] While

46 The complaint directs itself to the presence of American forces in Chad and Zaire, see U O Umozurike, 'The African Charter on Human and Peoples' Rights: Suggestions for more effectiveness', (2007) 13(1) *Annual Survey of International and Comparative Law* 179–190, at 183, see in particular footnotes 25 and 26. In the early years of the Commission' existence, a number of individual communications were also submitted against non-African States (see Frans Viljoen, 'Introduction to the African Commission and Regional Human Rights System' in Christof Heyns (ed) *Human Rights Law in Africa* (Vol 1) (Leiden, Nijhoff, 2004) 385 at 441.

47 Application 7/2023, *Democratic Republic of Congo v. Republic of Rwanda*, submitted on 20 August 2023, under Rule 44(2)(a), 44(5)(a) and 44(1).

48 By the start of 2023, the matter was listed on the Court's website as a 'pending contentious case', but no further information was provided. In its application, the DRC also requested that the case be dealt with through an accelerated process. (No such process is provided for under either the Court Protocol or the Court Rules.) Rwanda was required to respond within 30 days to the request for an accelerated procedure; and within 90 days to the substantive application, covering jurisdiction, admissibility, merits and reparations (Rule

little information about the substantive allegations are in the public domain, surrounding circumstances suggest that there would be some overlap between the substance of the earlier *DRC* case.[49] The submission of this inter-state case has to be seen against the background of the Nairobi and Luanda processes to mediate the conflict between the DRC and Rwanda, and efforts at mediation by, among others, the President of Angola.[50]

The Commission decided not to consider one of the other inter-state complaints placed before it (Communication 422/12, *Sudan v South Sudan*). The Commission received this communication, submitted under article 49 of the Charter by the Sudanese Advisory Council for Human Rights within the Presidency, on 7 May 2012. At its 13th Extraordinary Session, in February 2013, the Commission decided not to be seized with this communication. This decision was presumably taken because the Commission considered that South Sudan was not bound by the African Charter as this country, which only gained independence on 9 July 2011, had not at the time ratified it.[51] South

42(2)(a), 42(5)(a), 44(1) of the 2020 Court Rule). In its Ruling (Request for Expedited Procedure), the Court indicated that the case relates to the conflict between the DRC's army and a coalition comprising the Rwanda's armed forces and the M 23 rebel movement; and alleges, among others, the violation of the rights guaranteed under the African Charter to the life and physical integrity, human dignity, the prohibition of slavery, human trafficking, torture, development, a clean, healthy and sustainable environment, and the right of peoples to peace.

49 Ongoing cross-border conflict, insecurity, and allegations of aggression and 'incursion' by Rwandan armed forces into the eastern provinces of the DRC are reported (see eg Implementation of the Peace, Security and Cooperation Framework for the Democratic Republic of the Congo and the Region: report of the Secretary-General, S/2023/730, 3 October 2023 (paras 2, 8); Communiqué of the 1103rd Meeting of the Peace and Security Council held on 31 August 2022, on the Situation in the Eastern Democratic Republic of Congo (DRC).)

50 See eg Remadji Hoinathy, 'Eastern DRC peace processes miss the mark' *ISS Today* (8 February 2023) <https://issafrica.org/iss-today/eastern-drc-peace-processes-miss-the-mark> accessed 30 April 2024.

51 See Magnus Killander and Bright Nkrumah 'Human rights developments in the African Union during 2012 and 2013' (2014) 14 *African Human Rights Law Journal* 275 (raising the issue whether South Sudan as a successor State should not have been considered bound by Sudan's ratification; however, if a distinction is drawn between a successor State that continues its authority over the same territory as the 'mother' State, and a State that secedes from part of the territory of the 'mother' State, the answer may well be that South Sudan did not inherit all the international obligations of Sudan; this approach is borne out by practice, which eg required South Sudan to independently ratify the African Charter, which Sudan had ratified (already in 1986) while South Sudan was still a part of the 'original' Sudanese territory.

Sudan subsequently, in October 2013, deposited its instrument of ratification to the Charter. It is therefore possible for Sudan to resubmit this complaint.

The third complaint presented to the Commission, Communication 478/14, *Djibouti v Eritrea,* was withdrawn without a decision on the merits. The Commission declared it admissible at its 25th Extraordinary Session held in February 2019. However, before it could be heard on the merits, the matter was withdrawn at the instance of Eritrea, which indicated that this was 'in light of recent developments in bilateral relations between the two States …'.[52] The Commission closed the file at its 70th session in February 2022, and no decision in respect of this communication has been made public.

5 Analysis of *drc* Case

The only merits decision on an inter-state complaint is now looked at in some depth.[53]

5.1 *Admissibility*

The Charter requires, for an inter-state communications to be admissible, that local remedies be exhausted "if they exist", unless the procedure to achieve exhaustion would be unduly prolonged.[54] In the *DRC* case, since the actions of the respondent States took place in the DRC itself, the Commission's position is that the question of exhaustion of local remedies did not arise.[55] Another approach would have been to argue that exhaustion of remedies is not required because of the massive scale of the human rights violations. It should be recalled that the African Commission in the exercise of its protective

52 52nd and 53rd Activity Report of the African Commission on Human and Peoples' Rights, covering the period 6 December 2021 to 9 November 2022, p 10; <https://achpr.au.int/en/documents/2023-06-08/52nd-and-53rd-combined-activity-reports> accessed 30 April 2024.

53 There are obviously more aspects of the case that justify analysis, such as the issue of provisional measures. The Commission did not request provisional measures in the DRC case. While the Commission's competence to issue "provisional measures" in respect of individual communications is provided for in the Commission's 2010 Rules of Procedure (Rule 98), there is no similar provision for inter-state cases.

54 Art 50.

55 *DRC* case (n 8), para 63 ("The [African] Commission takes note that the violations complained of are allegedly being perpetrated by the Respondent States in the territory of the Complainant State. In the circumstances, the [African] Commission finds that local remedies do not exist, and the question of their exhaustion does not, therefore, arise").

mandate routinely exempts complainants from exhausting local remedies in the context of allegation of a series of serious and massive violations of human rights.[56] In this regard, it differs from the European system.[57]

Logically, in the context of an inter-state complaint, the 'local' in the term 'local remedies' may refer to the territory or jurisdiction of the complaining State or the respondent State. This logic gives rise to two questions. First: Should the complaining State (in this instance, the DRC) have endeavoured to hold the respondent States accountable under DRC law (that is, in its own territory under its own laws)? The second question is: Should the DRC have instituted proceedings against each of the respondent States before their own domestic courts, under their respective applicable laws?

In an analogous case, which is not an inter-state case as such, but has been brought by a Ghanain individual against the eight States that have accepted direct individual access to the Court, the African Court found that it would be 'unreasonable to require the Applicant to sue all the Respondent States in his own country, because this form of remedy is 'barred by sovereign immunity'.[58] It is equally unreasonable to seek recourse against each of the respondent States before their respective domestic judiciaries, as it would be very 'cumbersome' and time consuming to pursue remedies in all the respondent States. Some countries make it impossible for inter-state cases to be heard before domestic courts. Tanzania, for example, does not allow its domestic courts 'to entertain matters related to their obligations arising from international treaties'.[59] Attempts to exhaust local remedies would under those circumstances be futile, and are not required.

Under the African Charter, there is an admissibility requirement that an individual communication is only admissible before the Commission if it had not been *settled* by an international mechanism of dispute settlement.[60] This requirement is however not applicable to inter-state communications. In any event, if the Commission had applied this rule in this case, it would have had no problem finding the matter admissible, because the matter before the ICJ was, in 2003, *pending* and not yet *settled*.

56 See eg *Social and Economic Rights Action Centre* (SERAC) *and Another v Nigeria* (2001) AHRLR 60 (ACHPR 2001) para 38.

57 See Isabella Risini, *The inter-state application under the European on Human Rights* (Martinus Nijhoff, 2018) at 53 (noting that under the European system exemptions from exhaustion are more wide reaching in inter-state than in individual communications).

58 *Mornah v Benin, Burkina Faso, Côte d'Ivoire, Ghana, Mali, Malawi, Tanzania and Tunisia; Sahrawi Arab Democratic Republic and Mauritius Interveners*, Application 28/2018, judgment of 22 September 2022 (*Morocco Readmission* case), para 209.

59 *Morocco Readmission* case, para 210.

60 Art 56(7) of the African Charter.

5.2 *Substantive Findings*

On the substance, the Commission found all three respondent States in violation of articles 2, 4, 5, 12(1) and (2), 14, 16, 17, 18(1) and (3), 19, 20, 21, 22 and 23 of the African Charter. The question arose whether violations of international humanitarian law (IHL) fall within the Commission's mandate. In this regard, two relevant guiding principle are (i) that a communication must be 'compatible with' the African Charter and AU Constitutive Act;[61] and (ii) that the Commission must draw inspiration from relevant human rights instruments, including those adopted by UN specialised agencies.[62] In any event, the Commission in the *DRC* case does not find that IHL as such has been violated, but reads and interprets the African Charter, of which violations are found, in the light of IHL.[63]

5.3 *Multi-forum Litigation*

The *DRC* case was also submitted to the ICJ. However, the Commission makes no reference to the ICJ case, which was pending by the time the Commission reached its decision. In fact, the DRC submitted three cases related to the same subject matter to the ICJ. In February 1999, the case to the Commission against Burundi, Uganda and Rwanda was submitted. On 23 June 1999, the DRC submitted three separate cases against Burundi, Uganda and Rwanda to the ICJ. After the DRC had informed the ICJ of its intention to discontinue the proceedings instituted against Burundi and Rwanda, these two cases were struck off the ICJ's roll on 30 January 2001. On 28 May 2002, the DRC submitted a (new) case against Rwanda with the ICJ.

On 19 December 2005, the ICJ handed down its merits decision in the last of these cases, *DRC v Uganda*.[64] It found that the unlawful military intervention by Uganda in the DRC was a grave violation of the prohibition on the use of force expressed in article 2(4) of the United Nations Charter. The Court also held that the Uganda Peoples' Defence Forces (UPDF) troops had committed violations of international humanitarian law and human rights law, and that

61 Art 56(2) of the African Charter.

62 Art 60 of the African Charter.

63 See Frans Viljoen, 'The relationship between international human rights and humanitarian law in the African human rights system: An institutional approach' in Erika De Wet & Jann Kleffner (eds) *Convergence and Conflicts of Human Rights and International Humanitarian Law in Military Operations* (Pretoria University Law Press, 2014) 303; but also see Michaela Hailbronner, 'Laws in conflict: The relationship between human rights and international humanitarian law under the African Charter on Human and Peoples' Rights' (2016) 16(2) *African Human Rights Law Journal* 339 at 349–351.

64 ICJ, *Armed Activities on the Territory of the Congo (Democratic Republic of the Congo v. Uganda)* (*DRC v Uganda*).

these violations were attributable to Uganda. On Uganda's counter-claim, it found that the DRC violated its obligations under the Vienna Convention on Diplomatic Relations (by attacking the Embassy and committing acts of maltreatment against Ugandan diplomats at Ndjili International Airport).

On 13 May 2015, the DRC asked the Court to determine the amount of reparation owed by Uganda in the light of the failure of negotiations with Uganda on the question of reparations. On 1 July 2015, the ICJ observed that although the parties had tried to settle the question directly, they had clearly been unable to reach an agreement. It therefore required the parties to file written pleadings on the question of reparations. After obtaining the report by four independent experts and holding oral hearings, the ICJ delivered its judgment on reparations on 9 February 2022,[65] awarding US$225 million for damage to persons, US$40 million for damage to property, and US$60 million for damage related to natural resources.[66] The Court allowed Uganda to pay the total amount in five yearly instalments of US$65 million each, starting on 1 September 2022.[67] It was reported that on 1 September 2022, Uganda in fact paid – and the DRC received – the first instalment of US$65 million.[68]

Two striking issues emerge from this chronological overview:

First, the Commission took more than three years before it included the decided case in its annual activity report, which was made public after it had been authorised by the Executive Council in 2006. The African Commission seems to have been influenced by the fact that a similar case to the one decided by it was pending before the ICJ. To explain this delay, which stands as an aberration in the Commission's practice, it should be noted that the ICJ merits decision on the case against Uganda was handed down on 19 December 2005. This sequence of events begs the question: To what extent has the Commission's decision to make its finding public been influenced by the outcome of the ICJ case?

Uganda made the following argument during the proceedings before the African Commission: 'Uganda also noted that the Democratic Republic of Congo has accused Uganda in several other fora: the UN Security Council, the

65 ICJ, *Armed Activities on the Territory of the Congo (Democratic Republic of the Congo v. Uganda)*, Reparations, Judgment, I.C.J. Reports 2022, p. 13 <https://www.icj-cij.org/public/files/case-related/116/116-20220209-JUD-01-00-EN.pdf> accessed 30 April 2024 (*DRC v Uganda Reparations*).

66 *DRC v Uganda* (n 64), para 405.

67 Ibid, para 406.

68 Patrick Ilunga 'Uganda pays first $65m to DRC as war reparations', *The East African*, 12 September 2022, <https://www.theeastafrican.co.ke/tea/news/east-africa/uganda-pays-first-usd65m-to-drc-as-war-reparations-3945720> accessed 30 January 2024.

ICJ, the Lusaka Initiative, and the OAU. According to the respondent State, these actions "present a dilemma to the conduct of international affairs … and adjudication", undermining the credibility of these institutions and the [African] Commission as divergent opinions may be reached.'[69] Although there is no formal requirement that the matter cannot be brought before another dispute settlement mechanism, the Commission seems to have been aware and took this into account in timing the release of its own decision.

In any event, as indicated earlier, none of these procedures rendered the matter inadmissible before the Commission for having been 'settled' under a human-rights based international dispute-settlement procedure.[70]

5.4 *Conciliation and Friendly Settlement*

As the *DRC* case was submitted under article 49 of the Charter, there is no textual prerequisite of attempting to reconcile the parties. Taking heed of the circumstances of the case, the Commission concluded that an attempt at reconciliation would not be appropriate, as "such contacts will not be diplomatically either effective or desirable" in the particular case.[71] It added: "Indeed, the situation of undeclared war prevailing between the Democratic Republic of Congo and its neighbours to the east did not favour the type of diplomatic contact that would have facilitated the application of the provisions of Articles 47 and 48 of the [African] Charter."[72] However, the possibility of amicable settlement, set out in the Commission's rules, is still applicable but has not been used successfully in any of the relevant cases.[73]

5.5 *Inter-state and Individual Claims before the Commission*

There were no individual communications submitted related to the subject matter in the *DRC* case. It is hard to argue that the non-submission of such cases is due to practical difficulties arising from the massive and widespread nature of the violations. Although the widespread nature and multiplicity of the violations make for a complex and multi-pronged case, which may be labour-intensive and costly, there are ample examples of similar cases being successfully brought against States parties to the Charter,[74] including the DRC

---

69 *DRC* case (n 8), para 34.

70 Art 56(7) of the African Charter.

71 *DRC* case (n 8), para 61.

72 Ibid.

73 See 2020 Rules of Procedure of the African Commission, Rule 112.

74 See eg *Commission Nationale des Droits de l'Homme et des Libertés v Chad* (2000) AHRLR 66 (ACHPR 1995); *Malawi African Association and Others v Mauritania* (2000) AHRLR 149 (ACHPR 2000); *Sudan Human Rights Organisation and Another v Sudan* (2009) AHRLR 153 (ACHPR 2009).

(as Zaire).[75] Since the Charter does not prescribe a victim requirement, the Commission has from early on in its jurisprudence accepted that an *actio popularis* may be brought to address violations of a massive scale affecting large groups of people.[76] This approach flows logically from the collective nature of the 'peoples' rights', which are guaranteed under articles 19 to 24 of the Charter. The ease with which cases could have been submitted makes the lack of complaints all the more striking.

5.6 *Fact-finding and Resources*

To a large extent, the Commission relied on admissions or acknowledgements by the respondent States. It also held an oral hearing, at which Rwanda and Uganda were represented. The fact that Burundi presented no argument or evidence; and that Rwanda did not take part in the case beyond the admissibility phase to some extent hampered the ability to arrive at a full, authentic and authoritative picture. On the issue of harm by Uganda to the DRC's natural resources, the Commission found that the State's averments were reliably contradicted by the "Report of the Panel of Experts, submitted to the Security Council of the UN in April 2001 (under reference S/2001/357) identified all the Respondent States among others actors, as involved in the conflict in the Democratic Republic of Congo. The report provides evidence of the involvement of the Respondent States in the illegal exploitation of the natural resources of the Complainant State".[77]

5.7 *Reparations and Implementation*

Due to the delay in deciding the case, the situation had, by the time the merits decision was taken, to a large extent resolved itself. The Commission therefore took "note with satisfaction, of the positive developments that occurred in this matter, namely the withdrawal of the Respondent States armed forces from the territory of the Complainant State".[78] Perhaps to ensure that the process is fully completed, it urged the three States to withdraw their troops "immediately" from the DRC.[79] This recommendation begs the question whether the Commission communicated its 2003 decision to the States at that time (2003),

---

75 See eg *Katangese Peoples' Congress v Zaire* (2000) AHRLR 72 (ACHPR 1998); *Free Legal Assistance Group and Others v Zaire* (2000) AHRLR 74 (ACHPR 1995).

76 See *Social and Economic Rights Action Centre* (*SERAC*) *and Another v Nigeria* (2001) AHRLR 60 (ACHPR 2001), para 49.

77 *DRC* case (n 8), para 92.

78 *DRC* case (n 8).

79 Ibid.

or whether it only did so only when it was made public in 2006. Clearly, the effectiveness of a remedy such as the withdrawal of troops is time-sensitive.

The Commission also recommended that "adequate reparations" be paid, "according to the appropriate ways", "for and on behalf of the victims of the human rights" by the three States while their forces were in "effective control of the provinces". As with many other decisions of African Commission, it is unclear to what extent these reparations recommendations have been given effect by States.[80] However, available information strongly suggests that the government did not take any measures in response to the Commission's finding. On the other hand, reliable reports indicate that the ICJ's order for compensation is being adhered to, despite the initial expression of misgivings by the Ugandan government.[81] The open-ended and undetermined nature of the amount of reparations in the Commission's reparations finding contrasts sharply with the ICJ's elaborate and meticulously argued reparations order. Uganda's compliance can at least in part be ascribed to the meticulous research that went into determining the amount of compensation, and the extensive substantiation of all relevant issues in the ICJ's judgment.

6 Reasons for the Limited use of Inter-state under the African Regional System Complaints Thus Far

A major reason why the inter-state complaints procedure is underused across all systems and regions is because States are reluctant to be seen to engage in 'unfriendly' or hostile acts towards other States, in avoidance of antagonizing other States and provoking retaliatory measures. Also, the procedure is viewed as 'outdated' because 'other, quicker and less formalistic mechanisms' have become available to States though which they can 'vent their concern' about serious human rights violations in other States.[82] Against this background,

80 See generally Frans Viljoen and Lirette Louw, 'State compliance with the recommendations of the African Commission on Human and Peoples' Rights, 1994–2004' 101.1 *American Journal of International Law* (2007) 1–34; and Rachel Murray and Debra Long, *The Implementation of the Findings of the African Commission on Human and Peoples' Rights* (Cambridge University Press, 2015).

81 Uganda: ICJ decision on DRC unfair and wrong, The Independent, (<https://www.independent.co.ug/uganda-icj-decision-on-drc-unfair-and-wrong/> accessed 30 January 2024), containing a statement by the Ugandan regarding the ICJ judgment, dated 10 February 2022.

82 Nowak (n 3) at 274; see also eg art 7 of the EU Treaty, which provides for a more immediate way for States to address concerns of this nature; and the various possibilities within the ambit of the UN Human Rights Council.

some of the reasons for the dearth of inter-state cases submitted to either the African Commission or Court, in particular, are considered.

6.1 *Culture of Non-intervention; Preference for Non-confrontational and Non-judicial Dispute Resolution*

A primary reason for the reluctance of African States to complain against other African States lies in the general culture of non-intervention among African States.[83] One of the foundational values of both the Organisation of African Unity (OAU) and AU is "non-interference by any member State in the internal affairs of another".[84] For many years after its inception, the OAU adhered to a rigid notion of non-interference in the domestic affairs of other members States. For example, when then President of South Africa, Nelson Mandela, in 1993 criticised the human rights record in Sani Abacha-run Nigeria, in particular, the execution of Ken Saro-Wiwa, South Africa found itself at odds with most other African States,[85] causing a shift in South African foreign policy from an unequivocal human rights-based to a more multilateral approach.[86] This culture of non-interference has been reinforced in the African context by factors such as the weight attached to sovereignty in a post-colonial context,[87] and an overriding concern for unity and consensus within the OAU (and since its establishment, the AU). African leaders have over time shown great reluctance to openly criticise each other. At an institutional level, within the AU Executive Council, this disinclination has led to a practice *not* to "name and blame" states

83 See also Mumba Malila 'Daunting prospects: Accessing the African Court through the African Commission' (2011) 31 *Human Rights Law Journal* 61–72 at 68 (present diplomatic and political environment' making the use of art 5(1)(b) of the Court Protocol 'highly implausible').

84 Art 4(g) AU Constitutive Act; see also art 3(2) of the 1963 OAU Charter.

85 Thabo Mbeki, 'How Abacha humiliated Mandela' 29 February 2016 <https://www.politicsweb.co.za/opinion/how-abacha-humiliated-mandela--thabo-mbeki> accessed 30 April 2024 ('Undoubtedly our Government drew its own conclusions from this painful experience with regard to the complexities of the construction of inter-state relations, including as this relates to the effective promotion of human rights.')

86 See Mbulelo Shadrack Bungane, South Africa's Human Rights Diplomacy in Africa: 1994–2008, MA dissertation, University of Pretoria, 2103, <http://hdl.handle.net/2263/43686> accessed 30 April 2024 (noting a 'move away from unilateral action to reliance on multilateral forums to deal with human rights challenges; the development of continental norms and standards, as well as strengthening continental structures; and conflict resolution and post-conflict reconstruction and development in Africa').

87 See Scott Leckie 'The inter-state complaint procedure in international human rights law: hopeful prospects or wishful thinking?' (1998) 10 *Human Rights Quarterly* 249, at 263 (referring to African States' 'shared jealously of recently gained sovereignty').

that have not complied with the orders of the African Court.[88] The failure of the AU to invoke the possibility of intervening in member States under the 'responsibility to protect', codified in article 4(h) of the AU Constitutive Act, bears further testimony to this hesitance to outrightly confront other AU member States.[89]

Avoidance of intervening postures align with a preference for non-confrontational and non-judicial (including quasi-judicial) dispute mechanisms. This approach is facilitated by the availability within the continent of 'many other less contentious dispute settlement mechanisms ordinarily available to the States in dispute'.[90] One example is the African Peer Review Mechanism (APRM). Hansungule notes that the 'peer pressure' that States have committed themselves to 'is very similar to the processes' under articles 47 to 49 of the Charter.[91] The similarities are that in both processes a consultative review is undertaken of a State's record, based on information provided by both the government and independent experts. However, while the APRM covers governance in a very broad sense, the focus of inter-state complaints is much more specific on human rights. Importantly, the inter-state process may conclude with the finding of an independent expert-adjudicator, while the APRM involve governmental 'peers'. In any event, the APRM is a voluntary process, which has been accepted by only 37 AU member States.[92] APRM-related visits and reviews are also relatively few and far between.

Related to these factors is the nature of matters that are likely to be referred, and the existence of alternative channels to resolve these cases. Inter-state cases are most likely to be submitted in contexts where the relationships between States had seriously broken down, where there is conflict between States, and where military force may be used or international armed conflict is imminent or real. In these circumstances, the (quasi)-judicial route is – particularly within the African continent – not the most appropriate channel to explore.

88 The Court routinely indicated, in its Annual Reports, the States that have not complied with the Court's judgments, despite the provisions of art 31 of the Court Protocol, which requires the Court to specify 'the cases in which a State has not complied with the Court's judgment', read with the Executive Council's obligation under art 29(2) to 'monitor' the 'execution' of judgments.

89 See eg Dan Kuwali & Frans Viljoen (eds) *Africa and the Responsibility to Protect: Article 4(h) of the African Union Constitutive Act* (Routledge, 2013).

90 Malila (supra n 83) at 68.

91 Michelo Hansungule 'The African Charter on Human and Peoples' Rights ' in Abdulqawi A. Yusuf and Fatsah Ouguergouz (eds) *The African Union: Legal and institutional framework A manual on the pan-African organization* (Leiden Martinus Nijhoff, 2012) 417 at 441.

92 African Peer Review Mechanism (APRM), 'APRM Member States' <https://aprm.au.int/index.php/en/about/states> accessed 30 January 2024 (17 of these States have by the end of 2022 undergone any review).

Within the AU, such matters are best brought to the attention and resolved by the AU Peace and Security Council (AU PSC), thus reducing the need for recourse to inter-state complaints. Even before the AU PSC comes into play, the various regional economic communities are to be approached to endeavour to resolve such conflicts. For example, the SADC Organ for Politics, Defence and Security (Organ) was launched in June 1996 as a formal institution of SADC with the mandate to support the achievement and maintenance of security and the rule of law in the SADC region. Within ECOWAS, the Mechanism for Conflict Prevention, Management, Resolution, Peacekeeping, and Security has been established, and ECOWAS has played an influential role in numerous conflicts in West Africa. It would be difficult for African States to "leapfrog" or sidestep the role of these overlapping networks of conflict resolution, and to negate the importance of its belonging to these IGOs in which collectivity and solidarity are important constituent elements.

For the first twenty years in the life of the African Charter (1986–2006), the Commission was the only institution to which States could potentially submit cases against other States. Approaching the Court with an inter-state case only became possible after the entry into force of the Court Protocol and the Court's operationalisation in 2006. The absence of binding judicial recourse –'impossibility of judicial resolution' – could also count as a factor inhibiting genuinely concerned States from submitting instituting inter-state complaints.[93] With the advent of the Court, a judicial institution has been introduced to complement but not replace the Commission. The Court's jurisdiction is optional, and depends on the State accepting the formal bindingness of the Court Protocol. Writing in 1988, Leckie suggested that the remote prospect of a binding decision in an inter-state case may be a factor that would limit the use of this procedure.[94] While this factor may well account for the dearth of cases between 1986 and 2006, it does not account for the fact that only one of the States parties to the Court Protocol has since 2006 submitted an inter-state case to the Court. A relevant factor here may be the low level of implementation by States of the Court's judgments and the inaction of AU policy organs in response thereto.

6.2 *ICJ as Alternative Forum*

In so far as the judicial route is regarded as an option for resolving inter-state disputes, African States have over the years showed growing confidence in

93 Leckie (supra n 87) at 263.

94 Ibid: 'The impossibility of judicial resolution of human rights violations and the Commission's ability to make only recommendations will also limit the use of this procedural option.'

and greater openness to the ICJ. Initially, newly independent African States joined the UN, but very rarely approached the ICJ with inter-state cases.[95] One of the main reasons for this reticence to judicial resolution of disputes of an international nature was the deep mistrust of international law, which these States perceived to have colluded in legalizing and legitimizing colonial occupation and misrule.[96] Another was the underrepresentation of Africans on the Court.[97] An early exception contributed to deepen these misgivings:[98] In 1960, two African States – Ethiopia and Liberia – instituted proceedings against the Union of South Africa, as imperial power, before the ICJ.[99] They contended that the application of apartheid policies by South Africa in South West Africa (SWA), over which the League of Nations had granted it trusteeship, violated international law.[100] While in 1962 the ICJ dismissed all preliminary objections in the case,[101] including the objections by South Africa that the two States lacked standing, in 1966 the Court, instead of proceeding to a merits decision, revisited its previous finding and concluded, on highly contentious technical grounds,[102] that Ethiopia and Liberia lacked 'legal right or interest'.[103] The ICJ's surprising about-turn deeply disappointed not only the two States, but the Asia-Africa group more generally.[104] While this disinclination persisted

95 PM Munya 'The International Court of Justice and peaceful settlement of African disputes: Problems, challenges and prospects' (1998) 7(2) *Journal of International Law and Practice* 159–224.

96 See eg Siba N'zatioula Grovogui, *Sovereigns, Quasi Sovereigns and Africans: Race and Self Determination in International Law* (Minnesota: University of Minnesota Press, 1996).

97 At the time, only one of the 15 Judges were from an African State. The number of African ICJ Judges increased to two in 1963, and to three in 1973 (Munya (n 95) at 177–178.

98 See R Higgins 'The International Court and South West Africa: the implications of the judgment' (1966) 42 *International Affairs* 573–599.

99 The two States submitted two separate cases, which the ICJ on 20 May 1961 decided should be joined because they had the same interest in the proceedings.

100 Ethiopia and Liberia are not only the African States of the longest standing as sovereign entities, but were also, with the Union of South Africa and Egypt, the only African members States of the League of Nations; they brought the case as erstwhile members of the League.

101 *South West African Cases (Ethiopia v South Africa; Liberia v South Africa)* Preliminary Objections [1962] ICJ Report 318/9 (21 December 1962).

102 See TO Elias *Africa and the development of international law* (1998) 94.

103 *South West African Cases (Ethiopia v South Africa; Liberia v South Africa) Second Phase* [1966] ICJ Report 6 (18 July 1966) (finding that the two States lacked special, national interest in the mandate over the SWA, beyond the general legal interest of all League members).

104 It was within this group that the case was initiated as an opportunity to overcome frustration about the lack of effective international action despite the Court's Advisory Opinions on SWA (eg International Status of South West Africa (SWA), Advisory Opinion, 1950 I.C.J. (11 July)).

during the 1970s, in the early 1980s a change occurred. On the back of two advisory opinions favourable to decolonisation and self-determination,[105] the resolution of the *Continental Shelf* case between Tunisia and Libya,[106] and greater African representation in the Court's composition, the Court from the early 1980s received a slow but steady flow of cases from African States.[107]

A majority of cases filed by African States before the ICJ deal with border, territorial or maritime disputes and delineations.[108] Outside the ambit of these disputes, and beyond the SWA cases, only two contentious cases were submitted *by African States against African States*: the 'Great Lakes' situation involving the DRC and its neighbours;[109] and the *Diallo* case brought by Guinea against the DRC.[110] In the remaining cases, African States have submitted cases

105 *Legal Consequences for States of the Continued Presence of South Africa in Namibia (South West Africa) notwithstanding Security Council Resolution 276 (1970)*, Advisory Opinion, I.C.J. Reports 1971, p. 16; *Western Sahara, Advisory Opinion*, I.C.J. Reports 1975, p. 12. See also *Legal Consequences of the Separation of the Chagos Archipelago from Mauritius in 1965*, Advisory Opinion, I.C.J. Reports 2019, p. 95, in which the ICJ concludes that the decolonization of Mauritius was not conducted in a manner consistent with the right of peoples to self-determination.

106 Continental Shelf (Tunisia/Libyan Arab Jamahiriya) (concluded in 1982).

107 Between 1960 and 1979, 3 cases were submitted by African States; 1980–1989, 4 cases were submitted; 1990–1999, 10 cases; 2000–2009, 5 cases; 2010–2019, 7 cases, and 2020–2023, 3 cases, adding up to a total of 32 cases.

108 *Maritime Delimitation in the Indian Ocean (Somalia v. Kenya)* (concluded in 2021); Frontier Dispute (Burkina Faso/Niger) (concluded in 2013); Frontier Dispute (Benin/Niger) (concluded in 2005); *Land and Maritime Boundary between Cameroon and Nigeria (Cameroon v. Nigeria: Equatorial Guinea intervening)* (concluded in 2002); Kasikili/Sedudu Island (Botswana/Namibia) (concluded in 1999); *Maritime Delimitation between Guinea-Bissau and Senegal (Guinea-Bissau v. Senegal)* (concluded 1995); Territorial Dispute (Libyan Arab Jamahiriya/Chad) (concluded in 1994); *Arbitral Award of 31 July 1989 (Guinea-Bissau v. Senegal)* (concluded in 1991); Frontier Dispute (Burkina Faso/Republic of Mali) (concluded in 1986); Continental Shelf (Libyan Arab Jamahiriya/Malta) (concluded in 1985); Continental Shelf (Tunisia/Libyan Arab Jamahiriya) (concluded in 1982) (see also Application for Revision and Interpretation of the Judgment of 24 February 1982 in the Case concerning the Continental Shelf (Tunisia/Libyan Arab Jamahiriya) (*Tunisia v. Libyan Arab Jamahiriya*)).

109 *Armed Activities on the Territory of the Congo (Democratic Republic of the Congo v. Burundi)* (concluded in 2001); *Armed Activities on the Territory of the Congo (Democratic Republic of the Congo v. Rwanda)* (concluded in 2001); with *Armed Activities on the Territory of the Congo (Democratic Republic of the Congo v. Uganda)* (concluded in 2022); Armed Activities on the Territory of the Congo (New Application: 2002) (*Democratic Republic of the Congo v. Rwanda*) (concluded in 2006).

110 *Ahmadou Sadio Diallo (Republic of Guinea v. Democratic Republic of the Congo)* (concluded in 2012).

against erstwhile colonial powers (UK, Belgium and France),[111] Qatar,[112] as well as Myanmar and Israel.[113] The last two cases reveal an appetite to act in the common interest of States parties to human rights treaties, to uphold the shared values, locating these firmly within 'collective enforcement'.[114]

Uganda's reaction against the adverse finding by the ICJ in *Armed Activities on the Territory of the Congo (Democratic Republic of the Congo v Uganda)* embodies a bifurcated approach to international justice that is not uncommon among African States. As a matter of principle, it pledged its long-standing belief in 'the international system', but in response to the outcome in the specific case, it characterised the ICJ judgment on both the merits and reparations as 'undue interference' in 'African affairs'.[115]

6.3 *Lacklustre Performance of the African Commission*

One of the reasons for the death of inter-state complaints is the uninspiring outcome of the one decided inter-state communication in the *DRC* case. A four-year delay between the submission of the matter (in 1999) and the Commission's decision (in 2003) meant that the most pressing circumstances

111 *Northern Cameroons (Cameroon v. United Kingdom)* (concluded in 1963); *Arrest Warrant of 11 April 2000 (Democratic Republic of the Congo v. Belgium)* (concluded in 2002); *Questions of Interpretation and Application of the 1971 Montreal Convention arising from the Aerial Incident at Lockerbie (Libyan Arab Jamahiriya v. United Kingdom)* (concluded in 2003); *Questions of Interpretation and Application of the 1971 Montreal Convention arising from the Aerial Incident at Lockerbie (Libyan Arab Jamahiriya v. United States of America)* (concluded in 2003); *Certain Criminal Proceedings in France (Republic of the Congo v. France)* (concluded in 2010); *Certain Questions of Mutual Assistance in Criminal Matters (Djibouti v. France)* (concluded in 2028); *Immunities and Criminal Proceedings (Equatorial Guinea v. France)* (concluded in 2020); and *Request relating to the Return of Property Confiscated in Criminal Proceedings (Equatorial Guinea v. France)* (concluded in 2020).

112 *Appeal relating to the Jurisdiction of the ICAO Council under Article 84 of the Convention on International Civil Aviation (Bahrain, Egypt, Saudi Arabia and United Arab Emirates v. Qatar)* (concluded in 2020); *Appeal relating to the Jurisdiction of the ICAO Council under Article II, Section 2, of the 1944 International Air Services Transit Agreement (Bahrain, Egypt and United Arab Emirates v. Qatar)* (concluded in 2020).

113 *Rohingya Genocide* case (n 11); *Gaza Genocide* case (n 11).

114 See eg Statement by South Africa welcoming the provisional measures ordered by the International Court of Justice against Israel, 26 January 2024: 'South Africa will continue to act within the institutions of global governance to protect the rights … and to obtain the fair and equal application of international law to all, *in the interest of our collective humanity*' (emphasis added).

115 Uganda: ICJ decision on DRC unfair and wrong, The Independent, <https://www.independent.co.ug/uganda-icj-decision-on-drc-unfair-and-wrong/> accessed 30 April 2024, containing a statement by the Ugandan regarding the ICJ judgment, dated 10 February 2022.

have in fact already been resolved, or fundamentally changed by the time of the Commission's decision. A further three-year delay between the Commission's decision and its publication (in 2006) casts doubt on the factors motivating and guiding the Commission in its decisions. The sense of disillusionment resulting from non-implementation of the recommendations is exacerbated by the measures taken by Uganda to give effect to the ICJ's reparations order. A comparison between the reparations practices of the Commission and the ICJ shows up the Commission's weaknesses, and may undermine States' confidence in pursuing the Commission route. The submission by The Gambia is evidence of a 'belief' in the international system, pronounced in the context of return to respectability within the international community, and solidarity in transnational intergovernmental networks, in this case, the Organization of Islamic Cooperation.[116]

6.4 *Individual Communications as Alternative Means*

Another possible factor that may reduce the need for recourse to inter-state complaints is the prominence given by and the extent to which the African regional system is able to deal with massive or widespread violations.[117] It is understood that inter-state complaints in pursuit of the public interest are likely to be brought because 'effective remedies are not available' due to large number of complainants or the breakdown of the rule of law.[118] As the European system is less attuned to dealing with 'individual' complaints involving massive or large-scale violations, the inter-state mechanism has proven to be a useful outlet through which these concerns could be vented.[119]

---

116 *Application of the Convention on the Prevention and Punishment of the Crime of Genocide* (*The Gambia v Myanmar*), Provisional Measures, Order, 23 January 2020, <https://www.icj-cij.org/en/case/178> accessed 30 April 2024. See para 43 (Myanmar submitting that the OIC is the 'true applicant' in the proceedings, and that the OIC, which is not a State and 'cannot therefore have a reciprocal acceptance of jurisdiction with the respondent State, has used The Gambia as a "proxy" in order to circumvent' the restrictions to the Court's personal jurisdiction); but also see paras 45, 46 (the Court rejecting Myanmar's preliminary objection because it saw 'no reason why it should look beyond the fact that The Gambia has instituted proceedings against Myanmar in its own name).

117 See art 58 of the African Charter; and eg *Malawi African Association and Others v Mauritania* (2000) AHRLR 61 (ACHPR 2000) and *Free Legal Assistance Group and Others v Zaire* (2000) AHRLR 74 (ACHPR 1995).

118 Prebensen (n 2) 557.

119 See eg the submission in 1967, of Applications 3321-3323/67 and 3344/67, *Denmark, Norway, Sweden and the Netherlands v. Greece* (mass arrests, censorship, and martial law during the colonels' military dictatorship military following the 1967 coup d'état in Greece); and in 1982, Applications 9940-44/82, *France, Norway, Denmark, Sweden, and the Netherlands v. Turkey* (execution of numerous Turkish citizens, torture and illegal detention following military take-over and declaration of martial law in 1980).

Under the African system, with its explicit protection of peoples' rights,[120] and a very accommodating standing regime, including *actio popularis*, there is a lesser urgency for States to submit cases on behalf of groups of victims in other States. Also, the African Commission's jurisprudence has numerous examples of non-citizens instituting cases in other States parties to the African Charter,[121] thus limiting the urgency for States to intervene on behalf of their own citizens experiencing human rights violations in other States parties to the African Charter.

6.5 *Practical Concerns*

At a very practical level, and to some extent resulting from the factors highlighted above, there is a low level of knowledge and awareness about inter-state complaints. An increased appreciation for and interest in inter-state cases before the ICJ arising from the submission of and preliminary measures orders in the *Rohingya Genocide* and *Gaza Genocide* cases is likely to leave largely unaffected the general lack of awareness of the possibility of inter-state complaints or cases before AU human rights bodies. This knowledge gap extends to diplomats, government officials, lawyers and scholars.[122] The lack of awareness and understanding of the inter-state route through the African Court, specifically, is even more acute. While the *DRC* case has given relatively wide exposure to the possibility of an inter-state case being submitted to the Commission, there is little understanding of a similar competence to approach the Court. It is possible, though, that this may change over time, depending on the trajectory of the *DRC v Rwanda* case submitted to the Court in late 2023.

7 Blurring of Boundaries: The Distinction between Individual Complainants, Intervening Third Party States and Inter-state Complainants

The discussion on inter-state communications is premised on the existence of a clear distinguishing line between an 'inter-state' communication/case and an 'individual' communication/case. However, this is not always the case, especially in a context where NGOs (a broadened category of 'individuals', at least in the African system), may in fact not be representing civil society, but act

120 Arts 19 to 25 of the African Charter.

121 See *Rencontre africaine pour la defense des droits de l'homme v Zambia* Communication 71/92, and *Good v Botswana* Communication 313/2005.

122 Inter-state complaints or cases are rarely discussed in writing about the Commission or Court's mandate and operation.

at a government's behest.[123] A State may also avoid the inter-state complaints mechanisms by adjoining its arguments, as third party intervener, to those of an individual complainant/applicant.

In 1996, at a time of turmoil in Burundi, a Belgian-based NGO, the *Association pour la Sauvegarde de la Paix au Burundi,* instituted a complaint to the African Commission against Burundi's neighbouring States (Tanzania, Kenya, Uganda, Rwanda, Zaire (now DRC) and Zambia) for imposing sanctions against Burundi.[124] During the admissibility phase, the Commission observed as follows: "It would appear that authors of the communication were in all respects representing the interests of the military regime of Burundi".[125] However, the Commission dealt with the matter as an "individual communication". The decisions has been criticised on the basis that the logical consequence of the finding on the nature of the applicant should have been that the NGO be considered as an "under-cover" NGO and that the matter should have been dealt with as an inter-state communication.[126] Admitting NGOs that are 'screens' for governments as individual complainants risks 'the discrediting of civil society in Africa, in spite of NGO dynamism in the area of human rights, particularly in Africa'.[127]

A State party to the Court Protocol may also be admitted as an intervening third party State, when it is not a party to a dispute but 'has in interest in a case'.[128] As Ouguergouz points out,[129] the unfortunate wording of this provision confuses the joinder of cases and the intervention by third States.[130] What is at stake in article 5(2) is not the joinder of interrelated cases by the Court, but rather an intervention by a State on the basis of its interest in a case instituted by or against other States.

---

123 As a government 'organised' (or 'owned' or 'oriented') NGO or 'GONGO'; see Reza Hasmath, Timothy Hildebrandt and Jennifer YJ Hsu, 'Conceptualizing Government-organized Non-governmental Organizations' (2019) 15(3) *Journal of Civil Society* 267–284.

124 Communication 157/96, *Association pour la Sauvegarde de la Paix au Burundi v Kenya, Rwanda, Tanzania, Uganda, Zaire and Zambia* (*Burundi* case), published in the Commission's 17th Activity Report. See also Communications 233/99, 234/99 (joined), *Interights (on behalf of the Pan African Movement and others) v Eritrea and Ethiopia.*

125 *Burundi* case (n 124) para 63.

126 See Alain Didier Olinga, 'The embargo against Burundi before the African Commission on Human and Peoples' Rights (Note on Communication 157/96, Association for the Preservation of Peace in Burundi v Tanzania, Kenya, Uganda, Rwanda, Zaire and Zambia): recent developments' 5(2) *African Human Rights Law Journal* (2005) 424–432.

127 Olinga (n 126) at 428.

128 Art 5(2) of the Court Protocol.

129 Ouguergouz (n 39) at 115.

130 Art 5(2): 'When a State party has an interest in a case, it may submit a request to the Court to be permitted to *join*' (emphasis added).

The border line between an 'intervening' State and a State bringing an inter-state case can also be blurred. A individual case submitted directly to the Court under article 5(3) read with 34(6) of the Court Protocol illustrates a close alignment between the individual bringing the case and a State party to the Charter and Protocol acting as 'intervening State' in that matter – the Sahrawi Arab Democratic Republic (SADR).[131] This case claims that the eight respondent States – all the States that at the time had in place valid direct access declarations under article 34(6) of the Protocol – have violated the African Charter by allowing the African Union to readmit Morocco as a member. In particular, the case alleges that the readmission of Morocco violates the right to self-determination of the people of the SADR. Based on its interest in the case, the SADR was allowed to enter into the proceedings as an intervening State.[132] Since the SADR is a State party to the Court Protocol but has not accepted direct individual access to the Court, it did not qualify as a respondent State in the submitted case. The extent of overlap between the interest of the applicant (Mornah, a national of Ghana) and that of the SADR transpires from the fact that the contentions by Mornah and the SADR as intervening State were largely similar.[133] In important respects, the SADR presented much more extensive and fully developed arguments than the applicant.

The distinct impression is created that the individual application procedure was used as an avenue to bring the respondent States before the Court in what is essentially an inter-state case. Arguably, the Court would also have had jurisdiction if the SADR brought the case as an inter-state case against the respondent States. Because the SADR has been a State party to the Court Protocol since 2013, the Court would have had personal jurisdiction to hear such an inter-state case. Understandably, the SADR may have been reluctant to take such a confrontational stance against the eight States concerned, as the core of its quarrel – the denial of the right to self-determination of the Sahrawi

131 *Mornah v Benin, Burkina Faso, Côte d'Ivoire, Ghana, Mali, Malawi, Tanzania, Tunisia, Sahrawi Arab Democratic Republic and Mauritius Interveners*, Application 28/2018, judgment of 22 September 2022 (*Morocco AU Admission* case).

132 *Mornah v Benin & ors (intervention by Sahrawi)* (2020) 4 AfCLR 602 (ruling (on application for leave to intervene) of 25 September 2020.

133 The Court (in the *Morocco AU Admission* case, n 131, paras 120 & 121), reiterates its consistent jurisprudence that 'any person' can bring an application 'on others' behalf without a need to demonstrate victimhood or a direct vested interest in the matter', and highlights that all 'African citizens' have a vested interest in the right to self-determination because of its 'particular importance to the African society considering the continent's history of colonialism and military occupation'. As an applicant State in an inter-state case can be seen as embodying the interest of its 'citizens', the same broad approach to standing would likely be applied to the interest of applicant States.

people – is with Morocco (and not with the eight respondent States).[134] The most significant constraint in the way of an inter-state case against Morocco is the fact that Morocco has not become a party to either the African Charter or the Court Protocol.

Adjudicators should be alert that the couching of a case as an 'individual' case may conceal a State interest, and should, when required, inquire whether the case would not have been more appropriately presented as an 'inter-state' case, in line with the principle that the 'initiation of an inter-state complaint is dependent on the voluntary exercise of the sovereign will of a State party to the Charter, which decision can only be made by States in accordance with the Charter'.[135]

8 Conclusion

Textually, the African human rights system holds much promise that inter-state complaints or cases would feature as a significant means of redressing human rights violations on the continent. In fact, the African Charter is unique among human rights treaties in making both inter-state and individual communications a necessary consequence of becoming a State party. All States parties to the African Court Protocol have the competence to submit inter-state cases to the Court and accept that other States parties may lodge cases against them. Inter-state complaints may consequently be submitted both to the African Commission and the African Court, by 54 and 34 AU member States, respectively.

The considerable potential for the submission of inter-state cases has not been realised, with only three cases having been submitted to the African Commission, and one to the Court. Only one of these cases has thus far been decided on the merits. The reasons for the rare use of inter-state complaints lie, in the first place, in the general approach of African States towards resolving inter-country disputes. Even if a particular AU member State would be prepared to raise an issue related to human rights with another African State, its preference may well be to make use of mediation or negotiation, and diplomatic and political – rather than quasi-judicial or judicial – means. Within this context, inter-state complaints are likely to remain exceptional.

---

134 *Morocco AU Admission* case, n 131, para 17, the Court noting that 'the instant Application mainly relates to the rights and freedoms of the people of SADR'.

135 Communication 233/99-234/99, *Interights (on behalf of Pan African Movement and Citizens for Peace in Eritrea) v Ethiopia and Interights (on behalf of Pan African Movement and Inter African Group) v Eritrea*, 29 May 2003. Para 44.

Even if a State would in principle accept the suitability of approaching the Commission or Court with a human rights case, it may be dissuaded from submitting a case due to the Commission's disappointing record, and the fear that even the Court's judgments are not guaranteed effective implementation. Uncertainty about the prospect of effective case-handling may further impede submissions. It may also simply be that the option of pursuing inter-state complaints before regional bodies does not arise in the minds of government officials, lawyers and advisors, due to the relative invisibility and opaqueness of this procedure.

In the few instances of its application, the complaining State did not in the first place act to uphold the integrity of the African Charter system (in the name of 'collective enforcement'), but submitted the case to protect its national interests and the human rights of its own nationals. The submission of the *DRC* case was provoked by the complete breakdown in inter-state relations because of the illegal occupation and exploitation of the DRC's resources by forces from neighbouring States, and the dire situation in which its citizen found themselves in the eastern part of the country. The *DRC v Rwanda* case seem to relate to the ongoing threat to the national interest and security of the peoples of the eastern DRC.

Perhaps departing from an overly optimistic view of the African system, it is also possible that States do not experience the need to act in the 'collective public interest' because the Charter system is flexible and is able with ease to accommodate claims of massive violations. The Commission and Court allow for cases to be submitted by individuals and groups of individuals, and have been generous in exempting complainants/applicants from the exactitudes of exhausting local remedies. States may, on this basis, validate their non-submission of cases by pointing to the actual submission by victims of violations – and the concomitant findings – in these circumstances.

Against this backdrop, it seems unlikely that there will, in the near future, be a dramatic increase in the use of the inter-state mechanism under the African regional human rights system. However, the pending *DRC v Rwanda* case before the African Court may have a significant influence on this trend. In the context of greater awareness of the existence and potential relevance of the inter-state procedure, the resolution and impact of this first-ever inter-state case before the African Court may either be an accelerator for or discourage the submission of similar cases in the future.

Recent submissions by African States (The Gambia and South Africa) of two inter-state cases to the ICJ do not necessarily detract from this conclusion. These cases are against *non-African States* (Myanmar and Israel, respectively). Both cases are based on the principle of 'collective enforcement', as they seek to uphold the respondent States' human rights obligations, and invoke the standing of the applicant State to bring the case in the interest of all State parties (to the Genocide Convention). At the same time, the submission of these cases also aligns with the submitting States' broader geo-political ambitions. For The Gambia, submitting the case helps to distinguish the Adama Barrow era from the era of Yammeh's authoritarian rule, especially as his government's popular supports weakens, and aligns it with the agenda of the Organisation of Islamic Cooperation. For South Africa, submitting the case aligns with the African National Congress's long-standing support for Palestinian people's claims to self-determination, and bolster the government's foreign policy objective of contributing to a reconstructed new world order. The question thus remains whether the submissions of these two cases presages more frequent submission of inter-state cases by African States against African States before the ICJ.

African States may submit inter-state cases against each other before the ICJ, and have indeed done so. But they may also bring these cases to the African Court. Endowed with an expansive substantive jurisdiction, the African Court provides a plausible alternative or complementary forum for inter-state cases. The Court's jurisdiction is however limited to African States that have accepted its jurisdiction, and that are party to the relevant treaty that is invoked. So far, no African State has submitted a case against another African State on the basis of collective enforcement of the Charter, and certainly not related to genocide.

As far as the Genocide Convention is concerned, the African Court has jurisdiction over African States parties to the Genocide Convention.[136] By the end of 2023, 36 African States have become party to the Genocide Convention.[137] Most of them have also accepted the Court's jurisdiction.[138] Failure by Sudan to accept the Court's jurisdiction made it impossible for countries such as The Gambia and South Africa to submit an inter-state case in respect of the plausible genocide in the Darfur region of Sudan, in the early 2000s. Similarly, Ethiopia, another State in respect of which allegations of

136 Under art 3(1) of the Court Protocol, the Court has substantive jurisdiction over 'relevant human rights' treaties ratified by the States concerned.

137 *Convention on the Prevention and Punishment of the Crime of Genocide,* opened for signature 9 December 1948, 78 UNTS 277 (entered into force 12 January 1951) <https://treaties.un.org/pages/ViewDetails.aspx?src=TREATY&mtdsg_no=IV-1&chapter=4> accessed 30 April 2024 (18 African UN member States are not party to this Convention, as well as the Saharawi Arab Democratic Republic).

138 The following States have accepted the Genocide Convention but not the Court's jurisdiction: Cape Verde, Egypt, Ethiopia, Guinea, Liberia, Namibia, Seychelles, Sudan, Zimbabwe.

genocide have circulated, is not a party to the Court Protocol although it has ratified the Genocide Convention.

Unquestionably, African States parties to the Court Protocol may submit inter-state cases on a much wider array of human rights related topics than genocide, since the African Court's jurisdiction extends to all human rights treaties to which States parties have become party. Going by persistent non-compliance with adverse findings of the African Commission, the most egregious African violator-States may be identified. However, a number of them have not accepted the African Court's jurisdiction, even if they have at least become party to the African Charter.[139] From this perspective, the more frequent use of inter-state cases may serve as a disincentive to these States from ratifying the Court Protocol.

It remains to be seen whether the slowly emerging trend towards submitting inter-state cases will be reinforced by more African States submitting inter-state cases against other African States when Africa's people are exposed to grave or systematic human rights violations, especially when no complaints are forthcoming from individuals, groups or NGOs.

---

139 Eritrea presents probably the clearest example: The African Commission has strongly condemned the violations of freedom of information and access to information by the Eritrean government and called for release of detainees conduct of speedy and fair trials; and an end to the ban on private media in two communications (*Article 19 v Eritrea* (2007) AHRLR 73 (ACHPR 2007) para 108 & *Zegveld and Another v Eritrea* (2003) AHRLR 84 (ACHPR 2003) para 62). The government of Eritrea has however failed to implement the recommendations made by the Commission. The Commission in 2005 also adopted Resolution 91, condemning the arrest and continued detention of the victims of the 2001 crackdown, calling for their release and for Eritrea to comply with its international human rights obligations.

CHAPTER 5

The Path Less Taken? Interstate Conciliation and Human Rights

Eran Sthoeger

Abstract

Though provided for in several treaties, including three universal human rights treaties, resort to interstate conciliation has been sparse. In 2018, however, the first three human rights interstate conciliations were initiated under the International Convention on the Elimination of All Forms of Racial Discrimination (CERD). While two of these have been terminated by mutual agreement, the third, *Palestine v. Israel*, is ongoing after the CERD Committee has concluded that it has jurisdiction to establish a conciliation commission. This article examines how suited conciliation is to advance the goals of interstate communications in human rights treaties, as well as conciliation more broadly. It also tries to identify critical factors that may determine the success or failure of such conciliations, particularly by drawing on lessons learned from the recent conciliation between Timor Leste and Australia under the UN Convention for the Law of the Sea, which successfully concluded with a delimitation treaty.

Keywords

conciliation – international human rights – interstate communications – CERD – Palestine v. Israel – dispute settlement – Timor-Leste/Australia conciliation

 | DOI:10.1163/9789004712584_007

1 Introduction*

Conciliation between States is provided for in many treaties including some of the most central treaties to the international order, such as the Vienna Convention on the Law of Treaties (VCLT)[1] and the United Nations (UN) Convention on the Law of the Sea (UNCLOS).[2] Nevertheless, conciliation between States remains an uncommon phenomenon and only partially successful.[3] In 2016, the first interstate conciliation in decades, and first ever conciliation under UNCLOS, was initiated by Timor Leste against Australia. The conciliation successfully concluded with a delimitation treaty.[4]

Interstate conciliation is also provided for in the International Covenant on Civil and Political Rights (ICCPR),[5] Convention against Torture and Other Cruel, Inhuman or Degrading Treatment or Punishment (CAT)[6] and the International Convention on the Elimination of All Forms of Racial Discrimination (CERD).[7] It is one of various forms interstate communications found in universal human rights treaties. An interstate communication,[8] in the human rights context, is a formal allegation of noncompliance with a human rights treaty submitted by one or more State-parties against another State-party, to the body competent to receive such complaints under the treaty regime.[9] Interstate communications include procedures with binding judgments, such as filing an application before the International Court of Justice (ICJ),[10] or the European Court of Human Rights. The latter is also an example of a communication in a regional human rights treaty. This contribution, however, will focus on a particular

* The article refers to the *Timor Leste/Australia* conciliation in which the author represented Timor Leste (any views expressed in the article are exclusively those of the author).

1 (signed 23 May 1969, entered into force 27 January 1980) 1155 UNTS 331.

2 (signed 10 December 1982, entered into force 16 November 1994) 1833 UNTS 397.

3 Jean-Pierre Cot, 'Conciliation' (2006) MPEPIL, paras. 7,12, 35; Nicholas Butler, 'Arbitration and Conciliation Treaties' (2006) MPEPIL, para. 9.

4 Treaty between the Democratic Republic of Timor-Leste and Australia Establishing their Maritime Boundaries in the Timor Sea (signed 6 March 2018, entered into force 30 August 2019) (2018 Timor Sea Treaty).

5 (signed 16 December 1966, entered into force 23 March 1976) 999 UNTS 171.

6 (signed 10 December 1984, entered into force 26 June 1987) 1465 UNTS 85.

7 (signed 7 march 1966, entered in to force 4 January 1969) 660 UNTS 195.

8 While this contribution will use the term 'communication', 'terminology for State complaints under human rights treaties includes 'inter-State application', 'petition', 'communication', 'complaint', and 'affaire interetatique', see Risini and Ulfstein, 'Human Rights, State Complaints' (2022) MPEPIL, para. 2 <https://opil.ouplaw.com/display/10.1093/law:epil/9780199231690/law-9780199231690-e817> accessed 30 April 2024.

9 Ibid, para. 1; Scott Leckie, 'Inter-State Complaint Procedure in International Human Rights Law: Hopeful Prospects or Wishful Thinking?' (1988) 10(2) *Human Rights Quarterly* 249.

10 CERD, Art. 22.

form of interstate communication before human rights treaty bodies, that of conciliation, which does not produce a binding result.[11]

The reasons a State may choose to submit a communication alleging human rights violations by another State may vary.[12] States may have an interest in protecting a particular group of people in another State or in protecting the common interests of the international community in the protection of human rights.[13] States may also 'weaponize' such methods for self-interest and political reasons, unrelated to the subject matter of the communication.[14] Of course, the questionable motivation does not necessarily entail that the communication is unsubstantiated.[15]

Until recently, no State had ever submitted a non-judicial interstate communication under a universal human rights treaty against another State. Presumably, even when concerned with the human rights situation in another State, States fear that such action may invite retaliatory action,[16] or jeopardize a prosperous political and economic relationship with the breaching State, while human rights take the 'back seat'.[17] States, it appears, see such interstate communications as a hostile and unfriendly act and prefer to resort to other methods of response.[18] These may also include initiating binding procedures

11 CAT, Art. 21(1)(e); ICCPR, Art. 42(1)(a); CERD, Art. 12(1)(a).

12 For an in-depth discussion of these reasons see Merryl Lawry-White, 'Inter-State Human Rights Disputes before Dispute Resolution Mechanisms: inter-state communications mechanisms under UN human rights treats an option?' (2024) 13(1) *International Human Rights Law Review*.

13 Leckie, *supra* n 9, at 256–257,297–298; Risini and Ulfstein, *supra* n 8, paras. 32–33, 76; Dai Tamada, 'Inter-State Communication under ICERD: From ad hoc Conciliation to Collective Enforcement?' (2021) *12 Journal of International Dispute Settlement* 406.

14 Leckie, *supra* n 9, at 297–298; H. Kooijmans, 'Inter-State Dispute Settlement in the Field of Human Rights' (1990) 3 *Leiden Journal of International Law* 87, 90; Kooijmans, *supra* n 14, at 87; Patrick Thornberry, 'The Committee on the Elimination of Racial Discrimination (CERD)' in Frédéric Mégret, Philip Alston (eds., 2nd edn.), *The United Nations and Human Rights: A Critical Appraisal* (OUP 2020), at 321.

15 Thornberry, 'The Committee', *supra* n 14, at 321.

16 Ibid, at 266; Risini and Ulfstein, *supra* n 8, para. 33.

17 Leckie, *supra* n 9, at 252–255; Kooijmans, *supra* n 14, at 97; see also comments made by the Netherlands during CERD negotiations, see GA, 20th session, 3rd Committee: 1356th meeting (26 November 1965) UN Doc A/C.3/SR.1355, paras. 45–46.

18 Leckie, *supra* n 9, at 266; Rosana Garciandia and Philippa Webb, 'The UN's Work on Racial Discrimination: Achievements and Challenges' (2022) 25(1) Max Planck Yearbook of United Nations Law, at 228.

before international courts, where available.[19] Ultimately, just as self-interest and political considerations may drive a State to initiate a communication, so do such factors normally inhibit such action.[20]

In 2018, however, the first three human rights interstate communications ever were initiated under the CERD.[21] A conciliation commission was established by the CERD Committee in all three. While two of these have been terminated by mutual agreement, the third communication, *Palestine v. Israel*, is ongoing.

In light of these new developments, this contribution looks at the potential of conciliation in the context of universal human rights treaties. Notwithstanding extra-legal political considerations a State may have,[22] it is prudent to assess how suited conciliation is to advance the legal objectives of interstate communications in human rights treaties and those of conciliation more broadly. The contribution also attempts to identify critical factors that may determine the success or failure of such conciliations in the human rights context. To do so, Part II will introduce conciliation as a method for the peaceful settlement of disputes, its brief history in international relations and its objectives. Part III, in turn, will introduce the features of interstate communication procedures in universal human rights treaties and their various goals. Building on the previous parts, Part IV will examine, first, the inherent structural compatibility of conciliation to fulfil the objectives of interstate communications. Second, considering lessons learnt from the successful *Timor-Leste/Australia* conciliation, it will try to identify particular factors that may contribute to the success or failure of the process. Some concluding thoughts will be shared in Part V.

---

19 *Application of the Convention against Torture and Other Cruel, Inhuman or Degrading Treatment or Punishment (Canada and the Netherlands v. Syrian Arab Republic)*, Joint Application instituting proceedings of 8 June 2023; *Application of the International Convention on the Elimination of All Forms of Racial Discrimination (Georgia v. Russian Federation), Preliminary Objections, Judgment* [2011] I.C.J. Reports 70; *Application of the International Convention for the Suppression of the Financing of Terrorism and of the International Convention on the Elimination of All Forms of Racial Discrimination (Ukraine v. Russian Federation), Preliminary Objections, Judgment,* [2019] I.C.J. Reports 558; *Application of the International Convention on the Elimination of All Forms of Racial Discrimination (Qatar v. United Arab Emirates)*, Preliminary Objections, Judgment, [2021] I.C.J. Reports 71; *Application of the International Convention on the Elimination of All Forms of Racial Discrimination (Armenia v. Azerbaijan)* of 16 September 2021; *Application of the International Convention on the Elimination of All Forms of Racial Discrimination (Azerbaijan v. Armenia)* of 23 September 2021.

20 Leckie, *supra* n 9, at 297–298.

21 Garciandia and Webb, *supra* n 18, at 226.

22 Lawry-White, *supra* n 12.

2 Conciliation in International Law

Interstate conciliation is more written about than practiced. Despite the recent *Timor-Leste/Australia* conciliation and the communications before the CERD Committee, this still holds true.

Conciliation was defined in the 1961 Resolution of the *Institut de Droit International* as –

> a method for the settlement of international disputes of any nature according to which a commission set up by the parties, either on a permanent basis or on an ad hoc basis to deal with a dispute, proceeds to the impartial examination of the dispute and attempts to define the terms of a settlement susceptible of being accepted by them, or of affording the parties, with a view to its settlement, such aid as they may have requested.[23]

Conciliation involves an element of fact-finding, after which the conciliators attempt to broker an amicable solution between the disputing parties, 'by agreement'.[24] Conciliation thus is a composite of enquiry and mediation.[25] Conciliation often has an institutional element and involves setting up a commission, making it more formalistic than good offices or mediation. The parties are sometimes represented by agents and counsel during conciliation. The process may end with a report submitted to the parties, which they can then accept or reject. The proceedings and their outcome are usually confidential and without prejudice to the legal positions of the parties.[26]

Conciliation was conceived first and foremost as a mechanism for compromise or amicable settlement of political disputes, at the expense of other aims, such as determination of State responsibility.[27] But, as Pellet

23 Institut de Droit International, *Règlement de la procédure de la conciliation internationale*, AnnIDI 49(2) (1961) 375, Art.1.

24 *Ukraine v* Russia, *supra* n 19, para. 110.

25 UN Office of Legal Affairs (Codification Division), *Handbook on the Peaceful Settlement of Disputes between States* (UN 1992), at 45; Alain Pellet, 'Peaceful Settlement of International Disputes' (2013) MPEPIL, para. 38 <https://opil.ouplaw.com/display/10.1093/law:epil/9780199231690/law-9780199231690-e70?prd=EPIL> accessed 30 April 2024.

26 Cot, *supra* n 3, para. 2.

27 Nadine Susani, 'Conciliation and Other Forms of Non-Binding Third Party Dispute Settlement' in James Crawford, Alain Pellet, Simon Olleson, Kate Parlett (eds), *The Law of International Responsibility* (OUP 2010), at 1102–1103.

notes, distinguishing between political and legal disputes is sometimes a futile process,[28] and compromise sometimes necessitates determinations of breach as the basis of an amicable solution.[29]

While more flexible, procedurally conciliation commissions resemble arbitral tribunals and the single most meaningful difference remains the inability of the commission to issue binding decisions. Conciliation is therefore a half-breed method for the settlement of disputes. It stands some way between diplomatic methods for the settlement of disputes and arbitral or judicial settlement.[30] Herein lies both the advantage and disadvantage of the procedure: on the one hand it tends to avoid legal determinations of culpability and any solution is dependent on it being acceptable to both parties. On the other hand, the non-binding result raises the question whether the arbitral-like process is useful at all.[31]

The role of the law in conciliation is somewhat ambiguous. One could argue that extra-legal solutions weaken international law, as they do not aim at ensuring strict compliance.[32] At the same time, conciliation may support the law if the conciliators give 'full weight (though not exclusive weight) to the legal rights of the parties. Indeed, in situations where the parties feel unable to commit themselves to prior acceptance of a binding award, it may be the only way to allow the law to play a useful role'.[33] Thus, conciliation can prove useful when a dispute is – at least partially – legal in nature, but the parties seek a politically accepted solution. Indeed, the little practice demonstrates that sometimes conciliation commissions had to first determine the legality of a State's actions before putting forth an acceptable solution to the parties.[34]

The introduction of compulsory conciliation in multilateral treaties, in what Cot terms codification treaties aimed at establishing common rules for a particular field of international law,[35] also serves a goal beyond the amicable

---

28 Pellet, *supra* n 25, para. 6.

29 Susani, *supra* n 27, at 1103.

30 Cot, *supra* n 3, paras. 2–3; Natalie Klein, 'Timor Sea conciliation: a harbinger of dispute settlement under UNCLOS?' in Helene Ruiz Fabri, Erik Franckx, Marco Benatar, Tamar Meshel (eds), *A bridge over troubled waters: dispute resolution in the law of international watercourses and the law of the sea* (Brill, Leiden 2020) 105–106; Kooijmans, *supra* n 14, at 89.

31 Ibid, at 1100–1102; Klein, *supra* n 30, at 105–106.

32 Susani, *supra* n 27, at 1103; Hersch Lauterpacht, *The Function of Law in the International Community* (Archon Books, Hamden 1966), at 260–269.

33 Derek Bowett, 'Contemporary developments in legal techniques in the settlement of disputes' (1983) 180 *Recueil des cours* 189–190.

34 Susani, *supra* n 27, at 1103.

35 Cot, *supra* n 3, para. 28

dispute settlement. The Commission is expected to rely – at least in part – on the relevant law of the regime and produce a record of the relevant facts and law.[36] It also introduces the possibility that a conciliation commission will need to determine its own competence, before proceeding to the merits of the dispute.[37] Though its main objective remains amicable settlement, like other dispute settlement mechanisms in such treaties, compulsory conciliation also serves to elucidate the application and interpretation of the legal regime more generally, like an advisory opinion.[38]

2.1 *The Timor-Leste/Australia Conciliation*

In 2016, Timor-Leste initiated the first ever compulsory conciliation under UNCLOS, which successfully culminated in a delimitation agreement. UNCLOS provides for three instances where compulsory conciliation can be attempted in lieu of the availability of compulsory procedures entailing binding decisions.[39]

In order to understand the commencement of conciliation by Timor-Leste and the ultimate settlement of the delimitation dispute, it is necessary to consider briefly the dispute's history.[40] The eastern half of the island of Timor (plus the enclave of Oé-Cusse Ambeno and the island of Atauro) was a Portuguese colony. The other half of the island, West Timor, belonged to the Dutch East Indies and later became part of Indonesia. In November 1975 Timor-Leste declared its independence from the colonial power Portugal but was quickly invaded and occupied by Indonesia. At that point, Australia had already concluded maritime agreements delimiting the seabed with Indonesia in the Timor Sea, leaving a 'gap' due south of Timor-Leste. Australia was the only state to recognize Indonesia's sovereignty over East Timor and, in 1989, it concluded the Timor Gap Treaty with Indonesia, establishing a Zone of Cooperation (ZOC) to exploit oil and gas in the Timor Sea. After a 1999 referendum on independence and a temporary UN administration, Timor-Leste regained its independence on 20 May 2002. On the same day, the Timor Sea Treaty between East Timor and Australia was signed. It established a Joint

---

36 Ibid, paras. 27–28.

37 Ibid, paras. 19–20.

38 Ibid, para. 28.

39 UNCLOS, *supra* n 2, Arts. 297–298.

40 The history was summarised in *Timor Sea Conciliation (Timor-Leste v Australia)*, Decision on Competence (2016) PCA Case No 2016–10, paras. 5ff; in *Timor Sea Conciliation (Timor-Leste v Australia)*, Report and recommendations of the compulsory conciliation commission between Timor-Leste and Australia on the Timor Sea (2018) PCA Case No 2016–10, paras. 8ff; and Elizabeth Exposto, 'The Timor Sea Conciliation and Treaty: Timor-Leste's Perspective', (2018) 36 *Australian Year Book of International Law Volume* 45–51.

Petroleum Development Area (JPDA) as a resource-sharing arrangement between the parties instead of the ZOC.

Just prior to, and in anticipation of, Timor-Leste's regaining of its independence, on 22 March 2002, Australia amended its acceptance of the Optional Clause under the ICJ Statute and made a declaration under Article 298(1)(a)(i) of UNCLOS precluding any recourse by Timor-Leste to the ICJ or to the binding dispute settlement mechanisms of UNCLOS for the determination of its maritime boundaries with Australia.

Negotiations over maritime boundaries between the parties did not progress. Instead, on 12 January 2006, the parties concluded the Treaty between Australia and the Democratic Republic of Timor-Leste on Certain Maritime Arrangements in the Timor Sea (CMATS), which was a revenue sharing arrangement for the Greater Sunrise oil and gas field, an area straddling the eastern limit of the JPDA. CMATS was intended to last for 50 years (and extended the lifetime of the Timor Sea Treaty to 50 years). Most relevant to the competence of the Conciliation Commission, it contained a moratorium on boundary negotiations and third-party dispute settlement of permanent maritime boundaries for its duration.

Against this backdrop, on 11 April 2016, Timor-Leste instituted the compulsory conciliation procedure against Australia over the delimitation of the Timor Sea. Australia challenged the competence of the Commission and requested to bifurcate the proceedings so as to address its competence as a preliminary issue. Timor-Leste objected to bifurcation and, at the same time, was eager to use the conciliation process as an opportunity to discuss its historic claims *vis-à-vis* Australia publicly, as would have been the case in proceedings before the ICJ. At a procedural meeting with the Commission on 28 July 2016, it was agreed that the Commission would hold a public session at which the parties could set out their positions on the dispute and its background,[41] followed by a private hearing on 29–31 August 2016 on both the question of bifurcation and on the competence question itself.[42] Afterwards, the Commission unanimously dismissed Australia's jurisdictional objections on 19 September 2016.[43] The Commission issued its final report on 9 May 2018,[44] after the parties successfully concluded a delimitation treaty on 6 March 2018,[45] in the presence of the UN Secretary-General in New York. In

41 This hearing was streamed live and publicly aired in Timor-Leste. See <https://files.pca-cpa.org/pcadocs/2016-08-28_PCA.mp4> accessed 26 October 2022.

42 *Timor Sea Conciliation*, Report, *supra* n 40, para. 36.

43 *Timor Sea Conciliation*, Competence, *supra* n 40.

44 *Timor Sea Conciliation*, Report, *supra* n 40.

45 2018 Timor Sea Treaty, *supra* n 4.

addition to establishing the maritime boundary between the parties this treaty also established a resource-sharing arrangement for Greater Sunrise.[46]

3 Interstate Communications in Human Rights Treaties

Several types of interstate communications are found in the universal human rights treaties. While they vary in form, they share common goals.

3.1 *Forms of Interstate Communications with Non-binding Outcomes in Human Rights Treaties*

Interstate communication procedures with non-binding outcomes are found in most universal human rights treaties: the CERD; the ICCPR; the CAT; the International Convention on the Protection of the Rights of All Migrant Workers and Members of Their Families (CMW);[47] the International Convention for the Protection of All Persons from Enforced Disappearance (CED);[48] the Optional Protocol to the International Covenant on Economic, Social and Cultural Rights (ICESCR);[49] and the Optional Protocol to the Convention on the Rights of the Child on a Communications Procedure (CRC).[50]

In several of these treaties, a State can file a declaration accepting the competence of the Committee to receive communications from other States that have filed similar declarations.[51] The exact procedures before the various treaty bodies are not detailed. Generally speaking, a State may bring an interstate communication before the treaty body committee against another State that has accepted its competence when, in its view, the latter State has failed to comply with its obligations under the relevant treaty, and the parties have failed to resolve the matter bilaterally.[52]

46 Ibid, Annex B, Art 7.

47 (signed 18 December 1990, entered into force 1 July 2003) 2220 UNTS 3.

48 (signed 20 December 2006, entered into force 23 December 2010) 2716 UNTS 3.

49 (signed 10 December 2008, entered into force 5 May 2013) 2922 UNTS 29.

50 (signed 19 December 2011, entered into force 14 April 2014) A/RES/66/138.

51 Optional Protocol to the CRC, Art. 12; ICCPR Art. 41; Optional Protocol to the ICESCR, Art. 10; CMW, Art. 76; CED, Art. 32.

52 No such requirement in CERD, see Art. 11(1), although the Committee initially acts as an intermediary and only considers the substance of the communication after the State parties fail to reach an agreed solution within a six months period, see Art. 11(2); see also Michał Balcerzak, 'Special character of human rights obligations and the jurisdiction of the Committee on the Elimination of Racial Discrimination in the Palestine v. Israel case' (2020) 40 *Polish Yearbook of International Law* 97.

The CAT, ICCPR and CERD also provide for the possibility of conciliation. Under the CAT, the Committee can set up a compulsory ad hoc conciliation commission, without the prior consent of the parties.[53] Under the ICCPR, the Human Rights Committee (HRC) may initiate conciliation proceedings, but only with the consent of the parties.[54]

Under CERD, the Committee may establish a compulsory conciliation commission regarding an interstate communication without the States' prior consent.[55] After the Committee obtains the relevant information from the parties, the Chairman 'shall appoint an ad hoc Conciliation Commission'.[56] The CERD then provides the process for appointment of the conciliators,[57] the place of meetings[58] and that the commission can adopt its own rules of procedure.[59] The costs of the conciliation are to be borne equally by the parties.[60] Confidentiality is not mentioned with respect to proceedings under CERD. The Rules of Procedure adopted by the conciliation commission in *Palestine v. Israel* do stipulate, however, that the process will be confidential.[61] The CERD stipulates that the final report be circulated to all parties to the CERD, suggesting that it will also be made public.[62]

The conciliation provisions in both the ICCPR and CERD do not refer expressly to legal findings in the final report.[63] The CERD, for example, refers to 'findings on all questions of fact relevant to the issue between the parties and containing such recommendations as it [the conciliation commission] may think proper for the amicable solution of the dispute'.[64] While some read

53 CAT, Art. 21(1)(e). Though the States must have accepted the general competence of the Committee.

54 Art. 42(1)(a).

55 Art. 12(1)(a).

56 Ibid.

57 Art. 12(1).

58 Art. 12(1)(b)(4).

59 Art. 12(1)(b)(3); see also ICCPR, Art. 42.

60 ICCPR, Art. 42(12); CERD, Art. 12(1)(b)(6).

61 CERD Committee, Rules of Procedure regarding the hearings carried out pursuant to Article 11 (2019), reproduced in Report of the Committee on the Elimination of Racial Discrimination, (2019) UN Doc A/74/18, Annex II, Rule 5 (2019 RoP); CERD Committee, Inter-State communication submitted by the State of Palestine against Israel: Rules of Procedure (2022 RoP) (25 April 2022) UN Doc CERD/C/105/DR/59/2016/Rev.1, Rule 16.

62 CERD, Art. 13(3); CERD Committee, 2019 RoP, *supra* n 61, rules of procedure 35(2).

63 Risini and Ulfstein, *supra* n 8, para. 60.

64 Art. 13(1); see also CERD Committee, RoP, *supra* n 61, Rule 19.

this to exclude findings of breach by States,[65] others find that interpretation too restrictive.[66]

3.2 *The Objectives of Interstate Communications*

The treaty bodies' main objective is to incentivize and encourage compliance by States.[67] Compliance is also an objective specific to interstate communications, as can be seen by the drafting history.[68] In addition, the drafters viewed interstate communications as encompassing a collective responsibility of the international community to ensure rights are protected.[69] Today, some human rights are viewed as *erga omnes* obligations, that all States have an interest in ensuring compliance with.[70]

Interstate communications could also serve to ensure that non-complying States are held accountable for their human rights violations.[71] For the complaining State, as noted by the CERD, the interstate communication procedure is a 'procedural means available to States for drawing to the attention of the Committee situations in which they consider that some other State is not giving effect to the provisions of the Convention'.[72]

The text of the human rights treaties establishes that interstate communications are a way to assist State parties to amicably settle their disputes, in their interest as well as the interest of all parties to a treaty.[73] The CERD, for example, views the role of the conciliation commission as making

65 Risini and Ulfstein, *supra* n 8, para. 60.

66 David Keane, 'Towards an 'Amicable Solution' in the Universal Human Rights System: Inter-State Communications under the International Convention on the Elimination of Racial Discrimination' (Völkerrechtsblog, 28 April 2021) <https://voelkerrechtsblog.org/towards-an-amicable-solution-in-the-universal-human-rights-system/> accessed 30 April 2024, doi: 10.17176/20210428-100917-0.; Balcerzak, *supra* n 52, at 99.

67 David Keane, 'Mapping the International Convention on the Elimination of All Forms of Racial Discrimination as a Living Instrument' (2020) 20(2) *Human Rights Law Review* 253.

68 E.g., GA, 20th session, 3rd Committee: 1347th meeting (18 November 1965) A/C.3/SR.1347, paras. 33, 60, 75; GA, Draft International Covenants on Human Rights (13 December 1966) A/6546, paras. 181–183.

69 GA, A/C.3/SR.1347, *supra* n 68, para. 27; see also CERD Committee, Inter-State communication submitted by the State of Palestine against Israel: Jurisdiction of the Committee (12 December 2019) UN Doc CERD/C/100/5, para. 3.41; Tamada, *supra* n 13, at 423.

70 HRC, General Comment No 31(80): Nature of the General Legal Obligation Imposed on States Parties to the Covenant (26 May 2004) CCPR/C/21/Rev.1/Add.13, para. 2.

71 Balcerzak, *supra* n 52, at 96.

72 CERD Committee, General Recommendation 16 (1993) UN Doc INT/CERD/GEC/7488/E; see also Patrick Thornberry, *The International Convention on the Elimination of All Forms of Racial Discrimination: A Commentary* (OUP 2016) 55–56.

73 CERD Committee, CERD/C/100/5, *supra* n 69, paras. 3.41–3.42.

its 'good offices ... available to the States concerned with a view to an amicable solution of the matter on the basis of respect for this Convention'.[74] This is further supported by the negotiating history.[75] The ICJ in *Ukraine v Russia* stated that the objective of conciliation under CERD is amicable dispute settlement.[76] Moreover, the Court drew a parallel between conciliation under CERD and bilateral negotiations as 'two means to achieve the same objective, namely to settle a dispute by agreement'.[77] Similarly, the CERD Committee has opined that the procedure is 'conciliatory, opposite to adversarial ... it should be practical, constructive and effective'.[78]

It is worth noting that it is possible that the balance between the objectives of interstate communications in general may vary between particular treaties.[79] The CERD Committee, for example, viewed the automaticity and compulsory nature of the CERD's communication procedure as an indication of 'a stronger desire of the drafters of the Convention to set up protective measures to ensure that the provisions of the Convention are adequately observed and complied with by all States parties'.[80] Confidentiality of procedures, on the other hand, may be an indicator of emphasis on dispute settlement.[81]

Finally, as the practice of individual communications under human rights treaties demonstrates, the utilization of the interstate communication mechanisms may potentially contribute to the development of human rights law via interpretation and application.[82] At the same time, the recent conflicting views of the ICJ and the CERD Committee on the interpretation of CERD also raise issues of coherence and fragmentation.[83]

3.3 *Conciliation Practice Under the CERD*

On 8 March 2018, Qatar submitted the first ever interstate communications under a universal human rights treaty, by submitting two communications

74 CERD, Art. 12 (1)(a); see also ICCPR, Art. 42(1)(a); CAT, Art. 21(1)(e).

75 E.g., GA, 20th session, 3rd Committee: 1354th meeting (25 November 1965) A/C.3/SR.1354, paras. 48–49.

76 *Ukraine v. Russia, supra* n 19, para. 110; Tamada, *supra* n 13, at 415–416.

77 *Ukraine v. Russia, supra* n 19, para. 110; see also Tamada, *supra* n 13, at 415, 424.

78 CERD Committee, CERD/C/100/5, *supra* n 69, paras. 3.41, 3.50.

79 Balcerzak, *supra* n 52, at 105.

80 CERD Committee, CERD/C/100/5, *supra* n 69, pp. 10–11.

81 Jan Eiken, David Keane, 'Towards an Amicable Solution: The Inter-State Communications Procedure under ICERD' (2022) 21 *The Law and Practice of International Courts and Tribunals* 307.

82 Keane, 'Mapping', *supra* n 67, at 236–268, 253–254.

83 Geir Ulfstein, 'Who is the Final Interpreter in Human Rights: the ICJ v CERD?' (EJILTalk!, 22 February 2021) <https://www.ejiltalk.org/who-is-the-final-interpreter-in-human-rights-the-icj-v-cerd/> accessed 15 May 2023.

to the CERD Committee, against Saudi Arabia and the UAE, alleging that they had taken discriminatory actions against Qatari citizens, based on their nationality.[84] Qatar then submitted an Application before the ICJ under Art. 22 of the CERD against the UAE on 11 June 2018.[85] Against the opposition of the respondents, on 27 August 2019, the Committee decided that it has jurisdiction over the communications,[86] and that they are admissible.[87] The Committee concluded that differential treatment based on the nationality of legal persons can amount to racial discrimination,[88] and that the requirement of the exhaustion of local remedies does not have to be met when a 'generalized policy and practice' has been authorized.[89]

The Committee went on to establish conciliation commissions, with the cooperation of the parties, in both matters. Following the Al Ula Agreement between the parties – which included a provision to suspend all international proceedings – Qatar requested the suspension of both proceedings. The proceedings were accordingly suspended[90] and eventually terminated,[91] before the merits of the communications were determined.

In another submission, Palestine filed a communication against Israel on 23 April 2018, alleging violations of the CERD with regard to Palestinian citizens

84 See CERD Committee, Jurisdiction of the Inter-State communication submitted by Qatar against the United Arab Emirates (27 August 2019) UN Doc CERD/C/99/3; Decision on the jurisdiction of the Committee in respect of the inter-State communication submitted by Qatar against Saudi Arabia (27 August 2019) UN Doc CERD/C/99/5.

85 Saudi Arabia made a reservation on the ICJ'S jurisdiction under CERD, Art. 22.

86 CERD Committee, CERD/C/99/3, *supra* n 84, para. 60; CERD/C/99/5, *supra* n 84, para. 53.

87 CERD Committee, Admissibility of the inter-State communication submitted by Qatar against the United Arab Emirates (27 August 2019) UN Doc CERD/C/99/4; Decision on the admissibility of the inter-State communication submitted by Qatar against Saudi Arabia (27 August 2019) UN Doc CERD/C/99/6.

88 CERD Committee, CERD/C/99/4, *supra* n 87, para. 60–63; CERD/C/99/6, *supra* n 87, paras. 16–19; The ICJ rejected this view and reached the opposite conclusion see, *Qatar v. United Arab Emirates, supra* n 19, para. 71.

89 CERD Committee, CERD/C/99/4, *supra* n 87, para. 40.

90 Decision of the ad hoc Conciliation Commission on the request for suspension submitted by Qatar concerning the interstate communication Qatar v. the United Arab Emirates (5 March 2021) UN Doc INT_CERD_ISC_9381_E; Decision of the ad hoc Conciliation Commission on the request for suspension submitted by Qatar concerning the interstate communication Qatar v. the Kingdom of Saudi Arabia (5 March 2021) UN Doc INT_CERD_ISC_9382_E.

91 OHCHR, Qatar against United Arab Emirates: UN ad hoc Conciliation Commission terminates operation, 2 February 2023, <https://www.ohchr.org/en/press-releases/2023/02/qatar-against-united-arab-emirates-un-ad-hoc-conciliation-commission> accessed 30 April 2024.

living in the Occupied Palestinian Territory, including East Jerusalem.[92] Israel asserted that the Committee lacks jurisdiction to entertain the communication as there are no treaty relations between Israel and Palestine under the CERD.[93] (Upon Palestine's accession in 2014, Israel filed a declaration stating that it does not recognize Palestine and considers its 'request for accession as being without legal validity and without effect upon Israel's treaty relations under the Convention').[94] To assess this argument, the Committee requested advise from the UN Office of legal Affairs (OLA). The OLA memorandum, determined that by its statement, Israel excluded the existence of treaty relations, i.e., the creation of rights and obligations under the CERD – including the communication procedures – with Palestine. Therefore, OLA concluded, the CERD Committee did not have competence to entertain the communication.[95]

Disagreeing with Israel's position and OLA's assessment, on 12 December 2019, the Committee concluded that it had jurisdiction to proceed with the communication.[96] The decision was adopted with 10 votes in favor, three votes against, two abstentions, and one member not present.[97] The Committee acknowledged that 'under general international treaty law, a State party to a multilateral treaty may exclude treaty relations with an entity it does not recognize',[98] but added that 'certain treaty regimes, due to their particular character, may depart from those general principles'.[99] The Committee also considered that human rights, including racial discrimination, are of *erga omnes* character and that the latter is also a *jus cogens* norm.[100] While bypassing an ultimate decision on the existence of treaty relations between the parties,[101] it concluded that

> given the nature of racial discrimination and, consequently, of the obligations contained in the Convention that are subject to a collective

92 CERD Committee, CERD/C/100/5, *supra* n 69.
93 CERD Committee, CERD/C/100/5, *supra* n 69, paras. 2.12–2.16.
94 UN OLA, Transmission of the content of OLA Memorandum at the request of the Committee on the Elimination of Racial Discrimination (23 August 2019) UN Doc OLA INT_CERD_ISC_9360_E, para. 5.
95 UN OLA, *supra* n 94, para. 69.
96 CERD Committee, CERD/C/100/5, *supra* n 69.
97 To date, there has been only one other instance of a non-consensual decision of the Committee, see Keane, 'Mapping', *supra* n 67, at 236–268, 264–265.
98 CERD Committee, CERD/C/100/5, *supra* n 69, para. 3.13.
99 Ibid.
100 Ibid, at 7–10.
101 Balcerzak, *supra* n 52, at 421–422.

> guarantee and enforcement, a State party cannot bar another State party, through a unilateral action, from triggering an enforcement mechanism created by the Convention.[102]

The Committee added that conciliation under CERD is compulsory for all State parties.[103] It is triggered by one State party against another and Palestine and Israel are both parties to CERD, fulfilling the condition.[104] Finally, given the conciliatory nature of the mechanism, the Committee considered it should not take a formalistic approach towards its jurisdiction or block the possibility of agreement.[105]

Five members of the Committee adjoined a joint opinion, which essentially accepted OLA's position that the Committee cannot entertain the communication, noting that the majority position goes against the 'very essence of treaty law', and that the *erga omnes* or *jus cogens* character of certain rights cannot overcome the existing jurisdictional barrier.[106]

Israel also made admissibility arguments, mainly that Palestine had not met the requirement of exhaustion of local remedies. On 30 April 2021, the Committee rejected Israel's claims. Similar to its previous admissibility decisions above, it stated that exhaustion of local remedies does not apply in cases of a generalized policy, which are demonstrated by 'a repetition of acts and official tolerance'.[107] The Committee concluded that these have *prima facie* been demonstrated, basing itself on its own observations with respect to Israel's previous periodic reports.[108]

Israel in response criticized the Committee, stating that it 'has decided to apply a separate standard to Israel, and disregard both facts and law to reach a predetermined and agenda driven conclusion' and that 'Israel cannot expect to receive fair and non-discriminatory treatment from this body, and will conduct its relations with it accordingly'.[109] In an official statement, the US then Permanent Representative in Geneva stated that the decision showed 'disregard for treaty law [and] raises serious questions about the legitimacy of

102 CERD Committee, CERD/C/100/5, *supra* n 69, para. 3.37.

103 Ibid, para. 3.39.

104 Ibid, para. 3.40.

105 Ibid, para. 3.41.

106 Ibid, paras. 3.41–3.42.

107 CERD Committee, Inter-State communication submitted by the State of Palestine against Israel: decision on admissibility (30 April 2021) CERD/C/103/4, para. 62.

108 Ibid, para. 64.

109 Mission of Israel to the UN in Geneva, *Israel Reaction to CERD Decision on Admissibility*, 3 May 2021, <https://embassies.gov.il/UnGeneva/NewsAndEvents/MediaStatements/Pages/20210503-Israel-Reaction-to-CERD-Decision-on-.aspx> accessed 30 April 2024.

this process'.[110] At the same time, several writers have expressed support for the decision.[111]

The CERD Committee then proceeded to establish a conciliation commission. The five commission members – all members of the Committee – were appointed by vote in the Committee in accordance with article 12(1)(b), as no agreement was reached between the parties.[112] The Committee adopted its Rules of Procedure during its meetings on 19 January and 10 February 2022,[113] and at present the Committee continues its work, without Israel's participation.

4 What can Conciliation Offer Human Rights? Structural and Practical Considerations

Having regard to the nature and aims of interstate conciliation, this section will first assess the potential suitability of interstate conciliation to fulfil the goals of interstate communications, in principle. Then, it will examine what factors may determine the success or failure of interstate conciliation in the human rights context, in light of the *Timor-Leste/Australia* conciliation and *Palestine v. Israel*.

110 US Mission to International organizations in Geneva, *Statement on the decision of CERD regarding jurisdiction over an inter-state communication against Israel*, 6 January 2020, <https://geneva.usmission.gov/2020/01/06/statement-on-the-decision-of-cerd-regarding-jurisdiction-over-an-inter-state-communication-against-israel/> accessed 30 April 2024.

111 Eiken, Keane, *supra* n 81, at 315; Jan Eiken, 'Breaking new ground? The CERD Committee's decision on jurisdiction in the inter-State communications procedure between Palestine and Israel' (*EJIL:Talk!*, 29 January 2020) <https://www.ejiltalk.org/breaking-new-ground-the-cerd-committees-decision-on-jurisdiction-in-the-inter-state-communications-procedure-between-palestine-and-israel/> accessed 30 April 2024; Nora Salem, 'A Procedural Win in Palestine's Quest to Seek Justice for Israel's Apartheid Regime before the CERD' (*Opinio Juris*, 19 November 2021) <https://opiniojuris.org/2021/11/19/a-procedural-win-in-palestines-quest-to-seek-justice-for-israels-apartheid-regime-before-the-cerd/> accessed 30 April 2024; Balcerzak, *supra* n 52.

112 UN Committee on the Elimination of Racial Discrimination (CERD) Sets Up Ad Hoc Conciliation Commission – Press Release, 17 February 2022 <https://www.un.org/unispal/document/un-committee-on-the-elimination-of-racial-discrimination-cerd-sets-up-ad-hoc-conciliation-commission-press-release/> accessed 30 April 2024.

113 CERD Committee, RoP, *supra* n 61.

4.1 *Conciliation and interstate communications: structural compatibility*

Conciliation is first and foremost a process geared towards amicable resolution, an objective shared with interstate communications. As discussed below, achieving this goal is largely dependent on the will and interests of the parties in reaching such resolution.

Interstate communications before treaty bodies are also intended to promote compliance with human rights.[114] The CERD, for example, states that the settlement reached with the assistance of the conciliation commission should be 'on the basis of respect for this Convention'.[115] In its decision on jurisdiction in *Palestine v. Israel*, the CERD Committee opined that the compulsory nature of the procedure indicates a stronger emphasis on ensuring compliance than in other interstate communication procedures.[116]

A question may arise regarding the consequences of an amicable solution on compliance with human rights norms. If compliance with human rights ultimately depends on the will of States, a process that results in an agreed solution may promote compliance, particularly in a dispute that addresses structural incompatibilities, rather than a single violation.[117] In *Timor-Leste/Australia*, the agreement was viewed as 'an equitable solution consistent with those [UNCLOS'] legal provisions'.[118] The Commission noted that a "conciliation commission should not encourage parties to reach an agreement that it considers to be inconsistent with the Convention [UNCLOS] or other provisions of international law".[119] That said, it viewed its role in the following terms:

> The function of a commission is to assist the parties to reach an amicable settlement, not to pronounce for its own sake on questions of international law, and the Commission has frequently noted that it is not

---

114 Eiken, Keane, *supra* n 81, at 314–315.

115 Article 12(1)(a).

116 CERD Committee, CERD/C/100/5, *supra* n 69, paras. 3.38–3.39.

117 Helen Keller and Réka Piskóty, 'Friendly Settlements as the Sleeping Beauty in Inter-State Cases: Opportunities and Risks for the European Court of Human Rights' (*Völkerrechtsblog*, 28 April 2021) <https://voelkerrechtsblog.org/friendly-settlements-as-the-sleeping-beauty-in-inter-state-cases/> accessed 30 April 2024, doi: 10.17176/20210428-181222-0; Nicola Wenzel, 'Rethinking Friendly Settlements under the European Convention on Human Rights: Why We Should Design a New Friendly Settlement Procedure for Inter-State Cases', *Völkerrechtsblog*, 28 April 2021) <https://voelkerrechtsblog.org/rethinking-friendly-settlements-under-the-echr/> accessed 30 April 2024, doi: 10.17176/20210428-180705-0.; Garciandia and Webb, *supra* n 18, at 228.

118 *Timor Sea Conciliation*, Report, *supra* n 40, para. 291.

119 Ibid, para. 70.

> an arbitral tribunal with the power to make a binding ruling. It follows, for the Commission, that a conciliation commission need not as a matter of course engage with the parties on their legal positions, but may engage with these matters to the extent that so doing will likely facilitate the achievement of an amicable settlement.[120]

In practice, the Conciliation Commission did not take any strong positions on the law and encouraged the parties to abandon their legal positions as a necessary step for reaching a settlement.[121]

This may seem contradictory, but it is not. States are generally free under UNCLOS to settle their boundaries in any manner they choose, and thus the agreement reached in *Timor-Leste/Australia* can be said to reflect an equitable solution. Rarely can a delimitation agreement be seen as contrary to the law, if at all.

However, human rights law is not like other bodies of law: respect for human rights is non-negotiable.[122] But a compromise solution reached between two States regarding the observance of human rights may deviate from the standards set in the relevant treaty. Indeed, such settlements in the European context have been heavily criticized for this reason,[123] and the point was also made during the CERD negotiations.[124]

Eiken and Keane argue that a CERD conciliation commission must exercise oversight to ensure that an amicable solution reached is on the 'basis of respect for this Convention', in accordance with CERD Art. 12(1)(a).[125] And surely the conciliation commission can urge the parties to do so. But if the parties reach a compromise that does not conform to the CERD, what can the conciliators do? There does not seem to be a basis in the text of CERD for their report to criticise an amicable solution reached. Even if they did so, it is unlikely that the parties will reopen their agreement. Ultimately, a conciliation commission is powerless in this regard. Thus, in a legal regime where States are not free to diverge from the default rules, such as human rights, compromise solutions may undermine rather than uphold legal standards.

---

120 Ibid.

121 Ibid, paras. 64, 296.

122 Kooijmans, *supra* n 14, at 89–90.

123 Ibid; Risini and Ulfstein, *supra* n 8, para. 61; Keller and Piskóty, *supra* n 117; Already in the drafting of ICERD, the limits of conciliation were noted. Waldron-Ramsey (Tanzania) commented in the Third Committee: 'Conciliation ... was not particularly appropriate to the subject of the Convention.' (para 41).

124 GA, 20th session, 3rd Committee: 1346th meeting (17 November 1965) A/C.3/SR.1346, para. 41.

125 Eiken, Keane, *supra* n 81, at 330–332.

With respect to State responsibility, conciliation commissions have in the past made findings of fact and law, establishing a State's responsibility, for example as part of a process to find an agreed form of reparations.[126] Under UNCLOS, for example, findings on facts *and law* are to be included in the conciliation commission's final report. The conciliation provisions in both the ICCPR and CERD do not refer expressly to legal findings, being more focused on reaching an amicable solution.[127] Under CERD, the Committee may make 'findings on all questions of fact relevant to the issue between the parties and containing such recommendations as it may think proper for the amicable solution of the dispute'.[128] As noted above, views differ whether the mandate of the conciliation under CERD includes findings of breach;[129] and without breach, there cannot be State responsibility.[130] Furthermore, legal pronouncements are also critical to the extent that conciliation is also to contribute to human rights through interpretation and application.

In *Palestine v. Israel*, the Commission's Rules of Procedure refer both to the 'statement of facts' and 'findings of fact', perhaps indicating that the latter are also normative in nature.[131] Furthermore, the Rules give the Commission the 'power to interpret the provisions of the Convention'.[132] That the final report of a conciliation commission under CERD will likely become public, may also contribute to upholding State responsibility.[133]

Of course, regardless of how effective conciliation is to hold States accountable for human rights violations, at times it may be the only tool available, whether because the party in question has not consented to procedures with binding rulings or they are otherwise unavailable.[134] A State without better options may choose to initiate compulsory conciliation under CERD to push for findings of breach and consequent State responsibility, even if such recourse is limited in its effectiveness.

---

126 Susani, *supra* n 27, at 1103.

127 Risini and Ulfstein, *supra* n 8, para. 60.

128 Art. 13(1); see also CERD Committee, RoP, *supra* n 61, Rule 19.

129 See *supra* Part 3.

130 International Law Commission, Draft Articles on the Responsibility of States for Internationally Wrongful Acts, Yearbook of the International Law Commission, 2001, vol. II (Part Two), Art. 2.

131 CERD Committee, RoP, *supra* n 61; see also Eiken, Keane, *supra* n 81, at 337.

132 Ibid, Rule 1(3).

133 Eiken, Keane, *supra* n 81, at 307.

134 Such as by filing a reservation on the jurisdiction of the ICJ under the relevant treaty (like Saudi Arabia and Israel). See Veronica Botticelli, 'Making Something Out of (Almost) Nothing? Inter-State Human Rights Communications as Narrow Gateways for China's Accountability in the Xinjiang's Crisis' (2024) 13(1) *International Human Rights Law Review*.

∴

The above demonstrates that, from a structural standpoint, the compatibility of conciliation with the objectives of interstate communications cannot be answered in the abstract. The answer is dependent on the objectives being sought by the conciliation, which may differ in each instance.

4.2 *When Will Conciliation Succeed? Lessons from the Recent Past*

As just demonstrated, what a 'successful' conciliation entails in the human rights context is dependent on the objective sought. In addition to the inherent structural difficulties, there may be case-specific factors that may contribute or inhibit a 'successful' outcome. Some of these will be explored below, drawing on the dynamics that contributed to reaching an amicable solution in *Timor-Leste/Australia* and comparing those to the conciliations under CERD, particularly the pending *Palestine v. Israel* conciliation.

4.2.1 Flexibility and Versatility

The Conciliation Commission in *Timor-Leste/Australia* took a flexible and versatile approach towards its task, reflected in how it conducted the proceedings. For one, it held an extraordinary public hearing before it considered its competence, in order to satisfy Timor-Leste's desire to assert publicly its position.[135] On the other hand, the Commission also decided to hear arguments on bifurcation at the same time it heard arguments on its competence, thus *de facto* granting Australia's request to consider the Commission's competence separately from the merits. The hearing and the consequent Decision on Competence, in virtually all respects, were not dissimilar to the comparable stages in arbitral practice.[136] While not entirely free of criticism,[137] the Decision on Competence was unanimous (including the Australian-appointed conciliators),[138] members of the Commission were all legal experts in the

135 Exposto, *supra* n 40, at 52.

136 Gary Quinlan, 'Perspective of Australia' in Hao Duy Phan, Tara Davenport, Robert Beckman (eds), *The Timor-Leste/Australia conciliation: a victory for UNCLOS and peaceful settlement of disputes* (World Scientific, Singapore 2019), at 184–185.

137 Klein, *supra* n 30, at 116–122.

138 S Jayakumar, 'Compulsory dispute settlement and conciliation under UNCLOS' in Hao Duy Phan, Tara Davenport, Robert Beckman (eds), *The Timor-Leste/Australia conciliation: a victory for UNCLOS and peaceful settlement of disputes* (World Scientific, Singapore 2019), at 28.

field[139] and their Decision was based on mainstream application of treaty law and consistent with trends in UNCLOS jurisprudence,[140] giving it a degree of credibility.

Once the Commission established its competence and started its consideration of the substance of the dispute, its procedures became more flexible, and diverged from the legalistic model.[141] Its Rules of Procedure stated that it could conduct the proceedings 'as it considers appropriate',[142] and that flexibility was demonstrated throughout. Between July 2016 and February 2018 the Commission held nine 'formal' meetings with the parties, in various locations, including The Hague, Singapore, Copenhagen and Washington, DC.[143] Mostly, the Commission engaged bilaterally with each delegation during these meetings.[144] At times, the Commission met with both parties for a joint session.[145] In addition to these 'formal' occasions, there were constant 'informal' contacts between the parties and the Commission or some of its members. Throughout the process, the Commissioners engaged with the parties and made themselves available: they travelled across Timor-Leste and Australia to meet with key decision-makers and gain a first-hand impression of the issues underlying the dispute.[146] The Commission commented on the variety and modality of these meetings and how they were integral to reaching the final agreement:

> The Commission sought to engage with the Parties' representatives through formal and informal sessions, through conversations at the political level and working level, and through a nearly continuous flow of letters, e-mail communications, telephone calls, and text messages. The Commission also made extensive use of its Registry as an additional channel of communication with the Parties and to record and share within the Commission the details of informal contacts and conversations.

139 Quinlan, *supra* n 136, at 183–184.

140 Klein, *supra* n 30, at 122.

141 Ibid, at 184–185, 195.

142 *Timor Sea Conciliation*, Report, *supra* n 40, Annex 8, Rule 10; Robert Beckman, 'Composition of the Conciliation Commission and its role' in Hao Duy Phan, Tara Davenport, Robert Beckman (eds), *The Timor-Leste/Australia conciliation: a victory for UNCLOS and peaceful settlement of disputes* (World Scientific, Singapore 2019), at 58–60.

143 *Timor Sea Conciliation*, Report, *supra* n 40, paras. 36–92.

144 Ibid.

145 Ibid.

146 Ibid; Agio Pereira, 'Perspective of Timor-Leste' in Hao Duy Phan, Tara Davenport, Robert Beckman (eds), *The Timor-Leste/Australia conciliation: a victory for UNCLOS and peaceful settlement of disputes* (World Scientific, Singapore 2019), at 165.

> Many of the principal steps that were instrumental to bringing the Parties together occurred as much in late night conversations with various members of each delegation as in any formal meeting.[147]

Ultimately, all methods of communication were used, essentially at the discretion of what the Commission saw fit to successfully bring the parties together.[148]

In the three communications submitted under CERD, as in *Timor-Leste/Australia*, the Committee first dealt with the legal arguments of the parties concerning competence, before establishing the Conciliation Commission, similarly differentiating between 'legal' issues of competence and the substantive conciliation process, as prescribed in CERD Article 11. On the other hand, in its Decision on Jurisdiction in *Palestine v. Israel*, the Committee seemed to conflate conciliation before a CERD conciliation commission with preliminary matters of competence, when it considered that conciliation 'should be practical, constructive and effective' and, therefore, the Committee should not adopt a 'formalistic approach' to its jurisdiction.[149] This, despite the fact that jurisdiction is procedural by nature and despite the fact that the CERD creates a clear dichotomy between competence (a matter for the Committee) and the merits (a matter for the conciliation commission).

The Rules of Procedure in *Palestine v. Israel* state that the meetings will be held in Geneva, or any other location determined by the Conciliation Commission.[150] They also state that the Commission 'may' invite the parties to appoint representatives to attend its meetings, and that communication will be through the representatives of the parties in Geneva, and may be oral or in writing, separately or together.[151] Thus far, the Commission has met in Geneva to discuss preliminary issues.[152] On the face of it, the procedures of the CERD Commission seem more rigid than in *Timor-Leste/Australia*, although the Rules of Procedure do allow for some flexibility.[153]

147 *Timor Sea Conciliation*, Report, *supra* n 40, para. 295; see also Quinlan, *supra* n 136, at 184–185.
148 See also Quinlan, *supra* n 136, at 187–188; Exposto, *supra* n 40, 54.
149 CERD Committee, CERD/C/100/5, *supra* n 69, para. 3.41.
150 CERD Committee, RoP, *supra* n 61, Rule 6.
151 Ibid, Rules 13–14.
152 UN, State of Palestine against Israel: Conciliation Commission Holds First In-person Meeting, 6 May 2022, <https://www.un.org/unispal/document/state-of-palestine-against-israel-conciliation-commission-holds-first-in-person-meeting/> accessed 30 April 2024.
153 Garciandia and Webb, *supra* n 18, at 227–228.

4.2.2 Intensity and Proactivity

On top of versatility, the above also demonstrates a second feature in *Timor-Leste/Australia*, that is the intensity of the conciliation, reflected in the high number of formal and informal encounters during the process.[154] The intense level of engagement, though somewhat dictated by the 12 month timeframe given in UNCLOS for the process (which was exceeded with the agreement of the parties), was a direct result of the proactive approach of the Commission.[155] This activism was reflected both in the pace of the proceedings but also in their substance: the Commission regularly put forward papers and came up with suggestions for interim and final resolution as well as confidence building measures, purposely pushing the parties from their original positions.[156] As most meetings were held separately with each party, at most points only the Commission had full knowledge of the wider picture, giving a sense that it was the Commission that was in charge and leading the process.

Under CERD there is no set timeframe for the process, and the Commission's Rules state that the process will be completed 'within a reasonable time'.[157] At the time of writing, the *Palestine v. Israel* case was in its fifth year. Furthermore, though only time will tell, the CERD conciliation process seems more passive in nature. UNCLOS itself envisions a proactive process, as a conciliation commission is to 'hear the parties, examine their claims and objections, and make proposals to the parties with a view to reaching an amicable settlement'.[158] A CERD commission's mandate, on the hand, is to provide 'good offices' to the parties for amicable settlement and later on consider the matter based on the information provided, and making recommendations in its final report.[159]

4.2.3 Scope of the Dispute

A significant contributor to the success in *Timor-Leste/Australia* was that the Commission was able to learn and consider the interests of the parties and the motivations behind their legal positions on delimitation.[160] The Commission also allowed Timor-Leste, for example, to air its historical narrative publicly, which contributed to its trust in the Commission and the process.[161] Later

154 Exposto, *supra* n 40, at 54.
155 Quinlan, *supra* n 136, at 184; Jayakumar, *supra* n 138, at 22.
156 E.g., para. 293; Quinlan, *supra* n 136, at 187, 195.
157 CERD Committee, RoP, *supra* n 61, Rule 1(4).
158 UNCLOS, *supra* n 2, Annex V, Art. 6.
159 CERD Committee, RoP, *supra* n 61, Rules 2, 19.
160 On seeking to understand the underlying interests see Beckman, *supra* n 142, at 66–68.
161 Pereira, *supra* n 146, at 140, 156–158.

on, the Commission considered that in order to resolve the legal question of delimitation:

> [I]t proved essential that the Commission's mandate extended to the consideration of the Parties' broader, non-legal interests to the extent necessary for an amicable settlement. It became apparent to the Commission that any agreed outcome would also have to address in a comprehensive manner the development and exploitation of resources in the area and the Parties' respective rights and status.[162]

At the same time, the Commission did not set out to exercise its mandate on all issues dividing the parties. After a maritime boundary and resource-sharing scheme was agreed, the Commission did not take it upon itself to decide on the 'development concept' of the Greater Sunrise Special Regime, which would have entailed determining to which state's coastline the pipeline would be assigned, a matter that divided the parties.[163] Indeed, UNCLOS grants a conciliation commission the mandate to refer to 'any measures which might facilitate an amicable settlement of the dispute', supposedly including measures outside of the law on delimitation.[164]

Such flexibility on the scope of the dispute does not seem to exist in a human rights conciliation, where the subject matter is limited to rights under the treaty. In both the Qatar cases and *Palestine v. Israel*, the subject matter relates to rights under the treaty, but in the context of broader political and legal disagreements which do not fall within the mandate of a CERD conciliation commission.

4.2.4 Abandoning Legal Positions

Similarly, the success in *Timor-Leste/Australia* was a function of the Commission engaging on the law only to the extent necessary to reach an amicable solution, and urging the parties to move on from their legal positions as 'a mutually acceptable outcome' requires compromise.[165] While stating that it should not present the parties with suggestions that are contrary to the law, it emphasised that its task was 'to assist the parties to reach an amicable settlement, not to

162 *Timor Sea Conciliation*, Report, *supra* n 40, para. 291; Quinlan, *supra* n 136, at 188–189, 195; Pereira, *supra* n 146, at 139–140, 172; Jayakumar, *supra* n 138, at 22–23.

163 *Timor Sea Conciliation*, Report, *supra* n 40, paras. 217, 297.

164 UNCLOS, *supra* n 2, Annex V, Article 5; Beckman, *supra* n 142, at 57–58.

165 *Timor Sea Conciliation*, Report, *supra* n 40, paras. 70, 296; Beckman, *supra* n 142, at 64; Klein, *supra* n 30, at 135–136.

pronounce for its own sake on questions of international law'.[166] As noted by the Timorese Agent to the conciliation, the Commission hammered the message that 'notwithstanding the letter of the law, conciliation is not about which party is right or wrong', but rather it is a 'give and take' geared towards reaching an 'effective outcome'.[167]

As explained above, within the law of the sea, going beyond default rules ('the letter of the law') is unlikely to produce an amicable solution that is contrary to the law. This will equally apply to solutions introduced by a conciliation commission. The same cannot be said in the human rights context, where a conciliation commission could not (and should not) be expected to condone and, let alone, nudge the parties to circumvent their obligations under human rights law as a basis for agreement.

4.2.5 Trust Building

The history of the *Timor-Leste/Australia* dispute – compounded by Australia's objection to the Commission's competence – evidences that the parties started the conciliation in a status of reciprocal mistrust.[168] The Commission took it upon itself to rebuild that trust as its first priority, as well as the trust of the parties in the Commission.[169] The Commission took several steps to overcome this starting point. First, the Commission sought to minimize the negative effect of Australia's procedural objection by resolving the issue of competence as a preliminary matter, and in less than three weeks.[170] Thereafter, the first order of business for the Commission was for the parties to adopt 'confidence building measures', to move pass this animosity and build a foundation for compromise, 'a circuit-breaker to years of deadlocked negotiation and litigation'.[171] Furthermore, trust was necessary for the treaty drafting process: after the contours of the treaty were agreed, the parties drafted the detailed treaty bilaterally.[172]

In the case of Palestine and Israel, the events surrounding the Committee's decisions on competence – basing its competence on an 'unorthodox'[173]

---

166 Ibid, para. 70.

167 Pereira, *supra* n 146, at 174; see also Ben Huntley, Amelia Telec, Justin Whyatt, 'The Timor Sea Treaty: An Australian Perspective' (2018) 36 *Australian Year Book of International Law* 39, for a similar Australian perspective.

168 *Timor Sea Conciliation*, Report, *supra* n 40, para. 287.

169 Ibid; Pereira, *supra* n 146, at 173–174; Exposto, *supra* n 40, at 53.

170 *Timor Sea Conciliation*, Report, *supra* n 40, para. 287; Beckman, *supra* n 142, at 62–63.

171 Huntley, *supra* n 167, at 37; *Timor Sea Conciliation*, Report, *supra* n 40, paras. 287–289; Quinlan, *supra* n 136, at 187; Pereira, *supra* n 146, at 161–162; Beckman, *supra* n 142, at 66–69, 77–78; Klein, *supra* n 30, at 134.

172 Quinlan, *supra* n 136, at 189–191; Huntley, *supra* n 167, at 38.

173 Eiken, Keane, *supra* n 81, at 315.

interpretation of treaty law notwithstanding OLA's clear opinion; and the uncommon existence of a minority opinion in the Committee against its competence – are not the best starting point for building trust in the process. One might expect a body not comprised of legal experts[174] to 'conform to accepted methods of treaty interpretation; as a foundation for its competence to enhance the legitimacy of the process, within a procedure entirely dependent on the will of the parties to engage'.[175]

In any event, establishing trust between parties to a conciliation is highly dependent on the specific identity and relationship of the parties. For example, as noted above, the subject matter of a human rights conciliation may relate to only a fraction of the broader political and legal disagreements between the parties. Depending on the relationship, in some instances conciliation may serve as a first step in bringing the parties together to solve their wider differences. But in other cases, those wider underlying differences may negate the possibility of establishing trust between the parties even on a specific human rights aspect.

4.2.6 Interaction with Third Parties

Finally, where third parties' rights and interests are involved, the ability of a conciliation commission to receive input on their positions and even engage with them may be critical to a successful outcome. In *Timor-Leste/ Australia*, the Commission was made aware that there may be a third state (in that case Indonesia) with interests in the Timor Sea and welcomed any communications, through the parties as intermediaries, that enabled it to ascertain with confidence that its proposals would not affect third-party rights. Additionally, in its attempt to assist the parties in reaching agreement on a development concept, it interacted and met directly, with the blessing of the parties, with the private companies that had interests in Greater Sunrise.[176] Though ultimately no agreement on this was reached, it still proved useful, as the agreement reached on revenue sharing in the treaty will adapt to the eventual agreement on the development of the resource.

While both the ICCPR and CERD seem to limit the procedure to information provided by the parties,[177] the CERD Committee Rules of Procedure in

---

174 Thornberry, 'The Committee', *supra* n 14, at 311–312.

175 See Cot, *supra* n 3, para. 20; Geir Ulfstein, 'The Human Rights Treaty Bodies and Legitimacy Challenges' in Nienke Grossman, Harlan Grant Cohen, Andreas Follesdal, Geir Ulfstein (eds) *Legitimacy and International Courts* (CUP 2018) 290.

176 *Timor Sea Conciliation*, Report, *supra* n 40, para. 201; see also Beckman, *supra* n 142, at 74–77.

177 ICCPR, Arts. 41(1)(f), 42(6); CERD, Arts. 11(4), 12(8).

Palestine v. Israel refer to the possibility of obtaining information 'from any other relevant sources'[178] and the Commission retains the right to decide who attends its meetings, aside from the parties, thus allowing for at least some engagement with relevant third parties.[179]

Of the six elements identified as contributing to the success of the *Timor-Leste/Australia* conciliation, some could be said to be potentially available in human rights conciliations, such as the flexibility and intensity of procedures, as well as the ability to interact with third parties. Others, such as proactivity of the commission, are not excluded, though they find less support in the relevant provisions of human rights treaties, or the Rules of procedure in *Palestine v. Israel*, for example. Other elements, such as the mandate to expand the subject of the matter of the dispute beyond human rights or diverting from the law, seem to be incompatible with human rights conciliation. Some elements, such as trust building, may ultimately be case dependent.

An overarching theme with respect to the contribution of all six elements to the agreement reached in *Timor-Leste/Australia* was the parties' willingness to engage in good faith with the Commission and their common goal to successfully reach an agreement, above all else:

> both Parties ultimately preferred an amicable solution to the continuation of an unsatisfactory status quo. In this sense, the matter can be considered to have been ripe for resolution. In the Commission's view, it is in fact a significant benefit of conciliation that the proceedings were able to build on these aspirations for a positive outcome and preferable to a resolution of the dispute consisting merely of identifying a "winner" ... [180] the Parties did, through the conciliation, engage bilaterally in a constructive manner to achieve an equitable compromise.[181]

Each bilateral relationship is unique and multifaceted. But one reason that may have contributed to the fruitful engagement of the parties in *Timor-Leste/Australia* was something identified by the Committee itself: the dispute in the Timor Sea was *the* strain on an otherwise friendly – albeit complex – bilateral relationship.[182] In this context, despite Australia's initial hesitance, it ultimately

---

178 Rule 2(3).

179 Rule 12(3).

180 *Timor Sea Conciliation*, Report, *supra* n 40, para. 285.

181 Ibid, paras. 285, 289, 300.

182 See also Quinlan, *supra* n 136, at 175, 179–180; Pereira, *supra* n 146, at 171; Exposto, *supra* n 40, at 45.

decided to work together with Timor-Leste and the Commission to find a final resolution to the historic dispute, to the financial benefit of the parties and to finally remove that strain.[183] As the Timorese Deputy Agent in the conciliation put it, the process renewed the goodwill between the parties.[184] Of course, to renew goodwill, such goodwill must exist in the first place.

The relationship between Palestine and Israel is very different, in many ways. But surely it is undisputed that potential violations of CERD are but one element of an otherwise much wider historical, political and legal dispute. Thus, conciliation under the CERD is not an opportunity to settle an issue that has been hindering an otherwise healthy relationship. The conciliation's rocky foundation on issues of competence are unlikely to help in this regard. With respect to the two Qatar conciliations, their termination makes it difficult to ascertain how they would have played out. Had they continued to be considered on the merits, the ICJ's view – contrary to that of the CERD Committee – that the matters raised in the communications do not fall within the subject matter of the CERD, may have proven detrimental to the willingness of Saudi Arabia and the UAE to seek an amicable solution via the conciliation process.

The contribution of the elements surveyed in *Timor-Leste/Australia*, whether procedural ones like flexible meeting formats, or substantive ones like expanding the scope of the dispute or abandoning legal positions, cannot be denied. But the ability to incorporate these elements in a conciliation process – 'the latitude' given to the Commission – is ultimately dependent on the mutual willingness of the parties to allow a conciliation commission to do so.[185] For example, the extension of the timeframe of the conciliation; the Commission's direct engagement with third parties; the proactive and intense pace and flexibility of forms of communication. These were only possible because both parties were mutually invested in the process and saw potential in reaching an agreement, so they welcomed these measures. In that case as in others, if either party chooses not to seriously engage with the Commission, all of its efforts and tactics to reach a solution will be in vein.

The overarching lesson from *Timor-Leste/Australia* is that insomuch as human rights conciliation is geared towards an amicable settlement, success remains dependent on the will of the parties. As a senior member of the Australian delegation in the conciliation put it, the 'critical ingredient was political will. Conciliation will not work if one party simply stalls'.[186] The Agent

183 Quinlan, *supra* n 136, at 182–183, 185–186; Huntley, *supra* n 167, at 42; Klein, *supra* n 30, at 135.
184 Exposto, *supra* n 40, at 56–57.
185 Klein, *supra* n 30, at 212.
186 Quinlan, *supra* n 136, at 194.

for Timor-Leste shared this sentiment: 'good-faith engagement is an essential element in determining whether the conciliation can bear fruit'.[187]

5 Conclusions

This contribution sought to explore the potential of conciliation in meeting the objectives of interstate communications. Until recently, this question was purely academic. But with the successful conclusion of *Timor-Leste/Australia* and the first ever interstate communications submitted under the CERD, the question has become practically relevant, both for the pending *Palestine v. Israel* conciliation as well as for future ones.

Conciliation was conceived and remains primarily a third-party dispute settlement mechanism producing a non-binding result, in which a neutral party – the conciliation commission – assists the parties in reaching an amicable solution to the dispute. The emphasis, thus, is on agreement, not vindication of legal positions. The *Timor-Leste/Australia* example shows that conciliators have various tools at their disposal, and their utilization may contribute to achieving this ultimate objective of an agreed solution. At the same time, as conciliation does not produce a binding result, the conciliators efforts will be in vein if either party – or both – is unwilling to engage in good faith to reach what is inevitably a compromise solution. After initial hiccups, such good will was present in *Timor-Leste/Australia*. The inexistence of such will or inability to create it during a conciliation will doom any chance of agreement.

This truism is equally applicable in the human rights context. Where the parties are willing, conciliation may result in an amicable solution and the process 'has the potential for creative, structural remedies, providing a *sui generis* understanding of conciliation in the context of human rights'.[188] But, where no will exists, which is presumably the case in *Palestine v. Israel*, the process will not result in a solution to the alleged violations, and the questionable foundations of the decisions on competence will not assist in that regard.

A separate, though important question, is whether a compromise solution between States in a human rights conciliation, which does not or only partially conforms to their human rights obligations, is desirable in the first place.

When an amicable solution is out of reach, what then can be achieved by initiating a human rights conciliation? To some extent, conciliation may be

---

187 Pereira, *supra* n 146, at 139–174, 140; see also Beckman, *supra* n 142, at 81.

188 Eiken, Keane, *supra* n 81, at 341.

a vehicle to encourage compliance with human rights regimes in which all State-parties have an interest. Under CERD, for example, the findings of the Commission – which possibly include findings of violations – will be included in a final report circulated to all State parties.[189] Such findings may also serve as a basis for attempts to hold the breaching State responsible. As an aside, a detailed report will also contribute to the body of interpretation of CERD.

The knowledge that such a report is possible may have contributed to the will of Timor-Leste and Australia to find common ground.[190] In *Palestine v. Israel*, it is unlikely that findings of breach by the Commission will push Israel into compliance with those findings, considering it has already denounced the process as tainted, and considering the wider relationship between the parties. Nevertheless, for Palestine, the process may still serve some purpose. As one supportive writer put it:

> … what remains is that the ad hoc Conciliation Commission will be issuing a report on this matter, which will be distributed amongst all States parties to the ICERD. This may serve as another piece of the puzzle in Palestine's judicial quest to seek justice.[191]

The compatibility of conciliation in the human rights field is thus ultimately dependent on the objective a State is attempting to achieve.

Beyond all of these considerations, one must not forget the practical realities. While in no way diminishing the merits of a human rights conciliation, the decision to initiate (or not) such a process is political in nature. Indeed, politics are the art of the possible. Timor-Leste initiated conciliation against Australia not because it was certain that the process would succeed. It did so because it exhausted all other options after Australia refused to negotiate and blocked access to binding procedures. It did so because it had no other choice.[192] Other States may find themselves in the same position[193] and conclude that absent better options, human rights conciliation may be better than nothing.

189 Eiken, Keane, *supra* n 81, at 334.

190 Beckman, *supra* n 142, at 81–82; see also Eiken, Keane, *supra* n 81, at 339–340.

191 Salem, *supra* n 111; see also Eiken, Keane, *supra* n 81, at 314–315; Keane further suggests that such findings may have some effect on the obligations of third States, which is another objective of Palestine, see David Keane, 'Palestine v Israel and the Collective Obligation to Condemn Apartheid under Article 3 of ICERD' (2022) 23 Melbourne Journal of International Law 1.

192 Beckman, *supra* n 142, at 82; *supra* n 30, at 115; Exposto, *supra* n 40, at 50.

193 Cot, *supra* n 3, para. 22; Klein, *supra* n 30, at 140.

CHAPTER 6

Inter-State Communications before UN Human Rights Treaty Bodies: Testing the Waters for Collective Communications

Rosana Garciandia and Jean-Pierre Gauci

Abstract

The awakening of inter-state communications with the first ever three cases before the Committee on the Elimination of Racial Discrimination in 2018 has inspired new avenues of research about their potential and shortfalls. This chapter opens a new line of exploration, considering the mechanism's potential as an avenue for collective action at a time when many States are responding to violations of international law, even when not directly affected by those violations. Those responses have included massive third-party interventions (*Ukraine v Russia*), and the initiation of proceedings before the International Court of Justice by States not directly injured (*The Gambia v Myanmar, Canada and the Netherlands v Syrian Arab Republic, South Africa v Israel*). This chapter argues that enabling collective inter-state communications before UN treaty bodies could strengthen the mechanism as an avenue for treaty compliance and the protection of human rights, and for amplifying sovereign voices as part of peaceful dispute settlement processes.

Keywords

collective inter-state communications – amplifying sovereign voices – procedural efficiency – harmonization – third-party and joint proceedings – impartial conciliation commission

DOI:10.1163/9789004712584_008

1 Introduction

Most UN human rights treaties or protocols establish inter-state procedures,[1] allowing States to bring to the attention of the respective treaty bodies a breach of an obligation by another party without having to prove a direct interest in the case.[2] After attempts at negotiation,[3] this may lead to conciliation or good offices by those treaty bodies or an *ad hoc* conciliation commission. This avenue, which had laid dormant for decades, was activated with the first three cases in the history of the UN in 2018, all before the Committee on the Elimination of Racial Discrimination (CERD Committee).[4]

1 International Covenant on Civil and Political Rights (ICCPR) (art. 41–42); Optional Protocol to the International Covenant on Economic, Social and Cultural Rights (ICESCR) (art. 10); Convention Against Torture (art. 21); International Convention on the Elimination of All Forms of Racial Discrimination (ICERD) (arts. 11–13); International Convention on the Protection of the Rights of All Migrant Workers and Members of their Families (CMW) (arts. 76–77); Optional Protocol 3 to the Convention on the Rights of the Child (UNCRC) (art. 12); International Convention for the Protection of All Persons from Enforced Disappearance (ICAED) (art. 32).

2 The inter-state communications procedure is reciprocal, and therefore requires that the two parties have accepted the competence of the treaty body to receive communications.

3 No explicit mention is made in treaties or case law of whether attempts for negotiation need to be genuine or exhaustive. The CERD Committee has referred only to the reference in art. 11(3) of ICERD that the matter be adjusted to the satisfaction of both parties (*Palestine v Israel* (Decision on Admissibility) CERD/C/103/4 (30 April 2021)). The International Court of Justice, in *Georgia v Russia* (2011) and *Ukraine v Russia* (2019), has clarified what "negotiation" means, albeit in the context of art. 22 of ICERD (the compromissory clause) (*Application of the International Convention for the Suppression of the Financing of Terrorism and of the International Convention on the Elimination of All Forms of Racial Discrimination* (*Ukraine v Russian Federation*) (Pending) (Preliminary Objections) [2019] ICJ Rep 558 [116]–[117]).

4 *Palestine v Israel; Qatar v Saudi Arabia; Qatar v UAE*. The procedure is established under arts. 11–13 of ICERD. On ICERD, see Patrick Thornberry, *The International Convention on the Elimination of All Forms of Racial Discrimination: A Commentary* (OUP 2016).

The awakening of this mechanism has inspired new lines of research about its potential and shortfalls.[5] Building on that research, this chapter opens a new line of exploration, considering the mechanism's potential as an avenue for collective action in a moment when many States are reacting to violations of international law, even if they may not be directly affected by those violations. The world has witnessed the initiation of proceedings before the International Court of Justice (ICJ) in the case of *The Gambia v Myanmar*, the joint application by Canada and the Netherlands against Syria,[6] and most recently the application by South Africa against Israel.[7] In each of these cases, the applicant States have not been directly injured. Equally important, in an unprecedented use of third-party intervention, 33 States have submitted to the ICJ their declarations of intervention as third parties in ongoing proceedings in the case of *Ukraine v Russia*, and in June 2023, 32 of them were accepted at the preliminary objections stage.[8]

In the context of this possible paradigm shift in the international community, this chapter argues that enabling collective inter-state communications before UN treaty bodies could strengthen the mechanism as an avenue for treaty compliance and the protection of human rights, and for amplifying sovereign voices as part of peaceful dispute settlement processes. The methodology is based on: a) an analysis of the treaties and their travaux préparatoires and existing individual cases; b) a comparative analysis of collective action in different fora, including joinder of proceedings and third-party intervention before the ICJ, the International Tribunal on the Law of the Sea (ITLOS), regional human rights courts, arbitral tribunals (such as the International Centre for Settlement of Investment Disputes (ICSID)), and other fora; and c) consultation with experts and stakeholders (legal advisers to States, (current

5 Dai Tamada, 'Inter-State Communication under ICERD: From ad hoc Conciliation to Collective Enforcement?' (2021) 12 Journal of International Dispute Settlement 405; Gay McDougall, 'Introductory Note to Inter-State Communication submitted by the State of Palestine against State of Israel' (2020) 59 International Legal Materials 922.

6 *Application of the Convention Against Torture and Other Cruel, Inhuman or Degrading Treatment or Punishment* (*Canada and the Netherlands v Syrian Arab Republic*) (Pending) ICJ Press Release 2023/28 <https://www.icj-cij.org/sites/default/files/case-related/188/188-20230612-PRE-01-00-EN.pdf> accessed 6 October 2023.

7 *Application of the Convention on the Prevention and Punishment of the Crime of Genocide in the Gaza Strip* (*South Africa v Israel*) (Pending) ICJ Press Release 2023/77 <https://www.icj-cij.org/sites/default/files/case-related/192/192-20231229-pre-01-00-en.pdf> accessed 17 January 2024.

8 *Allegations of Genocide under the Convention on the Prevention and Punishment of the Crime of Genocide* (*Ukraine v Russian Federation*) (Pending) ICJ Order (2 June 2023) <https://www.icj-cij.org/sites/default/files/case-related/182/182-20230605-ORD-01-00-EN.pdf> accessed 30 April 2024.

or former) members of UN treaty bodies, civil society organisations, and academics from a variety of disciplines).[9]

The chapter proceeds in three parts. First, it explores a possible paradigm shift in how the international community reacts to human rights violations. Second, it looks at the potential of collective inter-state communications for treaty compliance, and for amplifying sovereign voices as part of peaceful dispute settlement processes. Third, it proposes specific ways in which the contours of collective action in inter-state communications should be defined to mitigate associated risks. The chapter considers the two main forms of collective action: joint inter-state communications, where all States involved are parties to the procedure, and third-party intervention, where two States are parties to the procedure and other States may join but not as parties. More informal forms of collective action are also considered briefly.

2 A Paradigm Shift in the International Community or an Optical Illusion?

Prior to the awakening of inter-state communications in 2018 before the CERD Committee, the literature was practically unanimous about the reasons for the absolute lack of inter-state case law before UN committees,[10] reflecting some States' perceptions of inter-state communications as an unfriendly act,[11] a

---

9 The consultation process was undertaken through written consultation and a workshop hosted by the King's College London Centre for International Governance and Dispute Resolution and the British Institute of International and Comparative Law.

10 Egon Schwelb, 'Civil and Political Rights: The International Measures of Implementation' (1968) 62 American Journal of International Law 827; Scott Leckie, 'The Inter-State Complaint Procedure in International Human Rights Law: Hopeful Prospects or Wishful Thinking?' (1988) 10 Human Rights Quarterly 249.

11 Meron explains that one of the reasons inter-state communications have been 'underutilised' is the perceived unfriendliness (Theodor Meron, *Human Rights and Humanitarian Norms as Customary Law* (Clarendon Press 1991) 152–153). This consideration reflects what is observed in the analysis of the travaux préparatoires. The Iraqi representative discussing the ICERD claimed that the adoption of an inter-state communication procedure 'might disturb international peace and impair friendly relations between States', with the potential of extending 'the cold war' by interfering in the domestic affairs of other States (UNGA Third Committee, 'Draft International Convention on the Elimination of All Forms of Racial Discrimination: Articles on Measures of Implementation' (19 November 1965) 20th Session, 1347th Meeting, [7]).

threat to national sovereignty[12] and the principle of non-interference,[13] and as a tool that could be used with mere political motivations.[14] Despite committees' emphasis on inter-state communications being conciliatory, not adversarial,[15] States have traditionally preferred not to escalate a human rights-related dispute if it could be resolved through diplomatic means or if other alternatives seemed more suitable and less cumbersome.[16] They have prioritized avoiding the risk of politicisation of inter-state procedures, leaving 'Pandora's box' closed[17] and opting for diplomatic action or sanctions[18] whenever another State party to a UN human rights treaty was deemed to be failing to comply with treaty obligations, particularly if the applicant's own direct interest was not affected.[19] This aligns with the 'individualist' approach that States have taken

12 During the negotiations for the ICCPR, those who considered the procedure of the Human Rights Committee contrary to national sovereignty found that 'no State party should set itself up as a judge of the domestic actions of another' (UNGA, 'Draft International Covenants on Human Rights' (1955) 10th Session, UN Doc A/2929, [62]).

13 During the negotiations for the ICCPR, the Ukrainian representative considered that any system other than the reporting system 'would introduce complications into the measures of implementation and ultimately yield negative results' (UNGA Third Committee, GAOR, 21st Session, 1415th Meeting (1966) UN Doc A/C.3/SR.1415, 219–222, 220 [8]). See also UNGA Third Committee, 'Draft International Convention on the Elimination of All Forms of Racial Discrimination: Articles on Measures of Implementation' (19 November 1965) 20th Session, 1347th Meeting, [6]–[7].

14 This resulted in the inclusion of the mechanism as voluntary in most UN treaties (except for the ICERD, which adopted a compulsory model) and in a relatively low number of States accepting the competence of committees to hear those cases (the competence of the respective committees to hear inter-state cases has been accepted by 50 of the 173 States parties to the ICCPR, 27 of the 171 States parties to the ICESCR, 63 of the 173 States parties to the CAT, 15 of the 50 States parties to the UNCRC, 4 of the 58 States parties to the CMW, and 28 of the 71 States parties to the ICAED. The highest rate is found in the 150 of the 189 States parties to the Convention on the Elimination of All Forms of Discrimination Against Women (CEDAW) accepting the competence of the CEDAW Committee to hear inter-state communications).

15 Human Rights Committee, 'General Comment 31 on the Nature of the General Legal Obligation Imposed on States Parties to the Covenant' (26 May 2004) UN Doc CCPR/C/21/Rev.1/Add. 13; Committee on the Elimination of Racial Discrimination, 'Inter-State Communication Submitted by the State of Palestine Against Israel: Decision on Jurisdiction' (16 June 2021) UN Doc CERD/C/100/5, [59].

16 Peter H Kooijmans, 'Inter-State Dispute Settlement in the Field of Human Rights' (1990) 3 Leiden Journal of International Law 87.

17 Tu Yunxin, 'On the Normative Structure of International Human Rights Treaties Monitoring Mechanisms and Its Legal Challenges' (2019) 18 Journal of Human Rights 511, 523.

18 'Magnitsky' sanction laws are a generalized type of domestic legislation that allow States to react to human rights violations by other countries. See: <https://www.humanrightsfirst.org/topics/global-magnitsky> accessed 30 April 2024.

19 Kooijmans, supra note 16, 89.

in international affairs for decades, avoiding overexposing themselves unless a violation directly affects them. As Leckie noted in the late eighties, '[S]tates prefer to pursue mutually acceptable policies' and 'quiet forms of diplomacy' 'when addressing human rights in other [S]tates if they have interests other than human rights in the country in question'.[20]

However, an analysis of recent developments in international litigation, coupled with the increase in inter-state human rights cases before the European Court of Human Rights (ECtHR),[21] suggest that a paradigm shift could be consolidating in international litigation, with potential implications for inter-state communications before UN human rights treaty bodies.

2.1 *From Reacting to Direct Injuries to Engaging with International Mechanisms when other States have been Affected*

Two litigation strategies have resulted in a strong sense of collective response. First, the strategy followed by the Gambia against Myanmar before the ICJ, initiating a case for Myanmar's violations of the human rights of the Muslim Rohingya population without being directly affected. This initiative, following from *Belgium v Senegal,* is based on the violation of *erga omnes partes* obligations[22] and could open a path to other litigation for similar situations, as recently observed in the joint application by Canada and the Netherlands against Syria under the Convention Against Torture,[23] and the application by

20 Scott Leckie, 'The Inter-State Complaint Procedure in International Human Rights Law: Hopeful Prospects or Wishful Thinking?' (1988) 10 Human Rights Quarterly 249, 252. See also Kooijmans, supra note 16, 87–88; Menno Kamminga, *Inter-State Accountability for Violations of Human Rights* (University of Pennsylvania Press 1992) 33.

21 Isabella Risini, Justine Batura and Lukas Kleinert, 'A "Golden Age" of Inter-State Complaints?: An Interview with Isabella Risini' (*Völkerrechtsblog*, 16 September 2020) <https://voelkerrechtsblog.org/a-golden-age-of-inter-state-complaints/> accessed 10 May 2024.

22 *Erga omnes partes* obligations are obligations 'under a multilateral treaty that a State party to the treaty owes in any given case to all the other States parties to the same treaty, in view of their common values and concern for compliance, so that a breach of that obligation enables all these States to take action' (Yoshifumi Tanaka, 'The Legal Consequences of Obligations Erga Omnes in International Law' (2021) 68 Netherlands International Law Review 1, 1–2, citing Institut de Droit International, 'Resolution: Obligations Erga Omnes in International Law' Krakow Session 2005 <https://www.idi-iil.org/app/uploads/2017/06/2005_kra_01_en.pdf> accessed 30 April 2024). *Belgium v Senegal* and *The Gambia v Myanmar* are two examples of *erga omnes partes* obligations giving standing to a State before the ICJ (ibid).

23 *Application of the Convention Against Torture and Other Cruel, Inhuman or Degrading Treatment or Punishment* (*Canada and the Netherlands v Syrian Arab Republic*) (Pending) (Application Instituting Proceedings) <https://www.icj-cij.org/sites/default/files/case-related/188/188-20230608-APP-01-00-EN.pdf> accessed 30 April 2024.

South Africa against Israel under the Genocide Convention.[24] It could also open such a path in cases involving violations of *erga omnes* obligations.[25] In *The Gambia v Myanmar*, the *erga omnes partes* nature of the allegedly violated obligations has allowed a State with no direct interest in the case to initiate proceedings against Myanmar. The recent joint application of Canada and the Netherlands instituting proceedings before the ICJ against Syria concerning a dispute under the Convention Against Torture[26] also materializes the avenue for State responsibility based on *erga omnes partes* obligations,[27] following many attempts to hold Syrian officials accountable under domestic legal frameworks.[28] South Africa's application also cites *The Gambia v Myanmar* for its points on *erga omnes partes*.[29] At the time of writing, the Court had issued five provisional measures against Israel and established its own prima facie

24 *Application of the Convention on the Prevention and Punishment of the Crime of Genocide in the Gaza Strip* (*South Africa v Israel*) (Pending) (Application Instituting Proceedings) <https://www.icj-cij.org/sites/default/files/case-related/192/192-20231228-app-01-00-en.pdf> accessed 30 April 2024.

25 International law has defined *erga omnes* obligations as those obligations owed to the whole international community, and therefore entitling any State to invoke the responsibility of other States for their breach (Tanaka, supra note 22; Pok Yin S Chow, 'On Obligations Erga Omnes Partes' (2021) 52 Georgetown Journal of International Law 469). Those are obligations of relevance, including, as recently clarified by the International Law Commission, the prohibition of genocide, the prohibition of racial discrimination, and the prohibition of slavery (See: <https://legal.un.org/ilc/texts/instruments/english/draft_articles/1_14_2022.pdf>). South Africa's application references both *erga omnes partes* obligations under the Genocide Convention and broader *erga omnes* obligations in relation to genocide (supra note 24, [133]).

26 Supra note 23.

27 The Court did accept the *erga omnes partes* argument for prima facie standing in its order for provisional measures: *Application of the Convention Against Torture and Other Cruel, Inhuman or Degrading Treatment or Punishment* (*Canada and the Netherlands v Syrian Arab Republic*) (Pending) (Request for the Indication of Provisional Measures: Order) General List No 188 (16 November 2023) <https://www.icj-cij.org/sites/default/files/case-related/188/188-20231116-ord-01-00-en.pdf> accessed 11 May 2024, [50]–[51], [57].

28 See, for example, the *Al-Khatib* trial in Germany (https://voelkerrechtsblog.org/the-end-of-the-al-khatib-trial/); proceedings in Sweden (https://www.ecchr.eu/en/case/sweden-criminal-complaint-against-assads-intelligence-officials/); and two joined cases before the plenary assembly of the French Cour de Cassation (https://www.ejiltalk.org/france-is-back-on-the-universal-jurisdiction-track/). This willingness at the domestic level could seem to suggest that those States may be open to intervening as third parties in the case before the ICJ. But that would be jumping too fast to conclusions, as one would need to factor in the diplomatic price that States may need to pay if they decide to go down that road.

29 Supra note 24.

jurisdiction.[30] Quoting the *The Gambia v Myanmar* case, the Court noted that 'any State party to the Genocide Convention may invoke the responsibility of another State party, including through the institution of proceedings before the Court, with a view to determining the alleged failure to comply with its obligations *erga omnes partes* under the Convention and to bringing that failure to an end'.[31] Nonetheless, as Hachem and Hathaway explain, '[i]f the ICJ does allow the case to proceed to the merits, it will further entrench *erga omnes partes* standing as an important new tool in enforcing international human rights law, making clear that its decisions in [the] *The Gambia* and the *Syria* cases were no outliers'.[32] Importantly, in its order on provisional measures, the Court noted that 'the Respondent [Israel] did not challenge the standing of the Applicant [South Africa] in the present proceedings'.[33] In a similar way, inter-state communication procedures do not require a direct interest or a connection to a particular victim for standing before UN treaty bodies,[34] which positions any State party to the treaty as, following this new trend, able, simply in their capacity as State party, to initiate an inter-State procedure against the violating State.

Second, massive third-party intervention under art. 63 of the Statute of the International Court of Justice (ICJ Statute) is ongoing in the case concerning *Allegations of Genocide under the Convention on the Prevention and Punishment of the Crime of Genocide (Ukraine v Russian Federation)* before the ICJ[35] and

30 *Application of the Convention on the Prevention and Punishment of the Crime of Genocide in the Gaza Strip (South Africa v Israel)* (Pending) (Request for the Indication of Provisional Measures: Order) General List No 192 (26 January 2024) <https://www.icj-cij.org/sites/default/files/case-related/192/192-20240126-ord-01-00-en.pdf> accessed 11 May 2024.

31 Ibid, [33]. For a discussion on the case, including provisional measures and what a hypothetical merits stage might look like, see EJIL: The Podcast!, 'Episode 23: Unhappy New Year! Genocide in the Courtroom' (15 January 2024) <https://www.ejiltalk.org/ejil-the-podcast-episode-23-unhappy-new-year-genocide-in-the-courtroom/> accessed 30 April 2024.

32 Alaa Hachem and Oona A Hathaway, 'The Promise and Risk of South Africa's Case Against Israel' (*Just Security*, 4 January 2024) <https://www.justsecurity.org/91000/the-promise-and-risk-of-south-africas-case-against-israel/> accessed 17 January 2024.

33 Supra note 30, [33].

34 Malcolm Langford, Cheryl Lorens and Natasha Telson, 'Inter-State Procedure', in Malcolm Langford and others (eds), *The Optional Protocol to the International Covenant on Economic, Social and Cultural Rights: A Commentary* (Pretoria University Law Press 2016) 147, 164, citing Kamminga, supra note 20.

35 *Allegations of Genocide under the Convention on the Prevention and Punishment of the Crime of Genocide (Ukraine v Russian Federation)* (Pending) ICJ Press Release 2022/35 <https://www.icj-cij.org/public/files/case-related/182/182-20220913-PRE-01-00-EN.pdf> accessed 30 April 2024.

in a separate case before the ECtHR,[36] in support of Ukraine's claims.[37] This, coupled with the expression of interest of the Netherlands, Canada, Germany, Denmark, the UK and the Maldives to intervene to support The Gambia against Myanmar before the ICJ, has led scholars to analyse the pros and cons of third-party intervention and its potential as a tool for *actio popularis*.[38] Germany has also announced that it intends to intervene in the *South Africa v Israel* case.[39] Beyond international litigation, the myriad of initiatives established in response to violations of international law by Russia in Ukraine[40] gives a sense of the momentum and of one particularly relevant feature for this chapter: the

---

36 There are 31 third-party interveners in the case *Ukraine and the Netherlands v Russia* before the ECtHR (nos. 8019/16, 43800/14, 28525/20 and 11055/22). See European Court of Human Rights, 'Update on the Third-Party Intervention Requests Granted in Inter-State Case *Ukraine and the Netherlands v Russia*' (Press Release No 082, 17 March 2023) <https://hudoc.echr.coe.int/app/conversion/pdf/?library=ECHR&id=003-7598878-10452070> accessed 11 May 2024.

37 *The Gambia v Myanmar* has also been described as a form of collective action, 'reflecting the will of the 57 states comprising the [Organisation of Islamic Cooperation (OIC)]', as 'it was the OIC that 'tasked' The Gambia with bringing the case (and the OIC membership funded it)'. See Michael Ramsden, 'Strategic Litigation before the International Court of Justice: Evaluating Impact in the Campaign for Rohingya Rights' (2022) 33 European Journal of International Law 441, 458.

38 Brian McGarry, 'Obligations *Erga Omnes* (*Partes*) and the Participation of Third States in Inter-State Litigation' (2023) 22 Law and Practice of International Courts and Tribunals 273; Brian McGarry, 'A Rush to Judgment? The Wobbly Bridge from Judicial Standing to Intervention in ICJ Proceedings' (2023) 100 Questions of International Law 5; Kyra Wigard, Ori Pomson and Juliette McIntyre, 'Keeping Score: An Empirical Analysis of the Interventions in *Ukraine v Russia*' (2023) 14(3) Journal of International Dispute Settlement 305.

39 For coverage and commentary on this, see Stefan Talmon, 'Germany Rushes to Declare Intention to Intervene in the Genocide Case brought by South Africa Against Israel Before the International Court of Justice' (*German Practice in International Law*, 15 January 2024) <https://gpil.jura.uni-bonn.de/2024/01/germany-rushes-to-declare-intention-to-intervene-in-the-genocide-case-brought-by-south-africa-against-israel-before-the-international-court-of-justice/> accessed 17 January 2024. See also EJIL: The Podcast!, supra note 31, 36:25–37:23.

40 In March 2022, a group of 39 States submitted a joint referral to the International Criminal Court, which had already expressed its intention to seek authorisation for opening an investigation. The collective referral, then joined by more States, allowed the prosecutor to proceed with the investigation, which led to arrest warrants being issued for Vladimir Putin and Maria Lvova-Belova in March 2023, with Eurojust's Joint Investigation Team playing a very important role in evidence gathering (See <https://www.icc-cpi.int/news/situation-ukraine-icc-judges-issue-arrest-warrants-against-vladimir-vladimirovich-putin-and> accessed 30 April 2024). Other collective initiatives include the establishment of an independent international commission of inquiry by the UN Human Rights Council (See <https://documents-dds-ny.un.org/doc/UNDOC/GEN/G22/277/44/PDF/G2227744.pdf> accessed 30 April 2024); a UN General Assembly (UNGA)

collective nature of action against Russia. The international community has taken a collective approach to this situation, joining forces to protect human rights and contribute to securing justice with an unprecedented collective legal response.[41]

These collective responses could consolidate a new paradigm, where the potential of existing mechanisms would be revisited to serve coordinated responses by the international community. Whether there is an actual paradigm shift, or this is only an optical illusion, will very much depend on the outcome of the proceedings initiated by South Africa, Canada and the Netherlands, Ukraine and the Gambia. In any event, having observed the collective reaction to human rights violations in Ukraine and the new spirit that *The Gambia v Myanmar* could bring to the fore, reactivating the *erga omnes partes* claims seen before in *Belgium v Senegal*, with some States ready to take a risk to protect human rights in others, this more 'collective' perspective could influence the perception and use of inter-state communications.

---

resolution supported by 141 member States demanding that Russia 'immediately, completely and unconditionally withdraw all its military forces from the territory of Ukraine within its internationally recognized borders' (See <https://daccess-ods.un.org/access.nsf/Get?OpenAgent&DS=A/RES/ES-11/2&Lang=E> accessed 11 May 2024); the suspension of Russia from the Human Rights Council, with the support of 94 member States (See <https://news.un.org/en/story/2022/04/1115782>, accessed 30 April 2024); a UNGA resolution on Russian reparations for Ukraine (See <https://news.un.org/en/story/2022/11/1130587> accessed 30 April 2024); initiatives at the EU level, such as the establishment of a joint investigation team with Ukraine into civilian killings (See <https://atalayar.com/en/content/eu-sets-joint-investigation-team-ukraine-civilian-killings> accessed 30 April 2024) and the EU Freeze and Seize Task Force (See <https://complyadvantage.com/insights/eus-freeze-and-seize-task-force-coordinates-international-action-against-russian-oligarchs/> accessed 30 April 2024); massive third-party intervention before the ICJ; initiatives by the Organization for Security and Co-operation in Europe (OSCE) (See <https://www.osce.org/files/f/documents/f/a/515868.pdf> accessed 30 April 2024); the creation of the International Centre for the Prosecution of the Crime of Aggression against Ukraine, which started its operations in May 2023, hosted by the EU Agency for Criminal Justice Cooperation (Eurojust) (See <https://www.eurojust.europa.eu/international-centre-for-the-prosecution-of-the-crime-of-aggression-against-ukraine> accessed 11 May 2024); and the support of the Council of Europe for the establishment of a special tribunal on the crime of aggression against Ukraine (See <https://www.coe.int/en/web/portal/-/secretary-general-joins-the-summit-of-leaders-for-creation-of-special-tribunal-on-the-crime-of-aggression-against-ukraine> accessed 30 April 2024).

41 As McGarry notes, 'mass participation is unprecedented in the Court's contentious cases'. (See Brian McGarry, 'Mass Intervention? The Joint Statement of 41 States on Ukraine v Russia' (*EJIL:Talk!*, 30 May 2022) <https://www.ejiltalk.org/mass-intervention-the-joint-statement-of-41-states-on-ukraine-v-russia/> accessed 30 April 2024).

As mentioned above, aligned with the literature before the awakening of inter-state communications, at the top of the list of reasons for the underuse of the mechanism continues to be its perceived adversarial nature and the potential adverse implications that an inter-state process could have for the diplomatic relations between two countries. This has maintained the perception of inter-state communications as a last resort mechanism. This new paradigm could influence States' choices, making inter-state communications more attractive as an option if stepping up in situations of serious human rights cases becomes a more common practice. Whilst inter-state communications do not require victimhood for standing, articulating the procedure as collective could result in more *actio popularis* cases,[42] especially when the resolution of a case may affect the interpretation of a provision in a treaty.[43] They could reduce the confrontational barrier associated with State-to-State communication procedures,[44] and offer a safe way to amplify the voices of the international community through a dispute settlement method which provides certain safeguards.

2.2 *The Potential Influence of these Two Litigation Trends on Inter-state Communications*

While not explicitly recognising this collective possibility,[45] UN treaties or rules of procedure do prohibit collective action. No amendment to the treaties would be necessary, although it would be helpful to explicitly include the collective avenue in rules of procedure. Collective inter-state procedures could take two forms: multi-party cases and third-party intervention. More informal forms of collective action, mirroring those in other fora,[46] could be amicus or requests of information from the treaty body.

---

42 Farid Ahmadov, *The Right of Actio Popularis before International Courts and Tribunals* (Brill 2018); François Voeffray, *L'actio Popularis ou la Défense de L'intérêt Collectif devant les Juridictions Internationals* (Graduate Institute Publications 2014).

43 Similar to what third-party States may be able to contribute in litigation before the ICJ under art. 63 of the ICJ Statute, one of the routes for third-party intervention. On third-party intervention before the ICJ, see Christine Chinkin, *Third Parties in International Law* (OUP 1993) 186–216; Juliette McIntyre, 'Procedural Values in the Intervention Procedure at the International Court of Justice' (2022) 1 *Ukrainian Law Review* 1.

44 As Leckie puts it for the ECtHR case of *Denmark, France, the Netherlands, Norway and Sweden v Turkey*, 'it appears that if there had not been a collective effort by the five states acting together the complaint may never have been filed' (Leckie, supra note 20, 295).

45 The relevant treaties use expressions such as 'both' or 'either', reflecting the presumed bilateral nature of inter-state communications.

46 Wood and Sthoeger explain that 'in addition to formal intervention', third-party States can get involved in inter-state litigation by 'transmitting a submission' to the court or tribunal, getting permission to attend otherwise closed hearings as observers, requesting early access to copies of the written pleadings, and even 'in more indirect ways, such

Multi-party cases would be the strongest form of collective action before UN treaty bodies, with multiple parties on either side of the procedure.[47] Two or more States could decide to join forces and initiate proceedings jointly against one or more 'injuring' States. There could also be the possibility for UN treaty bodies to combine cases, imposing collectiveness on the parties. Multi-party cases are a possibility before the ICJ[48] and other international courts and tribunals.[49] Although not widely used,[50] this collective form of dispute settlement articulates a formal channel for various claims to be presented jointly in court in an effective and coordinated manner. Enabling this for inter-state communications could facilitate an avenue for a coordinated collective response to human rights violations within the limits and rules of inter-state communication procedures, although the multiplicity of parties could,

---

as by publishing a comment or commissioning an article' (See Michael Wood and Eran Sthoeger, 'Third-Party Intervention and Involvement in Inter-State Arbitration' in Helene Ruiz Fabri and others (eds), *A Bridge over Troubled Waters: Dispute Resolution in the Law of International Watercourses and the Law of the Sea* (Brill Nijhoff 2020) 64–65).

47 Although inter-state communications are not a purely adversarial procedure, for simplicity we will refer to those States as 'applicant States' and 'respondent States'.

48 See arts. 36 and 47 of the Rules of Court of the International Court of Justice (ICJ Rules of Court).

49 European Court of Human Rights, 'Institution of Proceedings' (Practice Direction, issued 1 November 2003, as at 1 February 2022) [14]–[16]; Rules of Court of the European Court of Human Rights (ECtHR Rules of Court) (as at 28 March 2024) r 30; Rules of the International Tribunal for the Law of the Sea (adopted 28 November 1997, as at 25 March 2021) art. 47; Protocol to the African Charter on Human and Peoples' Rights on the Establishment of an African Court on Human and Peoples' Rights (adopted 10 June 1998, entered into force 25 January 2004) art. 5(2).

50 In the history of the ICJ, only one case has been initiated by more than one State (*Appeal Relating to the Jurisdiction of the ICAO Council under Article 84 of the Convention on International Civil Aviation (Bahrain, Egypt, Saudi Arabia and United Arab Emirates v Qatar)*) and against more than one State (*Monetary Gold Removed from Rome in 1943 (Italy v France, United Kingdom of Great Britain and Northern Ireland and United States of America)*). Factors which may lead States to opt for individual cases instead of multi-party cases include different approaches to legal argumentation (Wigard, Pomson and McIntyre, supra note 38), various 'political, strategic, evidential and factual' reasons (James Crawford, *State Responsibility: The General Part* (CUP 2013) 650), or the perception of multi-party litigation as an obstacle to community interests (Markus Benzing, 'Community Interests in the Procedure of International Courts and Tribunals' (2006) 5 Law and Practice of International Courts and Tribunals 369, 374–376; Paula Wojcikiewicz Almeida, 'Enhancing ICJ Procedures in Order to Promote Fundamental Values: Overcoming the Prevailing Tension between Bilateralism and Community Interests' in Massimo Iovane and others (eds), *The Protection of General Interests in Contemporary International Law: A Theoretical and Empirical Inquiry* (OUP 2021) 242–243).

amongst other issues, entail challenges concerning the potential success of the conciliation process that inter-state communications envisage.

Third-party intervention is the other main way in which collective action could be envisaged before UN treaty bodies, mirroring the functioning of third-party intervention in international litigation. Before the ICJ, third-party intervention under arts. 62 and 63 of the ICJ Statute,[51] which has traditionally been used to safeguard the legal interests of third parties or for harmonization of conventional rules, is increasingly being explored as a way for States to publicly and formally show support for another State or to condemn the conduct of another State in a universal forum. This practice has also been observed in the ECtHR, in the context of proceedings between Ukraine and the Netherlands and Russia, with 26 States intervening. The Court has since asked States to coordinate their work[52] and has published an amended version of the ECtHR Rules of Court in tandem with a Practice Direction on third-party intervention.[53] The Practice Direction notably states that information should be put 'as impartially and objectively as possible', should not 'express support

51 Through third-party intervention, the intervening State does not become a party to the proceedings, but the process allows those States to participate in the procedure in a restricted way and informs the Court that the legal rights of the intervener may be affected (George N Barrie, 'Third-Party State Intervention in Disputes before the International Court of Justice: A Reassessment of Articles 62 and 63 of the ICJ Statute' (2020) 53 Comparative and International Law Journal of Southern Africa 1, 6). In 1989, Nicaragua's application in the case between El Salvador and Honduras requested permission to intervene under the art. 62 procedure. In that request, it clarified that it did not want to intervene in the dispute concerning the land boundary, but all it wanted was to protect its rights in the Gulf of Fonseca, and to 'inform the Court of the nature of the legal rights of Nicaragua which are in issue in the dispute' (*Land, Island and Maritime Frontier Case* (*El Salvador/Honduras, Nicaragua intervening*) (Application for Permission to Intervene) [1990] ICJ Rep 92 [38]). The Court also permitted Equatorial Guinea to intervene as a non-party intervenor and later elaborated in its 2002 judgment that 'in fixing the maritime boundary between Cameroon and Nigeria, the Court must ensure that it does not adopt any position which might affect' the neighbouring States' rights: *Land and Maritime Boundary between Cameroon and Nigeria* (*Cameroon v Nigeria, Equatorial Guinea intervening*) (Counter-claims) [2002] ICJ Rep 303 [238].

52 European Court of Human Rights, 'Update on the Third-Party Intervention Requests Granted in Inter-State Case *Ukraine and the Netherlands v Russia*' (Press Release No 082, 17 March 2023) <https://hudoc.echr.coe.int/app/conversion/pdf/?library=ECHR&id=003-7598878-10452070> accessed 11 May 2024.

53 European Court of Human Rights, 'European Court Clarifies Third-party Intervention: Amendments to Rules of Court and New Guidelines' (Press Release No 84, 20 March 2023) <https://hudoc.echr.coe.int/app/conversion/pdf/?library=ECHR&id=003-7600935-10455264> accessed 11 May 2024.

directly for one or the other party',[54] and 'should relate solely to the aspects of the case that are relevant to [the State's] interest(s)'.[55] Batura observes that this idea of objectivity and not expressing support may not be so simple in practice.[56] Nevertheless, it does give some insight into how the ECtHR will seek to approach its collective instance.

The benefits to the parties and to intervening States have been analysed in light of existing practice,[57] flagging the support that intervention may bring to the parties,[58] and the practical benefits for the intervening States.[59] This form of participation would also enable a collective response, where third parties would signal themselves but be less involved in the case than in joint proceedings. A priori, this could be less disruptive to the conciliation process that inter-state communications envisage, and more feasible for States with limited budgets.

3 The Power of Group Action for the Aims of Inter-state Communications

Treaty compliance and the protection of human rights have traditionally been seen as the main aims of inter-state communications before treaty bodies. This perception expressed by many delegations during treaty negotiations[60]

54 European Court of Human Rights, 'Third-party Intervention under Article 36 § 2 of the Convention or under Article 3, Second Sentence, of Protocol No 16' (Practice Direction, issued 13 March 2023) [2].

55 Ibid, [34(a)].

56 Justine Batura, 'The Objective Friends of the Court—New Insights into the Role of Third Parties before the European Court of Human Rights' (*EJIL:Talk!*, 19 April 2023) <https://www.ejiltalk.org/the-objective-friends-of-the-court-new-insights-into-the-role-of-third-parties-before-the-european-court-of-human-rights/> accessed 30 April 2024.

57 Brian McGarry, *Intervening in International Justice: Third States before Courts and Tribunals* (CUP 2024).

58 The benefits for the party supported by third States come mainly from the possibility for intervenors to address arguments that that party has decided not to address, because of domestic policy arguments against it, or because strategically it has decided to prioritize another argument. They may also address arguments that that party does not have the capacity or expertise to address (consultation with experts).

59 In proceedings before the ICJ, the intervening States benefit at the practical level from the possibility of receiving copies of the pleadings and annexes ahead of the hearing (ICJ Rules of Court, art. 85(1)). They are also able to submit a written statement, to which the parties in the main proceedings can submit observations, and they can also submit observations during the course of oral proceedings (ibid, art. 85(3)).

60 As an example, during the drafting of the ICCPR, some States considered inter-state complaints as a system that would safeguard the provisions of the Covenant (See UNGA,

has consolidated with the work of treaty bodies, which has continuously acknowledged the potential of inter-state communications to 'ensure that the provisions of the [c]onvention are adequately observed and complied with by all States parties'.[61] It is argued here that the possibility of having inter-state communications with various applicant or respondent States, or allowing third-party intervention, could strengthen the mechanism's potential for ensuring treaty compliance and human rights protection. The study of inter-state communications has also led to the acknowledgment of other possible aims of inter-state communications, such as the settlement of a dispute, or the use of the mechanism to signal violating States and complying States. This section presents the benefits of that collective approach for these aims.

3.1 *Benefits for Treaty Compliance and the Protection of Human Rights: Procedural Efficiency and Harmonization*

One of the arguments traditionally used to support the existence of collective procedures in international law is procedural efficiency (or economy), seen as a core procedural value as it facilitates court decisions with 'the least amount of administrative obfuscation',[62] or 'at the earliest possible date and at the lowest possible cost to the parties'.[63] Joint proceedings and third-party intervention in inter-state communications could contribute to making the procedure more efficient for treaty compliance and human rights protection, by reducing the administrative burden and at the same time facilitating the consideration of a wider set of arguments by the treaty body or conciliation commission.[64] It would also lead to multiple applicant or respondent States building coordinated strategies, enhancing the efficiency of the process.[65]

'Draft International Covenants on Human Rights' (1955) 10th Session, UN Doc A/2929, [63]), representing an 'additional possibility of securing compliance' (See UNGA Third Committee, GAOR, 21st Session, 1415th Meeting (1966) UN Doc A/C.3/SR.1415, 219–222, 219 [3]).

61 UN Committee on the Elimination of Racial Discrimination, 'Inter-State Communication Submitted by the State of Palestine against Israel: Decision on Jurisdiction' (16 June 2021) UN Doc CERD/C/100/5, 10–11 [55].

62 Brooke Coleman, The Efficiency Norm (2015) 56 Boston College Law Review 1777, 1813–1814.

63 *Arbitral Award of 31 July 1989 (Guinea-Bissau v Senegal)* (Joint Dissenting Opinion of Judges Aguilar Mawdsley and Ranjeva) [1991] ICJ Rep 53, 124; CM Chinkin, 'Third-Party Intervention Before the International Court of Justice' (1986) 80 American Journal of International Law 495.

64 See supra note 58.

65 An interesting development to scrutinize in upcoming months will be whether third-party interventions in *Ukraine v Russian Federation* before the ICJ are dealt with jointly. Some States have even coordinated by making joint oral observations; Austria, Czechia, Lichtenstein, and Slovakia (beginning at 42) and Belgium, Croatia, Denmark, Estonia, Finland, Ireland, Luxembourg, Romania, and Sweden (beginning at 45) are two such

Similar arguments have been developed for collective action in other fora, such as the ICJ or ITLOS.[66] Third-party intervention has confronted the ICJ with a wider range of legal arguments, allowing it to fully explore the implications of cases. This has the potential of avoiding 'repetitive litigation on the same subject matter' and can 'provide adequate information for the Court to render a comprehensive judgment'.[67] In his separate opinion in the *Indonesia/Malaysia* case, Judge Weeramantry established that '[i]ntervention procedure both in domestic and international law is based, inter alia, on the need for the avoidance of repetitive litigation',[68] although recently the oral interventions of the large number of intervening States in the *Ukraine v Russian Federation* case in the preliminary objections phase were quite repetitive. The same has been established for ITLOS, where factors relevant to the exercise of the Tribunal's powers in respect of intervention are the good administration of justice, including the need for efficiency and the need to deal with the case as a whole.[69]

Collective communications would also enhance the mechanism's potential for compliance whenever the question at stake is one of interpretation of the treaty, where harmonization may be sought. In his separate opinion in the *Indonesia/Malaysia* case, Judge Weeramantry established that another basis for third-party intervention is 'the need for harmony of principle, for a multiplicity of cases involving the same subject-matter could result in contradictory determinations which obscure rather than clarify the applicable law'.[70] As McIntyre flags, ICJ third-party intervention case law is not so explicitly supportive of the harmonization narrative.[71] Indeed, the use of third-party intervention in *Ukraine v Russian Federation* before the ICJ could point in this direction, although the preliminary objections phase did not seem to support this proposition.

---

examples (See *Allegations of Genocide under the Convention on the Prevention and Punishment of the Crime of Genocide* (*Ukraine v Russian Federation*) (Pending) (Preliminary Objections) Verbatim Record 2023/15 <https://www.icj-cij.org/sites/default/files/case-related/182/182-20230920-ora-01-00-bi.pdf> accessed 23 October 2023).

66 Nienke Grossman, 'The Normative Legitimacy of International Courts' (2013) 86(1) Temple Law Review 61, 76; Wood and Sthoeger, supra note 46.

67 Tania Licari, 'Intervention under Article 62 of the Statute of the ICJ' (1982) 8 Brooklyn Journal of International Law 267, 271.

68 *Sovereignty over Pulau Ligitan and Pulau Sipadan* (*Indonesia/Malaysia*) (Separate opinion of Judge ad hoc Weeramantry) [2001] ICJ Rep 575, 635–643 [17]. See also Juan José Quintana, 'Litigation at the International Court of Justice: Intervention under Article 62 of the Statute' in Loretta Malintoppi and Eduardo Valencia-Ospina (eds), *International Litigation in Practice* (vol 10, Brill Nijhoff 2015) 838, 841.

69 Wood and Sthoeger, supra note 46, 75.

70 Supra note 68.

71 McIntyre, supra note 43, 14–16, 27–30.

In their declaration of intervention as third parties in the case, various States referred explicitly to the interpretation of the Genocide Convention as an issue of common interest,[72] and several States referred to *erga omnes* or *erga omnes partes* obligations.[73] This is consistent with the legal basis which all these States have used to substantiate their request to intervene: art. 63 of the ICJ Statute. Unlike art. 62,[74] which opens an avenue for intervention when the third State can prove an 'interest of a legal nature which may be affected by the decision in the case',[75] art. 63 does not require the intervening State to prove such interest.[76]

---

72 Lithuania, for example, mentioned that it 'shares with all the other contracting parties to the Genocide Convention a common interest in ensuring that the construction of its provisions – which contain obligations *erga omnes partes* – are properly interpreted, so as to avoid abusive interpretations and misuses of the Convention', and that 'the integrity of the Convention requires its proper interpretation' (See *Allegations of Genocide under the Convention on the Prevention and Punishment of the Crime of Genocide* (*Ukraine v Russian Federation*) (Pending) Declaration of Intervention of the Republic of Lithuania (22 July 2022) <https://www.icj-cij.org/public/files/case-related/182/182-20220719-WRI-02-00-EN.pdf> accessed 30 April 2024, [17]). New Zealand considered that 'issues raised in the case turn on a proper interpretation of' provisions of the Genocide Convention and reminded the Court that 'all States Parties to the Convention have an interest in the proper interpretation, application and fulfilment of those obligations' (See *Allegations of Genocide under the Convention on the Prevention and Punishment of the Crime of Genocide* (*Ukraine v Russian Federation*) (Pending) Declaration of Intervention by the Government of New Zealand (28 July 2022) <https://www.icj-cij.org/public/files/case-related/182/182-20220728-WRI-01-00-EN.pdf> accessed 30 April 2024, [12], [17]).

73 See, for example the references made in the following interventions in *Allegations of Genocide under the Convention on the Prevention and Punishment of the Crime of Genocide* (*Ukraine v Russian Federation*): Declaration of Intervention of the Federal Republic of Germany (1 September 2022) <https://www.icj-cij.org/public/files/case-related/182/182-20220901-WRI-01-00-EN.pdf> accessed 30 April 2024, [12], [13]; Declaration of Intervention of the United States of America (7 September 2022) <https://www.icj-cij.org/public/files/case-related/182/182-20220907-WRI-01-00-EN.pdf> accessed 30 April 2024, [9]; Declaration of Intervention of the Government of Italy (12 September 2022) <https://www.icj-cij.org/public/files/case-related/182/182-20220912-WRI-02-00-EN.pdf> accessed 30 April 2024, [14]; Declaration of Intervention of the Government of Australia (30 September 2022) <https://www.icj-cij.org/public/files/case-related/182/182-20220930-WRI-01-00-EN.pdf> accessed 30 April 2024, [26]; Joint Declaration of Intervention of the Governments of Canada and the Kingdom of the Netherlands (7 December 2022) <https://www.icj-cij.org/public/files/case-related/182/182-20221207-WRI-02-00-EN.pdf> accessed 30 April 2024, [11]–[12].

74 The differences between the procedures laid out in art. 62 and art. 63 have been commented on widely, given the practical and conceptual implications of the distinction. This has been the case also in ongoing proceedings in *The Gambia v Myanmar* and *Ukraine v Russian Federation*.

75 ICJ Statute, art. 62.

76 Leiden University and University of Geneva, 'Intervening in International Justice: Third States and *Ukraine v Russia*' (Webinar, 17 August 2022) <https://youtu.be/OWBQ2ojK3Jw> accessed 23 October 2023. It allows States to declare their intention to intervene and,

Art. 63, also applied only very occasionally, is an avenue for intervention when the third State has a weaker connection to the case, not necessarily a legal interest in the case but where the interpretation of the convention at stake may be of relevance to it. This leaves more leeway for States to intervene in cases where *erga omnes partes* or *erga omnes* obligations are to be interpreted, and points toward the role of the ICJ not only as the universal judicial organ of the UN settling disputes between parties but also shaping the content of multilateral treaties and clarifying and contributing to the progressive development of international law.[77] Notwithstanding the implications of the distinction between arts. 62 and 63 and the potential blurring of the line dividing them, analysed in other sections of this chapter, developments in this massive third-party intervention case present an opportunity for the ICJ to consolidate its recognition of collective action's contribution to harmonized treaty interpretation, legitimized by the participation in proceedings of other parties to the treaty. This gives other States the opportunity to contribute with their submissions 'their view on the treaty', in cases where the obligations of the treaty have been breached or in cases where the interpretation of treaty provisions is at stake.

Collective inter-state communications would give UN treaty bodies an excellent opportunity to hear the views of the parties to the treaty on an issue of interpretation, helping them reach a more legitimate and harmonized view of the treaty provisions, in line with the principles and techniques of interpretation applying to international human rights treaties. The harmonization argument is valid also for when the procedure is initiated against multiple respondent States, as (instead of isolated non-compliance) the case may be uncovering an issue of interpretation.

The values of efficiency and harmonization of the law, traditionally identified as benefits of collective action before the ICJ, are not the only relevant values to assess the convenience of a collective approach to inter-state communications. Other values should be observed when considering the implications of collective action before UN treaty bodies, including transparency, party autonomy, confidentiality, democratic legitimacy and

---

although it can be rejected by the Court and also challenged by a party to the case, it is more automatic (ICJ Rules of Court, art. 85) than the art. 62 avenue, where the State requests permission from the Court to intervene, usually after a hearing.

77 Armin von Bogdandy and Ingo Venzke, 'On the Functions of International Courts: An Appraisal in Light of Their Burgeoning Public Authority' (2013) 26 Leiden Journal of International Law 49, 56; Grossman, supra note 66, 76.

representation.[78] Now-President of the ICJ Judge Donoghue suggested in her dissenting opinion in *Nicaragua v Colombia* that the Court should consider reforming its treatment of non-party intervention (in relation to art. 62) to be more transparent and efficient.[79]

The protection of *erga omnes* obligations and the space that *actio popularis* may have before the ICJ are also worth scrutinizing, as they are for inter-state communications. This chapter touches below upon those aspects, to the extent that they are relevant to inter-state communications.

3.2 *Amplifying Sovereign Voices through Peaceful Dispute Settlement*

Beyond procedural efficiency and harmonization, collective inter-state communications could be a channel to amplify sovereign voices, which may already be expressing their views on human rights violations in other fora, through a procedure for the peaceful settlement of disputes. Sovereign actors with no direct connection to a case may decide to get involved in some way, to express their position on particularly grave violations or for other strategic purposes. This can unleash a cascade of political or diplomatic tensions which may escalate and create more problems in the international sphere than those it may be trying to solve, unless it is done through peaceful channels. It is therefore important to find ways to allow those voices to be heard and even amplified, but within a context of peaceful and constructive exchanges.

Conscious of those risks, States react to human rights violations by other States either through other collective processes, such as the Universal Periodic Review (UPR),[80] or through treaty-specific monitoring mechanisms. But it is not unusual to see States react also through coordinated sanctions, import

78 McIntyre, supra note 43; Wojcikiewicz Almeida, supra note 50; Gracious Avayiwoe, 'Towards Clarity: The 'May be Affected' Requirement and Non-party Intervention at the International Court of Justice' (2023) 14(1) Journal of International Dispute Settlement 110; Alina Miron and Christine Chinkin, 'Article 62' in Andreas Zimmerman and others (eds), *The Statute of the International Court of Justice: A Commentary* (3rd edn, OUP 2019) 1686.

79 *Territorial and Maritime Dispute (Nicaragua v Colombia)* (Application for Intervention) (Dissenting opinion of Judge Donoghue) [2011] ICJ Rep 348, 471 [57]-[59].

80 For an analysis of the UPR and its use, see Edward McMahon and Marta Ascherio, 'A Step Ahead in Promoting Human Rights? The Universal Periodic Review of the UN Human Rights Council' (2012) 18 Global Governance 231; Karolina M Milewicz and Robert E Goodin, 'Deliberative Capacity Building through International Organizations: The Case of the Universal Periodic Review of Human Rights' (2016) 48 British Journal of Political Science 513; Rochelle Terman and Erik Voeten, 'The Relational Politics of Shame: Evidence from the Universal Periodic Review' (2018) 13 Review of International Organizations 1; Valentina Carraro, 'Promoting Compliance with Human Rights: The Performance of the United Nations' Universal Periodic Review and Treaty Bodies' (2019) 63 International Studies Quarterly 1079.

bans or diplomatic measures.[81] Whilst those are valuable and legitimate courses of action, they are not considered dispute settlement methods and they therefore do not offer some of the safeguards which dispute settlement provides, necessary to ensure party autonomy and representation, or to reduce the political dimension present in other collective processes, such as the UPR.[82] Collective inter-state communications offer a path to amplify those voices with a quasi-judicialised[83] but flexible procedure with safeguards to join forces against human rights violations, while reducing the fear of confrontation traditionally associated with inter-state communications. Let us explore the two dimensions of what collective inter-state communications offer in this regard.

The first element, the quasi-judicial but flexible procedure with safeguards, is one that has also been explored in other conciliation experiences.[84] As Wood has identified, conciliation today displays quasi-judicial characteristics,[85] which presents an advantage when it comes to establishing safeguards to reduce the risk of politicisation despite the participation of multiple States in the procedure. A group of States may decide to collectively signal a behaviour as unacceptable or signal themselves as the 'good guys', sending a message to the world about collective condemnation or about them being good citizens.[86] This would be done with the flexibility that conciliation offers, but through a quasi-judicial procedure where an independent conciliation commission, whose decisions are to be respectful of international law, will put in place the necessary safeguards to mitigate the risk of politicisation.[87] As Tomuschat reminds us for the OSCE context, conciliation commissions have flexibility

81 Arne Vandenbogaerd, *Towards Shared Accountability in International Human Rights Law: Law, Procedures and Principles* (Intersentia 2016) 119, n 425.

82 McMahon and Ascherio emphasize the 'political nature of the process' which they describe as 'largely evolutionary, rather than revolutionary' and 'consensus driven' (supra note 80, 239–240). Terman and Voeten argue that 'the UPR is political by design' (supra note 80, 3).

83 Bernhard Zangl and others, 'Between Law and Politics: Explaining International Dispute Settlement Behavior' (2011) 18 European Journal of International Relations 369, 389–390.

84 Elizabeth Exposto, 'The Timor Sea Conciliation and Treaty: Timor-Leste's Perspective' (2019) 36 Australian Yearbook of International Law 43.

85 Michael Wood, 'Conciliation' in *Oppenheim's International Law* (OUP 2019).

86 McIntyre, supra note 43, 26–29. For an analysis of the potential of collective action for climate change, see Benjamin Norman Forbes, 'AOSIS v The World: A Blueprint for the First International Multi-Party Climate Change Case' (2021) 8 Groningen Journal of International Law 200.

87 On the advantages of replacing diplomatic proceedings by judicialized mechanisms in which independent third parties settle on the basis of international law, see Zangl and others, supra note 83, 370.

on the applicable law, but their decisions must 'remain within the framework of lawfulness and legitimacy defined by the ground norms of the present day international legal order'.[88] Those safeguards include party autonomy, equality between parties, a procedure in accordance with international law, and a balance between transparency and confidentiality.[89]

The second element, the fact that collective inter-state communications could make the procedure less confrontational, touches upon an issue that has traditionally been a ground for reluctance and critique of inter-state communications. The collective dimension of this new form of inter-state communications would reduce the fear of confrontation, as States would be joined or supported by others in their claims and therefore initiating an inter-state communication would be considered a less directly confrontational process. Applicant States may be more likely to initiate a procedure jointly, as collective action has the potential of reducing the fear of being identified as the State initiating proceedings against another one. The work of committees in this regard would also encourage a culture where inter-state communications are no longer perceived as confrontational, but rather as a peaceful dispute settlement method. Tomuschat refers, in his analysis of the OSCE conciliation procedure, to a climate of 'serenity' that would make conciliation a better avenue but has not yet been reached.[90]

Another avenue that States tend to take to react to sovereign human rights violations is litigation before the ICJ. In cases where both avenues are available, the interpretation of compromissory clauses such as art. 22 of ICERD becomes key to understanding how States may decide to proceed in terms of choices. As the Court has clarified in *Georgia v Russian Federation*[91] and *Ukraine v Russian Federation*,[92] having initiated an inter-state communication is no pre-requisite for proceedings before the ICJ, as the pre-conditions in that provision are to be interpreted as alternative, not cumulative. This leads to a scenario where States may prefer turning to the ICJ than to treaty bodies.[93]

---

88 Christian Tomuschat, 'Conciliation within the Framework of the OSCE Court of Conciliation and Arbitration: An Assessment from the Viewpoint of Legal Policy' in Christian Tomuschat, Riccardo Pisillo Mazzeschi and Daniel Thürer (eds), *Conciliation in International Law: The OSCE Court of Conciliation and Arbitration* (Brill Nijhoff 2017) 97.

89 Ibid, 90–92, 97, 101–102.

90 Ibid, 86.

91 *Application of the International Convention on the Elimination of All Forms of Racial Discrimination* (*Georgia v Russian Federation*) (Preliminary Objections) [2011] ICJ Rep 70.

92 *Application of the International Convention for the Suppression of the Financing of Terrorism and of the International Convention on the Elimination of All Forms of Racial Discrimination* (*Ukraine v Russian Federation*) (Preliminary Objections) [2019] ICJ Rep 558, [113].

93 See contribution by Merryl Lawry-White to this volume.

Yet, in addition to possible arguments on the specialization of treaty bodies,[94] from the perspective of the amplification of sovereign voices, inter-state communications could offer a more attractive pathway. So far, the ICJ has been quite reluctant to accept the use of third-party intervention as a path for *actio popularis*.[95] How the ICJ is to deal with massive third-party intervention is to be seen, as *Ukraine v Russian Federation* is the first case with such scale of intervention.

Interestingly, some declarations of intervention in *Ukraine v Russian Federation* refer to the *erga omnes* character of the obligation, instead of referring to those States' interest in the case. This strategy may be partly explained by the ICJ's historical reluctance towards intervention[96] and to *actio popularis*,[97] and may push forward a new notion of interest, leading to exploring the idea that it could be automatically subjective, even if that blurs the lines between arts. 62 and 63. It is also possible that the legal interest required under art. 62 may be more flexibly interpreted for cases related to *erga omnes* obligations.[98] The ICJ could shift towards a more open approach to using third-party intervention for *actio popularis*.

---

94 In the *Ahmadou Sadio Diallo* judgment on the merits, the ICJ referred to the Human Rights Committee as the 'independent body … established specifically to supervise the application of that treaty' and recognized that it should 'ascribe great weight' to the Committee's interpretation (*Ahmadou Sadio Diallo* (*Republic of Guinea v Democratic Republic of the Congo*) (Merits) [2010] ICJ Rep 639, 663–664 [66]. See further Sandy Ghandhi, 'Human Rights and the International Court of Justice in the *Ahmadou Sadio Diallo* Case' (2011) 11(3) Human Rights Law Review 527, 536). See also Nigel Rodley, 'The International Court of Justice and Human Rights Treaty Bodies' in Mads Andenas and Eirik Bjorge (eds), *A Farewell to Fragmentation: Reassertion and Convergence in International Law* (CUP 2015) 87.

95 McIntyre, supra note 43; Paula Wojcikiewicz Almeida, 'International Procedural Regulation in the Common Interest: The Role of Third-Party Intervention and Amicus Curiae before the ICJ' (2019) 18 Law and Practice of International Courts and Tribunals 163.

96 Atul Alexander and Shouvik Kumar Guha, 'Critical Analysis of Third-Party Intervention before the International Court of Justice' (2021) 8 Indonesian Journal of International and Comparative Law 441, 444; Inna Uchkunova, 'The Minotaur's Labyrinth: Third State Intervention before the International Court of Justice' (2014), 13 Law and Practice of International Courts and Tribunals 179. The fact that most of the relevant third-party intervention cases are typically bilateral disputes, such as territorial or maritime disputes, 'has probably influenced to a large extent the Court's cautious approach to this procedural institution' (Quintana, supra note 68, 849, n 11). This could definitely change after *Ukraine v Russian Federation.*

97 Andrea Gattini, 'Actio Popularis' in Hélène Ruiz Fabri (ed), *Max Planck Encyclopedia of International Procedural Law* (OUP 2019); Ingo Venzke, 'Public Interests in The International Court of Justice—A Comparison Between *Nuclear Arms Race* (2016) and *South-West Africa* (1966)' (2017) 111 American Journal of International Law Unbound 68, 68.

98 Consultation with experts. See also Miron and Chinkin, supra note 78, 1709.

But the Court may well decide to remain loyal to its previous position, limiting the potential of this avenue for collective action beyond the interest that intervening States may have in a case. In that scenario, collective inter-state communications would be the only judicialised but flexible avenue to turn to, in addition to regional human rights courts and advisory opinions (see below), which do not offer the advantages of a conciliation process.

The potential of collective inter-state communications as a channel to amplify sovereign voices with the safeguards that dispute settlement provides is consistent with the view that the aims of inter-state communications are multiple and evolving, with an increasing emphasis in their dispute settlement function and in their strategic use (i.e. providing an avenue for State responsibility and allowing States to signal themselves as a 'good citizen' or target another state as a 'bad citizen').

4 Shaping the Contours of Collective Inter-state Communications

Collective inter-state communications have potential for treaty compliance and for amplifying those sovereign voices (see section 3 above). But these benefits need to be considered cautiously[99] and assessed in balance with other aspects of the procedure.[100] Collective inter-state communications add a layer of complexity which comes with certain risks that would need to be mitigated for them to be a feasible and plausible option. The fact that in the two recently suspended inter-state cases on racial discrimination – *Qatar v UAE* and *Qatar v Saudi Arabia* – the CERD Committee decided not to hear the two cases jointly[101] is an indication that the collective dimension may not always work for inter-state communications. This section offers reflections on how some of those complexities or risks may be mitigated, by looking at the composition and impartiality of the conciliation commission, and the differences between third-party intervention and joint proceedings.

---

99 According to McIntyre, such potential advantage has not been so central to considerations by the ICJ, for example, on third-party intervention (McIntyre, supra note 43, 18).

100 On the need for a cautious approach to efficiency, see Fabien Gelinas and others (eds), *Foundations of Civil Justice: Toward a Value-based Framework for Reform* (Springer 2015) vii; Loukas Mistelis, 'Efficiency—What Else?: Efficiency as the Emerging Defining Value of International Arbitration: Between Systems Theories and Party Autonomy' in Thomas Schultz and Federico Ortino (eds), *The Oxford Handbook of International Arbitration* (OUP 2020) 349, 358.

101 The Committee made no mention of the reasons for this decision.

4.1 *Conciliation Commissions: Composition, Impartiality, and Functioning*

A study of ICERD, the only UN human rights treaty under which inter-state communications have been initiated to date, emphasizes the importance of appointing an impartial conciliation commission, integrated by highly recognised experts, and with guidance on its functioning and rules, but retaining a high degree of flexibility.[102] These features, which we also see mentioned in other frameworks envisaging conciliation,[103] become even more relevant when considering the possibility of having collective inter-state communications, to mitigate some of the associated risks that the collective dimension may pose. Three main risks need to be considered from this collective perspective, which may make an agreement more difficult to reach in multi-party conciliation or third-party intervention in these proceedings.

First, it may be more challenging to find a common ground solution acceptable to all parties. Second, if some of the parties want to use collective inter-state communications to amplify their voices signalling themselves or signalling others, there is a risk of politicisation. Third, connected also to this strategic use of the mechanism, any commission will have to strike the right (and difficult) balance between publicity and confidentiality. These potential problems could find their best solution through the appointment of a competent and independent conciliation commission which has clear rules to follow. As Wood emphasised for conciliation,[104] impartiality is the key to a conciliation commission's success, and that can only be reemphasised for collective inter-state communications. The rationale for mitigating these risks is also going to inform the decision on whether to articulate joint proceedings or third-party intervention (see section 4.2 below).

The need to find a common ground solution agreeable for various parties makes the work of the conciliation commission more challenging and may cause delays or procedural complication. This, however, does not make this avenue impractical. The need to reconcile multiple interests is a challenge that experts in international dispute settlement are well accustomed to, and one for which advanced techniques are available.[105] This type of challenge should

102 Eiken and Keane, supra note 5, in particular 323–326, 337–338.

103 United Nations Convention on the Law of the Sea (adopted 10 December 1982, entered into force 16 November 1994) 1833 UNTS 3, annex V, arts. 284, 297, 298; Convention on Conciliation and Arbitration within the Commission on Security and Cooperation in Europe (adopted 15 December 1992, entered into force 5 December 1994) 1842 UNTS 151 (Stockholm Convention), arts. 2–3, 18–25.

104 Wood, supra note 85.

105 John Merrills and Eric De Brabandere, *Merills' International Dispute Settlement* (7th edn, CUP 2022) 110–111; Exposto, supra note 84, 53–55.

inform the rules on who can be appointed as a member of the conciliation commission, particularly considering the skills and experience which may contribute better to resolving this complex challenge. Procedural complication may be solved with the flexibility that conciliation commissions have to set up procedural rules. As occurs with third-party intervention before the ICJ, a certain level of coordination between the interveners or parties holding similar positions may be necessary to make the commission's work more efficient.

The main tool to mitigate the risk of politicisation is again the independence and impartiality of the conciliation commission. As Tomuschat has expressed, 'the impact that a conciliation commission may have depends entirely on its independence and impartiality'.[106] The procedure to ensure such independence and impartiality may take different forms but usually follows a pattern where, as in the OSCE case, each party appoints a conciliator and the remaining members are elected in consultation with the parties, who can raise objections if there is any suspicion of bias.[107] Other considerations may also inform the appointment of members of a conciliation commission. In the ongoing inter-state communication between Palestine and Israel before the CERD Committee, the appointment of members of the *ad hoc* conciliation commission was also informed by geographic considerations, in an additional attempt to ensure fairness.[108] As Tomuschat explains for the OSCE process, ensuring fairness through the process to appoint an independent and impartial conciliation commission has the benefit that 'there is no 'unpleasant surprise'' or 'suspicion of bias [...] against the Court when it exercises conciliatory powers'.[109]

Finally, one of the biggest challenges that a conciliation commission will have to face when collective inter-state communications are initiated with, among others, the purpose of 'signalling' is striking the right balance between publicity and confidentiality. As Tomuschat considers in the OSCE context, confidentiality can be very important for conciliation, as it allows for commission members to be 'frank' and not have to worry about public and/or media perceptions.[110] However, if the parties (or at least some of them) are using this mechanism to signal themselves or to signal others, publicity is something that they are likely to want to avail themselves of. This may make the commission's decision on that balance more challenging, as the publicity associated with *actio popularis* would require higher levels of transparency

106 Tomuschat, supra note 88, 98.
107 Ibid, 90–92.
108 Eiken and Keane, supra note 5, 327–329.
109 Tomuschat, supra note 88, 90–92.
110 Ibid, 101.

than those ideal for dispute settlement.[111] This has also been acknowledged for third-party intervention before the ICJ, where 'sometimes publicity might disturb the proceedings',[112] and where for McIntyre 'the Court has persistently deferred to the parties' wishes.'[113] Deferring to the parties' wishes could be a way to ensure a good attempt at the right balance, mitigating politicisation and reputational risks, through the protection of party autonomy and equality of arms.[114] However, it is important that each conciliation commission establishes its own rules and principles, instead of being subjected to rigid rules which may make their endeavours more difficult.

An interesting development on this front could come from the development of model rules which treaty bodies could use, looking at questions such as:

- Who appoints conciliation commission members?
- What skills, qualifications and experience are required from members?
- How can independence be preserved once a commission has been established?[115]
- How can publicity and confidentiality be balanced?

4.2 *Third-Party vs Joint Proceedings*

The analysis in this chapter has addressed, so far, all forms of collective inter-state communication together. There are, however, notable differences between joint proceedings, third-party intervention, and more informal ways of collective action. This section flags some of those differences and reflects on the convenience of envisaging each of them as part of the UN inter-state communications mechanism. Given the lack of a victimhood requirement in inter-state communications, there is a fine line between joint proceedings

---

111 Consultation with experts.

112 McIntyre, supra note 43, 37.

113 Ibid.

114 In its order on third-party intervention in *Ukraine v Russian Federation*, the Court emphasized the need to 'organize the proceedings in a manner which ensures the equality of the parties', giving them both 'a fair opportunity and the necessary time to respond to the observations of the intervening States' (See Juliette McIntyre, Kyra Wigard and Ori Pomson, 'A Hot Potato: The ICJ's Order on the Admissibility of 32 Declarations of Intervention in *Ukraine v Russia*' (*EJIL: Talk!*, 13 June 2023) <https://www.ejiltalk.org/a-hot-potato-the-icjs-order-on-the-admissibility-of-32-declarations-of-intervention-in-ukraine-v-russia/> accessed 30 April 2024).

115 In the OSCE context, independence is maintained by having the parties to a dispute select from a pre-established list of qualified conciliators (art. 21(1) of the Stockholm Convention). These conciliators (who must be individuals with senior qualifications and experience in international law) are appointed by State parties for renewable six-year terms—and crucially, cannot be removed by the appointing State for the duration of their term (art. 3(2)-(3) of the Stockholm Convention).

and third-party intervention. The decision of States with no direct interest in the case on whether to join proceedings or intervene as a third party would depend on how the two options are articulated.

Joint proceedings are the most engaging and demanding form of collective inter-state communication that could be envisaged. One or more applicant States would initiate proceedings before a UN treaty body against one or more respondent States. In cases with multiple applicant States, there could be various affected States, various non-affected States, or a mixture of affected and non-affected States.[116] Whether a State decides to embark on this cumbersome, resource-intensive and rather risky procedure without a direct interest in the case remains very much dependent, as in *The Gambia v Myanmar*, on its own analysis of all the available options and their cost and potential, and the State's perception of their role in international human rights law and affairs. If a paradigm shift consolidates in the international community, we could see more of this, despite associated risks.[117] However, as indicated in section 4.1 above, a conciliation procedure with more than two parties may be more challenging, as it would be more difficult to achieve a positive outcome agreeable for all parties.

This may shift the balance of preferences towards third-party intervention, where the intervening States would not become a party to the proceedings but the process would allow those States to participate in the procedure in a restricted way and would inform the treaty body on how the outcome may affect the rights of the interveners.[118] Discussing inter-state arbitration, Wood and Sthoeger point out that there are no recent examples of third-party intervention in inter-state arbitration, and 'it seems to have been a widely held view that intervention should not be possible (…) unless the parties have expressly agreed to allow it, whether by general or specific agreement'.[119] Yet, they also acknowledge 'there is no principle of arbitration that precludes third-party intervention'.[120]

The same could be argued for conciliation, where there are no cases yet of third-party intervention, but it could be a more suitable way to provide a

116 This is possible because inter-state communications do not require victimhood for standing – only having accepted the competence of treaty bodies would be sufficient.

117 In addition to risks mentioned in section 4.1 above, there is a difficulty in maintaining consistency in legal position, which may have implications in terms of remedies and countermeasures. This is particularly the case in a scenario where directly affected and not directly affected applicant States join forces in proceedings.

118 See Chinkin, supra note 43.

119 Wood and Sthoeger, supra note 46, 68.

120 *Affaire du Guano* (*Chili v France*), Award (5 July 1901) XV UNRIAA 315–316, referred to in Wood and Sthoeger, supra note 46, 68.

collective avenue for conciliation than joint proceedings. Wood considers that 'in modern practice conciliation does display some quasi-judicial characteristics'.[121] Why not then embrace this form of collective action? The parties would remain in the driving seat, retaining control of the appointment of commission members, with third parties having no formal say on it (although in practice there could be certain influence of third parties in States parties' position or decision). This would also make it easier to achieve a common ground solution for the parties, as such a proposed solution does not have to be convincing or acceptable for third parties. It seems it could be more likely for States to be willing to intervene as third parties than through joint proceedings, despite the potential reputational risk associated with a rejection of intervention.[122] If the paradigm shift is not so radical, this could be an increasingly expected behaviour in States. As stated in section 3.1 above, if this trend consolidates, joint third-party interventions could become an attractive proposition, where the intervening States may coordinate with the State they support about their submissions, arguments and strategy. For this to consolidate, however, it would be important to set up clear rules on the grounds for intervention and bases for rejecting them.

In other fora, joinder of proceedings and third-party intervention still leave space for more informal types of collective action, mainly related to access to information, such as requesting access to information on a case before the ICJ despite not joining proceedings as a party or third-party intervenor.[123] However, one of the distinctive features of inter-state communications has been the discretion of the treaty body or conciliation commission to decide how much information is made available to non-parties, a decision usually based on what works best for the parties.[124] This principle, associated strongly with conciliation approaches to dispute settlement, reduces this option significantly in the case of inter-state communications, although not entirely. A treaty body or conciliation commission could make a decision in favour of

---

121 Wood, supra note 85.

122 A request for intervention may be denied or found inadmissible, which may have negative consequences at the domestic policy level, or from the international reputational perspective (consultation with experts). See also on confidentiality and reputational risk, Eiken and Keane, supra note 5, 307.

123 See Wood and Sthoeger, supra note 46; Wojcikiewicz Almeida, supra note 95, 163–188.

124 As observed by Eiken and Keane, supra note 5, 307, 'A "strict rule of confidentiality" is generally observed in conciliation proceedings to ensure the process does not in any way prejudice the legal positions of the parties in a future proceeding.'

this, although this would only make sense if it did not hamper the potential of the work of the conciliation commission.

Advisory opinions are another form of informal action that in this context can shed light on how collective action may also be shaped in other forms, beyond quasi-judicial processes. They bear mentioning, as they have 'proven an important tool for answering pressing questions facing the international community'.[125] Most recently, 57 States have filed written statements for the upcoming Palestine advisory opinion,[126] and there will presumably be similar (or even greater) levels of participation at the oral hearings in February 2024.[127] The request for an advisory opinion regarding the obligations of States in respect of climate change[128] is also likely draw a mass response. At the time of writing, the ICJ has authorised the Commission of Small Island States,[129] the EU,[130] the African Union,[131] the Organisation of African, Caribbean and Pacific States,[132] and the Pacific Community[133] to participate in proceedings. The advisory procedure thus demonstrates that there is a place for multilateral participation in the international legal order.

125 *The International Court of Justice: 75 Years in the Service of Peace and Justice* (United Nations 2022) 80.

126 *Legal Consequences arising from the Policies and Practices of Israel in the Occupied Palestinian Territory, including East Jerusalem* (Request for Advisory Opinion) ICJ Press Release 2023/43 <https://www.icj-cij.org/sites/default/files/case-related/186/186-20230807-pre-01-00-en.pdf> accessed 30 April 2024.

127 EJIL: The Podcast!, supra note 31, 30:50-31:13.

128 *Obligations of States in respect of Climate Change* (Pending) ICJ Press Release 2023/20 <https://www.icj-cij.org/sites/default/files/case-related/187/187-20230419-PRE-01-00-EN.pdf> accessed 30 April 2024.

129 *Obligations of States in respect of Climate Change* (Pending) ICJ Press Release 2023/32 <https://www.icj-cij.org/sites/default/files/case-related/187/187-20230622-pre-01-00-en.pdf> accessed 30 April 2024.

130 *Obligations of States in respect of Climate Change* (Pending) ICJ Press Release 2023/33 <https://www.icj-cij.org/sites/default/files/case-related/187/187-20230623-pre-01-00-en.pdf> accessed 30 April 2024.

131 *Obligations of States in respect of Climate Change* (Pending) ICJ Press Release 2023/42 <https://www.icj-cij.org/sites/default/files/case-related/187/187-20230718-pre-01-00-en.pdf> accessed 30 April 2024.

132 *Obligations of States in respect of Climate Change* (Pending) ICJ Press Release 2023/48 <https://www.icj-cij.org/sites/default/files/case-related/187/187-20230920-pre-01-00-en.pdf> accessed 30 April 2024.

133 *Obligations of States in respect of Climate Change* (Pending) ICJ Press Release 2023/70 <https://www.icj-cij.org/sites/default/files/case-related/187/187-20231124-pre-01-00-en.pdf> accessed 30 April 2024.

5 Concluding Remarks

As this chapter has highlighted, collective inter-state communications show potential as a means of strengthening the mechanism as an avenue for treaty compliance and human rights protection, and for amplifying sovereign voices in a peaceful way. We have proposed specific ways in which the contours of such collective action should be defined to mitigate the identified risks. The chapter has shown that this collective avenue, which is widely accepted (if not always utilised) in other fora, including the ICJ and regional human rights courts, could open a fresh avenue of engagement with this mechanism. Such engagement would embrace the potential of collective action as an effective path to treaty compliance and interpretation, and as a valuable channel through which States can raise their sovereign voices internationally in a peaceful and constructive way. This would require guaranteeing the independence of conciliation commissions through rules on appointment of their members that reduce associated risks, such as the risk of politicisation and of party inequality.

There would be a fine line between joint proceedings and third-party intervention in inter-state communications before UN treaty bodies, given the lack of a victimhood requirement. But if the paradigm shift in the international community consolidates, it is unlikely to do so in a radical way. The expectation is that we may see some sovereign behavioural change over time, but third-party intervention will emerge as more suitable than joint proceedings, and is probably more appealing to States without a direct interest in the alleged violations, at least for the medium term.

Acknowledgements

The authors would like to thank Ali Kamran Ahmed for excellent research assistance. Thanks to King's College London and its Centre for International Governance and Dispute Resolution (CIGAD) and to the British Institute of International and Comparative Law (BIICL) for their support for this research project.

CHAPTER 7

Inter-State Cases under ICERD as an Avenue to Protect Cultural Heritage

David Keane

Abstract

The most recent applications before the International Court of Justice (ICJ) under Article 22 of the International Convention on the Elimination of All Forms of Racial Discrimination (ICERD), Armenia v. Azerbaijan and Azerbaijan v. Armenia, both claim that the destruction of cultural heritage during the Nagorno-Karabakh conflict constitutes a violation of the Convention. The applications have met with enthusiasm that ICERD offers a potential new avenue for the protection of cultural heritage, as well as scepticism as to whether these claims fall within the scope of the treaty. Armenia and Azerbaijan bypassed the inter-State communications mechanism under Articles 11–13 before the Committee on the Elimination of Racial Discrimination (CERD), as they are legally entitled to do. But the CERD perspective remains important. First, the Articles 11–13 mechanism is available in relation to 182 States Parties, whereas due to reservations, the Article 22 mechanism is available only in relation to 157 States Parties. Second, CERD practice in relation to cultural heritage ought to inform the determination of the Court. This article investigates the CERD approach to the protection of cultural heritage. It draws in related questions such as whether religious cultural heritage comes under a treaty on racial discrimination; the applicability of these protections in situations of armed conflict; and ICERD's relationship with other specialised instruments. It offers conclusions as to what extent an avenue for the protection of cultural heritage under ICERD exists before the Committee and the Court.

 DOI:10.1163/9789004712584_009

Keywords

ICERD – racial discrimination – cultural heritage – religious cultural heritage – armed conflict – ICJ

1 Introduction

The most recent applications before the International Court of Justice (ICJ/the Court) under Article 22 of the International Convention on the Elimination of All Forms of Racial Discrimination (ICERD), *Armenia v. Azerbaijan* (2021) and *Azerbaijan v. Armenia* (2021), both claim that the destruction of cultural heritage during the Nagorno-Karabakh conflict constitutes a violation of ICERD.[1] Only Armenia requested provisional measures on this issue, forming the first hearings and decisions before the Court, hence its case will be the focus of this article. Armenia set out allegations that Azerbaijan is engaging in the destruction, erasure or falsification of Armenian cultural heritage, including the destruction of numerous relics of Armenian cultural heritage such as the Surb Astvatsatsin church, the historic Holy Saviour Ghazanchetsots Cathedral in Shushi, and 15th and 16th century Armenian cross-stones (*khachkars*).[2] In its December 2021 order on provisional measures, the Court considered that the rights allegedly violated satisfied the plausibility threshold, and that Azerbaijan must take 'all necessary measures to prevent and punish acts of vandalism and desecration affecting Armenian cultural heritage, including but not limited to churches and other places of worship, monuments, landmarks, cemeteries and artefacts.'[3] The case has yet to progress to the preliminary objections or merits stage, where questions of the scope of the treaty may be more substantively engaged beyond the relatively low bar of "plausibility" required for provisional measures.[4]

The Court's 2021 order has led to some excitement in the cultural heritage sphere as to a potential 'new, yet narrow, pathway for fighting cultural

1 *Application of the International Convention on the Elimination of All Forms of Racial Discrimination (Armenia v. Azerbaijan)*, Application Instituting Proceedings and Request for Provisional Measures, 16 September 2021 p. 44–50; *Application of the International Convention on the Elimination of All Forms of Racial Discrimination (Azerbaijan v. Armenia)*, Application Instituting Proceedings and Request for Provisional Measures, 23 September 2021 p. 44–56 and p. 70–74.

2 *Armenia v. Azerbaijan*, Ibid p. 44 paras 70–71, p. 46 paras 73–74.

3 *Armenia v.* Azerbaijan, Provisional Measures, Order, 7 December 2021 p. 391 para 92.

4 See further Massimo Lando, 'Plausibility in the Provisional Measures Jurisprudence of the International Court of Justice' (2018) 31(3) *Leiden Journal of International Law* 641–668.

destruction.'[5] It has been suggested that '[b]y recognizing that attacks on minority cultural heritage can be both a product of, and incitement to, racial hatred, the Court has opened the door for descendant communities to invoke the CERD treaty in defense of threatened sites'.[6] By contrast, others are not convinced about challenging the destruction of cultural heritage sites by pleading racial discrimination under ICERD, considering it 'an exercise in legal acrobatics'.[7] This scepticism is situated within a wider critique of the perceived use of Article 22 ICERD to bring situations of armed conflict and territorial dispute before the Court which, it is argued, have little to do with racial discrimination.[8] Judge Yusuf offered a dissenting opinion to the order in *Armenia v. Azerbaijan* that captures these concerns:

---

5 Simon Magakhyan, 'Cultural Desecration is Racial Discrimination' *Foreign Policy* 13 January 2022 <https://foreignpolicy.com/2022/01/13/armenia-azerbaijan-nagorno-karabakh-cultural-desecration-is-racial-discrimination/> accessed 30 April 2024. See also Alexander Herman, 'A New Take on Cultural Heritage at the ICJ – Armenia v. Azerbaijan' *The Institute of Art & Law* 17 February 2022 <https://ial.uk.com/new-take-icj/> accessed 30 April 2024.

6 Cornell University Department of Near Eastern Studies, 'World Court Decision sets "New Precedent" for Cultural Heritage Protection' *A&S Communications* 12 August 2021 <https://neareasternstudies.cornell.edu/news/world-court-decision-sets-new-precedent-cultural-heritage-protection> accessed 30 April 2024 [quoting Profs. Adam T. Smith and Lori Khatchadourian].

7 Fahrid Chishty, 'Is Cultural Desecration Racial Discrimination in International Law? Implications of the Order Indicating Provisional Measures in *Armenia v. Azerbaijan* [2021]' *Cambridge International Law Journal Blog* 24 March 2022 <http://cilj.co.uk/2022/03/24/is-cultural-desecration-racial-discrimination-in-international-law-implications-of-the-order-indicating-provisional-measures-in-armenia-v-azerbaijan-2021/> accessed 30 April 2024.

8 See *inter alia* Alain Pellet, 'Open Letter to my Russian Friends: Ukraine is Not Crimea' *Ejil: Talk!* 3 March 2022 <https://www.ejiltalk.org/open-letter-to-my-russian-friends-ukraine-is-not-crimea/> accessed 30 April 2024 – 'I do not believe in the Ukrainian accusations of racial discrimination before the ICJ – a pretext too often seized by States to try to circumvent the lack of jurisdiction of the World Court'; Filippo Fontanelli, 'The Disputes Between Armenia and Azerbaijan: The CERD Compromissory Clause as a One-way Ticket to Hague' *Ejil: Talk!* 11 November 2021 <https://www.ejiltalk.org/the-disputes-between-armenia-and-azerbaijan-the-cerd-compromissory-clause-as-a-one-way-ticket-to-hague/> accessed 30 April 2024 – 'CERD's open-ended texture beckons the CERD-ification of disputes that are only incidentally about race discrimination'; Yilin Wang, 'Warfare to Lawfare under CERD: Armenia v. Azerbaijan and Azerbaijan v. Armenia' *Opinio Juris* 9 November 2021 <http://opiniojuris.org/2021/11/09/warfare-to-lawfare-under-cerd-armenia-v-azerbaijan-and-azerbaijan-v-armenia/> accessed 30 April 2024 – '[t]he strategy is to cleverly re-characterize the dispute around racial discrimination in order to pass the step of jurisdiction *ratione materiae*'.

> The Court has thrown wide open the gates of the Convention on the Elimination of Racial Discrimination…to all kinds of claims that have nothing to do with its provisions or with its object and purpose. Through this Order, claims under humanitarian law have been given a home in CERD, whereas the law on the safeguarding of cultural heritage has been brought within the scope of CERD. This unprecedented approach risks transforming the Convention into a "fourre-tout"; a receptacle in which all sorts of asserted rights may be stuffed.[9]

Absent from the discussion to date is the perspective of the Committee on the Elimination of Racial Discrimination (CERD/the Committee). It may be noted that the Armenia and Azerbaijan applications bypassed the inter-State communications mechanism before CERD under Articles 11–13 ICERD, as they are legally entitled to do.[10] However, the CERD perspective remains important for two reasons. First, the Articles 11–13 mechanism before CERD is compulsory and available to all 182 States Parties to ICERD, whereas the Article 22 mechanism before the ICJ, due to reservations, is available only to 157 States Parties. Hence, CERD's views on whether ICERD protects cultural heritage are at a minimum of potential relevance in relation to 25 States Parties who could not be brought before the Court by another State Party, but could be brought before the Committee.[11] Second, CERD's position ought to inform the determination of the Court in this area. The Committee has been

9 *Armenia v. Azerbaijan*, Provisional Measures, Order, Dissenting Opinion of Judge Yusuf, 7 December 2021 p. 395 para 1. Judge Yusuf would repeat this position in a dissent to the later order on provisional measures issued by the Court against Azerbaijan in February 2023: 'A regrettable tendency seems to have developed, whereby any State that fails to find a valid basis of jurisdiction of the Court for its claims, but still wishes to bring a case before it, tries to stuff those claims into the framework of CERD.' *Armenia v. Azerbaijan*, Provisional Measures, Order, Dissenting Opinion of Judge Yusuf, 22 February 2023 p. 1 para 3.

10 In *Ukraine v Russian Federation*, the Court found the preconditions of Article 22 ICERD to be alternative rather than cumulative, meaning States Parties may seise the Court if they have satisfied the precondition of 'negotiation' and are not required also to go through the Articles 11–13 mechanism before CERD. See *Application of the International Convention for the Suppression of the Financing of Terrorism and of the International Convention on the Elimination of All Forms of Racial Discrimination* (*Ukraine v. Russian Federation*), Preliminary Objections, Judgment (8 November 2019), ICJ Reports 2019 p. 558, at p. 600 para 110.

11 Namely: Afghanistan, Bahrain, China, Cuba, Egypt, Equatorial Guinea, India, Indonesia, Iraq, Israel, Kuwait, Lebanon, Libya, Madagascar, Morocco, Mozambique, Nepal, Saudi Arabia, Singapore, Syrian Arab Republic, Thailand, Turkey, United States of America, Viet Nam and Yemen. United Nations Treaty Collection, Chapter IV.2 <https://treaties.un.org/pages/ViewDetails.aspx?src=IND&mtdsg_no=IV-2&chapter=4&clang=_en> accessed 30 April 2024.

monitoring the treaty since 1970, and has an expertise built over more than a half-century of practice that is important in determining the meaning and scope of the Convention in relation to the protection of cultural heritage. The views of the Committee do not bind the Court, but the ICJ will, according to its own jurisprudence, give them careful consideration and accord them great weight.[12]

With that in mind, this article examines whether ICERD provides an avenue for the protection of cultural heritage in reference to *both* CERD and the ICJ inter-State mechanisms. It considers Judge Yusuf's dissent to be a benchmark against which to test the scope of the treaty. Judge Yusuf is also a former Director of the Office of International Standards and Legal Affairs at the United Nations Educational, Scientific and Cultural Organization (UNESCO).[13] The dissent makes a number of arguments, but four may be identified in particular – that ICERD's provisions safeguard the rights and freedoms of human beings, not objects, and as a result '[c]onsiderations of race and racial discrimination cannot and do not apply to monuments, groups of buildings, sites and artefacts';[14] that *religious* cultural heritage such as cathedrals and churches do not fall within the scope of a treaty on *racial* discrimination;[15] that the protection of cultural monuments and sites falls within the ambit of other instruments, specifically UNESCO's 1954 Hague Convention for the Protection of Cultural Property in the Event of Armed Conflict (1954 Hague Convention) whose intergovernmental Committee has already been seised of the preservation of cultural sites in Nagorno-Karabakh;[16] and that other human rights bodies such as the European Court of Human Rights (ECtHR) also could not find such a link between the provisions of the European Convention on Human Rights (ECHR) and claims relating to cultural heritage, seen in its decision in *Ahunbay and Others v. Turkey* (2019) in which the destruction of the Hasankeyf archaeological and cultural heritage site in southeast Turkey was held not to violate the ECHR.[17]

---

12 *Application of the International Convention on the Elimination of All Forms of Racial Discrimination (Qatar v. United Arab Emirates)*, Preliminary Objections, Judgment (4 February 2021), ICJ Reports 2021, p. 71, at p.104 para 101; *Ahmadou Sadio Diallo (Republic of Guinea v Democratic Republic of the Congo)*, Judgment (2010) ICJ Reports p. 639, at p. 664 para 66.

13 As noted in Eleni Polymenopoulou, 'Cultural Rights in the Caselaw of the International Court of Justice' (2014) 27(2) *Leiden Journal of International Law* 447–464, at 449 n 11. See also Abdulqawi A. Yusuf (ed.) *Standard-Setting in UNESCO Vol. 1* (Martinus Nijhoff 2007).

14 Dissenting Opinion of Judge Yusuf (2021), supra n 9 p. 398–399 paras 13 and 15.

15 Ibid para 17.

16 Ibid paras 13–14.

17 Ibid para 16, citing *Ahunbay and Others v. Turkey*, Application no. 6080/06 (2019).

The article proceeds as follows. Section 2 considers whether ICERD protects cultural heritage, based on the text of the Convention and the practice of the Committee. It encompasses whether religious cultural heritage comes under the scope of ICERD as a treaty on racial discrimination. Section 3 reflects on the applicability of ICERD in armed conflict, the context in which the Armenia and Azerbaijan cases have arisen, including whether ICERD protects cultural heritage in armed conflict. Section 4 examines the relevance of other instruments to understanding the scope of ICERD, notably the 1954 Hague Convention as well as the ECHR. In conclusion, the article determines that from the perspective of CERD, the Convention clearly does protect cultural heritage, in peacetime and in armed conflict. As a result, the Articles 11–13 mechanism would offer an avenue to any of the 182 States Parties to ICERD to protect the cultural heritage of Convention groups in relation to any other State Party. Final remarks are addressed to the extent to which the position of CERD accords with the text, context and object and purpose of the treaty, and may as a result guide that of the Court.

2 CERD and the Protection of Cultural Heritage

International cultural heritage law is an open and composite field of international law,[18] in which the protection of cultural heritage by international human rights treaties has become increasingly recognised. In 2011, the UN Independent Expert in the Field of Cultural Rights, Farida Shaheed, identified a human rights-based approach to cultural heritage whereby 'a shift has taken place from the preservation/safeguard of cultural heritage as such, based on its outstanding value for humanity, to the protection of cultural heritage as being of crucial value for individuals and communities in relation to their cultural identity.'[19] In 2016, her successor as Special Rapporteur, Karima Bennoune, affirmed this link:

> the first mandate holder established how the right of access to and enjoyment of cultural heritage forms part of international human rights law, finding its legal basis, in particular, in the right to take part in cultural

18 Gabriele Gagliani, 'The International Court of Justice and Cultural Heritage: International Cultural Heritage Law through the Lens of World Court Jurisprudence?' in Anne-Marie Carstens and Elizabeth Varner (eds.) *Intersections in International Cultural Heritage Law* (Oxford University Press 2020) 223–242, at 223.

19 Farida Shaheed, 'Report of the UN Independent Expert in the Field of Cultural Rights: The Right to Access and Enjoy Cultural Heritage' UN Doc. A/HRC/17/38 (2011) p. 7 para 20.

> life, the right of members of minorities to enjoy their own culture and the right of indigenous peoples to self-determination and to maintain, control, protect and develop cultural heritage.[20]

Importantly, Special Rapporteur Bennoune identified the *legal basis* for the right to cultural heritage as 'the right to take part in cultural life'. As Yvonne Donders among others have noted, there are no explicit rights to cultural heritage in international human rights treaties.[21] Instead, a more narrowly framed right to participate – or to take part in – cultural life has been interpreted as engaging a right to cultural heritage. This right is articulated in Article 27(1) of the 1948 Universal Declaration of Human Rights (UDHR), whereby 'Everyone has the right freely to participate in the cultural life of the community'. Article 15(1)(a) of the 1966 International Covenant on Economic, Social and Cultural Rights (ICESCR) provides for 'the right of everyone to take part in cultural life', with similar formulations in later UN human rights treaties.[22] But the right would find its first expression in treaty form in ICERD, adopted on 21 December 1965, whose Article 5(e)(vi) prohibits racial discrimination in the enjoyment of: 'The right to equal participation in cultural activities'.

In fact, the earliest underpinnings of ICERD point to an understanding that the protection of the cultural heritage of Convention groups would be integral to the protection of the groups themselves. ICERD began as a UN response to a global outbreak of anti-Semitic incidents in the winter of 1959–60, known as the "Swastika epidemic". These incidents were directed not against Jewish individuals or groups of individuals, but against Jewish *property*:

> Set off by the apparently symbolic and widely publicised desecration of a synagogue in Cologne, Germany, on Christmas morning of 1959, an unprecedented wave of overt anti-Jewish incidents swept the world. By the following day, swastika paintings, the display of anti-Semitic slogans, and physical attacks on Jewish property had begun in the United States;

20 Karima Bennoune, 'Report of the Special Rapporteur in the Field of Cultural Rights: The Intentional Destruction of Cultural Heritage as a Violation of Human Rights' UN Doc. A/HRC/31/59 (2016) p. 12 para 50.

21 Yvonne Donders, 'Cultural Heritage and Human Rights' in Ana Filipa Vrdoljak and Francesco Francioni (eds.) *The Oxford Handbook of International Cultural Heritage Law* (Oxford University Press, 2020) 379–406, at 380.

22 See Article 13 of the 1979 Convention on the Elimination of Discrimination Against Women; Article 31 of the 1989 Convention on the Rights of the Child; and Article 43 of the 1990 International Convention on the Rights of Migrant Workers and their Families.

> within one month reports of such episodes had come from approximately 34 countries and almost every major capital city.[23]

This prompted a reaction from the UN Sub-Commission and Commission that led to the adoption of a series of resolutions, and ultimately the Convention itself.[24] The issue would be addressed by these UN bodies as one of 'manifestations' of racial prejudice and national and religious intolerance.[25] This language would be retained in several paragraphs of the Preamble to ICERD, in which the States Parties to the Convention, '[a]larmed by manifestations of racial discrimination still in evidence in some areas of the world', resolved to adopt 'all necessary measures for speedily eliminating racial discrimination in all its forms and manifestations'.[26] These preambular references to racial discrimination 'in all its forms and manifestations' appear to encompass attacks on the cultural heritage of Convention groups, such as the attacks on Jewish property from which the phrasing originates.

In terms of the operative articles, Article 1(1) ICERD defines racial discrimination in the 'political, economic, social, cultural or any other field of public life', thereby expressly referencing the 'cultural…field'. Article 5 provides a list of civil, political, economic, social and cultural rights, which are not stand-alone rights; rather, the obligations of State Parties admit no racial discrimination in the enjoyment of these rights.[27] Article 5(e) provides a list of economic, social and cultural rights, including – as with the UDHR and ICESCR – a single provision on cultural rights, the Article 5(e)(vi) 'right to equal participation in cultural activities'. Armenia would invoke this provision in *Armenia v. Azerbaijan* as entailing a right to the protection and preservation

---

23 Howard J. Ehrlich, 'The Swastika Epidemic of 1959–1960: Anti-Semitism and Community Characteristics' (1961–1962) 9(3) *Social Problems* 264–272, at 264.

24 See further 'Report of the Twelfth Session of the Sub-Commission on Prevention of Discrimination and Protection of Minorities' UN Doc. E/CN.4/800 (1960) p. 58–71; 'Report of the Thirteenth Session of the Sub-Commission on Prevention of Discrimination and Protection of Minorities' UN Doc. E/CN.4/815 (1961) p. 53–65; 'Report of the Seventeenth Session of the Commission on Human Rights' UN Doc. E/CN.4/817 (1961) p. 14–18.

25 For an overview of these actions, see 'Manifestations of Racial and National and Religious Hatred: Note by the Secretary-General' UN Doc. A/5129 (1962).

26 ICERD Preamble paras 9 and 10. The phrase appears also in para 5.

27 As emphasised in an early debate among CERD members on Article 5 – see further CERD, 'Meaning and Scope of Article 5 of the ICERD' UN Doc. A/9018 (1973) p. 12–20. For example, Mr. Dayal noted that 'Article 5 did not require States parties to implement all the rights which it enumerated, but simply required them to ensure that there was no discrimination on grounds of race in the exercise of those rights.' (at p. 15).

of Armenian cultural heritage.[28] Judge Yusuf would counter that an obligation for States Parties to protect cultural heritage sites does not arise from this provision.[29]

Patrick Thornberry observes of Article 5: 'The rights set out in Article 5, formulated using economical and porous language, made it almost inevitable that its interpretation and application would be influenced by developments in the broader international canon of human rights to which it is organically connected.'[30] It is important therefore to refer to this broader international canon to understand CERD's implementation of Article 5 in relation to cultural heritage. In that regard, ICESCR and the interpretive approach adopted by the Committee on Economic, Social and Cultural Rights (CESCR) have proven particularly influential on CERD's understanding of Article 5(e)(vi). Indeed, Judge Yusuf's dissent would also refer to ICESCR and the practice of CESCR.[31]

Article 15 is the only article in ICESCR devoted solely to cultural rights. Its key provision is Article 15(1)(a), the right of everyone '[t]o take part in cultural life'. CESCR's General Comment (GC) 21 is directed only to this provision, as per its title.[32] In GC 21, CESCR sets out a 'multifaceted content implicit in the concept of culture' in Article 15(1)(a).[33] It states: 'In the Committee's view, culture is a broad, inclusive concept encompassing all manifestations of human existence. The expression "cultural life" is an explicit reference to culture as a living process, historical, dynamic and evolving, with a past, a present and a future.'[34] GC 21 contains a number of specific references to the protection of 'cultural heritage' as part of this inclusive concept.[35] It provides an express obligation to: 'Respect and protect cultural heritage in all its forms, in times of war and peace'.[36] It has an emphasis throughout on minorities and indigenous peoples, and the need to protect their cultural heritage.[37] Marc-André Renold and

28 *Armenia v Azerbaijan*, Provisional Measures, Order, supra n 3 at p. 377 para 50. See also submission of Professor Pierre d'Argent on behalf of Armenia CR 2021/20 (14 October 2021) p. 45 para 3.

29 Dissenting Opinion of Judge Yusuf (2021), supra n 9 p. 399 para 16.

30 Patrick Thornberry, *The International Convention on the Elimination of All Forms of Racial Discrimination: A Commentary* (Oxford University Press 2016) 308.

31 Dissenting Opinion of Judge Yusuf (2021), supra n 9 p. 399 para 16.

32 CESCR General Comment 21, 'Right of everyone to take part in cultural life (art. 15, para. 1 (a), of the International Covenant on Economic, Social and Cultural Rights)' UN Doc. E/C.12/GC/21 (2009).

33 Ibid para 10.

34 Ibid paras 10–11.

35 Ibid paras 15(b), 37, 50(a) and (b), 53 and 54(b).

36 Ibid para 50(a).

37 Ibid paras 3, 7, 16(a) and €, 27, 32, 33, 36, 37, 49(d), 50(c), 52(a), (c) and (f), 53, 55(e) and 73, referring to indigenous peoples and/or minorities. References to the cultural heritage of these groups are emphasised in paras 37, 49(d) and 53.

Alessandro Chechi summarise: 'CESCR endeavored to articulate the obligation of state parties to ensure the protection of tangible and intangible cultural heritage within their jurisdiction, including the cultural heritage of minorities and Indigenous peoples, and the right to take part in cultural life as a freedom as opposed to mere opportunities to engage in cultural activities'.[38]

However, Judge Yusuf's dissent would cite GC 21 as indicative of CESCR's position that the protection of cultural heritage sites does *not* come under Article 15(1)(a) ICESCR. He finds:

> It should also be recalled that the United Nations Committee on Economic, Social and Cultural Rights, in its Comment No. 21 on Article 15, paragraph 1 (a), of the International Covenant on Economic, Social and Cultural Rights does not establish a direct link or consequential relationship between the broader and unqualified "right of everyone to take part in cultural life" and the protection of cultural and religious sites by State authorities.[39]

This is surely not reflective of CESCR's position, since GC 21 makes precisely this direct link. Having set out an obligation to 'protect cultural heritage in all its forms, in times of war and peace', it refers specifically to sites and monuments: 'Such obligations include the care, preservation and restoration of historical sites, monuments'.[40] This approach is seen also in the position of CERD. Thornberry signals that '[t]he influence of the work of CESCR on the practice of CERD in this respect is notable'.[41] He underlines that the reference in Article 5(e)(vi) to *participation* in cultural activities 'is only one expression amidst a critical mass of references to 'culture' in the archive of the Committee. CERD broadly recognises the extended sense of culture as that which animates the spirit of communities.'[42] Thus, CERD has interpreted Article 5(e)(vi) in this extended sense as protecting the cultural heritage of Convention groups, in line with CESCR's interpretation of the textually similar Article 15(1)(a) ICESCR.

The CERD archive is replete with measures taken to protect the cultural heritage of Convention groups. This began in the 1970s with CERD first raising

38 Marc-André Renold and Alessandro Chechi, 'International Human Rights Law and Cultural Heritage' in James Cuno and Thomas G. Weiss (eds.) *Cultural Heritage and Mass Atrocities* (Getty Publications: Los Angeles, 2022) 396–410, at 402.

39 Dissenting Opinion of Judge Yusuf (2021), supra n 9 p. 399 para 16.

40 CESCR GC 21, supra n 32 para 50(a).

41 Thornberry, supra n 30 at 384.

42 Ibid 385.

with Peru the need 'to protect the rich cultural heritage of the non-European element of the population',[43] and has continued across five decades of practice. Thus, it asked of China information on 'measures to protect the Tibetan cultural heritage'.[44] It requested from Pakistan information on Government policies for 'the preservation of the cultural heritage of the various pre-Islamic civilizations represented in Pakistan'.[45] It sought detailed information from Guatemala on indigenous communities including 'their physical existence and cultural heritage',[46] seeing the two as linked. It expressed concern to Venezuela about insufficient measures 'to prevent the destruction of the indigenous cultural heritage'.[47] It considered the effect of mining on the cultural rights of the Tsaatan people in Mongolia, calling for a plan to ensure 'mining operations do not harm the cultural heritage of the affected ethnic groups'.[48]

CERD recommendations refer also to the protection of objects, sites and monuments as part of cultural heritage obligations. For example, the Committee criticised Georgia for a 'lack of effective preservation of the cultural heritage and monuments of minorities (art. 5).'[49] It expressed concern to Saint Lucia that 'the cultural rights of the indigenous peoples are allegedly threatened by the destruction of sacred and cultural sites and objects', issuing a recommendation to ensure 'remedies [are] available to members of indigenous peoples to contest the destruction of their sacred and cultural sites'.[50] Its examination of the Russian Federation considered '[r]eports of the destruction of and damage to Crimean Tatar cultural heritage, including tombstones, monuments and shrines, and the lack of information on investigations carried out into such allegations and on other measures to prevent such vandalism'.[51]

States Parties have also understood that they have obligations in relation to cultural heritage. Thus, Colombia reported to CERD: 'Colombia was a multiracial society and attached a great deal of importance to defending the cultural heritage of all indigenous communities.'[52] Similarly, the delegate of Australia informed the Committee: 'With reference to the Aboriginal cultural

43 UN Doc. A/31/18 (1976) p. 28 para 79.
44 UN Doc. A/38/18 (1983) p. 112 para 467.
45 Ibid p. 92 para 367.
46 UN Doc. A/50/18 (1995) p. 55 para 315.
47 UN Doc. A/51/18 (1996) p. 66 para 475.
48 UN Doc. CERD/C/MNG/CO/23–24 (2019) para 25.
49 UN Doc. A/66/18 (2011) p. 43 para 16. These recommendations relate to the cultural heritage of the Azeri and Armenian minorities in Georgia.
50 UN Doc. A/59/18 (2004) p. 88 para 450.
51 UN Doc. CERD/C/RUS/CO/25–26 (2023) para 23(b).
52 UN Doc. A/47/18 (1993) p. 40 para 143.

heritage, the representative declared it essential that skeletal remains in museums around the world be returned. He supported the policy of "keeping places", controlled by Aboriginals, for sacred objects.'[53] Under the heading "The right to equal participation in cultural activities", Mauritius reported on the establishment of *Aapravasi Ghat* where indentured workers landed and were received upon disembarkation as a 'national, regional and international heritage site', and the *Le Morne* Cultural Landscape symbolizing the resistance of runaway slaves as a 'national, regional and international memorial site'.[54] The Committee in turn welcomed the inscription by Mauritius 'of *Aapravasi Ghat* and of *Le Morne* as heritage sites with a view to protect and promote the cultural heritages of slave and indentured labourer descents'.[55]

In the 1990s CERD evolved a new mechanism, the early warning and urgent action (EWUA) procedure, aimed at preventing existing situations escalating into conflicts or responding to violations requiring immediate attention.[56] This procedure has been deployed by the Committee to protect cultural heritage under immediate threat. For example, in relation to the indigenous Subanon community of the Philippines, CERD engaged the State Party on measures taken 'to protect the community from acts of violence and attacks on their property, sacred sites and institutions'.[57] This action was in support of Subanon opposition to the destruction of a sacred site, Mount Canatuan, by a gold mining company.[58] With regard to the Mi'kmaq people of Nova Scotia, Canada, the Committee highlighted acts carried out by non-indigenous fishers who were trying to obstruct the group's traditional fishing activities by the 'burning and destruction of their property, including lobster traps, lobster processing facilities and work vehicles'[59] – thus acting to protect ordinary objects of cultural significance. In relation to the Mapuche people in Chile, the Committee responded to information received that the sacred site of Chinay in the Villarrica National Park had been desecrated, 'including the destruction

53 UN Doc. A/46/18 (1992) p. 61 para 243.

54 UN Doc. CERD/C/MUS/15–19 (2012) p. 10 paras 39–40 and p. 25–26 paras 133–134.

55 UN Doc. A/68/18 (2013) p. 61 para 7(a).

56 UN Doc. A/48/18 (1993) Annex III 'Prevention of Racial Discrimination, including Early Warning and Urgent Procedures' p. 126–130; UN Doc. A/62/18 (2007) Annex III 'Guidelines for the Early Warning and Urgent Action Procedure' p. 115–120.

57 CERD, 'Letter to H.E. Ms. Erlinda F. Basilio' 7 March 2008 (early warning and urgent procedure).

58 For a review of this action and reflections on its results, see Cathal Doyle, 'CERD, the State, Mining Corporations and Indigenous Peoples' Rights: The Experience of the Subanon in the Philippines' in David Keane and Annapurna Waughray (eds.) *Fifty Years of ICERD: A Living Instrument* (Manchester University Press 2017) 182–206.

59 CERD, 'Letter to H.E. Ms. Leslie Norton' 30 April 2021 (early warning and urgent procedure).

of the sacred statue, the *rewe*, both a symbol and a sacred location.'[60] Clearly, in the eyes of the Committee, considerations of racial discrimination *do* apply to cultural sites and artefacts such as the *rewe*, and it will act to provide them with urgent protection.

A further question is whether *religious* cultural heritage falls under the scope of ICERD, a treaty on *racial* discrimination. Armenia's application incudes religious sites, such as Ghazanchetsots Cathedral in Shushi. Judge Yusuf's dissent found that 'it is not tenable, in my view, to assert that "religious heritage", in the sense of churches, cathedrals or other places of worship are plausibly protected under CERD.'[61] The definition of racial discrimination in Article 1(1) ICERD covers only 'race, colour, descent and national or ethnic origin', and religion does not obviously fall within its ambit. The early resolutions of the UN Sub-Commission and Commission in response to the "Swastika epidemic" discussed above related to manifestations of racial prejudice *and* religious intolerance, but the issues were later split in the Third Committee, where two resolutions were adopted calling for the preparation of draft declarations and conventions dealing separately with racial discrimination and religious intolerance.[62] Judge Yusuf would note as a result that 'it is well known that the drafters of CERD decided not to address religious discrimination or religious intolerance in this Convention'.[63]

Yet the drafters of the Convention did address religion, where it has a link with racial discrimination. This is seen in Article 5(d)(vii) ICERD, whereby States are required to eliminate racial discrimination in the enjoyment of the 'right to freedom of…religion'. The Committee has engaged the phrase "ethno-religious" to capture the groups and situations that come under its scope under this provision. It stated this mandate clearly in concluding observations to Georgia:

> Religious questions are of relevance to the Committee when they are linked with issues of ethnicity and racial discrimination. In this connection, and while acknowledging the effort made by the State

60 CERD, 'Letter to H.E. Mr. Juan Eduardo Eguiguren' 10 May 2019 (early warning and urgent procedure).

61 Dissenting Opinion of Judge Yusuf (2021), supra n 9 para 17.

62 General Assembly resolution 1780 (XVII) 'Preparation of a Draft Declaration and a Draft Convention on the Elimination of all Forms of Racial Discrimination' UN Doc. A/5217 (1962) p. 32; General Assembly resolution 1781 (XVII) 'Preparation of a Draft Declaration and a Draft Convention on the Elimination of all Forms of Religious Intolerance' UN Doc. A/5217 (1962) p. 33.

63 Dissenting Opinion of Judge Yusuf (2021), supra n 9 p. 399 para 17.

> Party to fight ethno-religious violence, the Committee remains concerned about the situation of ethno-religious minorities, such as the Yezidi Kurds (Art. 5).[64]

Likewise, it stated in relation to Tanzania: 'the Committee is concerned about the lack of information on the ethno-religious composition of the State Party's population and about allegations of tensions between ethno-religious groups (arts. 5 and 7).'[65] Importantly, CERD's mandate in relation to religion would form part of its 2007 Reporting Guidelines issued to all States Parties to the treaty, in which '[t]he Committee would like to recall the possible intersectionality of racial and religious discrimination… which may lead to discrimination on ethnic grounds against members of specific religious communities'.[66] More recent reports show CERD raising ethno-religious groups as a matter of course. For example, CERD raised the issue of biased policing against ethno-religious groups in Jamaica.[67] It expressed concern that ethno-religious groups in Cameroon are being subjected to grave human rights violations perpetrated by security forces.[68] It highlighted the extensive 'persecution of those practising Afro-Brazilian religions' in Brazil.[69]

Since ethno-religious groups come under the scope of ICERD, their cultural heritage also finds protection under the Convention. This may include churches, graveyards or other such sites. As noted, the desecration of Jewish cemeteries was an early influence on the call in the UN bodies to adopt ICERD, and following its entry into force, the Committee would continue to monitor this issue. A State report from Italy saw CERD discuss 'three or four cases of desecration of Jewish cemeteries'.[70] Similarly, a State report from Poland saw the Committee express deep concern at 'the continued incidence of anti-Semitic activities in the State party, including the desecration of Jewish cemeteries'.[71]

64 UN Doc. CERD/C/GEO/CO/3 (2005) para 18.

65 UN Doc. CERD/C/TZA/CO/16 (2005) para 20.

66 UN Doc. CERD/C/2007/1 (2007), 'Guidelines for the CERD-specific Document to be submitted by States Parties under Article 9, paragraph 1, of the Convention' p. 10.

67 UN Doc. CERD/C/JAM/CO/21–24 (2022) para 24.

68 UN Doc. CERD/C/CMR/CO/22–23 (2022) paras 22–25: 'Situation of ethnic, ethnolinguistic and ethno-religious groups and indigenous peoples in the context of crises and the security situation'.

69 UN Doc. CERD/C/BRA/CO/18–20 (2022) paras 43–44. For a brief discussion of this issue, see Robert Muggah, 'Evangelical gangs in Rio de Janeiro wage "holy war" on Afro-Brazilian faiths' *The Conversation* 16 December 2019 <https://theconversation.com/evangelical-gangs-in-rio-de-janeiro-wage-holy-war-on-afro-brazilian-faiths-128679> accessed 30 April 2024.

70 UN Doc. A/50/18 (1998) p. 22 para 88.

71 UN Doc. A/64/18 (2009) p. 87.

In recommendations to China, CERD emphasised the 'preservation of places of worship' of a number of China's minority nationalities:

> Taking into consideration that a distinctive religion is essential to the identity of several minority nationalities, concern is expressed with regard to the actual enjoyment of the right to freedom of religion in the State, particularly in the Muslim parts of Xinjiang and in Tibet, including the preservation of places of worship and the exercise of religious rights by members of all ethnic groups.[72]

The reference to religion as an essential component of minority identity is notable. Later in the same report, the Committee raised serious 'allegations of destruction by the State of mosques, Buddhist and Lama temples and other places of worship of the minority nationalities.'[73] The Committee has likewise expressed concern to Egypt at 'violence against ethno-religious minorities, particularly the violence that has resulted in the destruction of Coptic property and churches.'[74] Its concluding observations to Brazil raised the 'desecration of religious sites' as part of the persecution of Afro-Brazilian religions.[75] In sum, the destruction or desecration of cemeteries, churches, temples and other religious sites is seen by CERD as falling within the scope of the Convention, where it forms part of the cultural heritage of ethno-religious groups. Obligations of States Parties can include the protection of these sites from attacks. Remedies can involve restoration in the event of their damage or destruction, as with the Committee's call to Brazil for 'the rebuilding of destroyed religious sites'.[76]

3 The Applicability of ICERD Protections in Armed Conflict

While ICERD may protect cultural heritage, it is necessary to consider whether these protections are applicable in armed conflict. Notably, there has been some discussion in light of applications under Article 22 ICERD as to the relevance of the treaty to situations of armed conflict. Bruno Simma described *Georgia v. Russian Federation*, the first application under Article 22, as a juridical *Nebenkriegsschauplatz*, an ancillary theatre of conflict and as far from

---

72 UN Doc. A/51/18 (1996) p. 58 para 404.
73 Ibid para 417.
74 UN Doc. CERD/C/EGY/CO/17–22 (2016) para 21.
75 Supra n 69 para 43(b).
76 Ibid para 44(e).

a "pure" human rights case as one can get.[77] James Crawford commented of the same case that 'in *Georgia v. Russian Federation* … the doubt was whether that dispute really concerned racial discrimination, however broadly defined, or whether Article 22 was being used as a device to bring a wider set of issues before the Court'.[78] These doubts have arisen also in the context of the Ukraine, Armenia, and Azerbaijan applications.[79]

To a certain extent, they are understandable in that none of ICERD's operative articles address armed conflict. In addition, ICERD contains no provision comparable to Article 4 of the International Covenant on Civil and Political Rights (ICCPR), or Article 15 ECHR, in which certain of its provisions may be derogated from '[i]n time of war or other public emergency threatening the life of the nation'.[80] This may mean that all of the provisions of ICERD are non-derogable and apply at all times in all States Parties, including in a situation of armed conflict. It may also mean *e contrario* that ICERD was never intended to be applied in armed conflict. A similar discussion has arisen under ICESCR which, like ICERD, lacks a derogations clause. It has been argued that this does not necessarily mean that ICESCR's provisions apply in armed conflict.[81] However, CESCR, along with other international bodies, have affirmed the applicability of ICESCR in armed conflict.[82] Similarly, CERD has affirmed ICERD's applicability in armed conflict. But first, it is worth emphasising that

---

77 Bruno Simma, 'Human Rights before the International Court of Justice: Community Interest Coming to Life?' in Holger Hestermeyer *et al* (eds.) *Coexistence, Cooperation and Solidarity* (Brill 2011) 577–603, at 588 and 594.

78 *Obligations concerning Negotiations relating to Cessation of the Nuclear Arms Race and to Nuclear Disarmament (Marshall Islands v. India)*, Judgment 5 October 2016, Dissenting Opinion of Judge Crawford p. 521 para 18, quoted in Callista Harris, 'Claims with an Ulterior Purpose: Characterising Disputes Concerning the "Interpretation or Application" of a Treaty' (2019) 18 *The Law & Practice of International Courts and Tribunals* 279–299, at 281 n 7.

79 See commentaries supra n 8. See also 'An Interview with Alain Pellet', *Volkerrechtsblog* 4 July 2022 <https://voelkerrechtsblog.org/i-resigned-because-russia-had-become-an-absolutely-indefensible-client/> accessed 30 April 2024, in which Pellet describes Ukraine's 2017 application as an 'abusive pretext', with the phrase hyperlinking to Judge Yusuf's dissent in the *Armenia v Azerbaijan* case.

80 Article 15 ECHR. Article 4(1) ICCPR contains a similar phrase but does not refer to 'war', reading: 'In time of public emergency which threatens the life of the nation (…)'.

81 Michael J. Dennis, 'Application of Human Rights Treaties Extraterritorially in Times of Armed Conflict and Military Occupation' (2005) 99(1) *American Journal of International Law* 119–141, at 140–141.

82 For an overview see UN High Commissioner for Human Rights, 'Protection of Economic, Social and Cultural Rights in Situations of Armed Conflict' UN Doc. E/2015/59 (2015) p. 5 para 12 *et seqq*.

this is supported by the Convention text. In particular, the Preamble to ICERD reads in its paragraph 7:

> Reaffirming that discrimination between human beings on the grounds of race, colour or ethnic origin is an obstacle to friendly and peaceful relations among nations and is capable of disturbing peace and security among peoples and the harmony of persons living side by side even within one and the same State.

The history of this provision underscores its importance in reading the Convention. It originates in the drafting of the 1963 UN Declaration on the Elimination of All Forms of Racial Discrimination, which would form the basis for the drafting of ICERD. In the Third Committee, Tunisia sought to include an understanding of racial discrimination in draft Article 1 of the Declaration as a 'threat to international peace and security'.[83] Mr. Razgallah (Tunisia) explained his country's amendment on the basis that apartheid South Africa was steadily strengthening its armed forces.[84] Citing a rise in South Africa's defence budget from $60 million in 1961 to $168 million in 1963, he concluded that its Government was 'on a war footing'.[85] He continued: 'in view of the solidarity felt by all the African peoples vis-à-vis the population of South Africa – which thus found itself, as it were, on the defensive – it was clear that South Africa represented a potential hotbed of armed conflict'.[86]

Tunisia's amendment was supported by African States, such as Mali and Liberia.[87] Mrs. Diallo (Mali) commented that 'racial discrimination…was not only an attack on human rights but also a threat to international peace and security'.[88] It was opposed by Western States such as Denmark, 'for it was the prerogative of the Security Council to determine what was a threat to international peace and security.'[89] The United States indicated that it would be compelled to refrain from supporting the Declaration if the Tunisian amendment were adopted.[90] Tunisia did not withdraw its amendment, but

83 UN Doc. A/C.3/L.1080, in UN Doc. A/C.3/SR.1220 3 October 1963 p. 46 para 33.

84 UN Doc. A/C.3/SR.1216 1 October 1963 p. 23 para 2.

85 Ibid.

86 Ibid.

87 Ibid p. 26 para 31 (Mrs. Diallo (Mali)) and p. 28 para 59 (Mr. Doe (Liberia)).

88 Ibid p. 25 para 30.

89 Ibid p. 28 para 51 (Mr. Refslund Thomsen (Denmark)).

90 UN Doc. A/C.3/SR.1220 p. 45 para 28. Mrs. Dick (USA) explained that '[t]o characterize situations involving racial discrimination as threats to international peace and security was inaccurate and served no useful purpose.' She rejected any notion that racial relations in her own country constituted a threat to international peace.

rather opted to revise it, replacing 'threat to international peace and security' with the phrase 'as a fact likely in certain cases to disturb peace and security among peoples.'[91] The US proposed substituting 'capable of' for 'likely', which was accepted.[92] The phrase would form part of Article 1 of the 1963 Declaration, which reads:

> Discrimination between human beings on the ground of race, colour or ethnic origin is an offence to human dignity and shall be condemned as a denial of the principles of the Charter of the United Nations, as a violation of the human rights and fundamental freedoms proclaimed in the Universal Declaration of Human Rights, as an obstacle to friendly and peaceful relations among nations *and as a fact capable of disturbing peace and security among peoples*.[93]

The drafting of ICERD, based on the Declaration text, would make two further changes to this provision. First, it would move it to the Preamble, since Article 1 ICERD was to address the definition of racial discrimination. Second, an amendment in the Third Committee from thirteen Latin American States added 'as well as the harmonious coexistence of persons even within one and the same state', bringing an internal as well as an international dimension.[94] The resultant text formed paragraph 7 of the Preamble, quoted above, which even followed the Declaration text in listing only three grounds ('race, colour or ethnic origin') instead of the five grounds that would appear in the Article 1(1) definition. In the Sub-Commission, Mr. Capotorti (Italy) would single out the importance of this provision in an overall description of the Preamble: 'It stated the convictions on which the draft convention was based, [and] pointed out the connexion between the elimination of racial discrimination and international peace and security'.[95]

Preambular paragraph 7 understands racial discrimination as having the *capability* of disturbing peace and security. There is a clear threshold implied

91 UN Doc. A/C.3/L.1080/Rev.1, in UN Doc. A/C.3/SR.1223 7 October 1963 p. 59 para 24.
92 Ibid paras 25 and 30, with 'in certain cases' then being dropped as unnecessary.
93 UN Doc. A/RES/18/1904 (1963) [emphasis added].
94 UN Doc. A/C.3/L.1226 and Corr.1, in A/C.3/SR.1301 12 October 1965 p. 70 para 46. The amendment was described by the Argentinian delegate (Mr. Beltramino) as 'stressing the importance of racial tolerance for domestic peace'. (A/C.3/SR.1300 p. 63 para 3).
95 UN Doc. E/CN.4/Sub.2/SR.409 7 February 1964 p. 4.

in this term, which individual acts of racial discrimination would not reach.[96] Nevertheless, the African and Latin American States were committed to having a clause in the Convention that recognized the link between racial discrimination and conflict, both international and internal, a position the Western States would come to accept. Following the adoption of ICERD in 1965 by the General Assembly, the delegate of Cameroon 'rejoiced that States, by acceding to the Convention... would be reaffirming that discrimination between human beings was an obstacle to friendly and peaceful relations among nations and was capable of disturbing peace and security among peoples'.[97] But the delegate of the US also stated that 'the elimination of all forms of racial discrimination and respect for the individual were inseparable from the cause of peace.'[98] The capability of racial discrimination to disturb peace and security would be quickly recognized by CERD, which would affirm 'the integral relationship, emphasized *inter alia* in paragraph 7 of the preamble, between racial discrimination and international conflicts'.[99]

CERD began its work in 1970, and the question of its competence in relation to a situation of armed conflict soon arose. In its initial State report in 1971, the Syrian Arab Republic referred to violations of Article 5 ICERD in the territories occupied by Israel in the Golan Heights.[100] This led to divergent views in the Committee on a number of points, including its competence in relation to a situation of armed conflict. CERD member Mr. Sukati found that inasmuch as 'a state of belligerency' existed between certain Arab States and Israel, 'it was inappropriate for the Committee to involve itself in such a situation'.[101] Mr. Haastrup agreed, that 'the treatment of the population of the occupied Golan Heights should be defined not in terms of racial discrimination but in terms of the laws of war.'[102] Mr. Sukati then challenged the Committee to decide

96 See also comments of Sir Samuel Hoare (United Kingdom) during debates on the draft Declaration in the Commission on Human Rights, that 'while some forms of racial discrimination...definitely jeopardized friendly relations and international peace and security, he did not believe that a single act of racial discrimination would necessarily do so.' (UN Doc. E/CN.4/SR.767 3 March 1964 p. 5).

97 UN Doc. A/C.3/SR.1373 14 December 1965 p. 499 para 52 (Miss Luma (Cameroon)). She further described the Convention as a frontal attack on apartheid policies in South Africa and Southern Rhodesia which were 'a threat to world peace'. (at para 51).

98 Ibid p. 498 para 44 (Mr. Goldberg (USA)).

99 UN Doc. A/32/18 (1977) p. 14 para 43.

100 'Report of the Committee on the Elimination of Racial Discrimination', UN Doc. A/8418 (1971) p. 9 para 37.

101 Ibid p. 20 para 81(ii).

102 Ibid.

whether or not the question fell within its sphere of competence, before deciding what action to take.[103]

The ensuing discussion saw a range of views expressed. Messrs. Tarassov and Sayegh considered that racial discrimination, as defined in Article 1 of the Convention, was involved.[104] Mr. Ortiz-Martin was 'not sure' whether the usual criteria relating to human rights and racial discrimination in normal times of peace could be applied.[105] Sir Herbert Marchant believed that a 'political inter-State conflict' was involved in the case, and not racial discrimination.[106] Mr. Aboul Nasr observed that 'the Convention did not differentiate between war and peace and did not allow racial discrimination during war any more than it did in peacetime.'[107] A proposal was put to a roll-call vote where the Committee's competence in relation to the situation in the Golan Heights was affirmed, by 9 votes to 4, with 1 abstention.[108] This decision should be seen as an important precedent. It established that a situation of armed conflict did not displace the applicability of ICERD and the competence of the Committee. It affirmed that the treaty applies equally in times of war and in times of peace and cannot be suspended or derogated from. However, it recognised also the role of other international bodies, setting out in paragraphs 2 and 3 the actions of competent organs of the UN.[109] Thus, while the Committee affirmed the applicability of the treaty to a situation of armed conflict, its scope is limited to practices of racial discrimination and not to wider breaches of international law.

The Committee would apply the treaty sporadically to situations of armed conflict in the 1970s–80s.[110] This was not without occasional State

103 Ibid.

104 Ibid. Mr. Tarassov drew attention to 'a conscious and deliberate policy calculated to depopulate the occupied territories of their Arab inhabitants', while Mr. Sayegh contended that the fact that the native inhabitants of the Golan Heights had been denied the right to return to their homes was sufficient to show a clear case of racial discrimination existed.

105 Ibid p. 23 para 81(viii).

106 Ibid.

107 Ibid.

108 Ibid para 82. In favour: Messrs. Dayal, Getmanets, Aboul Nasr, Resich, Rossides, Sayegh, Tarassov, Tomko and Valencia Rodriguez. Against: Messrs. Haastrup, Marchant, Ortiz-Martin and Sukati. Abstention: Mr. Partsch. The text of the Decision is reproduced in para 83 (CERD Decision 4 (iv)).

109 Ibid para 83: '2. The Committee takes note also of the resolutions adopted by the competent organs of the United Nations, and of the reports of the Committees set up by the General Assembly and by the Commission on Human Rights to investigate the situation, to which the report submitted by the Syrian Government makes reference. 3. The Committee wishes to draw the attention of the General Assembly to this situation.'

110 See for example UN Docs. A/9018 (1973) p. 41 (Pakistan) and A/40/18 (1985) p. 75 (Afghanistan).

contestation. For example, Pakistan's report, referring to events in (then) East Pakistan, asserted that 'at no time was the imputation of racial discrimination or differentiation a component of these grievances ... [and] even the widest interpretation of the Convention on the Elimination of Racial Discrimination, and the Committee's functions under it, would exclude its competence to consider these issues'.[111] The Committee disagreed, finding that 'certain ethnic questions were involved in the conflict under reference', and as a result it could not endorse that section of Pakistan's report.[112]

The 1990s saw a shift in tone, with the emergence of ethnic conflicts that clearly engaged groups protected by the Convention. CERD wrote in its 1992 annual report to the UN Secretary-General: 'The year 1991–1992 has seen fearful sequences of killings deriving from discrimination based on race, colour, descent and national and ethnic origin in several regions of the world.'[113] The report discussed ethnic conflicts in Burkina Faso, Burundi, Ghana, Rwanda and the former Yugoslavia. CERD would often cite Article 5(b) ICERD in relation to these situations of conflict, which prohibits racial discrimination in '[t]he right to security of person and protection by the State against violence or bodily harm, whether inflicted by government officials or by any individual, group or institution'. For example, in 1992 in view of reports of ethnic conflict in Burundi and Rwanda, it requested further information from these Governments 'in particular the provisions of Article 5(b)'.[114] The following year, it stated in relation to the Sudan: 'Concerning Article 5(b) of the Convention...members of the Committee noted reports alleging mass killings and extrajudicial executions of civilians in the Nuba mountains, where the Government's programme of military action appeared to amount to ethnic cleansing.'[115] CERD even engaged its EWUA procedure to conduct field missions of Committee members to two States Parties experiencing conflict in this period, the [then] Federal Republic of Yugoslavia and Croatia; these remain the only field missions ever conducted by the Committee.[116]

---

111 Ibid p. 41 para 164.

112 Ibid.

113 UN Doc. A/47/18 (1993) vi.

114 Ibid p. 70 Decision 1 (41) and 2 (41).

115 UN Doc. A/48/18 (1994) p. 32 para 108.

116 UN Doc. A/49/18 (1995) p. 6 para 22 and p. 7 para 28. CERD offered its good offices in the form of a mission of its members, which was accepted. The Committee then sent a good offices mission consisting of three CERD members, Messrs. Ahmadu, Rechetov and Wolfrum, to the Federal Republic of Yugoslavia; and a second mission consisting of one CERD member, Mr. Yutzis, to Croatia. A 2007 review of the EWUA guidelines retained

CERD also regularly invoked the rules of International Humanitarian Law (IHL) at this time, as catalogued by David Weissbrodt.[117] For example, in relation to Chechnya, CERD expressed alarm over the disproportionate use of force by the Russian armed forces and condemned 'all violations of human rights and of international humanitarian law'.[118] With regard to Rwanda, the Committee welcomed reports that members of the Rwandan Patriotic Army had been tried for 'grave human rights and humanitarian law violations that appear to have had an ethnicity-motivated character'.[119] Since the 2000s, the Committee's references to IHL have become less frequent. This is likely a result of the evolution of international criminal law and more recently the growth of commissions of inquiry of the Human Rights Council, which often carry a specific IHL mandate. In that light, CERD's focus on IHL in the 1990s may be seen as a bridging of an accountability gap that had narrowed considerably by the end of the decade. The Committee played an important role in this process. This is seen in its General Recommendation (GR) 18 (1994), which urged that an international tribunal with general jurisdiction be set up to prosecute the perpetrators of genocide, crimes against humanity and grave breaches of the Geneva Conventions, as a response to 'racially and ethnically motivated massacres and atrocities occurring in different regions of the world'.[120] As Weissbrodt observes, GR 18 'anticipated the creation of the International Criminal Court'.[121]

Today, we see CERD's continued concern with armed conflict where it affects the rights of Convention groups under the treaty. For example, it noted that 'violence in Colombia has been largely concentrated in areas where indigenous and Afro-Colombian communities live; that increasingly these communities have been targeted by armed groups'.[122] In relation to the Philippines, it highlighted 'persistent violent clashes between security forces and non-State

the potential for CERD field missions: 'The measures to be taken by the Committee under the early warning and urgent action procedure may include … To offer to send to the State party concerned one or more of the members of the Committee'. (supra n 56 (2007) p. 118 para 14(d)).

117 David Weissbrodt, 'The Approach of the Committee on the Elimination of Racial Discrimination to Interpreting and Applying International Humanitarian Law' (2010) 19(2) *Minnesota Journal of International Law* 327–362.

118 UN Doc. A/50/18 (1998) Decision 1 (46) 'Report requested urgently from the Russian Federation' p. 6 para 25.

119 UN Doc. A/53/18 (1998) p. 22 para 11.

120 CERD, 'General recommendation XVIII on the establishment of an international tribunal to prosecute crimes against humanity' UN Doc. A/49/18 (1994) p. 117–118.

121 Weissbrodt, supra n 117 at 350.

122 UN Doc. A/54/18 (1999) p. 47 para 463.

armed forces, which disproportionately affect ethnic, ethnoreligious and ethno-linguistic minority groups and indigenous peoples, particularly in the regions of Mindanao and Negros island'.[123] In observations to Cameroon, it expressed concern at 'inter-ethnic conflicts in Bawock and Bali Nyonga', citing Article 5(b).[124]

CERD's supervisory role in armed conflict extends to the protection of the cultural heritage of Convention groups. Indeed, this is illustrated in recent concluding observations to Azerbaijan, issued in August 2022, in which the Committee affirmed a number of positions evident in its practice. It began by recalling that 'in situations of armed hostilities, the applicability of international humanitarian law does not preclude the application of international human rights law, including the Convention, which operates independently.'[125] It then expressed concern in relation to 'reports on the destruction of and damage to Armenian cultural heritage, including churches and other places of worship, monuments, landmarks, cemeteries and artefacts, and the lack of information on investigations conducted on such allegations'.[126] It concluded by recommending that Azerbaijan 'facilitate the mission proposed by UNESCO to draw a preliminary inventory of significant cultural properties, and strengthen its efforts to preserve these sites while ensuring effective and meaningful consultation with ethnic Armenian communities'.[127]

These concluding observations to Azerbaijan emphasise a number of points from the perspective of CERD. First, that the Convention applies *independently* in armed conflict, so that the potential applicability of IHL does not displace ICERD.[128] Second, that the scope of the treaty engages the protection of the cultural heritage of Convention groups, including in armed conflict. Third, that this extends to ethno-religious cultural heritage such as churches and cemeteries. Fourth, that obligations under other legal regimes, including the 1954 Hague Convention, may assist in interpreting or fulfilling ICERD obligations, so that cooperation with specialist agencies such as UNESCO may be considered as necessary for the proper implementation of Convention

123 UN Doc. CERD/C/PHL/CO/21–25 (2023) p. 4 para 15.
124 UN Doc. A/65/18 (2010) p. 37 para 20.
125 UN Doc. CERD/C/AZE/CO/10–12 (2022) para 4.
126 Ibid para 4(b).
127 Ibid para 5(c). The UNESCO mission is that referenced infra n 133.
128 The Committee would stress this also in recent concluding observations to the Russian Federation: 'In the light of the ongoing armed conflict in Ukraine initiated by the State party on 24 February 2022, the Committee recalls that, in situations of armed conflict and hostilities, the applicability of international humanitarian law does not preclude the application of international human rights law, including the Convention, which operates independently.' UN Doc. CERD/C/RUS/CO/25–26 (2023) para 4.

rights. This final aspect warrants exploring in more detail. It points to a potential complementary relationship between ICERD and other instruments in the realm of cultural heritage protection. It accords with the approach long-established by CERD that does not view the treaty in isolation, but rather as operating within a wider international legal environment.

4 ICERD and Other Instruments

An initial point to raise is why claims in relation to cultural heritage in armed conflict have arisen before the ICJ under Article 22 ICERD, in light of the existence of a *lex specialis* via the 1954 Hague Convention. In particular, why would States not access the dispute resolution mechanisms provided by UNESCO? In that regard, Sabine von Schorlemer observes that 'surprisingly little State practice exists with regard to the use of existing dispute settlement procedures within UNESCO'.[129] In general, an overview of UNESCO dispute settlement mechanisms shows a long-standing tendency for common agreement, i.e. "joint seizure", whereby *both* Parties have to agree recourse to a dispute settlement procedure.[130] In that vein, the 1954 Hague Convention does not provide for unilateral seizure of a dispute settlement mechanism that would give a conflicting Party the autonomy to instigate action.[131] If either State Party prefers not to resort to dispute settlement, as is often the case, there is no subsidiary mechanism within the 1954 Hague Convention to provide for a solution.[132] This is not to underestimate the efficacy of the range of mechanisms within the 1954 Hague Convention framework, including good offices, conciliation and the intergovernmental Committee, the latter, as noted by Judge Yusuf in his dissent, having set up an independent technical mission to Nagorno-Karabakh.[133] However, this mission could only progress

129 Sabine von Schorlemer, 'UNESCO Dispute Settlement' in Yusuf (ed.) supra n 13 73–103, at 74.

130 Ibid 85–86.

131 Ibid 86. The author highlights a minor exception in Article 14(6) of the Regulations for the Execution of the 1954 Hague Convention, which allows a High Contracting Party to lodge an objection to the registration of cultural property by another High Contracting Party that may then proceed to arbitration.

132 Ibid 94.

133 Declaration of the Committee for the Protection of Cultural Property in the Event of Armed Conflict of the Second Protocol to the 1954 Hague Convention, 'Ensuring Cultural Property Protection in and around Nagorno-Karabakh and Setting-up an Independent Technical Mission' C54/20/15.COM/Declaration 11 December 2020 <https://unesdoc.unesco.org/ark:/48223/pf0000380348> accessed 30 April 2024.

'with the agreement of all concerned Parties',[134] and gaining agreement from Azerbaijan for such a mission has been problematic, as highlighted by Heghnar Watenpaugh:

> UNESCO has made insistent requests to conduct a fact-finding mission in Azerbaijani-controlled areas regarding all groups' cultural heritage. Azerbaijan rebuffed these requests, then seemed to redirect UNESCO to focus on destruction by Armenians instead. A fact-finding mission has still not materialized, despite Azerbaijan's past collaborations with UNESCO, and the fact that one of UNESCO's longstanding goodwill ambassadors is Azerbaijan's vice president who is also the country's first lady.[135]

These obstacles were also raised by Armenia in provisional measures hearings before the Court: 'UNESCO has still not been able to access Armenian cultural sites, with its Assistant Director-General declaring on 21 December 2020: "Only the response of Azerbaijan is still awaited for UNESCO to proceed with the sending of a mission to the field."'[136] Hence, ICERD may be of particular use where a State is rebuffing the joint mechanisms proposed under the UNESCO framework. This explains the recourse to ICERD from a practical perspective, but it does not address the question of the scope of the treaty. As Judge Yusuf's dissent argues, the Court may still view the 1954 Hague Convention as providing the 'appropriate legal framework for the protection of cultural heritage in the context of armed conflicts'.[137]

The relationship between international human rights treaties and IHL has been addressed previously by the Court. In its well-known passage from the Advisory Opinion on *Nuclear Weapons*, the ICJ held in relation to the ICCPR: 'The Court observes that the protection of the [ICCPR] does not cease

---

134 Ibid para 7: 'Welcomes the UNESCO's initiative, taken in conformity with Article 23 of the 1954 Hague Convention, to carry out as soon as possible an independent technical mission, *with the agreement of all concerned Parties*, with the aim of assessing the status of the cultural property in all its forms as a prerequisite for the effective protection of heritage'. [emphasis added].

135 Heghnar Watenpaugh, 'International Court of Justice Lawsuits May Impact Heritage Protection' *Newsweek* 14 October 2021 <https://www.newsweek.com/international-court-justice-lawsuits-may-impact-heritage-protection-opinion-1639037> accessed 30 April 2024.

136 *Armenia v. Azerbaijan*, Submission of Professor Pierre d'Argent supra n 28 p. 52 para 30.

137 Dissenting Opinion of Judge Yusuf, supra n 9 p. 398 para 14.

in times of war.'[138] In its later Advisory Opinion on the *Wall*, affirmed in its judgment in *Armed Activities on the Territory of the Congo*,[139] the ICJ further held:

> [T]he Court considers that protection offered by human rights conventions does not cease in case of armed conflict ... As regards the relationship between international humanitarian law and human rights law, there are thus three possible situations: some rights may be exclusively matters of international humanitarian law; others may be exclusively matters of human rights law; yet others may be matters of both these branches of international law. In order to answer the question put to it, the Court will have to take into consideration both these branches of international law, namely human rights law and, as *lex specialis*, international humanitarian law.[140]

However, Nancie Prud'homme cautions that 'the exact stance of the Court on the interplay between human rights and humanitarian law is difficult to unscramble, as the judges did not offer specific guidance on how to subdivide the rights into these categories.'[141] Contrasting views may emerge from the differing interpretations of the *lex specialis* principle: 'On the one hand, *lex specialis* has been used...to interpret human rights in light of international humanitarian law. On the other hand...the *lex specialis* device has been employed to promote the primacy of humanitarian law over human rights and the idea that in situations of armed conflicts international humanitarian law should be applicable to the exclusion of international human rights law.'[142] Hence, the Court may view the 1954 Hague Convention as applicable to the exclusion of ICERD in the realm of cultural property in armed conflict, in line with the first 'situation' outlined in the *Wall* opinion.

138 *Case Concerning the Legality of the Threat or Use of Nuclear Weapons*, Advisory Opinion (1996) ICJ Reports p. 240 para 25. The passage continues: 'except by operation of Article 4 of the Covenant whereby certain provisions may be derogated from in a time of national emergency.' As noted, ICERD has no derogations clause.

139 *Armed Activities on the Territory of the Congo (Democratic Republic of Congo v. Uganda)*, Judgment (2005) ICJ Reports p. 168 para 216.

140 'Legal Consequences of the Construction of a Wall in the Occupied Palestinian Territory' (2004) ICJ Reports p. 178 para 106: '... save through the effect of provisions for derogation of the kind found in Article 4 of the ICCPR'.

141 Nancie Prud'homme, '*Lex Specialis*: Oversimplifying a More Complex and Multifaceted Relationship?' (2007) 40(2) *Israel Law Review* 356–395, at 377, citing also Dennis, supra n 81 at 133.

142 Prud'homme, Ibid 369–370.

At this point, it is important to distinguish the legal basis for the Court's views in *Nuclear Weapons*, the *Wall* and *Armed Activities*, from the application in *Armenia v. Azerbaijan*. In *Nuclear Weapons*, the question asked by the General Assembly of the Court referred to 'international law' in general, which clearly included IHL.[143] In the *Wall*, the General Assembly also referred to the 'rules and principles of international law'.[144] In *Armed Activities*, the Court's jurisdiction was founded on the declarations of acceptance of the compulsory jurisdiction of the Court made by the two States, under which the Court had a mandate to assess claims of violations of human rights *and* IHL.[145] In *Armenia v. Azerbaijan*, the Court's jurisdiction is founded only on Article 22 ICERD, which relates to a dispute with respect to the interpretation or application of ICERD. Hence, the question for the Court *prima facie* is whether the protection of cultural heritage in armed conflict falls within the scope of ICERD. The existence of a *lex specialis* via the 1954 Hague Convention appears not relevant to this question. The Court is not deciding which legal regime is more appropriate to address certain issues before it, but rather whether this aspect of the dispute relates to the application of ICERD.

If the ICJ determines that the protection of cultural heritage in armed conflict falls within the scope of ICERD, it may then consider the role of the 1954 Hague Convention in interpreting or fulfilling the relevant Convention provisions. It may do so on the basis that these are obligations accepted by the Parties to the dispute (where this is the case); or that these are customary rules;[146] or that the harmonisation of international law requires such an approach.[147] If it determines that the protection of cultural heritage in armed conflict does not fall within the scope of ICERD, then it ought to do so on the

---

143 UN Doc. A/RES/49/75[K] (1994).

144 UN Doc. A/RES/ES-10/14 (2003). Hence, the Court took into consideration these branches of international law '[i]n order to answer the question put to it'.

145 *Armed Activities*, supra n 139 'Overview of the Case'.

146 See for example Benjamin Charlier, 'The ICRC and the Protection of Cultural Property' *International Conference on the 20th Anniversary of the 1999 Second Protocol of the 1954 Hague Convention* (2019) 64 <https://www.ohchr.org/sites/default/files/Documents/Issues/CulturalRights/Activities/Geneva2019-ConferenceProceedings.pdf> accessed 30 April 2024: '[C]ultural property is protected in time of war by a wide range of international instruments … The fact that this protection has now been crystallized under international customary law is not disputed.'

147 For example, the ECtHR has emphasised the need to interpret the Convention 'in harmony with other rules of international law of which it forms part … [which] applies no less to international humanitarian law.' *Georgia v. Russia (II)*, Application no. 38263/08 (2021) para 94.

basis of the text, context and object and purpose of the Convention, and not the existence of another treaty regime that addresses these questions. This would be in line with its jurisprudence, where there is an established approach for determining whether a dispute concerning the interpretation or application of a treaty exists. As set out by Callista Harris: 'Consistently, the Court has not characterised disputes brought before it: the Court has not enquired into the true object of a claim or assessed whether the relative weight of a dispute lies with the treaty invoked or with rules of international law external to that treaty. The Court has simply asked whether the acts complained of fall within the provisions of the relevant treaty.'[148]

Hence, the question for the Court is not whether a more appropriate *lex specialis* exists, but whether the protection of cultural heritage falls within the scope of ICERD. In that light, and as extensively evidenced, it is clear that CERD views the protection of the cultural heritage of Convention groups in peacetime and in armed conflict as falling within the scope of the Convention. However, the interpretations of CERD in relation to the scope of the treaty, as with the decisions of any human rights body, do not bind the Court. The Court's dictum in its judgment in *Diallo* remains an important reference point, whereby the Court stated in relation to the Human Rights Committee that 'it believes that it should ascribe great weight to the interpretation adopted by this independent body', in order to achieve 'the necessary clarity and the essential consistency of international law'.[149] Nevertheless, in *Qatar v. United Arab Emirates*, which was before CERD under Articles 11–13 and the ICJ under Article 22 in parallel proceedings, the Court's February 2021 judgment chose not to follow CERD's earlier August 2019 admissibility decision on the meaning of the Article 1(1) term 'national…origin' as inclusive of "nationality".[150] This disjunction was criticised in dissenting opinions,[151] and more widely by

148 Harris, supra n 78 at 286.

149 *Diallo*, supra n 12.

150 *Qatar v. United Arab Emirates*, supra n 12 p. 105–106 paras 104–105. Contrast with *Qatar v. United Arab Emirates*, CERD/C/99/4 (2019) p. 13–14 paras 53–63.

151 *Qatar v. United Arab Emirates*, Dissenting Opinions of Judges Bhandari and Robinson supra n 12 p. 133–145 and 146–156. According to Judge Bhandari: 'The Judgment provides no compelling reason as to why it has chosen to depart from the reasoning in *Diallo* in this dispute, despite the fact that CERD remains "the guardian of the Convention". (at p. 141 para 21); According to Judge Robinson: 'There is no reason why the Court should not attach great weight to the recommendations of CERD (which is properly seen as the guardian of the Convention), if they are not in conflict with international human rights law or general international law'. (at p. 150 para 13).

commentators,[152] but it serves to emphasise that the Court will offer its own views that may depart from those of UN treaty bodies, including CERD.

The majority judgment in *Qatar v. United Arab Emirates* stated only that it had 'carefully considered' the position taken by CERD.[153] Hence, we may expect the Court to carefully consider the viewpoint of the Committee in relation to the scope of the treaty. We may also expect the Court to attach 'great weight' to that viewpoint. However, it does not necessarily follow that the Court will find that ICERD protects cultural heritage. The ICJ will deploy the standard Vienna Convention on the Law of Treaties methodology of text, context and object and purpose, and CERD interpretations must fit this formula in order to guide Court decision-making.[154] In that regard, it is submitted that ICERD does protect the cultural heritage of Convention groups based on the text of the Convention, specifically Article 5(e)(vi). This provision may be read in the context of preambular paragraph 7, which affirms the Convention's applicability to situations of armed conflict. Such a reading is arrived at in light of the object and purpose of the Convention, the elimination of racial discrimination 'in all its forms and manifestations', which includes attacks on cultural property, artefacts and sites. Indeed, the object and purpose of the Convention could hardly be achieved without the protection of the cultural heritage of Convention groups, as CERD practice abundantly illustrates. But it remains to be seen what the Court will determine and how it may apply the Vienna formula.

The Articles 11–13 inter-State communications mechanism before CERD remains a potential pathway for the protection of cultural heritage under ICERD via inter-State litigation. As noted, the Articles 11–13 mechanism has a wider jurisdictional reach than Article 22 since it applies to all 182 States parties to ICERD. Indeed, a *Foreign Policy* article in the wake of the ICJ's 2021

---

152 See Cathryn Costello and Michelle Foster, 'Race Discrimination Effaced at the International Court of Justice' (2021) 115 *AJIL Unbound* 339–344, concluding that the Court's 'misinterpretation of CERD suggest the ruling may come to be relegated to the annals of legal missteps'. (at 344); Geir Ulfstein, 'Qatar v. United Arab Emirates' (2022) 116(2) *American Journal of International Law* 397–403, noting that the Court had 'the possibility of demonstrating the real legal weight of pronouncements of such bodies and its willingness to engage in a dialogue with them. It failed to live up to both expectations.' (at 401–2)

153 *Qatar v. United Arab Emirates*, supra n 12 p.104 para 101.

154 See comments of James Crawford and Amelia Keene: 'the Court is prepared to adopt a liberal and flexible approach to interpretation where the crucible of the text, context and purpose permits.' James Crawford and Amelia Keene, 'Interpretation of the Human Rights Treaties by the International Court of Justice' (2020) 24(7) *The International Journal of Human Rights* 935–956, at 950.

order suggested it could be used by Greece to 'apply to the ICJ under the new ruling to challenge Turkey's ongoing conversion of Greek cathedrals to mosques'.[155] Whatever the potential merits of such a claim, Turkey is one of the 25 States Parties to ICERD that has a reservation to Article 22, and so the ICJ could not have jurisdiction. However, such an application could be brought before CERD. The Articles 11–13 mechanism is not legally binding,[156] but it involves the compulsory appointment of a 5-member ad hoc Conciliation Commission who may or may not be members of CERD and could include for example external experts in the realm of cultural heritage.[157] While the 1954 Hague Convention also contains means of conciliation,[158] this is not compulsory, since under the Hague Convention 'the Parties to a dispute must agree to participate in the…conciliation process.'[159] Furthermore, it is confined to situations of armed conflict. Thus, Articles 11–13 offers a means by which any of the 182 States Parties to ICERD may be compelled to engage in a process of conciliation in relation to the protection of cultural heritage by any other State Party, in peacetime or in armed conflict. The CERD process of conciliation results in a settlement agreement, or a report with findings of fact and recommendations, which could include facilitation of a UNESCO mission or other forms of cooperation with UNESCO experts.

A final aspect to note is the views of the ECtHR. Judge Yusuf's dissent cites its decision in *Ahunbay and Others v. Turkey*, in which '[t]he European Court of Human Rights also could not find such a link between the provisions of the European Convention on Human Rights and claims relating to cultural heritage sites or artefacts'.[160] The case related to the construction of the Ilisu dam on the Tigris river in southeastern Turkey, which ultimately destroyed the 12,000 year-old Hasankeyf archaeological and cultural heritage site.[161] The ECtHR found the case to be inadmissible (incompatible *ratione materiae*): 'the Court

155 Magakhyan, supra n 5. The reference is to the 2020 conversion of the Hagia Sophia which has been followed by further such conversions of Byzantine churches and condemned inter alia by UNESCO. See for example Theresa Mechemer, 'Turkey Controversially Converts Hagia Sophia From Museum Into Mosque' *Smithsonian Magazine* 13 July 2020 <https://www.smithsonianmag.com/smart-news/turkey-turns-hagia-sophia-museum-mosque-drawing-criticism-180975300/> accessed 30 April 2024.

156 Article 13(2) ICERD.

157 Articles 12(1)(a) and (b) ICERD.

158 Article 22 of the 1954 Hague Convention.

159 Von Schorlemer, supra n 129 at 77.

160 Dissenting Opinion of Judge Yusuf (2021), supra n 9 p. 399 para 16.

161 See further Bahar Aykan, 'Saving Hasankeyf: Limits and Possibilities of International Human Rights Law' (2018) 25(1) *International Journal of Cultural Property* 11–34.

currently saw no "European consensus", or even any trend among Council of Europe member States, potentially necessitating a reworking of the scope of the rights in question or allowing the Court to infer from the provisions of the Convention a universal individual right to the protection of a specific cultural heritage.'[162] But there are reasons why this decision should not be determinate of the scope of ICERD.

First, the decision was complicated by the question of standing. Hasankeyf lies in southeast Turkey, where the nation's Kurdish people, the country's largest ethnic and linguistic minority, are concentrated.[163] As Durrie Bouscaren emphasises, 'The majority of residents uprooted by the dam project are Kurdish, and the waters cover several sites deemed significant to Kurdish culture and history.'[164] In fact, Kurdish oral histories and traditions reference Hasankeyf.[165] Yet the applicants in *Ahunbay* were not Kurdish and were not from the region, hence did not qualify as victims for the purposes of the ECHR. They argued for standing based on Hasankeyf being part of the heritage of all mankind, but as Berenika Drazewska notes, 'the reluctance of the ECtHR to side with this view can probably be explained by its mistrust of *actio popularis*'.[166] Ultimately, the European Court declined to find 'a *universal* individual right to the protection of a *specific* cultural heritage'[167] – in other words, that any person could access the Court in relation to cultural heritage of a certain status. Drazewska reflects that the case may have had a better chance of prevailing if the petition 'had been filed by a member (members) of the Kurdish minority residing in Hasankeyf, and therefore directly affected by its destruction.'[168]

162 *Ahunbay and Others v. Turkey*, supra n 17. See also ECtHR Research Division, 'Cultural Rights in the Case-law of the European Court of Human Rights' (2011), affirming that 'the Court has never recognised the right to the protection of cultural…heritage as such' (at p. 19 para 35). However, note that in *Sargsyan v Azerbaijan* (Application no. 40167/06), the ECtHR did recognise that 'the applicant's cultural and religious attachment to his late relatives' graves in Gulistan may also fall within the notion of "private and family life".' (at para 257)

163 Durrie Bouscaren, 'The UNESCO Site That Never Was' *Sapiens* 29 April 2020 <https://www.sapiens.org/archaeology/hasankeyf/> accessed 30 April 2024.

164 Ibid.

165 Berenika Drazewska, 'Hasankeyf, the Ilisu Dam, and the Existence of "Common European Standards" on Cultural Heritage Protection' (2018) 2(4) *Santander Art and Culture Law Review* 89–120, at 102.

166 Ibid 113.

167 *Ahunbay and Others v. Turkey*, supra n 17 para 25. [emphasis added]

168 Drazewska, supra n 165 at 114.

Second, the decision acknowledged that the cultural heritage of minority groups and indigenous peoples *is* protected by international human rights law. The ECtHR, in declaring the application inadmissible, distinguished *Ahunbay* from 'international protection as it currently stands which usually concerns situations and regulations appertaining to the cultural rights of national minorities and the right of indigenous peoples to conserve, control and protect their cultural heritage'.[169] Thus, the European Court recognised that 'cultural heritage rights would seem to be intrinsically linked to the specific status of individuals belonging to national minorities or indigenous peoples.'[170] Given ICERD relates specifically to minorities and indigenous peoples as Convention groups, *Ahunbay* would appear to support a reading of the Convention as protecting their rights to cultural heritage. CERD's many actions to protect the cultural heritage of minorities and indigenous peoples under the Convention have been documented above.

Third, and from a practical perspective, Hasankeyf illustrates gaps in the protective regime afforded by UNESCO which led *Ahunbay* to petition the ECtHR. Attempts were made to engage UNESCO protections with a range of opposition groups led by *Doğa Derneği* (Nature Society) campaigning for Hasankeyf's inscription as a UNESCO World Heritage Site.[171] However, the Turkish government did not take any action to nominate Hasankeyf as a world heritage site, as announced publicly by the Director of UNESCO's World Heritage Center.[172] UNESCO in turn cannot compel Turkey to nominate a site such as Hasankeyf. The ECHR was not an alternative to UNESCO protections, but rather a last resort, with the ECtHR the final barrier to the submergence of the site forever as well captured by Bouscaren: 'In February of 2019, however, a chamber of seven judges rejected that application and sealed the town's fate.'[173] Aykan, writing one year prior to the ECtHR's judgment, also considered that 'the only possibility that remains to save Hasankeyf from destruction seems to be the decision that could come from the European Court of Human Rights'.[174] As *Ahunbay* illustrates, there should be little doubt of the significance of a failure to find that cultural heritage falls within the scope of a human rights treaty, be it the ECHR or ICERD. International human rights treaties offer a potential

169 *Ahunbay and Others v. Turkey*, supra n 17 para 23.

170 Ibid para 24.

171 Pinar Aykac, 'Absent Presents: Musealisation of the Historic Town of Hasankeyf as a Manifestation of "Absent Heritage"' (2023) *Journal of Architectural Conservation* 1–18, at 11.

172 Ibid.

173 Bouscaren, supra n 163.

174 Aykan, supra n 161 at 12.

avenue by which States which fail to protect cultural heritage under existing UNESCO standards, or actively engage in its destruction, may be compelled to come before an international court or body by individuals, NGOs and civil society, or other States Parties.

5 Conclusion

This article has examined whether ICERD protects the cultural heritage of Convention groups. From the perspective of CERD, it clearly does. The Committee's approach is based on the text of the Convention, specifically Article 5(e)(vi). It may be read in the context of preambular paragraph 7, which affirms the applicability of the Convention's provisions in armed conflict. It is arrived at in light of the object and purpose of the Convention, the elimination of racial discrimination 'in all its forms and manifestations'. The existence of a *lex specialis* in the 1954 Hague Convention does not displace the applicability of ICERD. Rather, these rules may inform any consideration of whether the Article 5 right has been violated, as well as the potential fulfilment of ICERD obligations through cooperation with UNESCO bodies, seen in CERD's recent concluding observations to Azerbaijan.

As a result, CERD's inter-State communications mechanism under Articles 11–13 would appear to be available to any of the 182 States Parties to ICERD seeking to protect the cultural heritage of Convention groups under threat or attack in another State Party. It remains to be seen whether the ICJ will take a similar view of the scope of the Convention. But a position that views ICERD as relating only to "human beings" and not their cultural heritage appears at odds with a treaty that has never drawn such sharp distinctions, since those first attacks on Jewish property in the winter of 1959–60 and across five decades of CERD practice.

More generally, Simma cautions that 'human rights violations viewed from an inter-State perspective can only bring to the fore very limited aspects of these problems'.[175] Most human rights violations are committed against a perpetrator's own population, and the preparedness of States to bring violations before the ICJ or other bodies has always been limited.[176] Threats

175 Bruno Simma, 'International Court of Justice' in *Elgar Encyclopaedia of Human Rights* (2022) 7.

176 Ibid.

to the cultural heritage of ICERD groups will arise much more frequently in a domestic rather than an inter-State context. Thus, the most far-reaching protections of cultural heritage under ICERD will always be that provided through the State reporting, individual communications and the early warning and urgent action procedure. The latter in particular may warrant greater attention, as a means of protecting the cultural heritage of Convention groups from urgent threats.

CHAPTER 8

Making Something Out of (Almost) Nothing?

Inter-State Human Rights Communications as Narrow Gateways for China's Accountability in the Xinjiang's Crisis

Veronica Botticelli

Abstract

With an ever-increasing number of reports denouncing systematic mistreatments against Uyghurs and other Muslim ethnic minorities detained in Xinjiang 're-education' camps, the time is ripe for the international community to explore possible judicial and quasi-judicial avenues to hold China to account. Excluding from the present analysis unilateral sanctions, as well as possible investigations and proceedings before international criminal tribunals, this article focuses on the role of inter-State human rights communications in securing justice. Given China's enduring reluctance to engage in dispute settlement mechanisms – particularly by formulating reservations to compromissory clauses enshrined in human rights treaties –, the quest for accountability poses significant challenges. By broadening the inquiry to alternative avenues, such as the inter-State quasi-judicial communication procedure under both the ICERD and the ILO's Constitution, as well as addressing the feasibility of requesting an ICJ's advisory opinion as an inter-State case in disguise, it is still possible to envisage narrow pathways that might be worth pursuing.

Keywords

human rights – Xinjiang – Uyghurs – inter-State communications – UN monitoring bodies – International Labour Organization

 | DOI:10.1163/9789004712584_010

1 Introduction

Since early 2017, several investigative and research reports issued by various NGOs, think-tanks and media outlets, alongside accounts from victims and civil society groups, have extensively denounced ill-treatment and widespread human rights abuses allegedly perpetrated by the People's Republic of China (hereinafter, 'China') in respect to Uyghurs and other predominantly Muslim ethnic minority communities detained in so-called 're-education' camps located in the Xinjiang Uyghur Autonomous Region ('Xinjiang Province', 'Xinjiang' or 'XUAR').[1]

Alleged violations have been mainly perpetrated in the context of arbitrary detention and constant surveillance of approximately one million individuals belonging to the above-mentioned ethnic minorities. According to available official documentation, through the institution of these 're-education' camps, China is attempting to significantly affect the assimilation of ethnic minority groups in the society, and to dismantle their sense of cultural distinctiveness.[2] Nonetheless, mass internment 'merely' constitutes the means through which China is implementing its policy of abuses in XUAR. Indeed, after being informed of increasing allegations on the Xinjiang's situation, on August 2022, the United Nations' Office of the High Commissioner for Human Rights published a comprehensive report (hereinafter, 'OHCHR Report') which clearly demonstrates that practices such as torture and other cruel and inhuman

---

1 See A Zenz, 'Wash Brains, Cleanse Hearts: Evidence from Chinese Government Documents About the Nature and Extent of Xinjiang's Extrajudicial Internment Campaign', (7) *The Journal of Political Risk*, 2019; Asia-Pacific Centre for the Responsibility to Protect, *Genocide and Crimes against Humanity in Xinjiang? Applying the Legal Tests*, Report, November 2020, <https://r2pasiapacific.org/files/5818/applying_legal_tests_xinjiang_nov2020.pdf> accessed 30 January 2024 ('APR2P Centre Report'); B Van Schaack, M Wang et al, '*Break Their Lineage, Break Their Roots*: China's Crimes against Humanity Targeting Uyghurs and Other Turkic Muslims', *Human Rights Watch & Mills Legal Clinic of Stanford Law School*, 19 April 2021; D Tobin, L T Murphy, R Thum, R Harris, J S Finley, 'State Violence in Xinjiang: A Comprehensive Assessment. A Submission of Evidence to The Uyghur Tribunal', *University of Manchester, SOAS University of London, Newcastle University, Helena Kennedy Centre for International Justice, Sheffield Hallam University*, 1st Hearings, London, 4–7 June 2021, available online; OHCHR Assessment of Human Rights Concerns in the Xinjiang Uyghur Autonomous Region, People's Republic of China, 31 August 2022, <https://www.ohchr.org/en/documents/country-reports/ohchr-assessment-human-rights-concerns-xinjiang-uyghur-autonomous-region> accessed 30 April 2024 ('OHCHR Report').

2 J Smith Finley, 'Securitization, Insecurity and Conflict in Contemporary Xinjiang: Has PRC Counter-terrorism Evolved into State Terror?', (38) *Central Asian Survey* (2019), 1, 2–3.

treatment of detainees,[3] practices of sexual violence and forced organ harvesting and sterilization,[4] the forced separation of children from their parents, coercive birth controls and enforced disappearances,[5] the progressive destruction of Uyghurs' and other Muslim minorities' religious and cultural heritage,[6] enslavement and forced labour have extensively occurred in the region,[7] with the majority of these repressive policies still carried out at the time of the publication of the OHCHR Report,[8] and purportedly still ongoing at the present time.[9]

The available evidence is likely sufficient to raise serious concerns as regards the existence of grave and repetitive violations of obligations enshrined in various human rights treaties ratified by China. Moreover, in recent months, the debate has shifted from *whether* abuse is occurring in the Xinjiang Province to *what* abuses amount to.[10] The multilateral treaties which may have been violated are, *inter alia*, the Convention on the Prevention and Punishment of the Crime of Genocide ('Genocide Convention'),[11] the Convention on the Elimination of All Forms of Racial Discrimination (ICERD),[12] the Convention Against Torture and Other Cruel, Inhuman or Degrading Treatment or Punishment (UNCAT),[13] the Convention on the Elimination of All Forms of Discrimination Against Women (CEDAW),[14] the Convention on the Rights

---

3 OHCHR Report, 23–27.

4 *Ibid.*, 32–36.

5 *Ibid.*, 40–42.

6 *Ibid.*, 25–30.

7 *Ibid.*, 36–40.

8 *Ibid.*, at 2.

9 Cf. Declaration of the United Nations' High Commissioner of Human Rights, Mr. Volker Türk, delivered at the 54th Session of the Human Rights Council, 11 September 2023; the full statement is available at https://www.ohchr.org/en/statements/2023/09/turk-human-rights-are-antidote-prevailing-politics-distraction-deception accessed 30 April 2024.

10 S Ryan, 'Atrocity Crimes in Xinjiang: Moving Beyond Legal Labels', (13) *Global Responsibility to Protect* (2021), 20.

11 *Convention on the Prevention and Punishment of the Crime of Genocide*, 9 December 1948, 78 UNTS 277 ('Genocide Convention').

12 *International Convention on the Elimination of All Forms of Racial Discrimination*, 21 December 1965, 660 UNTS 195 ('ICERD').

13 *Convention Against Torture and Other Cruel, Inhuman or Degrading Treatment or Punishment*, 10 December 1984, 1465 UNTS 85 ('UNCAT').

14 *Convention on the Elimination of All Forms of Discrimination Against Women*, 18 December 1979, 1249 UNTS 13 ('CEDAW').

of Child (CRC),[15] the Convention on the Rights of Persons with Disabilities (CRPD),[16] the Slavery Convention,[17] the International Labour Organization's Conventions No. 29 on Forced Labour,[18] No. 105 on the Abolition of Forced Labour,[19] and No. 111 on Discrimination (Employment and Occupation)[20] (hereinafter also referred to as 'ILO Convention No. 29', 'ILO Convention No. 105', 'ILO Convention No. 111').

Therefore, the current situation in Xinjiang requires – and has already acquired – widespread attention. However, if it is true that several States have taken important yet 'disaggregated' steps in ensuring China's accountability for the widespread abuses in the Xinjiang Province, such as the so-called 'U.S. Uyghurs Human Rights Policy Act' adopted by the United States,[21] 'Magnitsky-style' unilateral sanctions jointly enacted by the United States, the European Union and Canada[22] (to which China has recently 'reacted' by placing 'counter-sanctions'),[23] or other symbolic actions,[24] it is equally true that there has so far

15 *Convention on the Rights of the Child*, 20 November 1989, 1577 UNTS 3 ('CRC').

16 *Convention on the Rights of Persons with Disabilities*, 13 December 2006, A/RES/61/106, Annex I ('CRPD').

17 League of Nations, *Convention to Suppress the Slave Trade and Slavery*, 25 September 1926, 60 LNTS 253, Registered No. 1414 ('Slavery Convention').

18 International Labour Organization (ILO), *Forced Labour Convention*, C29, 28 June 1930 ('ILO Convention No. 29').

19 International Labour Organization (ILO), *Abolition of Forced Labour Convention*, C105, 25 June 1957 ('ILO Convention No. 105').

20 International Labour Organization (ILO), *Discrimination (Employment and Occupation) Convention*, C111, 15 June 1960 ('ILO Convention No. 111').

21 Cf. Uyghur Human Rights Policy Act of 2020 § 2, 22 U.S.C. § 6901 (2020), calling on the executive branch to impose unilateral sanctions against several Chinese entities, officials, and other persons whom the U.S. President identifies to be allegedly responsible for atrocities and other human rights violations in Xinjiang.

22 Cf. J Emtseva, 'Sanctioning the Treatment of Uighurs in China: Targeted Sanctions and Accountability Avenues for Human Rights Violation in Xinjiang', *Verfassungsblog*, 25 April 2021; for an analysis of the impact of Magnitsky-style sanctions on ensuring the protection of human rights, see V Kerr, JP Sexton, 'Human Rights and Security: Unpacking the Elusive Nature of Magnitsky Sanctions', 11 *Asser Research Paper* (2022) 7.

23 European Parliament, 'China countersanctions on EU targets', 22 March 2021; 'China sanctions US-based Xinjiang Monitor', *Aljazeera News*, 27 December 2023.

24 For instance, in November 2018, fifteen foreign ambassadors decided to issue a joint letter expressing concerns about China's practice of incarceration of Muslim ethnic communities; a brief summary of the letter's content can be found here: https://www.cbc.ca/news/politics/chinacanada-uighurs-letter-1.4906522, accessed 30 April 2024. A year later, in October 2019, the United Kingdom's permanent representative to the UN called on China to uphold its domestic legislation and international obligations in order to ensure the respect of fundamental rights; the full statement and its content can be retrieved here: https://www.gov.uk/government/speeches/joint-statement-on-xinjiang, accessed 30 April 2024.

been a lack of coordinated efforts on the possible seizure of an international court or quasi-judicial monitoring body to assess China's responsibility,[25] with limited legal actions against Chinese officials promoted by non-state actors before the International Criminal Court (ICC), facing procedural challenges due an alleged lack of sufficient evidence.[26]

Therefore, the option of lodging a judicial proceedings against China before an international court has never been seriously considered. This reluctance could be partly justified by the fact that China, although having ratified all the 'core' UN human rights conventions, has formulated a significant number of reservations to the compromissory clauses enshrined therein. Moreover, China has consistently rejected any quasi-judicial competence of the treaty-based monitoring mechanisms to examine inter-State communications.[27] Therefore, the feasibility for States to lodge a case against China is, if not completely nullified, at least significantly limited and, accordingly, particularly challenging.[28] This (apparent) deadlocked scenario has also represented

---

25 See M Schiavenza, 'Why Aren't More Countries Confronting China Over Xinjiang?', *ChinaFile*, 14 January 2020, <https://www.chinafile.com/reportingopinion/viewpoint/why-arent-more-countries-confronting-china-over-xinjiang> accessed 30 April 2024.

26 Press Release, 'Uyghur Genocide and Crimes Against Humanity: Submission of New Evidence to ICC Including Witness Testimony from inside the Camps', East Turkistan Government in Exile, 20 June 2020, <https://east-turkistan.net/uyghur-genocide-and-crimes-against-humanity-submission-of-new-evidence-to-icc-includes-witness-testimony-from-inside-camps/> accessed 30 April 2024; Press Release, 'East Turkistan National Awakening Movement, Uyghur Genocide and Crimes Against Humanity: Credible Evidence Submitted to ICC for the First Time Asking for Investigation of Chinese Official', 6 July 2020, <https://nationalawakening.org/press-release-uyghur-genocide-and-crimes-againsthumanity-credible-evidence-submitted-to-icc-for-the-first-time-asking-for-investigationof-chinese-officials> accessed 30 April 2024; cf. International Criminal Court, The Office of the Prosecutor, Report on Preliminary Examination Activities 2020, 18–20, <https://www.icc-cpi.int/news/report-preliminary-examination-activities-2020> accessed 30 April 2024; A Garwood-Gowers, 'China and the Uighurs: Options for Legal Accountability', 13 *Global Responsibility to Protect* (2021) 24.

27 China has formulated reservations as regards both individual complaint mechanisms and inquiry procedures enshrined in UN human rights treaties, alongside entering many reservations to their substantive provisions. This widespread reluctance has been repeatedly blamed by most international legal scholars; however, for a justification of China's decision to formulate reservations to human rights treaties, with particular reference to the ICESCR and the CRC, cf. J Wu, 'Is China Playing by the Rules? Assessing China's Reservations to International Human Rights Treaties', 19 *Chinese Journal of International Law* (2002) 253.

28 The few available analysis on the possibility for States to having recourse to the available inter-State mechanisms as regards the Xinjiang's crisis focuses their attention mainly to the ICERD communication system enshrined in Articles 11–13, given its compulsory nature; *ex multis*, cf. F Capone, 'Le violazioni dei diritti umani nello Xinjiang: tra la reazione della Cina e il lento risveglio della comunità internazionale', 8 *Quaderni di SIDIBlog* (2021) 23, 33.

of the main reasons that lead to the establishment of alternative accountability mechanisms, such as the so-called 'Uyghur Tribunal', an independent peoples' tribunal instituted in order to investigate ongoing atrocities and possible genocide against the Uyghurs and other Turkic Muslim populations. Among the various goals and objectives that the Uyghur Tribunals might want to achieve, its foremost *raison d'être* lies in the acknowledgment of the actual 'impossibility' of bringing the People's Republic of China to any formal international court – among others, as regards any possible contentious proceedings lodged before the ICJ under the Genocide Convention –, joined by the assertion (only apparently incontrovertible, as it will be examined) according to which «there is no known route to any other court that can deal with the issues before the tribunal».[29]

A further explanation for this impasse could be that no 'directly' affected State can be identified in the *cas d'espece*, as the alleged abuses are taking place in the exact same territories placed under the jurisdiction of the State that is committing them. However, a significant number of inter-State human rights cases has flourished in the last decade,[30] with many proceedings recently initiated before human rights courts[31] and quasi-judicial

29 Uyghur Tribunal's Webpage, 'About' Section, <https://uyghurtribunal.com/abouttribunal/> accessed 30 April 2024.

30 On the concept of 'community interest' in international law, see generally, *ex multis*, CJ Tams, *Enforcing Obligations* Erga Omnes *in International Law* (CUP, Cambridge 2005); G Gaja, 'The Protection of General Interests in the International Community', 364 *Recueil des Cours* (2011); E Benvenisti and G Nolte (eds), *Community Interests Across International Law* (OUP, Oxford 2018). On the potentials of community interest litigation, as well as its related recent 'explosion', see R Wolfrum, 'Enforcing Community Interests Through International Dispute Settlement: Reality or Utopia?', in U Fastenrath et al (eds), *From Bilateralism to Community Interest: Essays in Honour of Bruno Simma* (OUP, Oxford 2011), 1132; Y Suedi and J Bendel, 'Public Interest Litigation: a pipe dream or the future of international litigation?', in J Bendel and Y Suedi (eds), *Public Interest Litigation in International Law* (Routledge, London 2023), 34.

31 A completed and updated list of all inter-State applications decided by the ECtHR or currently pending before it is available at: https://www.echr.coe.int/inter-state-applications, accessed 30 April 2024. For a comprehensive assessment of the mechanism, as well as for a critical evaluation of the relevant case-law, see I Risini, *The Inter-State Application Under the European Convention on Human Rights: Between Collective Enforcement of Human Rights and International Dispute Settlement* (Leiden/Boston, Brill 2018); for a welcoming attitude towards the increasing of inter-State complaints before the ECtHR, see I Risini, J Batura, L Kleinert, 'A 'golden age' of inter-state complaints?: An interview with Isabella Risini', *Völkerrechtsblog*, 16 September 2019; on the importance of adopting a more cautious approach to the phenomenon, see instead P Palchetti, 'Ricorsi interstatali in materia di diritti umani: uno strumento da maneggiare con cura', 15(2) *Diritti umani e diritto internazionale* (2021) 361, 367.

bodies,[32] as well as before the ICJ,[33] not only by States 'directly' affected by the violation(s), but – quite surprisingly – by States other than the injured one, given their status as parties to a multilateral convention containing obligations *erga omnes partes*.

Against this backdrop, the present contribution intends to broaden the analysis by assessing advantages and drawbacks of resorting to the available yet underexplored inter-State communication mechanisms set out in human rights treaties in the context of the Xinjiang's current crisis.

The present analysis is structured in four different Sections. Following this introduction as Section 1 of the article, Section 2 offers a comprehensive overview of the international human rights law substantive framework applicable to the alleged mistreatments of Uyghurs and other Muslim ethnic minorities. Section 3 then proceeds to identify three main inter-State communication mechanisms, tailoring these procedural solutions to the substantive legal terms which can be most useful to bring the violations within the scope of application of these treaties. In particular, the paper argues that States should prioritize the activation of the compulsory inter-State communication mechanism set out in Articles 11–13 ICERD, while also considering the possibility of requesting an advisory opinion from the ICJ through the General Assembly or other UN organs, such as the Economic and Social Council (hereinafter, ECOSOC). Section 3 also delves into the hardly considered option of resorting to the inter-State supervisory procedure envisaged in Articles 26–34 of the Constitution of the International Labour Organization (ILO), highlighting the effectiveness and flexibility of its system of 'direct contacts' or 'good offices' which could be implied to rectify the situation in the State receiving the complaint. Section

32 *Qatar v. Kingdom of Saudi Arabia*, 8 March 2018, UN Doc. CERD-ISC 2018/1; *Qatar v. United Arab Emirates*, 8 March 2018, UN Doc. CERD-ISC 2018/2; *Palestine v. Israel*, 23 April 2018, UN Doc. CERD-ISC 2018/3. Cfr. CERD Information Note on Inter-State Communications, 30 August 2018, <https://www.ohchr.org/en/press-releases/2018/09/cerd-information-note-inter-state-communications> accessed 30 April 2024. For a comprehensive analysis on the drafting history, functioning and recent practice of the ICERD inter-State communication mechanism, see J Eiken and D Keane, 'Towards an Amicable Solution: The Inter-State Communications Procedure under ICERD', 21(2) *The Law and Practice of International Courts and Tribunals* (2022) 302.

33 M Longobardo, 'The Standing of Indirectly Injured States in the Litigation of Community Interests before the ICJ: Lessons Learned and Future Implications in Light of *The Gambia v. Myanmar* and Beyond', 24(5) *International Community Law Review* (2022) 476; *Application of the Convention on the Prevention and Punishment of the Crime of Genocide* (*The Gambia v. Myanmar*), Preliminary Objections, Judgment, ICJ Reports 2022, p. 477; *Application of the Convention against Torture and Other Cruel, Inhuman or Degrading Treatment of Punishment* (*Canada and The Netherlands v. Syrian Arab Republic*), Joint Application instituting proceedings, 8 June 2023.

4 considers all the inter-State communication options, trying to identify the more suitable one in order to achieve the main purpose of ascertaining China's responsibility for the alleged violations.

2 Human Rights Violations in the Xinjiang Province: A Comprehensive Legal Assessment

While several international experts have preferred to adopt a more cautious approach–characterizing China's alleged abuses in the Xinjiang Province by referring to various non-legal categories such as 'state of terror',[34] terrorism (as replacing a so-called 'counterterrorism' policy, whose adoption has been declared in several official statements issued by the Chinese Government),[35] and 'modern colonialism'–[36] the ever-increasing awareness of the international community *vis-à-vis* the widespread pattern of violations perpetrated against Uyghurs and other Muslim ethnic minorities is demonstrated by the growing number of official documents or research papers providing for a comprehensive legal framework of the alleged unlawful conducts.[37] These studies are critical

34 SR Roberts, 'The Biopolitics of China's "War on Terror" and the Exclusion of the Uyghurs', 50 *Critical Asian Studies* (2018) 232, 233.

35 R Topal, 'An Empirical Assessment of China's Counterterrorism Efforts and Securitization of Turkic Muslims', 46 *Studies in Conflict & Terrorism* (2023) 1745.

36 D Anand, 'Colonization with Chinese Characteristics: Politics of (In)security in Xinjiang and Tibet', 38 *Central Asian Survey* (2019) 129, 136.

37 Cf. OHCHR Report; APR2P Centre Report; Congressional-Executive Commission on China, 2019 Annual Report, <https://www.cecc.gov/sites/chinacommission.house.gov/files/documents/2019AR_XINJIANG.pdf> accessed 30 April 2024; Bar Human Rights Committee of England and Wales, Briefing Paper: Responsibility of States under International Law to Uyghurs and other Turkic Muslims in Xinjiang, China, July 2020, available online (until 27 September 2023), <https://barhumanrights.org.uk/bhrc-publishes-new-report-outlining-the-responsibility-of-states-under-international-law-to-uyghurs-and-other-turkic-muslims-in-xinjiang-china/> accessed 30 April 2024; as regards specific violations concerning systematic forced labour, modern slavery and human trafficking of Uyghurs and other Muslim minorities, affecting Xinjiang's international supply chains of a variety of industries, including agriculture, electronics, textiles and apparel, sporting goods, and new energy; A Crawford and LT Murphy, 'Over-Exposed: Uyghur Region Exposure Assessment for Solar Industry Sourcing', Sheffield, UK: Sheffield Hallam University Helena Kennedy Centre for International Justice, 2023, available online; LT Murphy, K Salcito, Y Uluyol, M Rabkin et al., 'Driving Force: Automotive Supply Chains and Forced Labor in the Uyghur Region', Sheffield, UK: Sheffield Hallam University Helena Kennedy Centre for International Justice, December 2022, available online; LT Murphy, N Elimä, and D Tobin, '*Until Nothing Is Left*: China's Settler Corporation and its Human Rights Violations in the Uyghur Region. A Report on the Xinjiang Production and Construction Corps', Sheffield, UK: Sheffield Hallam University Helena Kennedy Centre for International Justice, 2022,

insofar as they attempt at 'matching' the reported mistreatments with the relevant China's international obligations concerning human rights, either treaty-based or of a *jus cogens* character. For the purposes of this study, it is therefore useful to provide some essential background on the most frequently reported violations. This will help to identify and further investigate the available inter-State communication mechanisms, either of a contentious or advisory nature, which can be activated to address – and, hopefully, to end – the ongoing situation.

2.1 *Possible Genocide: An Almost 'Probatio Diabolica'*

Commonly referred to as the 'crime of crimes',[38] the legal definition of genocide, also reflective of customary international law,[39] is provided in Article I of the Genocide Convention, that describes it as the commission of certain prohibited acts with an intent to destroy, in whole or in part, a national, ethnical, racial, or religious group as such. Article II comprises an exhaustive list of five prohibited genocidal acts, including: a) killing members of the group; b) causing serious bodily or mental harm to members of the group; c) deliberately inflicting on the group conditions of life calculated to bring about its physical destruction in whole or in part; (d) imposing measures intended to prevent births within the group; or (e) forcibly transferring children of the protected group to another group.[40] Any of these conducts are punishable insofar as they are directed against members of a protected group and are committed with the specific intent (also referred to as *dolus specialis*) to destroy a protected group, in whole or in part.[41]

---

available online; LT Murphy, J Vallette, and N Elimä, 'Built on Repression: PVC Building Materials' Reliance on Labor and Environmental Abuses in the Uyghur Region', Sheffield, UK: Sheffield Hallam University Helena Kennedy Centre for International Justice, 2022, available online.

38 *Prosecutor v. Jean Kambanda (Judgment and Sentence)*, International Criminal Tribunal for Rwanda (hereinafter, ICTR), ICTR 97-23-S, 4 September 1998, para. 16.

39 *Advisory Opinion Concerning Reservations to the Convention on the Prevention and Punishment of the Crime of Genocide*, International Court of Justice (ICJ), 28 May 1951, ICJ Reports 1951, p. 15, 23. See also *Prosecutor v. Radislav Krstić (Trial Judgment)*, International Criminal Tribunal for the former Yugoslavia (hereinafter, ICTY), ICTY IT-98-33, 2 August 2001, para. 580.

40 The circumstance according to which the five genocidal acts included in Article II of the Genocide Convention must be understood as a *numerus clausus* has been repeatedly emphasized by several authors; among others, see WA Schabas, *Genocide in International Law: The Crime of Crimes* (CUP, Cambridge 2009), 176; G Mettraux, *International Crimes: Law and Practice; Volume 1: Genocide* (OUP, Oxford 2019), 285.

41 *Prosecutor v. Rutaganda (Judgement and Sentence)*, ICTR, ICTR-96-3-T, 6 December 1999, para. 60.

In respect to the ongoing situation in the Xinjiang Province, there is evidence of varying strength that each of the five genocidal acts might have occurred. Nevertheless, significant doubts remain as to whether the necessary specific intent can be established on the basis of sufficiently compelling evidence.

Firstly, China is responsible for having directly killed, either through actions or omissions, a significant number of members belonging to the minority groups, with evidence reporting the deaths of several Turkic minority Muslims detained in 're-education' camps, as well as the deliberate killings of Uyghur new-borns in XUAR's hospitals.[42] Secondly, there are extensive and reliable reports demonstrating serious bodily or mental harm inflicted to Uyghurs and other Muslim community members detained in the camps, deriving from acts of torture, inhuman and degrading treatment, persecution and sexual violence, eventually leading them to death.[43] Thirdly, reliable evidence reveals widespread practices of forced sterilization, forced birth control, and abortions regularly inflicted against Uyghurs and other Muslim ethnic communities. Although the Genocide Convention does not provide for an express classification of conducts amounting to measures intended to prevent births within the group, the case-law of *ad hoc* international criminal tribunals clarified that sexual mutilation, practices of sterilization, forced birth control, separation of the sexes and prohibition of marriages represent all relevant measures amounting to the prohibited conduct described in Article II(d) of the Genocide Convention.[44] This conclusion is also strengthened by several Chinese documents showing a dramatic birth rate decrease in Uyghur regions between 2015 and 2018, together with an impressive number of women targeted for sterilization or the implementation of intrauterine devices (IUD s) in recent years, as well as a significant increase in women 'in menopause'.[45]

As regards the possible configuration of other genocidal acts prohibited by Article II, the available evidence is less robust than that establishing the existence of the above-described acts. Indeed, it is still unclear whether the conditions within Xinjiang 're-education' camps, reportedly including inhuman treatments such as overcrowding, food and sleep deprivation, and forced labour undertaken by Uyghurs and other Muslim communities amount

42 H Gulchehra and H Shohret, 'Xinjiang Hospitals Aborted, Killed Babies Outside Family Planning Limits: Uyghur Obstetrician', *Radio Free Asia*, 17 August 2020.

43 OHCHR Report, paras. 74–75.

44 *Prosecutor v. Kunarać* (Judgment), ICTY, IT-96-23-T and IT-96-23/1-T, 22 February 2001, para. 322; *Prosecutor v. Jean-Paul Akayesu* (Appeal Judgment), ICTR, ICTR-96-4-A, 1 June 2001, para. 507.

45 A Zenz, 'Sterilizations, IUD s, and Mandatory Birth Control: The CCP's Campaign to Suppress Uyghur Birthrates in Xinjiang', June 2020 [updated on 21 July 2020].

to life conditions deliberately inflicted to the group with the intention to bring its physical destruction in whole or in part pursuant to Article II(c).[46] Similarly, there is evidence that forcible transfer of children of the group to another group as provided for in Article II(e) has occurred in Xinjiang, as many NGOs and press reports disclosed several instances in which Uyghur children have been taken away from their communities in Xinjiang and placed into special boarding schools, usually after their parents have been detained.[47] However, additional evidence is needed to establish the exact nature and scale of the separation that has occurred between Uyghur children and their parents.

As anticipated, a finding of genocide also requires evidence of a specific intent to destroy, in whole or in part, a protected group as such. Given that mere knowledge of a genocidal programme is not sufficient, proving the existence of the necessary mental element for the purpose of ascertaining China's international responsibility for genocide can be difficult. For these reasons, international courts and tribunals have developed principles as to when the relevant purpose can be inferred. For instance, in *Bosnia v. Serbia* the ICJ affirmed that the *dolus specialis* to destroy the group in whole or in part must be convincingly demonstrated by reference to circumstances, unless a general plan to that end can be proven.[48] Similarly, in *Croatia v. Serbia*, the ICJ held that the applicant State had to establish the existence of a pattern of conducts from which the only conclusion to be drawn is the existence of a clear intent of the respondent State to destroy a protected group.[49]

Accordingly, international legal scholarship and relevant case-law have confirmed that the definition of destruction corresponds to the most 'extreme' forms of genocide, namely the physical and biological destruction of the protected group,[50] without taking into account other minor conducts, such as the destruction of the national, linguistic, religious, and cultural identity, which

46 *Prosecutor v. Sikirica et al.* (*Judgment on Defence Motions to Acquit*), ICTY, IT-95-8-T, 3 September 2001; *Prosecutor v Jelisić* (*Judgment*), ICTY, IT-95-10-T, 14 December 1999; *Case Concerning the Application of the Convention on the Prevention and Punishment of the Crime of Genocide* (*Bosnia and Herzegovina v. Serbia and Montenegro*) (Judgment), ICJ Reports 2007, p. 43, para. 354 (hereinafter, '*Bosnia v. Serbia*').

47 A Qin, 'In China's Crackdown on Muslims, Children Have Not Been Spared', *The New York Times*, December 28, 2019; Y Wang and D Kang, 'China treats Uighur kids as orphans after parents seized', *Associated Press*, September 21, 2018; L Zaili, 'Children of Arrested Uyghur Families Strictly Supervised', *Bitter Winter*, 29 September 2018.

48 *Bosnia v. Serbia*, para. 373.

49 *Application of the Convention on the Prevention and Punishment of the Crime of Genocide* (*Croatia v. Serbia*) (Judgment), ICJ Reports 2015, p. 3, para. 407.

50 R Lemkin, *Axis Rule in Occupied Europe: Laws of Occupation, Analysis of Government, Proposals for Redress* (Columbia University Press, New York 1944), 87–89; see also WA Schabas, *Genocide in International Law: The Crime of Crimes* (CUP, Cambridge 2009), 272.

could not be qualified as genocide within the meaning of the Convention, but could arguably be considered as evidence of such intent, also amounting to cultural genocide.[51]

When it comes to acknowledging the existence of the genocidal intent in the context of the violations allegedly perpetrated in the Xinjiang Province, there is growing evidence as to the existence of a possible intent to destroy the Uyghurs and other Muslim ethnic communities. According to several sources,[52] as well as drawing from the evidence presented and discussed before the 'Uyghur Tribunal', genocidal intent can be inferred, *inter alia*, from public speeches issued by certain Chinese Government's senior officials, in light of the credible evidences that they put in place a specific State policy in relation to Uyghurs and other ethnic minorities of XUAR and that, by doing so, those officials must have express a necessary genocidal intent.[53] However, applying the narrower interpretation of the intent to destroy developed and currently valid under international law, doubts remain as to whether inferences as to the existence of the genocidal intent can be drawn from the above described conducts. Indeed, as argued by some scholars, the idea of 're-education' which lies at the heart of the creation of Xinjiang camps appears to be based on the intention to convert Uyghurs and other Muslim ethnic communities rather than to destroy them physically or biologically.[54]

Furthermore, available evidence as to the implementation of birth control measures in XUAR allows inferences of a specific intent to destroy at least a significant part of the group. As already pointed out, official documents reveal a serious decline in Uyghur women's natural births, combined with an increase

---

51 *Bosnia v. Serbia*, para. 344. The list of prohibited genocidal acts is deemed to be exhaustive; cf. WA Schabas, *Genocide in International Law, cit.*, 174–175.

52 Among others, see A Macdonald QC, J McArthur, N Hart, L Aboagye (Essex Court Chambers), 'International Criminal Responsibility for Crimes Against Humanity and Genocide against the Uyghur Population in the Xinjiang Uyghur Autonomous Region', 26 January 2021, para. 127.

53 A Ramzy, C Buckley, 'Absolutely No Mercy: Leaked Files Expose How China Organized Mass Detentions on Muslims', *The New York Times*, 16 November 2019; International Consortium of Investigative Journals (ICIJ), 'Exposed: China's Operating Manuals for Mass Internments and Arrest by Algorithm', 24 November 2019; A Zenz, 'Wash Brains, Cleanse Hearts', *cit.*; A Zenz, 'The Xinjiang Papers: An Introduction', 27 November 2021; A Macdonald QC, J McArthur, N Hart, L Aboagye (Essex Court Chambers), 'International Criminal Responsibility for Crimes Against Humanity and Genocide against the Uyghur Population in the Xinjiang Uyghur Autonomous Region', cit., paras. 189–196.

54 J Slawotsky, 'Is China Guilty of Committing Genocide in Xinjiang?', 20(3) *Chinese Journal of International Law* (2021), 625, 627.

in China's resources dedicated at preventing births through abortions and sterilizations, killing of new-borns, forced insertion of IUD s and separation of sexes.[55] Even though there is currently no direct proof of such genocidal policy, the necessary mental element can be deduced from facts which cumulatively demonstrate the existence of such intent beyond reasonable doubts.[56]

Further uncertainties also remain when it comes to apply the specific genocidal intent to the forcible transfer of Uyghur children from their original ethnic group to other groups.[57] In this regard, several authors have argued that such acts could amount to a form of cultural genocide, therefore demonstrating an intent to destroy a protected group *only* in a cultural sense.[58] Available evidence concerning practices of systematic birth suppression could nevertheless be regarded as useful in establishing that a specific genocidal intent is the only possible inference available from the pattern of persecutory conducts.

Whether or not China could be hold accountable for the crime of genocide as a principal perpetrator, its international responsibility may be nevertheless ascertained for having disregarded its general obligations to prevent and punish genocide set forth in Articles IV, V and IV of the Genocide Convention. In this respect, available evidence and reports satisfy the requirement of establishing a 'serious danger' that genocide had been or will be perpetrated. Therefore, since there is no existing information about any efforts within China to investigate the conducts potentially constituting the crime of genocide, nor to charge or prosecute those who may be held directly responsible for genocide or other forms of participation to the crime envisaged in Article III of the Genocide Convention, a possible request for an ICJ's advisory opinion could be helpful in order to ascertain whether and to what extent China's actions in Xinjiang constitute a violation of the peremptory norm prohibiting genocide, and what would be legal consequences of such a finding for China and for States other than China, with a view of putting an end to the alleged atrocities.

55 A Zenz, 'Sterilizations, IUD s, and Mandatory Birth Control', *cit.*; G Hoja and S Hoshur, 'Xinjiang Hospitals Aborted, Killed Babies Outside Family Planning Limits: Uyghur Obstetrician', *Radio Free Asia*, August 17, 2020.

56 *Bosnia v. Serbia*, para. 189; *Prosecutor v. Brđanin (Judgment)*, ICTY, IT-99-36-T, 1 September 2004, para. 970; *Prosecutor v. Tolimir (Judgment)*, ICTY, IT-05- 88/2-T, 12 December 2012, para. 745.

57 A Qin, 'In China's Crackdown on Muslims, Children Have Not Been Spared', *The New York Times*, 28 December 2019.

58 WA Schabas, *Genocide in International Law*, cit., at 294.

2.2 *Human Rights Abuses Against Uyghurs and Other Muslim Minorities: A Smoke that Does Actually Come from a Fire*

This section will identify the other human rights treaty-based obligations allegedly violated by China in the context of the ongoing Xinjiang's crisis.[59]

First and foremost, China's mistreatment of Uyghurs and other Muslim ethnic communities disregards several ICERD treaty obligations. At the outset Article 1 ICERD defines racial discrimination as any distinction, exclusion, restriction, or preference based on race, colour, descent, or national or ethnic origin, which has the purpose or effect of nullifying or impairing the recognition, enjoyment, or exercise, on an equal footing, of human rights and fundamental freedoms. There are serious accounts, articulated by human rights experts and monitoring bodies over the years,[60] including the Committee on the Elimination of All Forms of Racial Discrimination ('CERD Committee'),[61] that Uyghurs and other Muslim ethnic minorities have been discriminated. These accounts are based on *prima facie* evidence of discriminatory treatment, carried out through frequent profiling, monitoring, and specific targeting in workplace settings by Uyghur administrative and political leaders and, more generally, by law enforcement bodies; forcible separation of children from their families and assimilation into non-Uyghur groups; removal of Chinese identity documents; destruction of ethno-cultural and religious symbols and worship places; measures prohibiting practice and observance of religious beliefs, as well as forcible assimilation of Uyghurs and other Muslim minorities into practices going against their will; displacement and re-population of Uyghur

59 For a brief overview which considers China's possible violation of its human rights obligations under the Universal Declaration of Human Rights, the ICERD, the ICESCR, and the CAT, see G O'Connell, 'How China Is Violation Human Rights Treaties and its own Constitution in Xinjiang', *Just Security*, August 19, 2020.

60 European Parliament, Resolution of 9 June 2022 on the human rights situation in Xinjiang, including the Xinjiang police files, 2022/2700 RSP, available online; United Nations, OHCHR, 'Xinjiang Report: China must address grave human rights violations and the world must not turn a blind eye, say UN experts', 7 September 2022, available online; CERD Committee, Concluding International Labour Organization (ILO), Application of International Labour Standards 2022, Report of the Committee of Experts on the Application of Conventions and Recommendations, International Labour Conference, 110th Session, 2022, at 515.

61 Committee on the Elimination of All Forms of Racial Discrimination (CERD), Concluding Observations on the Combined Fourteenth to Seventeenth Periodic Reports of China (including Hong Kong, China and Macao, China), CERD/C/CHN/CO/14–17), 30 August 2018; cf. also CERD Committee, Prevention of Racial Discrimination, Including Early Warning and Urgent Action Procedure, Decision 1(108), 108th Session, 14 November – 2 December 2022, 2940th Meeting, 23 November 2022.

and other regions with Han Chinese; repression of Uyghurs language rights and simultaneous imposition of the Chinese Mandarin language, among others.[62] In so doing, China has shown an unambiguous preference for one ethnic group over another, thereby disregarding its treaty obligations under Articles 2, 3, 4, 5, and 6 ICERD, among others. Therefore, as it will be discussed more in details below, notwithstanding China's reservation to the compromissory clause in Article 22 CERD, the alleged violations could be brought to the attention of the CERD Committee through the compulsory inter-State communication procedure outlined in Articles 11–13, which is conciliatory and quasi-judicial in its nature and functioning, and aims to achieve an amicable solution between the States Parties involved in the dispute.

Furthermore, China's pattern of violations could also have breached several of its treaty-based human rights obligations. Therefore, in light of China's long-standing preference to opt out of any treaty provisions referring inter-State disputes to international courts and tribunals, the request of an advisory opinion to the ICJ could provide the only appropriate way to tackle the issue, similar to the approach adopted as regards genocide allegations.

The current crisis in Xinjiang reveals widespread violation of China's treaty obligations under the ICESCR,[63] whose Article 1 establishes that all peoples have the right to self-determination and the ability to freely determine their political status and pursue their economic, social, and cultural development. In the context of mass imprisonment and widespread abuses occurring in XUAR, China has regularly denied Uyghurs and other Muslim minorities the right to self-determination granted to them under international law. Indeed, legislative measures imposed by the Chinese Government have resulted in a series of policies that Uyghurs and other Muslim minorities would never have spontaneously chosen if they had been able to govern themselves.[64] Furthermore, detailed reports have revealed that detainees have been forcedly employed without little or no remuneration in mass factories producing consumer goods, thus violating both Articles 6(1) and 7 ICESCR, according to which the fundamental right to work must be based on free choice and acceptance, and employees must benefit from favourable, healthy and safe

62 A Zenz, 'China Didn't Want Us to Know. Now Its Own Files Are Doing the Talking', *The New York Times*, 24 November 2019; C Shepherd, 'Fear and Oppression in Xinjiang; China's War on Uighur Culture', *Financial Times*, 12 September 2019.

63 Committee on Economic, Social and Cultural Rights (ECOSOC), Concluding Observations, 22 March 2023, <https://tbinternet.ohchr.org/_layouts/15/treatybodyexternal/Download.aspx?symbolno=E%2FC.12%2FCHN%2FCO%2F3&Lang=en> accessed 30 April 2024.

64 G Bovingdon, *The Uyghurs: Stranger in Their Own Land* (Columbia University Press, New York 2010), 79.

working conditions, receiving an economic treatment proportional to the amount of their work.

Alongside arbitrary mass detention and forced employment perpetrated in Xinjiang's camps, regular investigations conducted to ascertain the existence of indoctrination tactics adopted to re-educate detainees on Chinese history, culture, and language, on the one hand, as well as the increasing number of deaths and health related issues suffered by internees, on the other hand, lead to believe that China has violated also Articles 2, 6, 7, 12, and 13 ICESCR.[65]

Furthermore, China has allegedly breached several obligations enshrined in CEDAW. Indeed, the account of practices adopted to deliberately target women of Uyghur and other Muslim ethnic communities' heritage raise concerns as to the existence of a gender-oriented discrimination. As already anticipated, cases of forced sterilization are recurrent in XUAR camps, with women being subject to intrusive surgical procedures preventing them from bearing children. Moreover, women of childbearing age, with or without children, have been all subject to either massive sterilization programs or to the family planning Chinese policy.

In addition to that, women and young girls are allegedly forced to take medication preventing them from menstruating, as well as to take drugs and other medicines causing them serious illnesses and loss of consciousness. Another dossier reports on the practice of confiscating of travel documents and imposing abortion on Uyghur women that attempted to renounce their Chinese citizenship and give birth elsewhere.

Finally, various news channels have denounced mass sexual assaults and torture occurring to several women in Xinjiang's camps. Testimonies reveal that women have been subject to rape and sexual assault by Chinese male personnel employed in detention facilities, by means of electronic batons used for vaginal penetration.[66] Given that, there is sufficient and concordant evidence that China has violated Articles 3, 6, 12, and 16 CEDAW.

65 G Shih, 'China's mass indoctrination camps evoke Cultural Revolution', *AP News*, 17 May 2018.

66 A Ferris-Rotman, 'Abortions, IUDs and Sexual humiliation: Muslim women who fled China for Kazakhstan recount ordeals', *Washington Post*, 7 October 2019, <https://www.washingtonpost.com/world/asia_pacific/abortions-iuds-and-sexual-humiliation-muslim-women-who-fled-china-for-kazakhstan-recount-ordeals/2019/10/04/551c2658-cfd2-11e9-a620- 0a91656d7db6_story.html> accessed 30 April 2024; A Ferris-Rotman, A Toleukhan, E Rauhala, and A Fifield, 'China accused of genocide over forced abortions of Uighur Muslim women as escapees reveal widespread sexual torture', *The Independent*, 6 October 2019, <https://www.independent.co.uk/news/world/asia/china-uighur-muslim-women-abortions-sexual-abuse-genocide-a9144721.html> accessed 30 April 2024.

To assess whether China could be held accountable for having committed torture, Article 1 UNCAT defines 'torture' as any act by which severe pain or suffering, whether physical or mental, is intentionally inflicted on a person for any reason based on discrimination of any kind when such pain or suffering is perpetrated by or at the instigation of, or with the consent or acquiescence of a public official or other person acting in an official capacity. Concerning Xinjiang's current crisis, former Uyghur detainees have reported severe conditions in 're-education' camps as involving overcrowded cells, indoctrination driving some to suicide, prolonged solitary confinement, food, and sleep deprivation as punishment, systematic beatings, electrical shock treatment, rape, and sexual humiliation and other forms of physical and mental abuse.[67] Available evidence suggests that most of these practices meet the necessary severity threshold, described by international courts as varying according to factual circumstances, giving weight to factors such as the consistency and context of the infliction of pain, as well as premeditation and purpose, but in any case requiring a significant degree of pain and suffering. It remains unclear whether the conditions in which detainees are confined in Xinjiang's camps satisfy this threshold. The CAT Committee held that conditions of detention may amount to torture,[68] but international practice suggests that this is more likely to be considered as cruel and inhuman treatment.[69] Notwithstanding this, reports of pain inflicted during interrogations as a coercive method of information extraction and as a punishment *technique* are very likely to demonstrate the existence of severe physical or mental pain and suffering. Moreover, the CAT Committee observed that, when it comes to preventing and punishing the crime of torture, China's criminal law only mentions physical

---

67 'At Least 150 Detainees Have Died in One Xinjiang Internment Camp: Police Officer', *Radio Free Asia*, 29 October 2019, <https://www.rfa.org/english/news/uyghur/deaths-10292019181322.html> accessed 30 April 2024; 'Uyghur Father of Two Dies After Falling Ill in Xinjiang Re-Education Camp', *Radio Free Asia*, 12 April 2018, <https://www.rfa.org/english/news/uyghur/father-04122018153525.html> accessed 30 April 2024; 'Uyghur Teenager Dies in Custody at Political Re-Education Camp', *Radio Free Asia*, 14 March, 2018, <https://www.rfa.org/english/news/uyghur/teenager-03142018154926.html> accessed 30 April 2024; 'Elderly Uyghur Woman Dies in Detention in Xinjiang Political Re-Education Camp', *Radio Free Asia*, 24 May 2018, <https://www.rfa.org/english/news/uyghur/woman-05242018164854.html> accessed 30 April 2024.

68 Committee Against Torture (CAT), Summary Account of the Results of the Proceedings concerning the Inquiry on Turkey, UN Doc. A/48/44/Add.1, 1993, para. 52.

69 Association for the Prevention of Torture and Centre for Justice and International Law, Torture in International Law, A Guide to Jurisprudence (2008), available online, 5, 140; *Prosecutor v Simić et al.* (Judgment), ICTY, Trial Chamber II, Case No IT-95-9-T, 17 October 2003, para. 97; *Prosecutor v Blagojević et al.* (Judgment), ICTY, Trial Chamber I, Case No IT-02-60-T, 17 January 2005, para. 609.

abuse, without including the infliction of mental pain and suffering, thereby indirectly tolerating such conducts.[70] Consequently, it is reasonable to assume that China has breached its obligations under Articles 1, 2, 10, and 16 UNCAT, among others.

Moreover, China has allegedly disregarded various fundamental rights and freedoms of children, as set out in the CRC, as well as those granted to disabled people by the CRPD. Indeed, reports of forced separations of Uyghur and other Muslim minorities children from their parents, often as a consequence of the latter's arbitrary detention, the subsequent placement of these children in state-run education institutions, denying their families visitation rights or any other communication, as well as the prohibition on the speaking of the Uyghur language and practice of Islam, and the imposition of Chinese language, history, and culture, subjecting them to what has been defined as 'cultural engineering', raise serious concerns that China is not fulfilling its human rights treaty-based obligations under Articles 1, 2, 3, 5, 9, 12, 14, 20, and 34 CRC, whose main aim is to safeguard the best interest of children against any possible discrimination that can offend their human dignity.[71] Lastly, China has allegedly violated CRPD provisions, even though this claim is, at the current stage, more difficult to prove.[72] CRPD intends to promote, protect, and ensure the enjoyment of human rights by all persons with disabilities, of whom China has always claimed to be a guarantor. However, starting from 2012, several NGOs have reported allegations of people with disabilities working in abusive or exploitative conditions,[73] with other documents reporting, even before that date, on the difficulties faced by eleven workers, most of whom had mental and psychological disabilities, employed at a factory in Toksun County, a Xinjiang's territory.[74] It is therefore possible, considering these allegations,

70 Committee Against Torture (CAT), *Concluding Observations on the Fifth Periodic Report of China*, CAT/C/CHN/CO/5, 3 February 2016.

71 Human Rights Watch, 'China: Xinjiang Children Separated from Families: Return Minors Housed in State-Run Institutions to Relatives', 15 September 2019, <https://www.hrw.org/news/2019/09/15/china-xinjiang-children-separated-families> accessed 30 April 2024; Human Rights Watch, 'China: Children Caught in Xinjiang Crackdown: Reunite Families; End Mass Arbitrary Detention', 16 October 2018, <https://www.hrw.org/news/2018/10/16/china-children-caught-xinjiang-crackdown> accessed 30 April 2024.

72 MA Stein, 'China and Disability Rights', 33 *Loyola of Los Angeles International and Comparative Law Review* (2010) 7, 7–8.

73 Human Rights Watch, 'China: Submission to the UN Committee on the Rights of Persons with Disabilities', 12 April 2012, <https://www.hrw.org/news/2012/04/12/china-submission-un-committee-rights-persons-disabilities> accessed 30 April 2024.

74 T Branigan, 'Chinese Agency 'Sold Disabled Workers into Slave Labour', *The Guardian*, 14 December 2010, <https://www.theguardian.com/world/2010/dec/14/china-disabled-workers-slave-labour-claim> accessed 30 April 2024.

that China is currently engaging in forced labour of people with disabilities belonging to Uyghur and other Muslim ethnic minorities, thereby disregarding its obligations under CRPD.

2.3 *Forced Labour and (Modern) Slavery as Serious Concerns in Xinjiang's Crisis: A Need for a Reappraisal*

This section intends to address whether and to what extent the allegations of forced labour and slavery formulated against China amount to a violation of its human rights treaty obligations under both the 1926 Slavery Convention and the ILO Convention No. 105.

First, according to the definition provided in Article 1 of the 1926 Slavery Convention, slavery is the legal status or condition of a person over whom any or all powers attaching to the right of ownership are exercised. The same definition, reflective of customary international law, is reproduced almost *verbatim* in Article 7 of the ICC Statute, that qualifies the act of 'enslavement' committed as a part of widespread or systematic attack against a civilian population as a crime against humanity if perpetrated in the context of trafficking of persons, particularly women and children. As concerns forced labour, instead, Article 2(1) of the ILO Convention No. 105 explains this expression as referring to every form of work or service which is exacted from any person under the menace of any penalty, and for which the said person has not offered himself voluntarily.

Despite frequent misunderstandings between these two legal notions, slavery and forced labour should be conceived as distinct concepts under international law.[75] Indeed, as recognized by several commentators, slavery comprehends more than just forced labour, while not all forms of forced labour can be classified as slavery.[76] Indeed, slavery, whose related prohibition has been conferred the status of peremptory norm by, *inter alia*, the ICJ,[77] implies a complete system of ownership, which should have a permanent character.

75 International Labour Organisation (ILO), 'What is Forced Labour, Modern Slavery and Human Trafficking', <https://www.ilo.org/global/topics/forced-labour/definition/lang--en/index.htm> accessed 30 April 2024.

76 A Jordan, 'Slavery, Forced Labor, Debt Bondage, and Human Trafficking: From Conceptual Confusion to Targeted Solutions', 2 *Center for Human Rights & Humanitarian Law* (2011).

77 Cf. Vienna Conference, Yearbook, Vol. II, 1966, at 247; *Barcelona Traction, Light and Power Co., Ltd. (Belgium v Spain)*, ICJ Reports 1971 (5 February 1971), para. 32; on the topic see among others A Bianchi, 'Human rights and the magic of *jus cogens*', 19(3) *European Journal of International Law* (2008) 491, 495; A Cassese, 'For an enhanced role of *jus cogens*', in A Cassese (ed) *Realizing Utopia: The Future of International Law* (OUP, Oxford 2012), 162; D Shelton, *Jus Cogens* (OUP, Oxford 2021), 86.

Although slavery can be often perceived as a historical relic of the past, whose eradication has been achieved by the international community already at the beginning of the 19th century through the adoption of the 1926 Slavery Convention, it must be recalled that more than 40 million people are nowadays victims of contemporary forms of slavery, servitude, or other slavery-like practices, that have been comprehensively labelled as 'modern slavery'. This expression encompasses a variety of prohibited conducts: alongside those explicitly prohibited under the 1926 Slavery Convention, modern slavery could come into being whenever allegations of widespread human trafficking (as defined by the 2000 Palermo Protocol),[78] forced labour (as described by the 2014 Protocol to the ILO Convention No. 29),[79] and child labour (as prohibited by both the 1999 ILO Convention on Worst Forms of Child Labour and the above mentioned CRC)[80] can be validly demonstrated.[81]

Available reports alleging the existence of a regime of forced labour sponsored by China and imposed on Uyghurs and other Muslim ethnic minorities have systematically refrained from implying both legal terms 'slavery' and 'enslavement'. However, in recent times, international experts have submitted reports based on an increasing amount of credible evidence likely sufficient to accuse China for having implemented a so-called 'modern slavery exploitation machine' on Xinjiang's ethnic, religious and linguistic minorities, thus distorting fair and free trade and seriously violating international labour standards and, more generally, basic fundamental rights, with several reports denouncing a state-sponsored systematic practice of forced labour imposed on Uyghurs interned in so-called 'Vocational and Educational Training Camps' (VETC s) for the purpose of carrying out labour-intensive sweatshops.[82] To this

---

78 UN General Assembly, Protocol to Prevent, Suppress and Punish Trafficking in Persons, Especially Women and Children, Supplementing the United Nations Convention against Transnational Organized Crime, 15 November 2000.

79 International Labour Organization (ILO), Protocol of 2014 to the Forced Labour Convention, 1930 (P029).

80 Cf. Article 32 CRC, according to which: «States Parties recognize the right of the child to be protected from economic exploitation and from performing any work that is likely to be hazardous or to interfere with the child's education, or to be harmful to the child's health or physical, mental, spiritual, moral or social development».

81 On the concept of 'modern slavery' see *inter alia* P Webb, R Garciandia Garmendia, 'State Responsibility for Modern Slavery: Uncovering and Bridging the Gap', 68(3) *International Comparative Law Quarterly* (2019) 539, 540.

82 Cf. International Labour Organization (ILO), Individual Case (CAS), Discussion, 2022 Publication, 110th Session, 1958 Discrimination (Employment and Occupation) Convention (No. 111); for a detailed analysis of this long-standing practice, already implemented starting from 2017, see instead C Buckley and A Ramzy, 'China's Detention Camps for Muslims Turn to Forced Labor', *The New York Times*, 16 December 2018.

end, it is worth emphasizing that the Xinjiang Production and Construction Corps (XPCC), a Chinese state-owned enterprise and paramilitary organization located in the Xinjiang Province charged of the administration of its own prison system and factories, has seized rural lands of indigenous farmers and allocated them for industrial exploitation.[83] As a consequence of this land-grabbing-alike phenomenon, the XPCC has forcedly employed local Uyghur and Muslim ethnic minorities in cotton harvesting and textile production.[84] Moreover, much of the cotton fabricated in the detention facilities, which has been estimated to represent approximately the 34% of China's overall cotton output, is also absorbed into global supply chains and found in garments worn by people throughout the world, raising concerns as to the involvement of fifty intermediary manufactures and more than a hundred well-known international brands corporations as possible complicit in the abuses.[85] Additional international reports identified at least twenty-seven factories located in nine different Chinese provinces having been found to regularly employ Uyghur labour forces which have been forcibly transferred from XUAR since at least 2017. Even though China keeps saying that these labour transfers should be regarded as poverty alleviation measures,[86] research raises serious concerns as to the fact that the labour schemes implied in the VETCs are not voluntarily chosen by the internees.[87] According to a report recently issued by the ILO, Xinjiang's workers are enduring a rigorous and ghettoized life under a military-style management, experiencing constant surveillance carried out both physically and through electronic devices.[88]

83 A general report on the XPCC's role and influence in the Xinjiang Province is provided by LT Murphy et al, 'Until Nothing is Left: China's Settler Corporation and its Human Rights Violations in the Uyghur Region', Sheffield Hallam University (United Kingdom), Helena Kennedy Centre, *cit.*; see also V Xiuzhong Xu et al, 'Uyghurs for Sale: 'Re-Education', Forced Labour, and Surveillance Beyond Xinjiang', *Australian Strategy Policy Institute*, 28 February 2020, https://www.aspi.org.au/report/uyghurs-sale accessed 30 April 2024.

84 For a comprehensive assessment of this practice, see LT Murphy et al, 'Laundering Cotton: How Xinjiang Cotton is Obscured in International Supply Chains', Sheffield Hallam University (United Kingdom), Helena Kennedy Centre, *cit.*, 9 ff.

85 E.g. Worker Rights Consortium, 'WRC Issue Brief: Inditex Linked to Companies Complicit in Uyghur Forced Labour', 4 November 2020, available online; on the matter, see generally A Kelly, 'Virtually entire fashion industries complicit in Uyghur forced labour, say rights groups, *The Guardian*, 23 July 2020.

86 H Davidson, 'Clues to scale of Xinjiang labour operation emerge as China defends camps', *The Guardian*, 18 September 2020.

87 OHCHR Report, paras. 47–48.

88 Application of International Labour Standards 2022 Report III (Part A) Report of the Committee of Experts on the Application of Conventions and Recommendations International Labour Conference 110th Session, 2022, 689.

Against this backdrop, it is reasonable to assume that the working conditions applied to Uyghurs and other Muslim minorities align with most (if not all) of the ILO's indicators of forced labour.[89] Therefore, China's pattern of violations deliberately breaches its treaty-based obligations under ILO Conventions No. 29, 105 and 111.

3 Staring at the (Almost) Empty Shelves: Rediscovering Inter-State Human Rights Communications as Avenues to Ensure China's Accountability in Xinjiang

The present section intends to rebut the 'apparent' lack of available inter-State adjudicative mechanisms often put forward by scholars when addressing the current situation in Xinjiang, presenting several alternative legal solutions to tackle the alleged violations.

The first subparagraph delves into the possibility of requesting an advisory opinion to the ICJ, based on an initiative of the General Assembly or of other UN organs or specialized agencies. Even though they do not have binding force, advisory opinions carry significant authority and weight, having been found to have 'legal effect'.[90] In recent times, there has also been a resurgence in the use of powerful instruments to enforce community interests and persuade violating States to amend their conduct.[91] Nevertheless, as it will be argued, they still represent a highly politically sensitive option that rests on a compromise often difficult to achieve.

The second subparagraph then shifts the analysis to the feasibility for States other than China to lodge a complaint before the CERD Committee, thus resorting to the compulsory inter-State communication mechanism enshrined in Articles 11–13 ICERD, with a view of ending China's impunity as concerned the alleged racial discrimination policy carried out against Uyghurs and other Muslim ethnic minorities. In this vein, attention will be paid to both

89 International Labour Organization, ILO's indicators of forced labour, <https://www.ilo.org/global/topics/forced-labour/publications/WCMS_203832/lang--en/index.htm> accessed 30 April 2024.

90 International Tribunal for the Law of the Sea (ITLOS), *Dispute Concerning Delimitation of the Maritime Boundary between Mauritius and Maldives in the Indian Ocean (Mauritius/Maldives)*, Preliminary Objections, Judgment, 28 January 2021, para. 205.

91 JA Hofbauer, 'Not Just a Participation Trophy? Advancing Public Interests through Advisory Opinions at the International Court of Justice' 22(2) *The Law and Practice of International Courts and Tribunals* (2023) 234.

the potential and disadvantages of having recourse to this type of inter-State procedure.

Finally, a third subparagraph examines the rather underexplored, yet effective, inter-State monitoring mechanism provided for in Articles 26–34 of the ILO Constitution. These provisions establish a complex, adversarial and somewhat 'hybrid' dispute settlement procedure, characterized by a significant investigative component, whose functioning and concrete implementation are jointly supervised by a Commission of Inquiry and a Governing Body. Even though the activation of this mechanism by the ILO Constitution's Contracting States Parties has been rather infrequent, in 2022 the Governing Body adopted several measures to condemn Myanmar's reluctance to abolish forced labour.[92] Therefore, it is not unrealistic to envisage that States may be interested in following this path with regards to the Xinjiang's crisis as well.

Before delving into the analysis of the various inter-State communication mechanisms considered for the present analysis, some caveats are necessary to set the context for the discussion. As briefly mentioned, China's (apparent) obstruction of all inter-State complaint procedures and, more generally, the perceived inadequacies of treaty-based enforcement mechanisms have been replaced by the widespread adoption of unilateral human rights sanctions – i.e., unilateral economic sanctions enacted to promote human rights abroad and to punish their violations[93] – imposed to Chinese heads of State and other high-ranking government officials, mainly subject to an asset freeze and to a travel ban.

This reveals two crucial aspects, which must not be overlooked. Generally, China considers that States should be able to freely choose the means of settling a dispute rather than disputes being subject to compulsory adjudication of international tribunals or other quasi-judicial bodies. For this reason, China has historically regarded negotiation and conciliation to be the appropriate means for settling disputes involving its 'core interests', which include issues of sovereignty and territorial integrity. However, over time, there has been a gradual shift in China's approach over trade and investment disputes. For instance,

92 Governing Body of the International Labour Organization (ILO), GB.344/INS/12/Decision, Decision concerning the Report of the Director-General on developments in Myanmar, including information on potential follow-up action by the 110th Session of the International Labour Conference.

93 As argued by several scholars, there is no well-established definition of 'human rights sanctions'; see C Portela, 'Targeted sanctions against individuals on grounds of grave human rights violations – impacts, trends and prospects at EU level' (2018), Study Commissioned by the European Parliament's Subcommittee of Human Rights 14; I Bogdanova, *Unilateral Sanctions in International Law and the Enforcement of Human Rights* (Brill, Leiden 2022), 223.

China has developed strong trust in the WTO system, perceiving it as a genuine level playing field where it can succeed, and strongly asserting itself in disputes threatening its economic and ideological interests. There is some evidence that China's increased acceptance of, and assertiveness before, international adjudication extends beyond trade and investments, to other areas in which its core interests are engaged.[94] As mentioned, China has never been a party to a contentious case before the ICJ. But in 2009, for the first time, it made both written and oral submission in the proceedings regarding the *Kosovo* Advisory Opinion, a case concerning the competing interests of the territorial integrity of a State and a minority group's wish for independence under the general principle of self-determination: an issue that, of course, presents significant overlaps and similarities with the Xinjiang's ongoing situation. Given the above, it can therefore be optimistically assumed that the various inter-State avenues identified in this study could represent appropriate forums where to achieve a compromising solution. On the one hand, an advisory proceedings before the ICJ will certainly be helpful in spreading awareness on the current crisis, while allowing China to engaging with the Court and support its own interests without having the risk of an adverse decision made against it. On the other hand, the treaty-based inter-State communication mechanisms established in both the ICERD and the ILO Constitution, avoiding a strong 'confrontational' approach and relying heavily on conciliatory procedures – but, at the same time, significantly departing from the forms and methods of human rights *soft* diplomacy – could seem more 'acceptable' to China, that may therefore be more inclined to have its conduct scrutinized by quasi-judicial bodies with a view of achieving an amicable solution with the applicant States, thus avoiding the threat of future contentious proceedings.

With regard to the unilateral sanctions enacted *vis-à-vis* Chinese heads of State and other senior government officials, one might wonder whether and to what extent the enjoyment of immunity may create potential tensions with the effective functioning of inter-State communication mechanisms, also in respect of the long-standing dilemma of the appropriateness of lifting state immunity for grave human rights violations on the basis of a *jus cogens* exception.[95] Against the background of their contested legality, as well as their

94 See further H Moynihan, 'China's Evolving Approach to International Dispute Settlement', The Royal Institute of International Affairs, Chatham House, March 2017, <https://www.chathamhouse.org/sites/default/files/publications/research/2017-03-29-chinas-evolving-approach-international-dispute-settlement-moynihan-final.pdf> accessed 30 April 2024.

95 On the topic, see extensively P Webb, 'Human Rights and the Immunities of State Officials', in E De Wet and J Vidmar (eds), *Hierarchy in International Law: The Place of Human Rights* (OUP, Oxford 2012), 114–147.

intricate relationship with the field of human rights, it seems difficult to affirm that the imposition of unilateral sanctions against State officials could in any way interact with a possible inter-State communication and be used as a valid exception in order to contrast any possible determination of State responsibility, for two main reasons. Firstly, as will be seen in more detail below, inter-State communication mechanisms, either of a 'official' or 'in disguise' nature, are not able to engage the international responsibility of the State, as they are conceived as conciliatory mechanisms.[96] Secondly, the emerging doctrine of conceptualising human rights as a 'common concern of humankind' – entailing a duty to cooperate and to secure compliance especially in instances of grave and systematic violations threatening international peace and security – has recently been regarded as an instrument for providing legitimacy to unilateral economic sanctions, offering a suitable framework for addressing the problem of non-reciprocal interests, as well as redefining rights and obligations in the field of human rights.[97]

3.1 *The 'One-Size-Fits-All' Solution? A Reference to the ICJ for an Advisory Opinion*

As anticipated, bearing in mind the consensual nature of international contentious jurisdiction,[98] China's alleged violations of human rights treaty-based obligations cannot be ascertained by the ICJ in a bilateral dispute, as China does not currently provide the Court with the necessary jurisdiction pursuant to Article 36(1) of the ICJ Statute, having formulated a conspicuous number of reservations to the compromissory clauses included in every core human rights treaties considered for the present study. In this respect, an exception can be formulated as regards the ICERD, whose compromissory clause set out in Article 22 has been reserved by China, but whose inter-State communication mechanism enshrined in Articles 11–13 cannot be avoided by means of reservations, as Article 20(2) clearly states.[99] Moreover, in the

96 Cf. E Decaux, 'The Potential for Inter-State Conciliation within the Framework of the UN Treaties for the Protection of Human Rights', in C Tomuschat, M Kohen (eds), *Flexibility in International Dispute Settlement: Conciliation Revisited* (Leiden, Brill Nijhoff, 2020), 39–82.

97 See among others I Bogdanova, *Unilateral Sanctions in International Law and the Enforcement of Human Rights*, cit., 306.

98 Cf. C Tomuschat, 'Competence of the Court, Article 36', in A Zimmermann et al (eds), *The Statute of the International Court of Justice: A Commentary* (OUP, Oxford 2019), 656–657.

99 Article 20(2) ICERD provides as follows: "A reservation incompatible with the object and purpose of this Convention shall not be permitted, nor shall *a reservation the effect of which would inhibit the operation of any of the bodies established by this Convention* be allowed. A reservation shall be considered incompatible or inhibitive if at least two thirds of the States Parties to this Convention object to it" (emphasis added).

case of a contentious proceeding as regards Xinjiang's atrocities, it is unlikely that China will spontaneously recognize the Court's competence pursuant to Article 36(2) of the ICJ Statute.[100] As a result, resorting to the ICJ contentious jurisdiction is not a suitable solution to end the alleged atrocities.

While most scholars have emphasized the impossibility of resolving this deadlocked scenario, given the unavailability of all contentious proceedings before the ICJ established by human rights treaties, scant attention has been paid to the alternative strategy of invoking the Court's advisory jurisdiction, especially when public interests are at stake.[101] Since its establishment, the ICJ has received 28 requests for advisory opinions, as of early 2023. While it is true that most advisory decisions have been issued in the early years of the Court's activity,[102] it is also true that this instrument is currently undergoing a revival, thus being far from constituting an ineffective relic of the past.

Against this background, while several authors and international judges have recently expressed some scepticism as concerns the recent resurgence of the (ab)use of the advisory 'route' to bring before the Court contentious matters in the absence of consent to adjudication by interested States,[103] other commentators have instead welcomed this trend.[104]

---

100 S Oda, 'The Compulsory Jurisdiction of the International Court of Justice: A Myth? A Statistical Analysis of Contentious Cases', 49 *International Comparative Law Quarterly* (2000) 251; B Simma, 'How Has Article 36 (2) of the ICJ Statute Fared?', in T Giegerich and UE Heinz (eds), *A Wiser Century? Judicial Dispute Settlement, Disarmament, and the Laws of War 100 Years after the Second Hague Peace Conference* (Duncker & Humblot, Berlin 2009), 455.

101 R Higgins, *A Comment on the Current Health of Advisory Opinions From 50 years of the International Court of Justice: Essays in honour of Sir Robert Jennings* (OUP, Oxford 2009); A Nollkaemper, 'International Adjudication of Global Public Goods: The Intersection of Substance and Procedure', 23(3) *European Journal of International Law* (2012) 769, 771.

102 M Pomerance, 'Seeking Judicial Legitimation in the Cold War: U.S. Foreign Policy and the World Court, 1948–1962', 4 *Indiana International and Comparative Law Review* (1995) 303; D Akande, 'Selection of the International Court of Justice as a Forum for Contentious and Advisory Proceedings (Including Jurisdiction)', 7(2) *Journal of International Dispute Settlement* (2016) 320, 339.

103 Cf. *Legal Consequences of the Separation of the Chagos Archipelago from Mauritius in 1965*, Advisory Opinion, ICJ Reports 2019, p. 96, International Court of Justice; Dissenting Opinion of Judge Donoghue; Declaration of Judge Tomka.

104 E.g. M Benzing, 'Community Interests in the Procedure of International Courts and Tribunals', 5(3) *The Law and Practice of International Courts and Tribunals* (2006) 369; L Boisson de Chazournes, 'Advisory Opinions and the Furtherance of the Common Interest of Mankind', in L Boisson de Chazournes et al (eds), *International Organization and International Dispute Settlement: Trends and Prospects* (Brill/Nijhoff, Leiden 2002), 105; R Wolfrum, 'Enforcing Community Interests through International Dispute Settlement: Reality or Utopia?', in U Fastenrath et al (eds), *From Bilateralism to Community Interest, cit.*, 1134.

Considering the recent resurgence of advisory jurisdiction before international courts and tribunals, the ICJ could thus issue an advisory opinion on the current situation in Xinjiang, allowing States considerable room for *manoeuvre* as regards the subject matter of the request. In this regard, Article 65(1) of the ICJ Statute thus provides that the Court may give an advisory opinion on *any legal question* at the request of whatever body may be authorized by, or in accordance with the UN Charter to make such a request.[105] Article 96 of the UN Charter provides that the General Assembly, Security Council, or other organs and specialized agencies of the United Nations that are authorized by the General Assembly may request an advisory opinion.

Given the above, two main questions must be addressed to determine whether and to what extent an advisory opinion can validly be requested from the ICJ to address the current situation of serious abuses and violations in Xinjiang. First and foremost, which could be the designated UN body or specialized agency to articulate the request? Furthermore, should the question be generally grounded on *jus cogens* norms, or should it be better based on selected human rights treaty-based obligations?

When answering the first question, it is worth noting that – similar to the recent Russian aggression in Ukraine, when any initiative under Chapter VII of the UN Charter was blocked by the Russian veto[106] – it is very unlikely that the UN Security Council could request an ICJ's advisory opinion on Xinjiang's current situation, given China's permanent status and associated veto power.[107] However, the UN has at its disposal two alternative mechanisms through which an advisory opinion might be sought.

The first and, perhaps, promptest solution is to request an advisory opinion from the ICJ through the General Assembly. Nonetheless, it is still unclear whether the request for an advisory opinion would require a simple majority vote or, rather, a two-thirds majority vote.[108] According to Article 18 of the UN

105 P D'Argent, 'Article 96 UN Charter', in A Zimmermann et al (eds), *The Statute of the International Court of Justice: A Commentary, cit.*, at 1795. It is interesting to observe that in the relevant provisions of the UN Charter the ICJ Statute, the expression 'legal questions' replaces 'dispute or question' previously implied in both the Covenant of the League of Nations and the Statute of the Permanent Court of International Justice; see M Shaw, *Rosenne's Law and Practice of the International Court: 1920–2015*, Vol. II, (Brill/Nijhoff, Leiden 2016), Chapter 15, para. II.244.

106 E.g. D Howell, 'Council at War: Russia, Ukraine and the UN Security Council', *EJIL:Talk!*, 25 February 2022.

107 A Rizvi, 'Uighur Crisis Highlights Flawed Structure of UN Security Council', *Jurist*, 10 July 2020.

108 S Rosenne, *The Law and Practice of the International Court: 1920–1966* (Martinus Nijhoff, Leiden 1997), 301.

Charter, decisions of the General Assembly as regards so-called 'important questions' are adopted by two-thirds of the members present and voting.[109] When specifying some of the matters included in the category of 'important questions', however, Article 18 does not mention a request for an advisory opinion. Practice does not provide further clarification on the majority required for the adoption of a General Assembly's decision including a request for an advisory opinion. Nonetheless, with the notable exceptions of the *South-West Africa*[110] and *Nuclear Weapons* advisory opinions,[111] both qualified by the then-President of the General Assembly as 'other questions' requiring a simple majority, on all occasions the General Assembly decided to request an advisory opinion by a majority in excess of two-thirds, reaching unanimity only once, in the case of the 1948 *Reparations* Advisory Opinion.[112]

When applying the above-described framework to the Xinjiang's situation, it is highly predictable that, as recently happened in cases of advisory opinions requested to enforce community interests, a two-thirds majority would be required. Although it must be admitted that reaching such a high threshold implies a rather delicate diplomatic and political compromise, recent practice demonstrates that achieving this goal is not impossible. Therefore, States should seriously consider requesting an advisory opinion to the ICJ within the General Assembly to finally address Xinjiang's current crisis.

In this respect, seeking an advisory opinion through the UN General Assembly has the advantage of having no constraints as to the subject matter of the question(s), insofar as the latter should be qualified as *legal* questions in nature, either abstract or concrete, concerning the definition and interpretation of any possible matter of international law – the resolution of which could require the cumulative or disjunctive application of treaty-based provisions and customary international law (including *jus cogens* norms) –,[113] and regardless their political implications.[114] Given the widespread pattern of

109 On the meaning of 'decisions' in this context, see the report of the Secretary-General in 5 GAOR, Annexes, a.i. 49 (A/1356) summarized in *UN Repertoire ad* Art. 18, para. 18.

110 *South-West Africa, Advisory Opinion Concerning the International Status*, Advisory Opinion, ICJ Reports 1950, p. 128.

111 *Legality of the Threat or Use of Nuclear Weapons*, Advisory Opinion, ICJ Reports 1996, p. 226.

112 UN General Assembly, *Reparation for injuries incurred in the service of the United Nations*, 1 December 1949, A/RES/365.

113 *Accordance with International Law of the Unilateral Declaration of Independence in Respect of Kosovo*, Advisory Opinion, ICJ Reports 2010, p. 403, para. 25; *Legality of the Threat or Use of Nuclear Weapons*, Advisory Opinion, ICJ Reports 1996, p. 226, para. 13; *Western Sahara*, Advisory Opinion, ICJ Reports 1975, p. 12, paras. 15–19.

114 *Kosovo Advisory Opinion*, para. 27.

atrocities perpetrated against Uyghurs and other Muslim ethnic communities, requesting an advisory opinion through the UN General Assembly might be a 'one-size-fits-all' solution, insofar as it would allow the ICJ to address a variety of matters at stake without the need for States other than China to strategically fit the question into the narrow 'bottlenecks' of compromissory clauses set out in human rights conventions which, as previously noted, have been reserved by China.

However, the General Assembly should not be envisaged as the exclusive forum for seeking an ICJ's advisory opinion on the XUAR's crisis. Among the UN bodies and other specialized agencies, a leading role could be exerted by the ECOSOC. According to a resolution adopted in 1946, the ECOSOC has been granted a general authorization to request advisory opinions *only* on legal questions arising within the scope of its activities.[115] While this can represent a significant limit for ECOSOC's action, in the case at stake many human rights violations allegedly perpetrated by China actually fall under the ICESCR's subject-matter. Moreover, unlike the described uncertainty as regards the General Assembly's necessary majority to adopt a resolution asking for an advisory opinion, Article 67(2) of the UN Charter provides that decisions of the ECOSOC shall be adopted by a majority of the members present and voting. In contrast to Article 18 of the UN Charter, this provision does not distinguish between the various questions. Thus, the term 'decision' must be interpreted as including all types of ECOSOC's actions requiring a vote for their adoption. Accordingly, since there is no categorization among the different issues, the applicable voting method would be that of simple majority.[116] This flexibility could represent the main advantage of seeking an ICJ's advisory opinion through the ECOSOC. Contrary to the General Assembly, where achieving a two-thirds majority of its one hundred-ninety-three member States can be difficult, the ECOSOC counts fifty-four member States. Therefore, reaching majority on a resolution asking for an advisory opinion from the ICJ should, in principle, be simpler within the ECOSOC than in other international fora.

However, two factors appear to be conditioning and, thus, discouraging the activation of the ECOSOC's pathway. Firstly, of the twenty-nine advisory proceedings defined and currently pending before the Court, it is worth noting

---

115 3 ECOSOC OR Plenary 37, 1946. For the original draft resolution, which was slightly amended later, see Annexes (E/131/Rev.1).

116 E Chaitidou, 'The Economic and Social Council, Voting, Article 67', in B Simma, DE Khan, G Nolte, A Paulus and N Wessendorf (eds), *The Charter of the United Nations: A Commentary* (Vol. II) (OUP, Oxford 2012), 1732.

that the ECOSOC has sought an advisory opinion only twice.[117] Indeed, except for the *Namibia* Advisory Opinion, where the request has been submitted through a historical resolution adopted by the Security Council, all other advisory proceedings have been promoted by the UN General Assembly. Secondly, counting on a restricted number of voting member States has already proved to be a 'double-edged sword' as regards the Xinjiang's crisis, since it significantly hindered the adoption of first condemnation measures. Indeed, in October 2022, the UN Human Rights Council rejected a resolution to hold a debate addressing the Xinjiang's crisis by a narrow margin of nineteen votes against – including many African States and, quite surprisingly, several members of the Organisation of Islamic Cooperation (OIC), which normally promotes the rights of Muslim minorities abroad[118], seventeen in favour and eleven abstentions.[119] Despite its formal rejection, there are some good reasons to be cautiously optimistic. As the vote was narrow, a possible future debate on the issue might just swing the other way, as new countries has meanwhile taken their seats, and hesitant members can be persuaded otherwise, especially in consideration of several follow-up initiatives to denounce the ongoing situation largely endorsed not only, as expected, by Western governments, but also from a range of Global South governments, including Paraguay, Guatemala, Liberia and Eswatini, Palau and Nauru.[120]

117 *Applicability of Article VI, Section 22, of the Convention on the Privileges and Immunities of the United Nations*, Advisory Opinion, ICJ Reports 1989, p. 177; *Difference Relating to Immunity from Legal Process of a Special Rapporteur of the Commission on Human Rights*, Advisory Opinion, ICJ Reports 1999, p. 62.

118 For instance, while the Indonesian delegate affirmed that his country does not want to look away from the suffering of fellow Muslims, it voted no because of impartiality. Similarly, Pakistan, which in July 2022 introduced the latest resolution on the human rights of Rohingya Muslims in Myanmar and has been a strong supporter of any investigation into the rights of Palestinians, equally referred to the importance of non-interference.

119 A/HRC/51/L.6, 40th Meeting, 51st Regular Session, Human Rights Council, Debate on the Situation of Human Rights in Xinjiang Autonomous Region China, Submitted by United States of America, Canada, Denmark, Finland, Iceland, Norway, Sweden, United Kingdom, <https://geneva.usmission.gov/2022/10/06/introducing-draft-decision-l-6-debate-on-the-situation-of-human-rights-in-the-xinjiang-uyghur-autonomous-region-china-hrc51/> accessed 30 April 2024; Cf. A Zammit Borda, 'The Debate on the Debate on Xinjiang at the Human Rights Council: Three Framing', *EJIL:Talk!*, 18 November 2022.

120 Cf. L Charbonneau, 'Record Number of States Condemn China's Persecution of Uyghurs: Joint Statement Calls on Bejing to End Rights Violations in Xinjiang', *Human Rights Watch*, 31 October 2022; 'Human Rights Violations in Xinjiang: Joint Statement at the UN Third Committee', 9 November 2023 (Last Update), Government of the United Kingdom (Foreign, Commonwealth & Development Office), <https://www.gov.uk/government/speeches/joint-statement-on-human-rights-violations-in-xinjiang-at-the-un-third-committee> accessed 30 April 2024.

Summing up the above, it is therefore reasonable to assume that States parties can reach an agreement for requesting an advisory opinion from the ICJ, preferably through the UN General Assembly, to obtain a general and unambiguous condemnation of China's alleged abuses in the Xinjiang Province. At the current stage, it is admittedly hard to unravel the 'conundrum' on whether and how States Parties to the UN General Assembly would vote on a request for an advisory opinion. At the same time, the situation is far from being definitely settled, as the geopolitical scenario of inter-State relations could rapidly change. Therefore, it may be worthwhile to play the advisory opinion 'card'.

3.2 *Of Making Compromises and Threading the ICERD 'Needle': Making the Most Out of the (Only) Compulsory Inter-State Human Rights Communication Mechanism*

As already argued, many of the mistreatments allegedly inflicted to Uyghurs and other Muslim minorities infringe several human rights granted by ICERD to individuals and ethnic groups. The CERD Committee has been entrusted with a range of procedural instruments, which States Parties to the Convention could – and, arguably, should – activate to ascertain China's international responsibility regarding the Xinjiang's crisis. The present section of the paper delves into the advantages and potential drawbacks of resorting to its inter-State communication mechanism.

Together with the 'traditional' individual communication procedure set forth in Article 14, ICERD also establishes two different inter-State mechanisms, entrusted with different functions. Firstly, Article 22 ICERD allows recourse to the ICJ for the adjudication of disputes concerning the interpretation and application of the Convention; however, China has included a reservation to this provision, exempting itself from being sued by other States before the ICJ. Secondly, Articles 11–13 ICERD set out an inter-State communication procedure before the CERD Committee. An advantage of this monitoring mechanism is that it applies to all States Parties upon ratification of or accession to the ICERD, regardless of any explicit expression of consent.[121] This mechanism automatically applies to all States, without any need to conclude a prior agreement for the CERD Committee to be seized with a communication. This is a distinctive feature among the different inter-State communication systems

121 On the contrary, article 14 of the ICERD stresses that "A State Party *may* at any time declare that it recognizes the competence of the Committee to receive and consider communications from individuals or groups of individuals within its jurisdiction claiming to be victims of a violation by that State Party of any of the rights set forth in this Convention" (emphasis added).

established in other UN human rights treaties, which have been conceived as optional: both States involved in the procedure must have agreed to the competence of the quasi-judicial monitoring body to consider such petitions.[122] Compulsory inter-State procedures can be traced only at a regional level, as provided for in Article 33 of the European Convention on Human Rights and Articles 45–61 of the African Charter on Human and Peoples' Rights.[123]

In its decision on jurisdiction rendered in *Palestine v. Israel*, the CERD Committee described the inter-State communication mechanism of Articles 11–13 as a 'unique instrument to settle inter-State disputes, set up for the common good of all States Parties'.[124] Furthermore, the potential of the CERD inter-State communication mechanism is bolstered by Article 20(2) ICERD, which provides that reservations whose effect would inhibit the operation of any of the treaty-bodies are not allowed. Although this provision does not specify which CERD institutions qualify as 'treaty bodies', it is nonetheless unambiguous that the CERD Committee must be included in this category.[125]

Moreover, unlike other contentious proceedings, the ICERD inter-State communication mechanism incorporates a process of conciliation that develops independently of the CERD Committee, through the appointment of an *Ad Hoc* Conciliation Commission.[126] As such, the procedure should not be regarded as an instrument to ascertain the international responsibility of a State but, rather, it is 'designed' to issue non-binding recommendations with a view of achieving an amicable solution. As further reaffirmed by the UN Human Rights Committee in its General Comment No. 31, an inter-State communication is aimed at drawing attention to possible violations of human rights by other States Parties and to calling on them to comply with their

122 S Leckie, 'The Inter-State Complaint Procedure in International Human Rights Law: Hopeful Prospects or Wishful Thinking?', 10 *Human Rights Quarterly* (1988) 249, 253. The author points out that the generally optional nature and reciprocal basis of inter-State communications 'has and will continue to limit its utilization'.

123 For a comprehensive assessment of the fundamental jurisdictional requirements of inter-State complaint mechanisms in the field of international human rights law, see L Lixinski, 'On the Circumscribed and Problematic Resurgence of Inter-State Human Rights Cases', 3(2) *European Convention on Human Rights Law Review* (2022) 174.

124 *Palestine v. Israel*, Jurisdiction III, UN Doc. CERD/C/100/5, para 3.41.

125 Cf. P Thornberry, *The International Convention on the Elimination of All Forms of Racial Discrimination: A Commentary* (OUP, Oxford 2016), 467.

126 CERD Committee, Admissibility of the Inter-state communication submitted by Qatar against the United Arab Emirates, UN Doc. CERD/C/99-4, 30 August 2019, para. 49. The Committee relied on a precedent interpretation of Article 22 ICERD provided by the ICJ, which nonetheless did not involve parallel proceedings; in this regard, see BI Bonafè, 'Parallel Human Rights Proceedings Before International Courts and Monitoring Bodies', 15(2) *Diritti umani e diritto internazionale* (2021), 369.

obligations should, far from being considered as an unfriendly act, be regarded as an expression of legitimate community interest.[127]

While being 'dormant' for almost seven decades, the inter-State procedure was utilized for the first time ever in 2018; since then, it has been triggered on two further occasions. On 8 March 2018, Qatar lodged two inter-state proceedings against the Kingdom of Saudi Arabia and against the United Arab Emirates.[128] Immediately afterwards, on 23 April 2018, Palestine submitted a communication against the State of Israel. Even though States other than China may not be considered a 'directly injured party' in respect of any harm being inflicted on Uyghurs, they could nevertheless bring China before the CERD Committee through the inter-State communication mechanism. Indeed, the alleged discriminatory treatment inflicted to the Uyghurs and to other Muslim minorities could constitute a violation of *jus cogens* norms, as well as a matter of grave and serious concern to the international community as the prohibition on discrimination under ICERD would be considered *erga omnes* in character.[129]

Generally speaking, inter-State communications perform two main functions.[130] Firstly, they can be activated to safeguard the interests of States Parties *vis-à-vis* the protection of their citizens or nationals, resembling the diplomatic protection's traditional scheme. This has been considered by some authors as a *private* dispute settlement function, given that it concerns the individual and subjective rights and interests of a State. The prevalent *private* nature of this type of inter-State cases is demonstrated by the necessary prior exhaustion of domestic remedies before triggering the inter-State procedure. The other function performed by inter-State communications is to guarantee

127 UN Human Rights Committee (HRC), General Comment no. 31 [80], The nature of the general legal obligation imposed on States Parties to the Covenant, 26 May 2004, CCPR/C/21/Rev.1/Add.13,

128 D Keane, 'CERD Reaches Historic Decisions in Inter-State Communications', *EJIL:Talk!*, 6 September 2019.

129 Many authors have warmly welcomed the CERD Committee's interpretation of the prohibition of discrimination and related obligations as having an *erga omnes* character in its jurisdiction decision issued in *Palestine v. Israel*, essentially 'disregarding' the absence of any treaty relations between the two States Parties involved in the proceeding; see, among others, C Ragni, 'Il contenzioso interstatale sui diritti umani: questioni aperte e prospettive future', 15(3) *Diritti umani e diritto internazionale* (2021) 599, 608; for a slightly critical appraisal of this decision, see instead D Tamada, 'Inter-State Communication under ICERD: From *ad hoc* Conciliation to Collective Enforcement?', 12(3) *Journal of International Dispute Settlement* (2021) 425.

130 Two functions correspond to those which are private and public, impure and pure, 'interested' and 'disinterested' respectively.; cf. I Risini, *The Inter-State Application*, cit., 5; P Palchetti, 'I ricorsi interstatali', cit., 363.

the collective interests of States in promoting the protection of fundamental rights, irrespective of the nationality of those individuals affected. Although less frequent in practice, this latter type of procedure lies in the logic of international human rights regimes, serving the interest of the international community, and may be labelled as *actio popularis* or *public interest litigation*.[131]

The often-neglected availability of the ICERD inter-State communication mechanisms has yet to be 'tested' within the context of feasible international responses to human rights violations allegedly attributed to China. The first difficulty is that it requires the legal initiative of one or more State Parties to ICERD to lodge such a communication. In this regard, Article 11 ICERD sets out no limits in terms of *locus standi*, nor it requires to demonstrate the existence of a victim status, providing that any State party that considers that another State party is not giving effect to the provisions of the Convention may bring an inter-State complaint. If it is true that inter-State human rights proceedings are often initiated by directly affected States acting under a 'quasi-diplomatic protection' scheme on behalf of individuals, be they its nationals or other people placed under the State's jurisdiction, it is equally true that there are States 'indirectly' affected that have brought such complaints, as seen for example in *The Gambia v. Myanmar*, where the applicant State lacks any link to the Rohingya victims,[132] and more recently in *Canada and The Netherlands v. Syria*, where the claimant States jointly initiated proceedings to hold Syria accountable for its violations under UNCAT.[133]

Against this background, any of the 183 States Parties to ICERD could validly initiate an inter-State communication. Firstly, suitable candidates could be

---

131 S Leckie, 'The Inter-State Complaint Procedure in International Human Rights Law: Hopeful Prospects or Wishful Thinking?', *cit.*, 256–257; G Ulfstein and I Risini, 'Human Rights, State Complaints', *Max Planck Encyclopedia of Public International Law* (2011), para. 10; I Risini, 'The Inter-State Application under the European Convention on Human Rights: More Than Diplomatic Protection', in N Weiß and JM Thouvenin (eds), *The Influence of Human Rights on International Law* (Springer, London 2015) 69, 70.

132 *Application of the Convention on the Prevention and Punishment of the Crime of Genocide* (*The Gambia v. Myanmar*), Preliminary Objections, Judgment, ICJ Reports 2022, p. 477, para. 93–114; as regards the question of The Gambia's *locus standi* before the ICJ, which has been contested by the respondent State, cf. para. 108 of the judgment; concerning the legal standing of indirectly injured States before the ICJ, see again M Longobardo, *cit.*; P Urs, 'Obligations *erga omnes* and the question of standing before the International Court of Justice', 34(2) *Leiden Journal of International Law* (2021) 505, 515.

133 *Application of the Convention against Torture and Other Cruel, Inhuman or Degrading Treatment of Punishment* (*Canada and The Netherlands v. Syrian Arab Republic*), Joint Application instituting proceedings, 8 June 2023; for a brief comment on the importance of this judicial initiative, see L Hill-Cawthorne, 'The Responsibility of Syria under the Convention Against Torture before the ICJ', *EJIL:Talk!*, 6 October 2023.

those States 'directly' affected by China's policies, whose nationals are being interned in Xinjiang's 're-education' camps. Secondly, Article 11 ICERD could also be invoked by 'indirectly' or 'specially' affected States which have already shown an interest in protecting the human rights of Uyghurs and other Muslim minorities, as for example Western countries such as the United States, Canada, or any EU member States. Thirdly, any other State Party seeking to denounce the ongoing crisis in Xinjiang could validly initiate such a communication.

Despite the advantages of lodging an inter-State communication according to the ICERD, it is important not to disregard a few significant limitations of such a procedure. As already pointed out, the CERD Committee is a quasi-judicial body entitled to merely provide non-binding recommendations adopted in the form of 'views' which, as argue by several scholars, resemble more advisory decisions than enforceable judgments.[134] This does not indicate that these views have no normative effect at all, or that States can deliberately opt to disregard them with impunity. However, it is evident that the lack of a clear and unambiguous treaty-based obligations requiring States Parties to comply with the CERD Committee's decisions has several adverse impacts on compliance: indeed, the non-binding nature of the CERD Committee's recommendations is frequently by several Governments to justify their failure to take concrete actions to give effect to them.

3.3 *Taking the Road 'Less Travelled': Assessing Advantages and Pitfalls of the ILO's Inter-State Complaint Mechanism*

When it comes to addressing the available inter-State complaint mechanisms in the context of international human rights law, little or no consideration has been dedicated to the procedure outlined in Articles 24–36 of the ILO Constitution.[135]

At first glance, it can be understandable why the option of invoking this mechanism has been widely disregarded also as concerns the current Xinjiang's crisis. This decision may be partly justified taking into account that, until very recent times, China did not ratify two fundamental ILO Conventions that could be applicable to the situation at stake, namely ILO Conventions No.

---

134 T Buergenthal, 'The U.N. Human Rights Committee', 5 *Max Planck Yearbook of United Nations Law* (2001) 341, 397.

135 This is probably because most available analysis which attempt at providing for a comprehensive *tour d'horizon* with regards to the UN 'core' human rights treaties did not consider the ILO framework; cf. L Lixinski, cit.; E Decaux, 'The Potential for Inter-State Conciliation within the Framework of the UN Treaties for the Protection of Human Rights', in C Tomuschat, M Kohen (eds), *Flexibility in International Dispute Settlement: Conciliation Revisited*, cit., 39.

29 and No. 105, providing for the prohibition and punishment of all forms of forced or compulsory labour, either imposed as such or as a means of political or educational coercion, as well as of racial, social, national or religious discrimination.

However, in August 2022, China passed domestic legislation approving the ratification of these treaties. Therefore, the ILO inter-State procedure must now be included in the discussion on potential avenues for raising awareness and throwing further light on the current Xinjiang's crisis. Even though, as already observed regarding the ICERD inter-State communication mechanism, quasi-judicial proceedings cannot result in a binding and enforceable judgment establishing China's responsibility under general international law, they may facilitate the achievement of an amicable settlement or conciliation between the States concerned, leading to the implementation of several measures and recommendations aimed at ending violations.

Pursuant to Article 26(1) of the ILO Constitution, any Contracting State Party or the ILO Governing Body itself shall have the right to lodge a complaint with the International Labour Office if it is not satisfied that any other member is securing the observance of any ILO Convention which both have ratified.[136]

The wording of this provision highlights two main features of the instrument. Firstly, any of the 187 Contracting States Parties of the ILO, provided that they have ratified at least one of its Conventions– either classified as fundamental or a governance convention – can validly lodge an inter-State complaint.[137] Moreover, ILO's inter-State procedures can be triggered by a State's complaint about another State's conduct without requiring the latter's consent for the

136 In general, see M van Alphen Fyfe and GF Sinclair, 'Supervisory and Review Procedures: International Labour Organization (ILO)', *Max Planck Encyclopedia of International Procedural Law* (2020), available online.

137 According to the ILO, the eleven fundamental treaty instruments are the following ones: the 1948 Convention on the Freedom of Association and Protection of the Right to Organise (No. 87); the 1949 Convention on the Right to Organise and Collective Bargaining (No. 98); the 1957 Convention on the Abolition of Forced Labour (No. 105); the 1973 Minimum Age Convention (No. 138); the 1999 Convention on Worst Forms of Child Labour (No. 182); the 1951 Convention on Equal Remuneration (No. 100); the 1958 Convention on Discrimination (Employment and Occupation) (No. 111); the 1981 Convention on Occupational Safety and Health (No. 155); the 2006 Convention on the Promotional Framework for Occupational Safety and Health (No. 187). The ILO Governing Body has also designed other four Conventions as governance instruments: namely, the 1947 Labour Inspection Convention (No. 81); the 1964 Employment Policy Convention (No. 122); the 1969 Labour Inspection (Agriculture) Convention (No. 129); the 1976 Tripartite Consultation (International Labour Standards) Convention (No. 144).

process to be undertaken.[138] As emphasized by several scholars, this functioning could seriously impair procedural fairness, thus requiring a significant degree of proceduralization, including rules on confidentiality of proceedings and deliberations.[139]

However, the respondent State's consent is not completely circumvented, since Article 26(1) provides for a form of 'reciprocity' condition, insofar as a State could validly lodge a complaint against another State for alleged non-compliance with an ILO Convention if also the respondent State is a party to it.

Furthermore, similarly to what has just been noted as regards the ICERD inter-State communication mechanism, the initiation of such proceedings is not contingent upon the complaining State or its nationals suffering direct harm. Indeed, a State Party may have a general interest in ensuring the implementation, in the territories of other States, of ILO Conventions relating to the welfare of citizens of all other States, notwithstanding any effect upon its nationals or on its own direct interest in the matter.

Whenever a State Party notifies the ILO's Director General of its intention to invoke the inter-State complaint procedure, the matter is immediately referred to the ILO's Governing Body which, once it has completed the analysis of the petition, can adopt two main initiatives. In the first instance, it may transmit the complaint to the respondent State and invite the Government to submit its observation on the matter. If the ILO's Governing Body decides not to transmit the complaint, or if an unsatisfactory response is received, it may decide, on a discretionary basis, to appoint a Commission of Inquiry, constituted by three independent members and described by the ILO as its 'highest-level investigative procedure'. The Commission of Inquiry's primary task is to further examine the complaint and issue a final report with its findings on all factual questions relevant to determining the matter and containing recommendations as to the steps that should be taken to solve the situation. Once completed and signed, the report is final and it is communicated to the ILO's Governing Body, which transmits it to the State concerned for its acceptance or otherwise. Alternatively, a system of 'direct contacts' and 'good

---

138 N Valticos, 'The International Labour Organisation', in K Vasak (ed), *The International Dimension of Human Rights* (Westport, Connecticut 1982), 377.

139 Cf. E Osieke, *Constitutional Law and Practice in the International Labour Organisation* (Martinus Nijhoff, Dordrecht 1985); F Maupain, 'The ILO Regular Supervisory System: A Model in Crisis?', 10(1) *International Organizations Law Review* (2013) 117.

offices' managed by the ILO's Director General could be employed to address and rectify the situation in the respondent State.[140]

Despite the conciliatory and non-adversarial character of the ILO's inter-State complaint mechanism, as well as its considerable flexibility, the relevant procedure has been initiated only in six cases. Alongside their highly sensitive political implications, the ILO repeatedly justified the low number of complaints by emphasizing the *extrema ratio* nature of the procedure, which should only be activated when the periodical supervisory system of States' reports fails to produce concrete and fruitful results.

It is interesting to note that, of the six inter-State complaints received by the ILO, the very first two communications concern allegations of forced labour. The first procedure was initiated in 1961 by Ghana, calling into question Portugal's compliance with the ILO Convention No. 105 concerning the abolition of forced labour in its then-African colonial territories in Mozambique, Angola and Guinea.[141] While setting an 'obvious' precedent in the ILO's case-law, this complaint also provided preliminary elucidations on procedural aspects of the mechanism, particularly with reference to the appointment of a Commission of Inquiry carrying out fact-findings and, more generally, performing investigative functions. Furthermore, this case is significant insofar as it constitutes a distinct example of an *actio popularis*, given that Ghana was not bringing proceedings on behalf of its nationals with a view of safeguarding its own interests but, rather, it sought to denounce the systematic and widespread violation of international labour standards. In this regard, the final report published by the ILO's Commission of Inquiry was useful insofar as it advanced the general knowledge of forced labour throughout the African Continent, also addressing the 'state of health' of labour legislation in the colonial territories mentioned in the complaint and issuing a number of findings and recommendations directed to Portugal. Most importantly, immediately after the launch of the investigation, Portugal introduced structural amendments to its legislation and practice regarding the application of the ILO Convention No. 105. This is an explicit demonstration of the fact that, even if it does not culminate in a binding judgment enforceable *vis-à-vis* the violating State, the ILO's inter-State mechanism should nonetheless be regarded as an influential tool, capable of

140 L Sweptson, 'Human Rights Complaints Procedures of the International Labour Organisation', in H Hannum (ed), *Guide to International Human Rights Practice* (Pennsylvania Press, Philadelphia 1984), 77.

141 Cf. 'Report of the Commission to Examine the Complaint Filed by Government of Ghana Concerning the Observance by the Government of Portugal of the Abolition of Forced Labour Convention 1957 (ILO No. 105)', 45 International Labour Office Official Bulletin 1–253 (Supp. II, 1962).

inducing change in the conduct of States found to be in breach of international labour standards.

In late 1961, few months after the very first inter-State case, a second complaint had been brought by Portugal against Liberia as regards allegations of forced labour in violation of the ILO Convention No. 29.[142] Although the politically controversial background of the issue raised led the respondent State to fear a 'weaponization' of the ILO's inter-State complaint mechanism as a means of lawfare, a Commission of Inquiry was nevertheless appointed for this case as well.

As these two precedents clearly demonstrate, there is fertile ground for re-discovering the ILO's inter-State procedure as an effective and powerful instrument in the toolbox of the solutions for tackling the Xinjiang's crisis and seeking justice for Uyghurs and other Muslim ethnic minorities, particularly as regards allegations of forced labour. The brief examination of the two precedents dealing with the correct fulfilment of ILO Conventions No. 29 and No. 105 had demonstrated that the establishment of a Commission of Inquiry can achieve significant outcomes within a considerably short timeframe. Furthermore, the *Portugal v. Liberia* case suggests that, even though the institution of an inter-State complaint may often be politically motivated or allegedly so, the core issue of the procedure remains to determine whether the legal allegations are supported by factual circumstances and to ascertain State's violations of its obligations as regards international labour standards.

At present, the most relevant limitation to an immediate activation of the ILO's inter-State complaints mechanism concerning alleged breaches of ILO Conventions Nos. 29, 105, and 111 as regards the ongoing Xinjiang's crisis is related to the impossibility of enforcing China's reporting obligations at very short notice. Pursuant to both Article 28(2) of ILO Convention No. 29 and Article 4(2) of ILO Convention No. 105, these newly ratified ILO treaty instruments will become effective twelve months after their ratification registration date: as for China, both Conventions officially entered into force on August 23, 2023. In accordance with Article 22 of the ILO Constitution, it was scheduled that the initial annual reports from China, outlining the measures undertaken to implement each ratified convention, would be published in 2024. Nonetheless, the ILO's Committee of Experts on the Application of Conventions and Recommendations (CEACR) has noted, through the release of certain recent

142 Cf. 'Report of the Commission to Examine the Complaint filed by the Government of Portugal Concerning the Observance by the Government of Liberia of the Forced Labour Convention 1930 (ILO No. 29)', 46 International Labour Office Official Bulletin (Supp. II, 1963).

observations, the presence of potential non-compliance scenarios which, if corroborated, would constitute a violation of China's obligations under ILO Conventions Nos. 29 and 105. At the time of publication of this contribution, it appears that China has not yet provided a response to these observations.[143]

Recent practice concerning inter-State proceedings has demonstrated that there is still a widespread cautiousness among States in engaging in a complaint against a violating State without first exploring non-adversarial mechanisms such as follow-up reporting procedures. Therefore, the international community might deem it appropriate to wait at least for the release of China's first reports on the implementation of the ILO Conventions No. 29 and No. 105, and for the ILO's Governing Body to engage in a follow-up procedure upon identifying breaches relating to the international labour standards applied to Uyghurs and other Muslim minorities employed in XUAR's supply chains.

Nonetheless, there are no provisions in the ILO Constitution preventing from instituting an inter-State procedure pursuant to Article 26(1) without waiting for the 'prior exhaustion' of other monitoring instruments. As the well-known saying posits, justice delayed is often justice denied.

Therefore, the current situation in Xinjiang demands urgent action: with the clock that is ticking, and in the light of the limited procedural options available, the ILO's inter-State complaint mechanism should be regarded as a powerful avenue for accountability, and therefore States should seriously consider activating it without further delay.

4 Conclusion

The article has attempted to record all alleged mistreatments perpetrated against Uyghurs and other Muslim ethnic minorities in Xinjiang, with the main purpose of classifying them into substantive categories which could be validly invoked by States other than China in a circumscribed, yet suitable, set of inter-State proceedings, whether initiated directly or 'under disguise' through the advisory jurisdiction of international courts and tribunals.

In this regard, while navigating the 'minefield' of China's reservations to all compromissory clauses included in the UN core human rights conventions, as well as recalling China's reluctance to accept the quasi-judicial inter-State

143 Cf. Country Profiles, Observation (CEACR), Adopted 2024, Published 113rd ILC Session (2025), Forced Labour Convention, 1930 (No. 29) - China (Ratification: 2022); Observation (CEACR) , Adopted 2024, Published 113rd ILC Session (2025), Abolition of Forced Labour Convention, 1957 (No. 105) - China (Ratification: 2022).

monitoring procedures established by the same treaties, it has been found it appropriate to first consider China's actions and omissions as violations of *jus cogens* norms, on the one hand, and *erga omnes* (partes) obligations enshrined in both ICERD and ILO Conventions No. 29, 105, and 111 on the other hand.

Firstly, since all avenues to sue China before the ICJ for possible acts of genocide or torture allegedly occurring in Xinjiang are blocked, attention has been devoted to the alternative strategy of considering the ICJ as a possible forum where an advisory opinion might be sought, especially through an initiative of the UN General Assembly. For instance, a coalition of powerful Western States could ask the Court to verify whether and to what extent China's abuses in Xinjiang violate *jus cogens* obligations, such as the prohibition of genocide, torture, racial discrimination, forced labour or slavery, among others. Furthermore, an advisory opinion could help to better assess which are the legal consequences, as well as procedural obligations, for States other than China. Secondly, the focus has been shifted to two other 'specific' and useful, albeit often under-explored, monitoring procedures, such as the quasi-judicial inter-State communication mechanisms set forth in the ICERD and the ILO Constitution. While the former has become more attractive in practice, having been recently activated on three distinct occasions, the latter continues to be relatively neglected. Despite their restricted *ratione materiae* quasi-jurisdiction, being tasked with the supervision of the effective implementation of treaty-based obligations laid down in the ICERD and the many ILO Conventions, these mechanisms have nevertheless proved to be very effective. The application of rather deformalized, flexible, and non-confrontational methods has indeed enabled the achievement of an amicable settlement between the States parties concerned, allowing for the restoration of a situation of legality.

Given the above, as China's actions and omissions have repeatedly proved to breach a significant number of *jus cogens* norms and human rights treaty-based obligations, time is now ripe for the international community to finally address these violations directly by pursuing inter-State alternative solutions, following the (very welcoming) community interest litigation's wave that is currently sweeping away international courts and tribunals.

Index

www.ingramcontent.com/pod-product-compliance
Lightning Source LLC
Chambersburg PA
CBHW050523240926
51846CB00003B/670